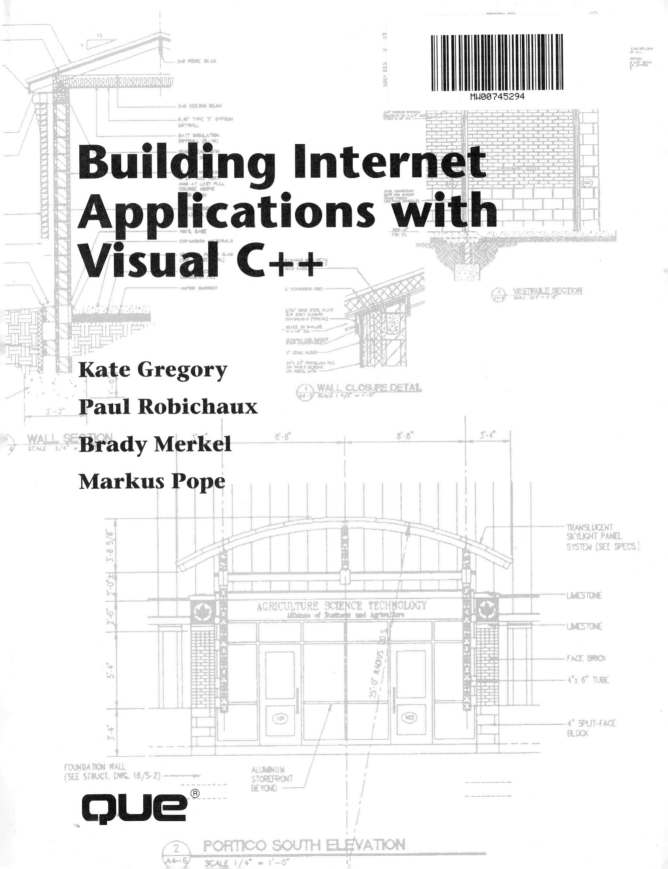

Building Internet Applications with Visual C++

Kate Gregory

Paul Robichaux

Brady Merkel

Markus Pope

MW00745294

que ®

Building Internet Applications with Visual C++

Copyright© 1995 by Que® Corporation.

Library of Congress Catalog No.: 95-69577

ISBN: 0-7897-0213-4

97 96 95   6 5 4 3 2 1

Interpretation of the printing code: the rightmost double-digit number is the year of the book's printing; the rightmost single-digit number, the number of the book's printing. For example, a printing code of 95-1 shows that the first printing of the book occurred in 1995.

All terms mentioned in this book that are known to be trademarks or service marks have been appropriately capitalized. Que cannot attest to the accuracy of this information. Use of a term in this book should not be regarded as affecting the validity of any trademark or service mark.

Screen reproductions in this book were created using Collage Plus from Inner Media, Inc., Hollis, NH.

President and Publisher: Roland Elgey
Associate Publisher: Joseph B. Wikert
Editorial Services Director: Elizabeth Keaffaber
Managing Editor: Sandy Doell
Director of Marketing: Lynn E. Zingraf

Dedication

To the husbands, wives, and children of all the Internet developers, from the seventies to today. You built it, too.

—Kate Gregory

I'd like to dedicate this book to my wife and son. Without their love and support, I'd be much the poorer, and I couldn't have written this book without them.

—Paul Robichaux

To my best friend, Logan Rayn, and her mother.

—Markus Pope

Credits

Title Manager
Bryan Gambrel

Acquisitions Editor
Fred Slone

Product Director
Steve Potts

Production Editors
Susan Ross Moore
Kelly Oliver

Editors
Kelli Brooks
Tom Cirtin
Amy M. Perry
Heather Stith

Assistant Product Marketing Manager
Kim Margolius

Technical Editor
Dan Dumbril

Technical Specialist
Cari Skaggs

Acquisitions Coordinator
Angela Kozlowski

Operations Coordinator
Patty Brooks

Editorial Assistant
Michelle R. Williams

Book Designer
Sandra Schroeder

Cover Designer
Dan Armstrong

Production Team
Stephen Adams
Angela D. Bannan
Jason Carr
Chad Dressler
Joan Evan
Amy Gornik
Darren Jackson
Damon Jordan
Daryl Kessler
Julie Quinn
Bobbi Satterfield
Michael Thomas
Jody York
Karen York

Indexer
Bront Davis

Composed in *Stone Serif* and *MCPdigital* by Que Corporation.

Acknowledgments

To my husband, Brian, and my wonderful children, Beth and Kevin—my heartfelt thanks once again for all the understanding and support. To Fred, Susan, and the other terrific Que people who made this happen, thank you for doing such a great job. And to all the software developers, RFC writers, and hard-working users who built the Internet into what it is today, my gratitude and appreciation are as big as the Net itself.

Kate Gregory

A number of people provided valuable advice and assistance while I was writing. I'd like to thank fellow Intergraphers Ted Briggs, Joyce Howell, and Lori Hufford. Lawrence McDonald provided valuable feedback on my early drafts, and Carl Ellison was particularly helpful with Chapter 13. Finally, my thanks to Fred Slone and the many other people at Que who were instrumental in actually getting this book into print.

Paul Robichaux

I'd like to thank Kate, Paul, and Brady for their excellent work on the project while I became extremely involved in labor and delivery! I'm now the father of a beautiful, demanding, screaming little girl—and being a father is the best thing that's ever happened to me, even surpassing the chance I've been given to work on several books for my publisher (sorry, Que).

In addition to Brady and Kate, I'd also like to thank Fred and all the other people at Que who've helped me throughout the book projects I've done. Oh, and also thanks to John. There are, of course, many other people that I need to thank, and you know who you are, so "Thanks." Well, that's about all the time I have; I've got to go change a diaper.

If you need me, just remember that I'm only a few packets away at **markus@datastorm.com.**

Markus Pope

About the Authors

Kate Gregory discovered the Internet in 1989, after hearing about it for years. She has been an active user since then, using all the services described in this book. She is a visible member of the Usenet community: a founding member of group-mentors, who help people create new newsgroups, and a regular in misc.kids and misc.business.consulting.

With her husband Brian, Kate has a computer consulting and software development business in rural Ontario, Canada. They develop Internet applications in Visual C++: the current project is a newsreader. She teaches Internet and C++ programming courses, and this is her second book for Que.

Kate can be reached at **kate@gregcons.com**.

Paul Robichaux is a software developer and author with a wide range of experience developing for and writing about desktop operating systems, applications software, and the Internet. He lives in Huntsville, Alabama, with his family.

Brady P. Merkel is a Senior Software Consultant with Intergraph Corporation in Huntsville, Alabama. His background includes extensive experience in software development, network connectivity, and Internet tools. One of his recent projects included the development of Intergraph Online, Intergraph Corporation's World Wide Web server. You can see his work at **http://www.intergraph.com.** Brady can be reached by e-mail at **bpmerkel@ingr.com.**

Markus Pope is a Quality Assurance Analyst with Datastorm Technologies, the makers of Procomm Plus. He got his start in computers at the wee age of 13 when he spent a lot of his free time (and not-so-much free time) sitting in front of a TI99/4a at Republic Junior High. Thanks to his friend Michael Coley, computers soon became Markus' sole purpose in life. Now married, and working for Datastorm for the past four years, Markus spends his time researching new stuff, playing on the Net, fishing, and acting silly for his little girl and her momma. If you need him, you can contact him via the Internet at **markus@datastorm.com.**

Nick Witthaus is a Quality Assurance Analyst with Datastorm Technologies, developing test plans, automating testing procedures, and manually testing software. Before this job, Nick worked in the Technical Support department of a major PC manufacturer. Nick holds a B.A. in Computer Science from the University of Missouri - Columbia.

Erik Jorgensen has been working with computers for more than 15 years. He now spends his time surfing the Internet and watching his daughter Jessika grow up much too quickly. He credits his mother and fathers for instilling in him the need to know how everything works. He currently lives in mid-Missouri with his wife Mary. He can be reached on the Internet at **erik.jorgensen@batboard.org.**

We'd Like to Hear from You!

As part of our continuing effort to produce books of the highest possible quality, Que would like to hear your comments. To stay competitive, we *really* want you, as a computer book reader and user, to let us know what you like or dislike most about this book or other Que products.

You can mail comments, ideas, or suggestions for improving future editions to the address below, or send us a fax at (317) 581-4663. For the online inclined, Macmillan Computer Publishing has a forum on CompuServe (type **GO QUEBOOKS** at any prompt) through which our staff and authors are available for questions and comments. The address of our Internet site is **http://www.mcp.com** (World Wide Web).

In addition to exploring our forum, please feel free to contact me personally to discuss your opinions of this book: I'm **75230,1556** on CompuServe, and I'm **bgambrel@que.mcp.com** on the Internet.

Thanks in advance—your comments will help us to continue publishing the best books available on computer topics in today's market.

Bryan Gambrel
Title Manager
Que Corporation
201 W. 103rd Street
Indianapolis, Indiana 46290
USA

Contents at a Glance

Internet Programming

Developing Applications

Appendixes

Contents

Introduction

Although the Internet itself isn't all that new, the fact that the general public can buy Internet access cheaply is. The growing Internet audience has attracted a lot of media attention and the interest of entrepreneurs eager to start or expand a business. How can you join the crowd and cash in?

One way is to take advantage of the enormous market for software that makes finding information with the Internet easy. This book shows you how to develop your own versions of the most popular Internet programs.

Of course, you don't have to plan a future in software development to want to know how the Internet works. This book shows you just how applications like e-mail and the World Wide Web do what they do. Think of it as a behind-the-scenes tour of the Internet.

Visual C++ is a good development language to use for this type of work because it makes Windows applications much easier to write. First of all, it has a built-in application framework that does much of the development work for the user interface, which frees you to focus on the Internet aspects of your programs. You'll learn more about this framework in Chapter 4, "Building a Windows Application Framework." The first full Internet application in this book (see Chapter 5, "Building an Internet Finger Application") requires you to write less than 100 lines of code to produce a complete Windows Internet application.

As you read this book, think about adding Internet aspects to ordinary programs, too. Imagine a financial calculator with a routine that gets the latest interest rates by connecting to the Internet, a contact manager that can send e-mail, or a word processor macro that delivers your manuscript electronically—the possibilities are endless, once you understand the basic Internet services. This book tells you everything you need to know.

What This Book Contains

This book is divided into parts to make it easy to find the information you need. Part I covers the background material you must understand before you can begin developing applications. Specifically, you'll learn the following:

- Chapter 1, "A Quick Tour of Internet Applications," shows you what the most popular Internet applications are and what they do.

- Chapter 2, "Understanding Internet Protocols," describes the protocols that applications use when talking to the Internet and what these protocols specify.

- Chapter 3, "Windows Sockets (WINSOCK.DLL)," explains what sockets are, how to use WINSOCK.DLL, and how to add a socket class to your application.

In Part II, you set to work building real Internet applications you can use right away. The applications in the first four chapters use the Single Document Interface (SDI), which is a little simpler to start with. In the last six chapters, you tackle Multiple Document Interface (MDI) applications and draw on the concepts that have already been established:

- Chapter 4, "Building a Windows Application Framework," demonstrates how the Visual C++ programming environment can dramatically reduce development time for a Windows application.

- Chapter 5, "Building an Internet Finger Application," creates a simple way to learn more about other Internet users.

- Chapter 6, "Building an Internet Whois Application," shows you another way to learn about users, and covers interface issues like changing fonts and resizing windows.

- Chapter 7, "Building an Internet FTP Application," develops a utility you can use to get text, program, and image files from all over the Internet.

- Chapter 8, "Building an Internet HTTP Server," creates a Web server that you can use to make your own Web page available throughout the Internet.

- Chapter 9, "Building an Internet IRC Application," demonstrates the Internet version of CB radio: live conversations with people all over the world.

- Chapter 10, "Building an Internet Gopher Application," creates an information-finding tool that can lead you into unexpected corners of the Internet.

- Chapter 11, "Building an Internet Electronic Mail Application," explains how mail travels the Net, and develops a mail reader that will send and receive messages for you.

- Chapter 12, "Building an Internet Newsreader Application," introduces you to the world of UseNet and builds a program to bring you into that community.

- Chapter 13, "Secure Communications on the Internet," explains cryptographic principles that are used in Internet programming, and demonstrates these principles in action.

- Chapter 14, "Building a Unique Internet Application—QSend," creates an application that is not in use on the Internet today. It extends OLE to enable transmission of spreadsheet charts, word processing documents, and similar "OLE objects" across the Internet.

Each programming chapter walks you through creating an Internet program and builds on the information that you learned in the previous chapters. Concepts aren't explained more than once unless they are related to a change you must make in the application you're currently developing.

In Part III, four appendixes cover material you may find useful:

- Appendix A, "Internet Port Assignments," summarizes the port numbers used by every Internet application.

- Appendix B, "Hypertext Markup Language," is an introduction to HTML, used to write Web pages.

- Appendix C, "Uniform Resource Locators," explains the URL as used on the World Wide Web.

- Appendix D, "Browsing the CD-ROM," covers the source files, documentation, and Internet applications found on the CD-ROM. These include all the source code discussed in the book, all the Internet specifications (called RFCs), the Windows Sockets specifications, and much, much more.

Who Should Read This Book

This book isn't for everyone. If you haven't heard of the Internet, don't have a computer that runs Windows, and have never programmed in any language, you're not ready yet. Some other Que books you should read first are:

- *Special Edition Using Windows 95*, to introduce the Windows 95 operating system.

- *Visual C++ by Example*, to get you started programming in Visual C++.

- *Special Edition Using the Internet*, to introduce you to the Internet.

You may be an experienced Windows programmer (in C, C++, or even Visual C++) who wants to learn about Internet programming. Or you may be an experienced Internet programmer (for UNIX, DOS, or other platforms) who wants to learn how to program applications for Windows. Perhaps you have been using the Internet for years, but you haven't ever developed Internet or Windows applications. If you fit any of these descriptions, you have something to learn from this book.

The four background chapters in this book are set up so that you can skip the ones that cover material you already know:

- If you are an experienced Internet user, you can skip Chapter 1, "A Quick Tour of Internet Applications."

- If you are an experienced Internet programmer, you can skip Chapter 2, "Understanding Internet Protocols." If you're new to Internet programming, you'll probably need to refer back to this chapter several times as you go through the rest of the book.

- Even if you've used sockets before, don't skip Chapter 3, "Windows Sockets (WINSOCK.DLL)," because you develop your own Windows socket class in this chapter.

- If you've ever built an application with Visual C++ (even if you just followed along with the tutorial on building Scribble that comes with Visual C++), you can skip Chapter 4, "Building a Windows Application Framework."

Even if you do know all about the preceding topics, consider skimming through the chapters anyway. You may learn something new.

What Tools You Need

First, you need a copy of Microsoft Visual C++ 2.1 or greater installed on your computer to produce 32-bit code. If you want to produce 16-bit code, you can use version 1.51 or greater, but be aware of instructions for 32-bit code, which don't apply. These instances are flagged with a special note, as explained in the following section on conventions.

Your computer also needs to be hooked up to the Internet. SLIP or PPP dial-up accounts are the best way to connect desktop Windows computers to the Internet. If you don't have such an account, get one. Your provider should give you some software that connects your computer to the Internet. You need to make this connection before you can run any of your programs.

Finally, you may also want to keep a notepad handy to scribble interface designs on. A comfortable chair is also important because you're going to enjoy writing Internet programs so much that you'll be spending a lot of time in front of your computer.

Conventions Used in This Book

One thing this book has plenty of is code. You can tell the difference between code and regular text because the code is in a special monospaced font. For example, you may see a line or two of code mixed in with the text like this:

```
int SomeFunction( int x, int y);
{
    return x+y;
}
```

Larger pieces of code will look like the following:

Listing 0.1

```
CHostDialog dialog(m_pMainWnd);
    if (dialog.DoModal() == IDOK)
    {
        AppSocket = new CSocket();
        if (AppSocket->Connect(dialog.m_hostname,119))
        {
            while (AppSocket->GetStatus() == CONNECTING)
            {
                YieldControl();
            }
            if (AppSocket->GetStatus() == CONNECTED)
```

(continues)

Listing 0.1 Continued

```
            {
            CString response = AppSocket->GetLine();
                SocketAvailable = TRUE;
            }
        }
    }
    if (!SocketAvailable)
    {
        AfxMessageBox("Can't connect to server. Please quit.",
                    MB_OK|MB_ICONSTOP);
    }
```

Remember, the code is only in the book so that you can understand the development process; you don't have to type in the code because it's all on the CD-ROM. Sometimes, the book shows several versions of a block of code to demonstrate the process of developing an application. In this case, the final version of the code is on the CD-ROM.

A code continuation character (➡) has been used when a code line is too long to fit within the margins of this book. This symbol simply indicates that due to page constraints, a code line has been broken that normally would appear on a single line.

Throughout the book, you come across various icons and boxes that highlight certain types of information.

Tips provide shortcuts or describe interesting features you might want to know about.

Notes explain subtle but important points. Make sure you read all the notes!

If you're using a 16-bit compiler (Visual C++ 1.51, for example), there will be times when the material in this book doesn't quite cover your situation. When that happens, you'll see a 16-bit note that explains what you need to do.

Part I

Introduction to Internet Programming

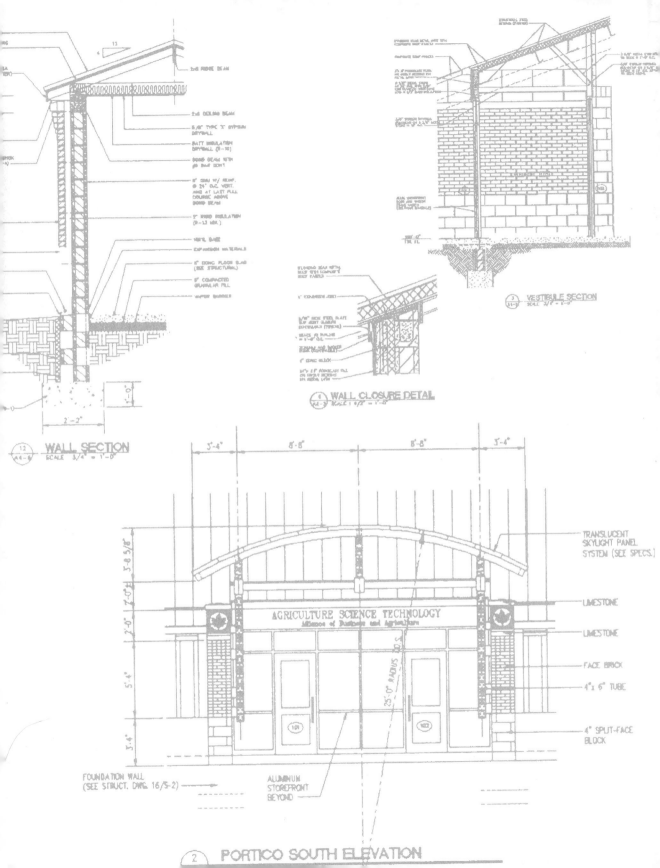

WALL SECTION
SCALE 3/4" = 1'-0"

2'-2"
1'-0"

WALL CLOSURE DETAIL
SCALE 1 1/2" = 1'-0"

VESTIBULE SECTION
SCALE 3/4" = 1'-0"

2nd RIDGE BEAM

2nd CEILING BEAM

5/8" TYPE "X" GYPSUM DRYWALL

BATT INSULATION DRYWALL (R-19)

BOND BEAM WITH #5 BAR CONT.

8" CMU W/ REINF. @ 24" O.C. VERT. AND AT EACH FULL COURSE ABOVE BOND BEAM

2" RIGID INSULATION (R-13 MIN.)

VINYL BASE

TOP MEMBRANE ON TERRAZZO

6" CONC. FLOOR SLAB (SEE STRUCTURAL)

6" COMPACTED GRANULAR FILL

VAPOR BARRIER

PORTICO SOUTH ELEVATION

3'-4"   8'-8"   8'-8"   3'-4"

TRANSLUCENT SKYLIGHT PANEL SYSTEM (SEE SPECS.)

LIMESTONE

LIMESTONE

FACE BRICK

4" x 6" TUBE

4" SPLIT-FACE BLOCK

AGRICULTURE SCIENCE TECHNOLOGY
Alliance of Business and Agriculture

3'-6 5/8"
2'-0 1/2"
2'-0"
5'-4"
3'-4"

25'-0" RADIUS

101   102

FOUNDATION WALL
(SEE STRUCT. DWG. 16/S-2)

ALUMINUM STOREFRONT BEYOND

Chapter 1

A Quick Tour of Internet Applications

You don't have to be an expert on every available Internet application before you can write your own. However, you do need to know the kinds of services that are available on the Internet in order to write useful applications for them. This chapter gives you a thumbnail sketch of the eight Internet services covered in this book:

- Finger

- Whois

- FTP

- HTTP (The World Wide Web)

- IRC

- Gopher

- E-mail

- UseNet News

Remember, even if you don't care about, say, FTP, you may want to read the chapter on it anyway to learn the concepts it covers—both Internet concepts and Windows programming concepts are sprinkled throughout the book.

The Client/Server Model

To understand how the Internet services work, you need to understand the client/server model. Internet services run over the Internet, which means that two programs are running whenever you access an Internet service. The program that runs on your desktop is called the *client program*. The program that runs on another machine, which could be on the other side of the world, is called the *server program*.

Server programs are not very exciting. They don't have a user interface. They must contain certain features; these features are laid out in Internet specifications called Requests For Comments, or RFCs. (Chapter 2, "Understanding Internet Protocols," deals with RFCs.) RFCs are cooperatively developed documents that define the behavior of each Internet service. (All the relevant ones are included on the CD-ROM that comes with this book.) Server programs wait for client programs to ask for something, and then they process the request, and send whatever was asked for or an error message. Really experienced Internet programmers can try to make server programs faster or more efficient, but beginners don't have much fun working with these programs.

Client programs have a lot more to offer. To start with, they have a user interface, which presents you with a programming challenge. You have to make the program user friendly but not expert hostile. The interface also needs to be intuitive for users with a wide range of backgrounds. Client programs have features not defined in the RFCs. For example, many Internet services send the user's e-mail address as part of the transmitted data. The RFCs don't specify how the client program must obtain this address. A smart programmer would have his program save the user's address to a file so that she wouldn't have to enter it every time she sent information. This is the sort of feature that determines whether people use your program or someone else's.

In this book, you'll be developing client programs almost exclusively. Just to show you that you're not missing anything, one server program is included as well. Because of space and time constraints, the client programs you'll be developing in this book are fairly basic. If you want to look at more complex versions of these programs, this chapter will point you to them. However, keep in mind that some of the basic programs you'll be developing are just as good as, even better than, the programs on the market today. You don't need to be a technological wizard to create a good program; you just need to come up with features that users want.

Finger

Finger is a service that asks hosts (Internet sites) about their users. It can get you a user ID at a certain site from a name or a name from a user ID; it can even find a phone number or office location. Sometimes it will tell you when a person last signed on or last read mail so that you can tell whether you're being ignored. Not every Internet host runs a Finger server program, and those that do may return little or no information. But many hosts will happily tell you about their users, even going so far as to list everyone who is signed on.

Finger clients are not exactly a burgeoning market. Next time you're at a party and people start discussing the Internet and what e-mail program and Web browser they use, ask them what Finger client they use, and then just watch as glazed looks steal across their faces. People on UNIX systems use the finger command, a Finger client that ships with UNIX. They may not have even thought of it as a client program in the usual sense. People who are not on UNIX systems have probably never heard of Finger, and that's a shame, because it's a useful little service. You'll develop your own Windows Finger client in Chapter 5, "Building an Internet Finger Application."

Whois

Whois asks a central registry about hosts. (You can also use it to ask about users, but why bother when you have Finger? Not everyone sends the sort of information to the registry that you would want about users, anyway.) You'll get a contact name, a phone number at the host (of the person who handles Internet access), often an address, and some information about the way the host is connected. You'll create your own Windows Whois client in Chapter 6, "Building an Internet Whois Application."

FTP

FTP stands for File Transfer Protocol. You can use FTP to transfer files from you to a customer, vendor, or friend, or from some public repository of information to your computer. For example, the RFCs are available by FTP.

In addition to being a Web browser, Netscape also has can FTP client program. All-in-one Internet packages include some fairly awful FTP client programs. For example, the *Trumpet* package of Internet applications includes `ftpw`, a bare-bones FTP program with a command-line interface (see fig. 1.1). In response to the `ftp>` prompt, the user types non-intuitive UNIX commands such as `ls` (for list files) and `cd` (for change directory). In contrast, the FTP application you develop in Chapter 7, "Building an Internet FTP Application," really looks like a Windows application, not a UNIX application running in a Windows edit box. I think you'll prefer it to any other client available.

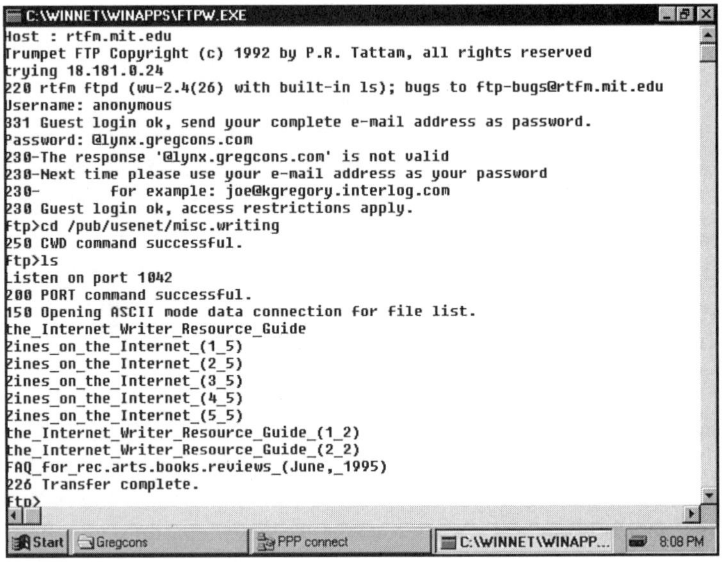

Fig. 1.1
The FTP site shown here, **rtfm.mit.edu**, contains text files that are related to the Internet and to UseNet news in particular.

```
C:\WINNET\WINAPPS\FTPW.EXE                                           _ □ ×
Host : rtfm.mit.edu
Trumpet FTP Copyright (c) 1992 by P.R. Tattam, all rights reserved
trying 18.181.0.24
220 rtfm ftpd (wu-2.4(26) with built-in ls); bugs to ftp-bugs@rtfm.mit.edu
Username: anonymous
331 Guest login ok, send your complete e-mail address as password.
Password: @lynx.gregcons.com
230-The response '@lynx.gregcons.com' is not valid
230-Next time please use your e-mail address as your password
230-        for example: joe@kgregory.interlog.com
230 Guest login ok, access restrictions apply.
Ftp>cd /pub/usenet/misc.writing
250 CWD command successful.
Ftp>ls
Listen on port 1042
200 PORT command successful.
150 Opening ASCII mode data connection for file list.
the_Internet_Writer_Resource_Guide
Zines_on_the_Internet_(1_5)
Zines_on_the_Internet_(2_5)
Zines_on_the_Internet_(3_5)
Zines_on_the_Internet_(4_5)
Zines_on_the_Internet_(5_5)
the_Internet_Writer_Resource_Guide_(1_2)
the_Internet_Writer_Resource_Guide_(2_2)
FAQ_for_rec.arts.books.reviews_(June,_1995)
226 Transfer complete.
Ftp>
```

| Start | Gregcons | PPP connect | C:\WINNET\WINAPP... | 8:08 PM |

HTTP (The World Wide Web)

Like all Internet services, the World Wide Web enables you to retrieve information. Kind-hearted people (or businesses planning to make money from you) put up Web pages and announce the location of these pages. Web pages contain information that their owners felt like making available to the public. It varies from useless, banal, insulting, and wrong to vital, up-to-the-minute, exciting, and priceless. The pages may include, among other things, text, pictures, and sounds. The pages can also include links to other pages. These links usually appear as an icon or an underlined word or phrase. When you click a link, you are taken to a related Web page.

If, for example, you are really into Lego blocks, not only can you put up a page with pictures of your best models, you can also add links to other people's Lego-related pages. Other people can add links on their pages that point to your page as well. Figure 1.2 shows a Web page about Lego. The underlined words are links to other Web pages, also about Lego.

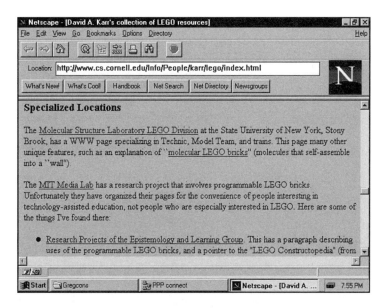

Fig. 1.2
This is David Karr's Web page about Lego as it appears in Netscape, a popular Web browser.

Figure 1.3 shows one of the Web pages for the LEGO division of the Molecular Structure Laboratory, reached by clicking David Karr's link. This full-size crane built entirely of Lego is typical of the sort of surprising images you can find on the Web. But the Molecular Structure Laboratory doesn't just provide pictures of amazing constructions: their Web page ends with a list of links, shown in figure 1.4. One of those links leads right back to David Karr's page. The connections back and forth between sites on a given topic explain why this collection of information is called a web.

The World Wide Web uses the *HTTP* (hypertext transfer protocol) to transfer information. HTTP client programs are usually called Web browsers. *Mosaic* was the first Web browser most people heard of, even though there were browsers before it. It was the first Windows-based browser and the first with a graphical interface. One glimpse of Mosaic in action was enough to convince many people they needed to jump on this technological bandwagon.

NCSA Mosaic, the original Windows Web browser, is still available at no charge. Several commercial versions of Mosaic are available as well, but today's most popular browser is *Netscape*. It's faster, lets you skip the oh-so-slow image loading that has turned off many dial-up users, and supports other Internet services as well as HTTP. In fact, some of the more popular pages now rely on Netscape features that are not in other browsers. Even if you don't write a Web browser, adding Web capabilities to any existing product is a twist that could send your product soaring. In Chapter 8, "Building an Internet HTTP Server," you develop a Web server that will make your pages available to other people's browsers.

Fig. 1.3

Clicking David Karr's link to the Molecular Structure Laboratory, LEGO division, leads to images like this one of a mobile crane.

Fig. 1.4

At the end of the Molecular Structure Laboratory Web page is another list of links, including a link back to David Karr's page.

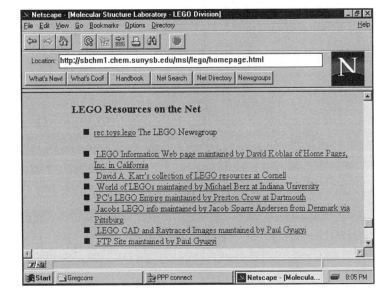

IRC

IRC (Internet Relay Chat) has been described as on-line CB radio. Conversations among large groups of people are carried on various channels. Users select the channel that interests them, and then join in. As each person types, her words appear on the screens of all the other people on that channel. Many large commercial online services, such as CompuServe and America Online, offer "chat rooms" with a similar kind of discussion.

IRC conversations are live, public, and unarchived. They're great for free-flowing chats, but they're not so great for business conversations. At times, people will arrange to join a specific channel at a specific time or issue a public invitation using News or the Web to join a channel. Most of the time, however, people looking for conversation just wander by and see what's happening on the channels they prefer. In Chapter 9, "Building an Internet IRC Application," you develop an IRC client to bring you into these worldwide conversations.

Gopher

These days, Gopher is usually explained as being "like the World Wide Web," but it actually predates the Web. *Gopher* is a series of links that lead to useful information like phone books or library catalogs. Gopher links are installed by administrators, whereas Web links are scattered among the information on user's home pages and aren't controlled by any one authority.

Because Gopher is more controlled, it isn't growing as fast and it usually isn't as much fun as the World Wide Web. From a business perspective, Gopher can be more useful than the Web, as you can see in figure 1.5. However, Gopher server programs are not as numerous as some other Internet applications. In Chapter 10, "Building an Internet Gopher Application," you create a Gopher client to burrow your way through Gopherspace.

Fig. 1.5

This list of Gopher
services offered by
Trent University
in Canada is
displayed using
the WinGopher
Gopher client.
Each selection
leads to a text file
or to another
menu.

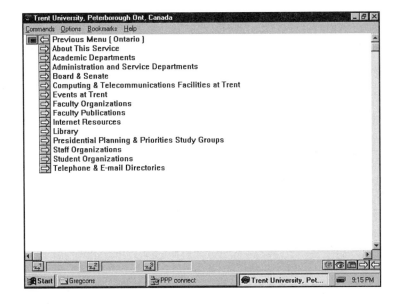

E-Mail

Electronic mail, known as *e-mail*, is a familiar concept to millions of people
who are not on the Internet, so it should come as no surprise that it's one of
the most popular services on the Internet. Writing a mail application is a big
job to tackle, which is why this book doesn't cover the subject until Chapter
11, "Building an Internet Electronic Mail Application." After all, e-mail is
popular because it does so much, and the interface is more complex than
other applications.

There are many e-mail applications available for Windows; probably the most
popular is *Eudora*. Figure 1.6 shows the interface of the shareware version,
one of the many Internet applications included on this book's CD-ROM.

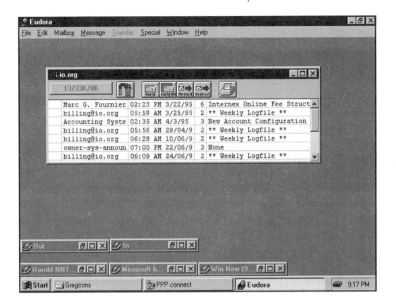

Figure 1.6
Eudora can have multiple mailboxes open at one time. This user keeps all mail related to a specific Internet service provider in one mailbox.

News

Explaining News, also called *UseNet* or *Internet newsgroups*, could take up a whole book. (I should know—I wrote one!) A simplified explanation is that News is typed conversations, like IRC, but because the messages are stored on all the machines around the Internet, it's not live. You can post a public message at 10 p.m. that asks a question, and then sign off and go to bed. At 11 p.m., someone may read your message and post an answer while someone else on the other side of the world does the same thing. The next morning you would see both answers; you might even see another message that disagrees with one of the answers. After a few days, or weeks on some sites, the messages are removed. Important messages are archived elsewhere.

News client programs are called newsreaders. A newsreader is one of the most difficult Internet applications to write. That's why it's almost the last project you'll be tackling in this book. It's also why most of the newsreaders for

Windows, whether commercial or shareware, are not very good. Many of them do not follow the specifications laid out for News, and those that do have other deficiencies. The most popular Windows newsreaders at the moment are *WinVN* (see fig. 1.7) and the *Trumpet newsreader* (see fig. 1.8). Many new newsreaders are coming onto the market now, but there's still room for a good one!

Fig. 1.7
The WinVN newsreader has windows for lists of newsgroups and for lists of articles. When a user double-clicks an article, it is displayed in another window. You can move or resize any of the windows.

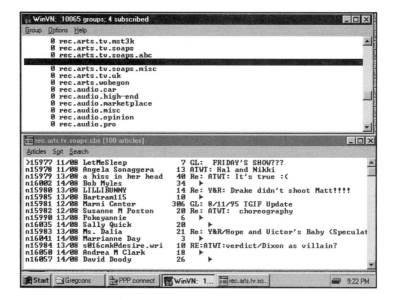

Fig. 1.8
The Trumpet newsreader has a slightly less flexible interface than WinVN.

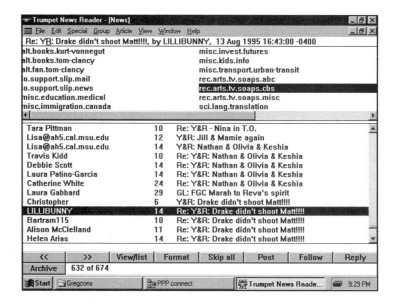

From Here...

Now you have some idea of what the standard Internet applications do, and how certain implementations of them look:

- Finger

- Whois

- FTP, illustrated with Trumpet's `ftpw`

- HTTP, illustrated with Netscape

- IRC

- Gopher, illustrated with WinGopher

- Electronic mail, illustrated with Eudora

- News, illustrated with WinVN and the Trumpet Newsreader

To actually write these applications, you need to know how they communicate with other programs on other Internet sites. The rules for this communication are called *protocols*, and they are discussed in the next chapter.

Chapter 2

Understanding Internet Protocols

To understand the protocols in use on the Internet, you must first understand Internet addressing because many protocols use addresses explicitly and addressing is the base of all operations on the Internet. After explaining how Internet addressing works, this chapter takes a brief look at many of the more popular protocols in use on the Internet. Each section introduces a protocol, covers some of the important points about using the protocol, and tells you where to find more information on the protocol.

In this chapter, you learn the following:

- How network addresses work on the Internet

- How TCP/IP works as the basic networking protocol for the Internet

- More technical detail on how the popular Internet application protocols, including Finger, Whois, FTP, HTTP (used for the World Wide Web), IRC, Gopher, SMTP, and NNTP, work

Internet Addressing

You are probably familiar with Internet addresses such as **oak.oakland.edu** (domain form) or **128.211.23.45** (numeric form), but you may not know exactly how these addresses are used, or exactly how they relate to the protocols in use on the Internet. Every host on the Internet has a unique address that distinguishes it from every other computer attached to the Internet. This addressing system is what allows information to be sent to individual computers hooked up to the Internet.

Internet addresses are 32-bit numbers that are usually separated into four 8-bit fields. The four fields of an Internet address are similar to the lines of a conventional postal address. Just as a mail carrier cannot deliver mail to you if you have no postal address, you cannot receive information on the Internet if you do not have an Internet address. One important difference between these two addressing systems is the order in which addressing information must be listed. Postal addresses list specific information first and then move on to more general information. For example, the first line of a postal address usually specifies an individual to which the letter is to be delivered, and the last lines are usually the city, state, and zip code information. Internet addresses start with the general information and then become more specific. In an Internet address, the first 8-bit field specifies the general network that a host is on (kind of like the city, state, and zip code information), and the last 8-bit field usually designates a specific computer or host on the network.

The other two fields of the Internet address can be used for either additional network identification or additional host identification. How these fields are used determines what type of Internet address you have. There are three types of Internet addresses: Class A, Class B, and Class C.

Class A addresses only use the first field for network identification and the remaining fields for host identification. Because 8-bits can only represent 256 unique numbers, giving all networks a Class A address would limit the total number of networks on the Internet to 256, which would not be practical. Only organizations or corporations with extremely large internal networks have Class A addresses. Addresses for machines on one of these large networks start with a number between 1 and 127.

Class B addresses use the first two 8-bit fields for network identification and the final two 8-bit fields for host identification. This system allows for many networks with many hosts. These addresses begin with numbers from 128 to 191. Most moderate to large size organizations and corporations have Class B addresses.

Class C addresses, as you may have guessed by now, use the first three 8-bit fields as network identification and the last 8-bit field for host identification. Class C addresses usually go to small organizations and corporations. They start with a number between 192 and 223. The numbers above 223 are reserved for future use. Figure 2.1 illustrates each class of address.

Now that you understand Internet addressing, you can learn how the low-level Internet protocols use addressing to communicate information to particular hosts. Internet addresses only solve part of the problem, that is, to identify each host uniquely. Once the host has a unique address, then it can establish connections to other hosts.

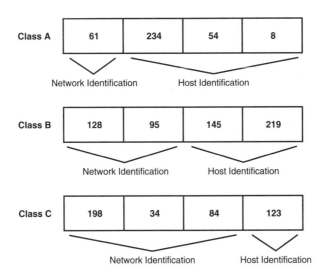

Fig. 2.1
Class A, Class B, and Class C addresses differ in how they identify networks and hosts.

Transmission Control Protocol/ Internet Protocol (TCP/IP)

Any discussion of protocols in use on the Internet should begin with the *Transmission Control Protocol/Internet Protocol* (*TCP/IP*). TCP/IP is the foundation for all the other protocols. As the name implies, TCP/IP is really two protocol standards that work in unison. As figure 2.2 on the next page shows, IP sits on top of the local network protocol, TCP sits on top of IP, and FTP and other protocols sit on top of TCP. The following sections explain what TCP and IP do.

Datagrams

Data transmission on the Internet usually occurs in chunks known as *datagrams*. A datagram is just a specific number of bytes that is sent together at one time. In order to understand why things need to be broken into relatively small chunks, consider the example of sending a file that is 20,000

bytes long. Sending a 20,000-byte file all at once would be impractical because it would consume a large amount of bandwidth for quite a long time. If
a host detected an error in the transmission, the entire 20,000-byte file would
have to be sent again, tying up the bandwidth another time. In order to
avoid this type of situation, a host may choose to break up this file into 20
1,000-byte datagrams and send them individually.

Fig. 2.2
The TCP/IP model
is a layered model.

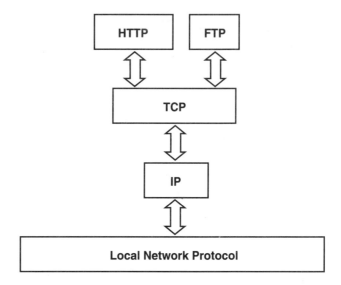

The size of a datagram is dependent upon the capabilities of the hosts
on each end of the transmission. If, for example, one host can support
1,500-byte datagrams and the other can only support 1,000-byte datagrams,
both sides will use 1,000-byte datagrams. You may have heard the term *packets* also being used to describe small groups of data. Often these two terms,
datagram and packet, can be used interchangeably. However, suppose that
one host has to send a file to another host and they agree to use 1,000-byte
datagrams. An intermediate network between the hosts can only handle
128-byte pieces of information. In this situation, the 1,000-byte datagram
must be broken up into 128-byte packets, transferred through the intermediate network, reassembled to a 1000-byte datagram, and then sent along to the
destination. The term *packet* is a generic term, referring to the physical representation of network information. Datagrams are a special case of packet,
referring specifically to the Internet Protocol. Datagrams are sometimes transmitted through other network media, in which they are encapsulated into
that medium's packet format, such as the 53-byte ATM (Asynchronous Transfer Mode) packet.

The following section examines the protocol responsible for managing datagrams, TCP.

Transmission Control Protocol (TCP)

Transmission Control Protocol's (TCP) main responsibilities are to perform the following tasks relating to communication between hosts:

- Breaking transmissions into datagrams

- Reassembling datagrams into their original form

- Ensuring that datagrams are in the correct sequence when reassembled

- Resending any datagrams that get lost or garbled in the transmission

TCP handles many of its chores with the aid of header information that is attached to the beginning of each datagram. The TCP header consists of numerous fields that contain information vital to the accurate transmission of datagrams across the Internet. The fields of the TCP header that you need to be most concerned with are the source port number, the destination port number, and the sequence number.

Because many people on a single host can carry on conversations with many other hosts, there needs to be a way to distinguish each conversation from the others and prevent any datagrams from going to the wrong user. When a TCP connection is established between two hosts, each host communicates to the other host through a specific TCP *port*. A port is really just a number signifying the conversation to which the incoming datagram belongs. The port number has no physical significance to a real communications port; it is just a logical representation. The source and destination port numbers simply tell where the datagram comes from (the source) and where the datagram is going (the destination). The sequence number tells the destination TCP module where the datagram belongs when the file (or whatever the datagrams represent) is reconstructed into its original form on the receiving host. This number is important because the Internet Protocol, which is explained in the next section, considers each datagram to be a separate entity, not part of a larger group. Internet Protocol does not care if the datagrams are sent in the proper sequence. It only cares that a datagram gets to the correct destination host.

Three other fields of the TCP header are mostly involved with the management of the datagrams. These fields include the checksum, the acknowledgment number, and the window. The checksum is used to verify that the datagram arrived at its destination in exactly the same form as it left the sender. A checksum can be computed by simply totaling the number of bytes in the datagram. The TCP checksum is a little more complicated than a simple total, but knowing the exact formula is not essential. The way a checksum works is that the sending TCP module computes a checksum and places this number into the appropriate field of the TCP header. When the destination host receives the datagram, the receiving TCP module computes its own checksum from the newly received datagram and compares it with the one placed in the header by the sending TCP module. If the two checksums do not match, the receiving TCP module notifies the sending TCP module of the error. The sending TCP module then resends the entire datagram to the receiving TCP module where the checksums are compared again. The process repeats until both checksums match.

The acknowledgment number is used to confirm the receipt of a datagram. The receiving TCP module must acknowledge each datagram that the sending TCP module sends. If the sending TCP module does not get this acknowledgment in a timely manner (usually a minute or so), it assumes that the datagram was lost somewhere and resends the datagram.

Because waiting for the acknowledgment of each datagram before sending any more would slow down transmission considerably, TCP uses a windowing system. This system allows the sending TCP module to send additional datagrams without having to wait for acknowledgment of each datagram it has sent to come back from the receiving TCP module. The amount of data that can be in transit at any one time is known as the *window size*. This windowing system prevents a fast computer from swamping a slow computer with data, which could result in the loss of some datagrams and cause the whole process to take an excruciating amount of time to complete.

The TCP header uses the window field to indicate how much data a host TCP module can still receive before its window is full. As the receiving TCP module receives datagrams, it decrements the number in the window field and sends a datagram back to the sending TCP module indicating the new window size. The receiving TCP module can relay both an acknowledgment and a change of window size in one single datagram. This consolidation cuts down on the amount of datagrams involved in a TCP transmission, thereby reducing the amount of time the whole transmission takes.

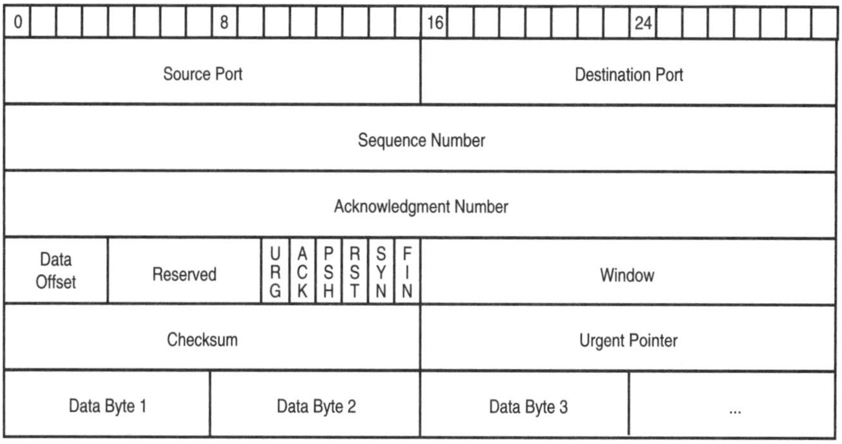

0							8								16							24							
Source Port															Destination Port														
Sequence Number																													
Acknowledgment Number																													
Data Offset		Reserved			U R G	A C K	P S H	R S T	S Y N	F I N	Window																		
Checksum															Urgent Pointer														
Data Byte 1					Data Byte 2					Data Byte 3						...													

Fig. 2.3
The TCP header includes the source and destination ports as well as a sequence number and checksum.

Internet Protocol

Internet Protocol (IP) is responsible for getting a datagram from point A to point B. A TCP module hands an IP module a datagram and the destination address of the host where the datagram is supposed to go. IP does not care about the contents of the datagram or the contents of the TCP header attached to the datagram. Its main concern is to find a route to the destination and send the datagram to that destination. An IP module adds its own header to the datagram in addition to the TCP header. The main fields of this new header that you need to be concerned with are the source and destination addresses, the checksum, the protocol, and the time to live.

The *source address* tells a receiving IP module the host from which this particular datagram came. The destination address tells an IP module, or an intermediate gateway, where to send this particular datagram. The IP checksum is used to ensure that the IP header is not damaged. Keep in mind that the IP checksum is not the same as the TCP checksum. The *IP checksum* only checks the accuracy of the IP header; the TCP checksum checks the accuracy of the datagram. Because other protocols besides TCP also use IP, the protocol field is needed to specify to which protocol this particular datagram goes. The *time to live* is a number that is decremented each time a host or gateway processes the datagram. This number is in place to prevent loops in which one datagram bounces back and forth between two hosts. If the time to live reaches zero, the receiving host discards the datagram, which causes the datagram to be resent.

To understand IP operation, consider an example of a datagram traveling from one host to another. Assume for this example that the datagram must travel through one intermediate gateway. The local IP module gets the datagram and destination address from the local TCP module. The local IP module looks at the destination address, sees that it is not local, tacks on the IP header, and sends the datagram to the gateway. The gateway receives the datagram, looks at the destination field of the header, makes some routing decisions, and sends the datagram to the local IP module of the destination host. That IP module then reads the IP header and sees that the datagram is to go to the TCP protocol; it strips off the IP header and sends the datagram to the correct protocol.

Fig. 2.4

The IP header includes the source and destination addresses.

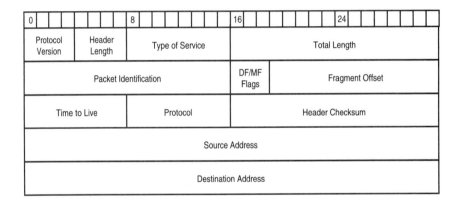

This brief explanation of how TCP/IP works should be enough for you to get started writing Internet applications. However, if you are interested in learning more about the nuts and bolts of TCP/IP, I encourage you to read RFC 791 and RFC 793 on IP and TCP respectively, available on the CD-ROM in the \RFC folder. There are also numerous books available that give in-depth coverage of TCP/IP and its use on the Internet.

The following sections deal with the application protocols you will be working with when you write Internet applications. Most application protocols are based on a simple 4-step client/server model. First the client makes a connection to a server. Then the client sends a request to which the server sends a response. Finally, the client closes the connection. The difference between application protocols lies primarily in the TCP/IP port number each one uses and the terms each protocol uses in the requests and responses. In fact, the word *protocol* actually refers to the exact syntax and language of the client/ server interchange.

Finger

Perhaps the most basic Internet application protocol is the Finger protocol. The Finger protocol is used to query hosts for information on users of that host. Finger follows the typical 4-step client/server model. Unlike most servers, the response of Finger servers does not need to adhere to a specific format, which means they can send just about anything. For example, they can send a user's full name, login name, terminal location, office location, office phone number, last login date, and so on. Finger servers may even send a user information file (also known as a *plan* file), which is usually a text file with information that the user wants sent to people who finger the account.

One of the more interesting applications of the Finger protocol is to use it to check on vending machines connected to the Internet. One university uses Finger to monitor the availability of soft drinks in a local dispenser. Yet another university can check the temperature and availability of coffee using Finger. I guess some students grew tired of climbing stairs only to find an empty vending machine. Thanks to Finger, they can check for refreshments remotely, and use their time more wisely.

In Chapter 5, "Building an Internet Finger Application," you learn about the technical details of the Finger protocol and create a Finger application. You can also find more information on the Finger protocol in RFC 1288 available on the CD-ROM in the \RFC folder.

Whois

The Whois protocol as it is now implemented is very similar to the Finger protocol. Whois follows the same basic 4-step client/server model. The Whois protocol is primarily used for obtaining information about a particular system or the users of that system.

The main Whois server for the Internet is located at InterNIC. This server contains contact information for each domain on the Internet. If you need to find out who owned the domain anyhost.com, you send a Whois message to the InterNIC Registration Services Host. You receive information on who owns that particular domain name and contact information for one or more people at that domain.

Chapter 6, "Building an Internet Whois Application," shows the Whois protocol in action. The details of the Whois protocol are also available in RFC 954 on the CD-ROM in the \RFC folder.

File Transfer Protocol

The File Transfer Protocol (FTP) has been in use since the early 1970s. It is also one of the essential protocols included when talking about the TCP/IP suite of protocols. FTP is used, as the name implies, to transfer files from host to host. *Anonymous FTP* is when you use FTP and specify the username *anonymous* upon connection. If prompted for a password, it is customary to provide your e-mail address, for logging purposes.

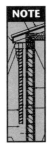 **NOTE** When transferring files, FTP can also perform translations on the files. This feature was designed to accommodate different operating systems, each of which has its own ASCII text file specification. For instance, UNIX systems use a line feed character at the end of each line, and PCs use a carriage return. When FTP is in *ascii* mode, it converts the end-of-line characters to the proper equivalent for the target system. Unfortunately, this feature can cause data corruption when you transfer a binary file. During a binary file transfer, FTP converts the end-of-line characters and effectively renders the file useless. To avoid this problem, always put FTP into *binary* mode first when transferring binary files.

The FTP protocol departs slightly from the typical client/server model used in Finger, Whois, and HTTP in that FTP uses two connections, a control connection and a data connection. FTP uses the control connection to send commands. This connection stays intact throughout the entire FTP session. FTP uses the data connection to transfer files. In Chapter 7, "Building an Internet FTP Application," you'll see this in action. RFC 959, on the CD as \RFC\RFC0959.TXT, is an excellent source for technical information on the FTP protocol.

World Wide Web

The World Wide Web (WWW) is actually a hypertext system implemented on a grand scale across the Internet. The system is made up of documents that contain links to other documents, files, or almost anything you can imagine. These documents, files, and so on are known collectively as Internet resources. By using a *Uniform Resource Locator (URL)*, you can find out where exactly each of these resources is located on the Internet. The following sections explain how URLs, *Hypertext Transfer Protocol (HTTP)*, *Multipurpose Internet Mail Extension (MIME)*, and *Hypertext Markup Language (HTML)* relate to the World Wide Web.

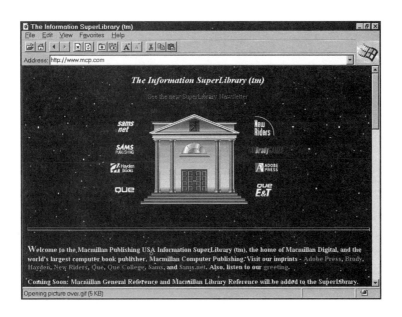

Internet Programming

Fig. 2.5
The World Wide Web serves as a new medium for businesses to reach new customers.

Uniform Resource Locators

Uniform Resource Locators (URLs) specify the exact location of any resource on the Internet that is part of the World Wide Web. You use an URL in a World Wide Web browser to identify and retrieve information. The format of an URL begins with a naming scheme specifier. This specifier indicates the Internet protocol you're using. Some common naming scheme specifiers are as follows:

Specifier	Protocol
ftp	FTP
http	HTTP
shttp	Secure HTTP
https	Another secure HTTP
gopher	Gopher
telnet	Telnet
news	UseNet News
nntp	UseNet News
wais	Wide Area Information Service
mailto	E-mail

Fig. 2.6
URLs serve as simple identifiers to resources on the World Wide Web.

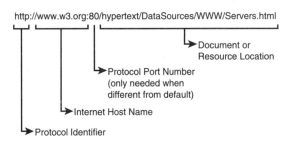

As illustrated in figure 2.6, the naming scheme is http, which indicates that this resource is located on an HTTP server. The rest of the URL includes the domain name (www.w3.org) and the path to the document. Appendix C, "Uniform Resource Locators," and RFC 1738 (on the CD in the \RFC folder) contain many examples of URLs and explain the correct URL syntax.

Hypertext Transfer Protocol

The Hypertext Transfer Protocol (HTTP) defines the standard for distributed, collaborative, hypermedia information systems. HTTP differs from the other protocols in that it allows the user to use embedded links within documents to find more information.

Like Finger and Whois, HTTP uses the simple 4-step client/server model. When a client sends a request for a document in HTTP, the server replies with status information, the type and size of the data, and information concerning many other attributes of the document. The server uses the Multipurpose Internet Mail Extension (MIME) to convey the file type.

Multipurpose Internet Mail Extension

The Multipurpose Internet Mail Extension (MIME) is a specification that allows the exchange of data in any format. Data senders use MIME to notify the receivers of the format of the enclosed data. MIME was originally developed to provide a standard way to send different types of data over Internet e-mail systems.

For e-mail, MIME information is transferred as part of the message headers. The following three headers are typically included:

■ *MIME-Version*. This header defines the version of MIME that is used, such as 1.0.

- *Content-Type.* The header defines the MIME type of the enclosed data, such as text/plain or video/mpeg.

- *Content-Transfer-Encoding.* This header defines the mechanism used to encode the data before it was sent, such as base64. Encoding is often required to send 8-bit binary data over 7-bit messaging systems.

In the World Wide Web, MIME is used in the HTTP request and response headers to define the format of information. When a Web browser requests a particular resource, the server responds with the MIME type of the data as well as the actual data. The browser can then take appropriate action, such as display the data within a window or execute an external program to handle the data. Servers typically base the MIME type on the file name extension of the requested information.

The MIME specification lists several MIME types. MIME types are categorized by a main type followed by a slash and a subtype. The list of MIME types continues to grow. If you need to define a new MIME type or subtype for your own purposes, prefix the type with the "x-" characters. Table 2.1 lists some example MIME types.

Table 2.1   Example MIME Types

MIME Type	Description
text/plain	Plain ASCII text
text/html	HTML text
application/msword	Microsoft Word document
application/x-powerpoint	Microsoft PowerPoint document (unratified)
audio/basic	Audio
video/mpeg	MPEG Video
image/gif	GIF picture
image/jpeg	JPEG picture

You can find more information about HTTP and MIME in Chapter 8, "Building an Internet HTTP Application." This chapter also shows you how to build an HTTP server. You can find the technical details of HTTP in the draft HTTP Internet specification included on the CD-ROM in the \RFC\DRAFTS folder. The MIME details are available in RFC 1521.

Hypertext Markup Language

The format of most of the documents sent on the World Wide Web is Hypertext Markup Language (HTML). HTML is a standard way of distributing hypermedia documents. An HTML document is really just a plain text document with HTML *tags* embedded within it. HTML tags inform the client that a particular section of the document should be displayed in a certain way. For example, the <TITLE> tag tells the client that the characters following the tag (up to the ending </TITLE> tag) are to be displayed as a title of the document. How the client displays the characters is really up to the client. Most clients allow the user to select the font, size, and color of any displayed text. In addition to <TITLE>, there are other text formatting tags such as <Hn>, where n is a number between 1 and 6, for headings and <P> for paragraphs.

One of the key features of HTML is the ability to include links to other documents within your document. If you want to add a link to another document on the same server, just use <A HREF="OtherPath/OtherDoc.html">Other Document</A>. The <A indicates that what follows is an *anchor* (basically just a link). The HREF="OtherPath/OtherDoc.html"> is the other half of the anchor declaration. The next string is what is displayed to someone viewing your HTML document. Finally, the </A> tag indicates the end of the anchor designation.

In addition to titles, headers, paragraphs, and links, there are tags for things such as in-line pictures and graphics, lists, menus, character formatting, and forms. For example, compare the following listing of HTML code and the results as displayed by a World Wide Web browser, as seen in figure 2.5.

```
<HTML><HEAD><TITLE>The Information SuperLibrary (tm)</TITLE></HEAD>
<BODY background="/home/nebula.jpg" text="#eeeeee" link="#00ff00"
vlink="#00ff00">
<H2><P ALIGN=CENTER><STRONG><I>The Information SuperLibrary (tm)</
p></I></STRONG></H2>
<a href="/general/news8/nl.html"><p align=center>
See the new SuperLibrary Newsletter</p></a><P ALIGN=CENTER>
<A HREF="/cgi-bin/imagemap/mcphome"><IMG BORDER=0 SRC="/home/
homenew.jpg" ISMAP ></P>
</A><HR SIZE=6><BR>
<STRONG><FONT SIZE=+2>W</FONT>elcome to the Macmillan Publishing
USA Information SuperLibrary (tm), the home of Macmillan Digital,
and the world's largest computer book publisher, Macmillan Computer
```

```
Publishing. Visit our imprints - <A HREF="/hayden/adobe.html">Adobe
Press</A>,
<A HREF="/brady">Brady</A>, <A HREF="/hayden"> Hayden</A>,
<A HREF="/newriders">New Riders</A>, <A HREF="/que">Que</A>,
<A HREF="/quecollege">Que College</A>, <A HREF="/sams"> Sams</A>,
and
<A HREF="/samsnet"> Sams.net</A>. Also, listen to our <A HREF="e-
door.au">greeting</A>.<P>
Coming Soon: Macmillan General Reference and Macmillan Library
Reference will be added to the SuperLibrary.<P>
...
</BODY>
</HTML>
```

For a complete guide to HTML tags, refer to Appendix B, "Hypertext Markup Language." You also can read the draft standard for HTML included on the CD-ROM in the \RFC\DRAFTS folder.

Internet Relay Chat

Internet users use the Internet Relay Chat (IRC) protocol to hold real-time conferences on many different topics. At any given time, you can find conversations on such subjects as computers, travel, politics, and everything in between. IRC enables users to communicate with IRC servers and enables these servers to communicate with other IRC servers.

The IRC servers are the mainstay of the entire system. They provide access points for clients so that clients can talk to each other, and they provide access points for other servers to form a distributed network.

The IRC protocol is a complex protocol. It specifies how client to server and server to server messages should be sent, acknowledged, and processed. For details on the IRC protocol, refer to Chapter 9, "Building an Internet IRC Application," or consult RFC 1459 in the \RFC folder on the CD-ROM.

Gopher

Gopher is a fairly simple protocol, much like Finger or Whois. However, just because Gopher is simple does not mean it isn't powerful. *Gopher* presents information to the user in the form of hierarchical lists similar to the way a file system is set up on a computer. Users can traverse these lists, going deeper and deeper into particular areas until they find the particular information they want. This delving or *burrowing* concept is where Gopher gets its name. Of course, the fact that it was developed at the University of Minnesota (home of the Golden Gophers) probably has something to do with it also.

If you want all the technical details for the Gopher protocol, read RFC 1438 available in the \RFC folder on the CD-ROM. Chapter 10, "Building an Internet Gopher Application," shows you how to build a Gopher application.

Simple Mail Transport Protocol

The Simple Mail Transport Protocol (*SMTP*) is the protocol used by two hosts to exchange Internet mail messages. Keep in mind that SMTP only covers the way mail messages are sent on the Internet, not the format of the messages themselves.

SMTP is based on a simple extension to the typical 4-step client/server model. Each SMTP connection uses multiple requests and responses. Instead of only a single transaction per connection, mail is sent from the client to the server until all the mail has been sent. This helps reduce the connection overhead when sending multiple messages to the same host.

Another protocol used to access Internet e-mail is the *Post-Office Protocol* (*POP*). POP enables you to access a mailbox on another server. Users who do not have the luxury of a full-time Internet connection can establish a full-time SMTP mailbox on their Internet Service Provider's server and use POP to retrieve the messages.

Chapter 11, "Building an Internet Electronic Mail Application," shows you how to build an SMTP and POP e-mail application. You can find more detailed information on SMTP in RFC 821. Information on POP is found in RFC 1725 in the \RFC folder on the CD-ROM.

Network News Transport Protocol

The *Network News Transport Protocol* (*NNTP*) is used, as you might expect, to carry news from one host to another. NNTP came about after the realization that storing news on a central server and allowing client applications to download only items of interest used far fewer resources than having all the news on each machine. NNTP provides a method of distribution, inquiry, retrieval, and posting of news articles between hosts. NNTP was designed with the UseNet news system in mind, but NNTP is easily adaptable to other news systems.

In a typical environment, news is transferred from host to host using a method known as *flooding*, which means that each host sends all its news to each host that it feeds. Because most hosts are fed by more than one host, this method results in many duplicated news items and wasted resources. You would think that a host should be able to ask the host it's feeding whether it already has the news items. This is generally possible except for a few transport mechanisms that are not interactive. For these mechanisms, flooding is the most efficient way of spreading the news. NNTP provides a method for every host to retrieve new news groups, retrieve new news articles, advise other hosts of new newsgroups, and advise other hosts of new news articles.

Chapter 12, "Building an Internet Newsreader Application," shows you how to build an NNTP application. If you want more technical information on NNTP, read RFC 977 available in the \RFC folder on the CD-ROM.

From Here...

This chapter examined many Internet protocols, including TCP/IP. TCP/IP forms the base upon which the application protocols, such as Finger, Whois, HTTP, FTP, IRC, Gopher, SMTP, and NNTP, sit. The next chapter looks at Windows sockets and explains how and why they are an integral of any Internet application that you write.

I

Internet Programming

Chapter 3

Windows Sockets (WINSOCK.DLL)

The key to Internet programming for Windows is sockets. Sockets, in general, means a set of functions to handle two-way communication using TCP/IP or other protocols. Windows Sockets, in particular, means the industry standard API developed by more than 20 vendors and released as an open networking standard to handle TCP/IP communications (though there are spaces left in the specification to handle other protocols later.) If you want to write Internet programs for Windows, you must know sockets and you must know Windows Sockets. This chapter answers some of the questions you may be asking yourself:

- What are sockets?

- What is the Windows Sockets API and where do I get one?

- How can I include sockets in a C++ program?

- What would I do with a socket class if I had one?

- How do I use sockets without CSocket and CAsyncSocket?

- How do I use MFC sockets if AppWizard won't include them?

What Are Sockets?

Sockets came from UNIX, and specifically from Berkeley UNIX (BSD) around 1980. A *socket* is a piece of software that can both send and receive data over a TCP/IP network. There are three important pieces of information about a socket: the IP address it is talking to, the port it is talking to at that address, and the socket type.

There's one thing about ports I have to make clear right away: these aren't ports like your serial or parallel port. They don't represent any hardware at all. They are just a convention used by the programs that are running on each of the communicating machines. TCP/IP enables my machine to be connected to many different Internet machines at once. For example, it is possible, all at the same time, for me to have a Web browser loading a big page while my newsreader is sorting and indexing a big list of news articles and an FTP program is downloading a big executable file. In the middle of all that, e-mail is arriving for me, and I turn my attention to it while all the other stuff loads and indexes and whatnot. All these different "conversations" between my machine and other machines on the Internet are happening on different ports. As was discussed in Chapter 2, "Understanding Internet Protocols," there are standard ports for standard Internet services such as the Web, News, FTP, and mail.

There are two types of sockets: *stream sockets* and *datagram sockets*. These correspond to the two main protocols wrapped up into TCP/IP: TCP and UDP. TCP communication proceeds like this: the two machines form a connection, data is exchanged over the connection, the connection is closed. UDP communication, on the other hand, does not involve a connection. One machine simply sends the other some material. Stream sockets implement TCP and are used where the applications are going to exchange a lot of data, or where the order in which data arrives is important. A classic example of a TCP application that would use stream sockets is FTP. Datagram sockets implement UDP and are used where the amount of data exchanged is small or the order is not an issue. The classic example here is a clock-updater that broadcasts its system time to a number of other sites.

Obtaining a Windows Sockets API

When someone says "the Windows Sockets API," as if there was only one, they are referring to the specification that all the vendors agreed on—that is, the names of the functions and what those functions do. For example, the specification states that there is a socket function called connect() which will "Initiate a connection on the specified socket."

You can't, however, execute a specification; you need actual code, raw or compiled. Many vendors provide a dynamic library called WINSOCK.DLL, which lets you call all the functions referred to in the specification. For example, the suite of programs generally referred to as Trumpet, by Peter Tattam, includes a WINSOCK.DLL with all these functions, and the other functions needed to actually establish a *SLIP* or *PPP* Internet connection across a telephone line. (SLIP stands for *Serial Line Internet Protocol*, and PPP stands for *Point-to-Point Protocol*.) Windows 95 and Windows NT also include a slightly different WINSOCK.DLL. In fact, I have six files, all with different sizes and date stamps, called WINSOCK.DLL, on the three computers in my office, as well as a file called WSOCK32.DLL, which is a 32-bit Winsock. Of course, they are all in different directories, so I can be sure the right one gets used by my Internet applications.

> If you don't have Windows 95 or Windows NT, you can still get a WINSOCK.DLL. There is a shareware copy of the Trumpet Winsock on the CD-ROM included with this book, in the folder \APPS\CONNECT\TWSK21F. Remember to register it if you use it.

The Windows Sockets API provides a level of abstraction between applications and the physical network. Figure 3.1 is a schematic of two Windows applications, an Internet client and an Internet server, communicating over the Internet using Windows Sockets. Of course, many of the programs your applications will communicate with will not be Windows programs. The sockets model abstracts the communication process for a variety of operating systems.

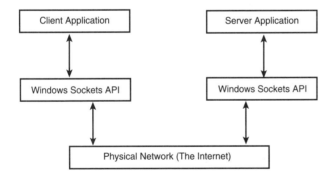

Fig. 3.1
These two applications, running under Windows on different machines, both use the Windows Sockets API to handle their communication.

Including Sockets in a C++ Program

The Winsock specification lists a great number of functions and their parameters. WINSOCK.DLL enables you to call those functions from anywhere in your program. You'll learn about these functions in a general sense, and then draw them together into a socket class that encapsulates the API.

Berkeley-Sockets Functions

Experienced sockets programmers from other operating systems will feel comfortable immediately with these functions: they have the same names and do the same tasks as the functions in the original Berkeley implementation of sockets for UNIX. These functions are:

- accept
- bind
- closesocket
- connect
- getpeername
- getsockname
- getsockopt, setsockopt
- htonl, htons, ntohl, ntohs
- inet_addr, inet_ntoa
- ioctlsocket
- listen
- recv, recvfrom
- select
- send, sendto
- shutdown
- socket

If you're not an experienced sockets programmer, the four functions htonl, htons, ntohl, and ntohs deserve special mention. They are used to convert large numbers that represent addresses. As you learned in Chapter 2, "Understanding Internet Protocols," Internet addresses can be represented as character strings or as four numbers separated by dots, like 198.53.145.3—the address of my Internet site. Each of these numbers is between 0 and 255, and so can be represented by an 8-bit number. The four of them together can be wrapped up into a 32-bit number, but unfortunately there are two ways to do it.

One way is to put the leftmost 8-bit number (198 for my machine) into the eight most significant bits of the 32-bit number, then the next eight bits into the second-most significant eight bits, and so on. This fills the 32-bit number from high end to low end and is called *big-Endian* order. The other is to put the leftmost number into the least significant eight bits and work your way up through the 32-bit number—this is called *little-Endian* order. For example, the address 0.0.0.1 would be converted to 1 in big-Endian order, or 16,777,216 (2 to the 24th power) in little-Endian order. If two machines with different orders need to exchange addresses and one passes a little-Endian number while the other is expecting big-Endian, there will obviously be a big problem getting communications established.

The Internet uses big-Endian order, but your machine may use little-Endian order (Intel machines are little-Endians; Motorola machines—including Macs—are big-Endians.). The socket function `htonl()` converts host addresses (32 bits stored in big- or little-Endian order depending on your host; the DLL is designed for a specific host—for example, an Intel machine) into network addresses—32 bits stored in big-Endian order. The `htons()` function does the same for 16-bit numbers. The reverse conversions are `ntohl()` and `ntohs()`.

Typically, these conversion functions are used when one site needs to pass an Internet address or port number to another site, and rarely in any other circumstances.

While you're learning about address conversions, `inet_addr()` converts a character string like `198.53.145.3` into a network address, and `inet_ntoa()` turns a 32-bit network address into an ASCII character string.

The rest of the Berkeley functions will be covered as you use them, later in this chapter.

Database Functions

Though these are called database functions, they don't necessarily look things up in a database—they might, for example, send a request to another machine on the Internet to look them up:

- `gethostbyaddr`
- `gethostname`
- `gethostbyname`
- `getprotobyname`

- `getservbyname`

- `getservbyport`

These functions enable conversion between cryptic numbers and codes, and recognizable keywords or names. The `gethostbyname()` function, for example, determines the network address (a 32-bit number) of the machine whose name (such as **ftp.microsoft.com**) is passed to it. To avoid hard-coding port numbers, you can call `getservbyname()` to convert a service name such as "ftp" into the corresponding port number—21 in this case.

Windows Extensions

Because Windows programming is message-based, it is *asynchronous*. That means that things don't necessarily happen in a specified order. One task does not always finish before another starts. When the operating system wants something done, perhaps a window redrawn, it sends off a message to the window ("redraw yourself") and then turns its attention elsewhere. When the window gets the message, it performs the action.

Typical sockets programming is *synchronous*. The program asks the socket to send some information, and then waits for an answer. To bring sockets into Windows requires a re-thinking of the ways these calls work. In the Windows world, the socket sends the request and arranges for a message to be dispatched when the answer arrives. While one part of the program is awaiting the response, other messages can be handled. Windows Sockets specifies another long list of functions, all of which operate asynchronously, including:

- `WSAAsyncGetHostByAddr`

- `WSAAsyncGetHostByName`

- `WSAAsyncGetProtoByName`

- `WSAAsyncGetProtoByNumber`

- `WSAAsyncGetServByName`

- `WSAAsyncGetServByPort`

- `WSAStartup, WSACleanup`

The first six functions are asynchronous versions of the similarly named database functions. They send a request for a host name or a service number or whatever, and rather than waiting for an answer, they rely on a message being sent with the response. Sockets programmers wouldn't refer to "waiting," though; *blocking* is the technical term for a socket function that may not return for some time while it awaits a response from the network.

To avoid blocking on any socket function, such as `recv()`, use `WSAAsyncSelect()`. This function enables your procedure to "register interest" in a network event, such as the socket being ready to be read. `WSASyncSelect()` sends a `WM_SOCKET_NOTIFY()` message to the socket when there is data to be read or the connection is complete.

There are two things the socket code can do when the socket is ready for the requested action. One way is to handle it locally—for example, filling an array with the characters coming over the connection, and wait for other objects to request the data from the array. The other is to generate another callback and just give a buffer of data to a message-handling routine in the object that told the socket to do the requested action.

The first method is better when the calling code can't do anything until it has the answer from the network. For example, the calling code might send a userid, wait until it has been accepted, and then send a password. The second method is better when you'd be able to multitask in between bits of data coming in—for example, if you are transferring a large file. You'll use both methods throughout this book because they both have their strengths and because you should get a chance to see both approaches.

`WSAStartup()` and `WSACleanup()` are very important functions. As their names imply, they must be called before starting to do any socket calls, and at the end of your program to clean up. Luckily, you don't have to call them directly—it's all taken care of behind the scenes.

Encapsulating Functions and Data into a Socket Class

As soon as the Windows Sockets specification was released, Internet programmers using C++ began to write "wrapper" classes for the functions in the API. Two such classes, `CSocket` and `CAsyncSocket`, are included with Visual C++ 2.1 and 1.52. Like many programmers, I had one of my own already and I see a few weaknesses in the ones Microsoft has provided. No problem! One of the nice things about C++ is inheritance. I've developed a socket class called `QSocket` that inherits from Microsoft's `CSocket` class, which in turn inherits from `CAsyncSocket`, as shown in figure 3.2.

Fig. 3.2
This inheritance diagram for the socket classes demonstrates the role of `QSocket`. It inherits from `CSocket`, which inherits from `CAsyncSocket`.

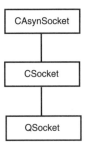

 If you don't have version 2.1 or 1.52 of Visual C++, there's a `QSocket` built from scratch on the CD-ROM included with this book. At the end of this chapter you learn what you have to do to use it.

Using a Socket Class

Perhaps the easiest way to demonstrate the use of a socket class is to list the public member functions of `QSocket` and then go through each of them in turn. The functions, as listed in the header file, are:

```
QSocket(BOOL create_socket = TRUE);  //constructor
BOOL Disconnect(void);

BOOL SetReceiveTarget(CWnd *window, UINT message);
void Send(const CString& data);
void SendRaw(const void* data, const int dataLen);
CString GetLine(void);
BOOL Listen(int back_log = 5);
QSocket *Accept();
void Linger();

SocketStatus GetStatus(void) { return CurrentStatus; }
CString GetErrorString(void) { return ErrorString; }
```

To understand what the functions do, it helps to look at the private data members of `QSocket`:

```
SocketStatus CurrentStatus;
CString ErrorString;

CStringList ReceiveLines;
CString RemainingReceive;
CStringList SendLines;
char *RawSendData;
int RawSendDataLength;
```

```
CWnd* ReceiveWindow;
UINT ReceiveMessage;
```

The `CStringList` variables are linked lists of `CStrings`, and are data being sent or received, broken into lines as indicated by CR-LF pairs. The `CWnd` pointer `ReceiveWindow` and the unsigned integer `ReceiveMessage` combine to show the socket how to `callback` the function that asked the socket to send or receive or whatever, when the response is ready. This message is also generated whenever the socket status changes, including when it goes into an error state or disconnects.

> `CString` and `CStringList` are discussed in Chapter 4, "Building a Windows Application Framework."

QSocket Constructor

The constructor looks like this:

```
QSocket::QSocket(BOOL create_socket)
  : CurrentStatus(UNINITIALIZED), ReceiveWindow(0),
    ReceiveMessage(0)
{
    if (create_socket)
    {
        if (Start())
        {
            CurrentStatus = DISCONNECTED;
        }
    }
}
```

`Start()` calls `Create()` and sets the status to ERRORSTATE if the `Create()` fails. The constructor changes the `Status` to DISCONNECTED if `Start()` succeeds. `Start()` could just as easily set the status in either case, but the code looks like this for historical reasons.

ConnectHelper

The next function in SOCKET.H is `Disconnect()`, but there's no `Connect()` function in there. That's because you inherit the `Connect()` function from `CSocket`. However, you override the protected function `ConnectHelper()`, which completes the final step of the connection. `Connect()` is split into two parts so that the first stage, determining addresses, is not overridden by derived classes, but the final few steps can be. Your protected `ConnectHelper()` function looks like this:

```
BOOL QSocket::ConnectHelper(const SOCKADDR* lpSockAddr,
                           int nSockAddrLen)
{
    CurrentStatus = CONNECTING;

    if (!AsyncSelect(FD_CONNECT))
    {
        SET_ERROR_VARS();
        return FALSE;
    }

    if (connect(m_hSocket, lpSockAddr, nSockAddrLen)
        == SOCKET_ERROR)
    {
        int err = GetLastError();
        if (err != WSAEWOULDBLOCK)
        {
            SET_ERROR_VARS();
            return FALSE;
        }
    }
    else
    {
        if (!AsyncSelect(FD_READ | FD_WRITE | FD_CLOSE ))
        {
            SET_ERROR_VARS();
            return FALSE;
        }

        CurrentStatus = CONNECTED;
        if (ReceiveWindow)
        {
            ReceiveWindow->SendMessage(ReceiveMessage,
                (WPARAM)SocketStatusChanged,(LPARAM)0);
        }
    }

    return TRUE;
}
```

AsyncSelect() is a CSocket function that calls WSAAsyncSelect() and arranges
for a standard message to be sent when the socket is ready for the required
action. When the socket is ready, a WM_SOCKET_NOTIFY message is sent to the
socket's hidden window, which then calls the appropriate virtual function of
the socket. These "overridable callbacks" are OnReceive(), OnWrite(),
OnOutofBandData(), OnAccept(), OnConnect(), and OnClose().

You start by calling AsyncSelect() and indicating you want to connect the
socket. If it returns FALSE, something is wrong and you bail out of the connection process.

The next call is to `connect()`, the API function that actually connects the socket to another machine on the Internet. If it returns an error that is not `WSAEWOULDBLOCK`, you have a problem and again you bail out of the connection process. If the error was `WSAEWOULDBLOCK`, it only means the connection will take a while to complete, so you have nothing else to do. Your `OnConnect()` method is called when the socket has connected. If there was no error, you actually connected right away. You then call `AsyncSelect()` again to indicate an interest in reading from, writing to, and closing this socket; as soon as it's ready for one of those three things, your `OnReceive()`, `OnWrite()`, or `OnClose()` methods are called.

At this point the socket is actually connected, so you set the status to CONNECTED. Since you make it possible to tell the socket who to `callback` after a successful connection, you pass that message along now by calling the `ReceiveWindow`'s Send Message method.

Disconnect

With connecting taken care of, you'll look at `Disconnect()`. It accomplishes the same purpose as the base class `Close()` function, but has a slight modification to enable the use of `Linger()`. The `Linger()` function is discussed later in this chapter. `Disconnect()` looks like this:

```
BOOL QSocket::Disconnect(void)
{

    // Allow socket related messages to be processed
    // before disconnect
    for (;;)
    {
        MSG msg;
        if (PeekMessage(&msg, NULL, 0, 0, PM_NOREMOVE)
        && msg.message != WM_QUIT)
        {
            if (PeekMessage(&msg, NULL, 0, 0, PM_REMOVE) )
            {
                TranslateMessage(&msg);
                DispatchMessage(&msg);
            }
        }
        else
        {
            break;
        }
    }
```

```
// You don't just call CSocket::Close() because you want to
// disable non-blocking mode before the closesocket() is
// called in the CAsyncSocket::Close().
// You disable the non-blocking mode so that when you have
// linger on you will block rather than return
// a WSAEWOULDBLOCK.
unsigned long nbIO = 0;
CancelBlockingCall();
AsyncSelect(0);

// disable non-blocking mode
ioctlsocket(m_hSocket, FIONBIO, &nbIO);

CAsyncSocket::Close();
m_hSocket = INVALID_SOCKET;

return TRUE;
}
```

The function starts with a *message pump*, which clears any outstanding messages that may affect this socket. For example, the message that indicates the socket is ready to give you the data you want to receive will trigger a call to OnReceive. You want all these messages to be processed before closing the socket.

Before you close the socket, you must disable non-blocking mode. In non-blocking mode, the call to Close() returns an error if there is still data to be sent. This defeats the purpose of Linger(), so it makes sense to turn off non-blocking mode before the call to Close(). You do that with a call to ioctlsocket(), but that call fails if there are any outstanding interests registered by previous calls to AsyncSelect(), so you must call AsyncSelect(0) first to cancel any such arrangements. But, still working backwards, before you can do that you should call CancelBlockingCall() to neatly dispose of any outstanding arrangements that were set up by earlier code.

So, putting these back in order, you call CancelBlockingCall() to get rid of previous calls, AsyncSelect() to cancel arrangements to call your functions when the socket is ready to transfer data, ioctlsocket() to disable non-blocking mode, and finally CAsyncSocket::Close() to actually close the socket.

Once the socket is closed, set the handle to INVALID_SOCKET to make sure no one can use it.

SetReceiveTarget

SetReceiveTarget() is the way that other objects arrange for callbacks. It looks like this:

```
BOOL QSocket::SetReceiveTarget(CWnd *window, UINT message)
{
    // Sets who to send all received data to.
    ReceiveWindow = window;
    ReceiveMessage = message;

    // Clear receive buffer as the data must be left over.
    ReceiveLines.RemoveAll();
    RemainingReceive = "";

    // Set up AsyncSelect.
    switch (CurrentStatus)
    {
        case CONNECTED:
            if (!AsyncSelect(FD_READ ¦ FD_WRITE ¦ FD_CLOSE ))
            {
                    SET_ERROR_VARS();
                    return FALSE;
            }
             break;

        case LISTENING:
            if (!AsyncSelect(FD_ACCEPT ))
            {
                    SET_ERROR_VARS();
                    return FALSE;
            }
             break;

        default:
            if (!AsyncSelect(FD_CONNECT ¦ FD_CLOSE ))
            {
                    SET_ERROR_VARS();
                    return FALSE;
            }
             break;
    }

    return TRUE;
}
```

This function sets the member variables that keep the window and message
to use for callbacks. It clears out anything in the CStringList ReceiveLines
and the single CString RemainingReceive, since the new callback function is
not going to want someone else's leftover data sent to it.

Now, you need to redo the AsyncSelect() if this socket has been created by
an accept call. It doesn't hurt to redo it anyway, so you do it here in
SetReceiveTarget(). Connected sockets announce they are interested in reading, writing, and closing; listening sockets are interested in accept calls, and
everything else is interested in becoming connected or closing.

Send

The Send() function sends a CString across the connected socket to the remote site. The code looks like this:

```
void QSocket::Send(const CString& data)
{
    if (data.GetLength() == 0)
    {
        return;
    }

    BOOL send_buffer_empty = SendLines.IsEmpty();

    SendLines.AddTail(data);

    if (send_buffer_empty)
    {
        int amt = SendLines.GetHead().GetLength();

         amt = CAsyncSocket::Send(SendLines.GetHead(), amt, 0);
        if (amt == SOCKET_ERROR)
        {
            int error = GetLastError();
            if (error != WSAEWOULDBLOCK
                && error != WSAEINPROGRESS)
            {
                SET_ERROR_VARS();
            }
        }
        else
        {
            if (amt == SendLines.GetHead().GetLength())
            {
                SendLines.RemoveHead();
            }
            else
            {
                // Only part of line was sent;
                // leave rest for later.
                const char *head = SendLines.GetHead();
                strcpy((char *)head, head+amt);
            }
        }
    }
}
```

This function accepts strings and adds them to the CStringList SendList. If
the list was empty, then there is no send request pending and you will have
to do a call to the CAsyncSocket function Send(). If there is something in
SendList already you need only tack your new data on the end; it will be sent
by the OnWrite function when the socket is ready.

`CAsyncSocket::Send()` returns the number of characters it was actually able to send—perhaps less than the entire line. The unsent portion is left in the first string in the list. This portion is sent by the `OnWrite()` function when the socket is ready, too.

SendRaw

This function is used for sending binary data, unlike `Send()`, which is line-oriented. The code looks like this:

```
void QSocket::SendRaw(const void *data, const int dataLen)
{
    char *sdata = new char[RawSendDataLength + dataLen];
    memcpy(sdata, RawSendData, RawSendDataLength);
    memcpy(sdata+RawSendDataLength, data, dataLen);
    delete RawSendData;
    RawSendData = sdata;

    RawSendDataLength += dataLen;

    while(RawSendDataLength > 0)
    {
        int amt_sent = CAsyncSocket::Send((char *)RawSendData,
        RawSendDataLength, 0);
        if (amt_sent == SOCKET_ERROR)
        {
            int error = GetLastError();
            if (error != WSAEWOULDBLOCK && error !=
            WSAEINPROGRESS)
            {
            SET_ERROR_VARS();
            }
            break;
        }
        else
        {
            RawSendDataLength -= amt_sent;
            memcpy(RawSendData, RawSendData+amt_sent,
            RawSendDataLength);
        }
    }
}
```

First, the buffer of characters that `data` points to is added to the end of `RawSendData`, and `RawSendDataLength` is incremented by `dataLen`. A call to `CAsyncSocket::Send()` will send an unknown number of these characters, so you need to check `amt_sent` to see how many actually went. To get these characters out of the `RawSendData` buffer, just copy the last part of the buffer back to the beginning, and adjust the `RawSendDataLength`.

GetLine

This is the pseudo-synchronous way of using an asynchronous socket. A call to GetLine() doesn't return to where it was called from until the socket has sent a full line (a CString containing a CR-LF pair), and it returns that line. However, it's not a truly blocking function because it pumps out Windows messages while it is waiting. Here's how it looks:

```
CString QSocket::GetLine(void)
{
    if (ReceiveWindow)
    {
        // You are in the wrong mode to use GetLine().
        return "";
    }

    while(CurrentStatus == CONNECTED && ReceiveLines.IsEmpty())
    {
        char temp[SOCK_BLOCK_SIZE+1];
        int amt = Receive(temp, SOCK_BLOCK_SIZE, 0);
        if (amt == SOCKET_ERROR)
        {
                SET_ERROR_VARS();
        }
        else if (amt == 0)
        {
            OnClose(0);
        }
        else
        {
            temp[amt] = 0;
            // Add to buffer you are using GetLine() mode.
            AddToReceive(temp, amt);
        }
    }

    if (!ReceiveLines.IsEmpty()) {
        return ReceiveLines.RemoveHead();
    }
    else
    {
        return "";
    }
}
```

Calls to GetLine() make no sense when there's a ReceiveWindow set up, so the first thing to do is to check that. Then, as long as the socket is connected but hasn't received a full line, you call the CSocket Receive() function (which does a message pump while waiting) hoping to fill the buffer temp. If Receive() returns 0, there is no more data for you and you might as well Close() the socket. If you received data, call AddToReceive() to parse temp

into lines separated by a CR-LF pair. It will not add a partial line into
`ReceiveLines`, keeping it in `RemainingReceive` for the next time through.
`AddToReceive()` is a long and uninteresting function—if you simply must see
it, the source code is on the CD-ROM in the folder \CODE\SOCKET. Look
through SOCKET.CPP for the function.

When you leave the `while` loop, if there is a line (or more) in the
`ReceiveLines` buffer, you return it. Note that if you had two lines to return,
the second will still be in `ReceiveList` and the next time `GetLine()` is called
you will never enter the `while` loop, but simply return that second line right
away.

Listen

`Listen()` arranges for a socket to respond to connection requests for a specific
local port. (The code that calls `Listen()` creates and binds the socket to a port
first.) This is how you arrange connections that are initiated by the remote
site rather than your own code. `Listen()` is primarily used when writing
server applications, as shown in the following segment of code:

```
BOOL QSocket::Listen(int back_log)
{
    if (ReceiveWindow != NULL)
    {
        // Receiving callbacks when status changes
        // so set up AsyncSelect
            if (!AsyncSelect(FD_ACCEPT))
        {
                SET_ERROR_VARS();
                return FALSE;
            }
    }

    if (!CAsyncSocket::Listen(back_log))
    {
        SET_ERROR_VARS();
        return FALSE;
    }

    CurrentStatus = LISTENING;

    return TRUE;
}
```

If the calling code is prepared to get callbacks when the socket accepts a connection, you call `AsyncSelect()` to say you want to be notified of accept
events. You then call `CAsyncSocket::Listen()` to issue the listen command.

Accept

Accept() is called when a socket is listening; it hands off a new incoming connection to a socket it creates for this purpose, then returns a pointer to that socket. Here's how it looks:

```
QSocket *QSocket::Accept()
{
    QSocket *return_socket = new QSocket(FALSE);

    // Do not get the address of remote end.
    if (!CSocket::Accept(*return_socket, NULL, NULL))
    {
        delete return_socket;
        return_socket = 0;
        SET_ERROR_VARS();
    }

    return_socket->CurrentStatus = CONNECTED;
    return return_socket;
}
```

You create the new socket but pass FALSE to the constructor so that Start() will not be called. You then call CSocket::Accept(), which fills in the socket handle of a real connected socket for the new connection. You set the status of this new socket to CONNECTED and return the pointer.

Linger

Sometimes asynchronous programming can cause a few headaches. For example, your program may call Send() or SendRaw() to send some data across the socket, and then call Disconnect() to close the socket, even though the data may not all have been sent. The solution to this is a call to Linger() before the close; this will keep the socket open until the last of the data has gone through. Here's how the code looks:

```
void QSocket::Linger(void)
{
    int what = 0;
    struct linger sL;
    sL.l_onoff = 1;
    sL.l_linger = 30;

    what = SetSockOpt(SO_LINGER, (char *)&sL, sizeof(sL));

    if (what == SOCKET_ERROR)
    {
        SET_ERROR_VARS();
    }
}
```

All this function really does is call SetSockOpt() from the Winsock API. It sets up a linger structure called sL and fills in l_onoff as 1 (any nonzero value turns lingering on) and l_linger as 30 (the number of seconds to allow for the last bit of data to be transferred). Once SetSockOpt() has been called, any future calls to Disconnect() will wait until the data has been sent before actually closing the socket.

Inherited Functions

There are three functions in CSocket that are just fine for your purposes: QSocket inherits them untouched. They are:

```
BOOL Connect(const CString& address, const int port);
BOOL GetSockName(SOCKADDR *sock_addr, int *addr_len);
BOOL Bind(const SOCKADDR *sock_addr, int addr_len);
```

Connect() handles the address that was passed and then calls ConnectHelper() as discussed previously. GetSockName() is just a wrapper for the Berkeley function getsockname(). Bind() must be called before Listen(); it ties an unconnected socket to a port on the local machine.

Using Sockets without *CSocket* and *CAsyncSocket*

If you're using versions of Visual C++ earlier than 2.1 or 1.52, you don't have the MFC classes. If you only want to execute the applications I've written, it doesn't matter what version of the compiler you have. But if you want to make a few changes, you'll find the code won't recompile without those MFC classes.

Don't worry; I've supplied a version of the QSocket class that behaves exactly like the QSocket that inherits from CSocket, but is written "from scratch" so it can be used by people who don't have the CSocket class. Here's how to use it:

As explained in Appendix D, "Browsing the CD-ROM," the CD-ROM has a subfolder for each of the applications in this book. Each subfolder has a copy of SOCKET.H and SOCKET.CPP. You need to copy the from-scratch versions of these files from the sockets folder (\CODE\SOCKET) to the folder of the application you are working on.

Next, open STDAFX.H in the application folder and delete the line:

```
#include <afxsock.h>        // MFC socket class
```

If the comment varies, delete the line anyway.

Internet Programming

Finally, open the source file for the object that inherits from `CWinApp` (typically this file has the same name as the project) and delete these lines from the `InitInstance()` function:

```
if (!AfxSocketInit())
{
    AfxMessageBox("Socket initialization failed.");
}
```

Now you can compile any changes and the from-scratch class will be used. It behaves exactly like the class that inherits from `CSocket`; the private implementation details have been changed, but not the public interface.

Using MFC Sockets if AppWizard Won't Include Them

In Visual C++ 2.1, the AppWizard automatically adds socket support if you request it. In version 1.52, the socket classes are available but AppWizard won't add the required code for you. You can do it yourself, though—just add the two fragments the 2.0 and 1.5 people were just instructed to remove! In STDAFX.H add:

```
#include <afxsock.h>        // MFC socket class
```

And in the object that inherits from `CWinApp`, add to the function `InitInstance()` these lines:

```
if (!AfxSocketInit())
{
    AfxMessageBox("Socket initialization failed.");
}
```

Now you can use those classes just as though AppWizard knew about them.

From Here...

The `QSocket` class is used by every application in this book. You can muddle by if you don't exactly understand what it does, but for true understanding of Windows Internet programming you must understand sockets. Now let's put them to work!

Part II

Developing Internet Applications

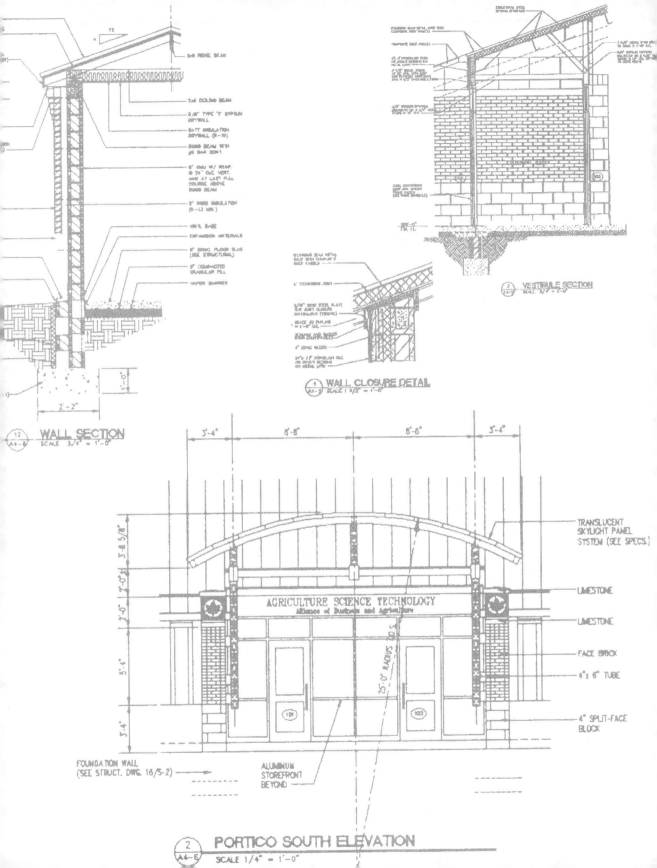

WALL SECTION
SCALE 3/4" = 1'-0"
12
A4-6

VESTIBULE SECTION
SCALE 3/4" = 1'-0"
3
A4-6

WALL CLOSURE DETAIL
SCALE 1 1/2" = 1'-0"
4
A4-6

AGRICULTURE SCIENCE TECHNOLOGY
Alliance of Business and Agriculture

TRANSLUCENT
SKYLIGHT PANEL
SYSTEM (SEE SPECS.)

LIMESTONE

LIMESTONE

FACE BRICK

4" x 6" TUBE

4" SPLIT-FACE
BLOCK

FOUNDATION WALL
(SEE STRUCT. DWG 16/S-2)

ALUMINUM
STOREFRONT
BEYOND

25'-0" RADIUS TO S.

PORTICO SOUTH ELEVATION
SCALE 1/4" = 1'-0"
2
A4-6

Chapter 4

Building a Windows Application Framework

Most Windows applications have a great deal in common; in fact, the user interface code is very similar for almost every Windows application. Menus, buttons, windows to put output into, edit boxes—all these Windows components recur in application after application. There's no way you're going to write them from scratch every time, is there? Well, because you're working with Visual C++, you don't even have to write them the first time! Visual C++ comes with the Microsoft Foundation Classes (MFC) and a collection of helpful dialogs called wizards. Just wait till you see what they can do for you. To quote the Class Library User's Guide (part of Microsoft's documentation for Visual C++), they "embody the accumulated wisdom of experienced programmers for the Windows environment." That means they make your job much, much easier. In this chapter, you learn about:

- Standard C++ classes anyone can use: MFC

- Automatic code generation with AppWizard

- Standard interface features everyone needs, already written

- Documents, Views, and how they work together

- Windows Messages and event notification

- Using AppStudio to create dialog boxes and menus

- Automatic code generation with ClassWizard

- Coding, compiling, and testing in the Visual C++ working environment

II

Developing Applications

The Microsoft Foundation Classes (MFC)

The Microsoft Foundation Classes are a collection of C++ classes that save your reinventing the wheel. Some of them are useful as base classes for your own objects, while others can be used as-is, especially CString, collection classes, and CTime.

Useful Base Classes

Classes you inherit from include CDocument, CView, CWnd, and CDialog. You learn more about these as the chapter progresses. These classes encapsulate Windows-specific concepts and save you a great deal of programming effort, as you'll see.

 Microsoft class names all start with "C" for class.

CString

Few programs can be written without using strings of some sort, and the MFC class CString is a pretty good implementation of the typical collection of string-handling functions. CString isn't perfect, and many C++ programmers have their own string classes, but it's a very good start. It's much easier to manipulate CString objects than to use char* variables as you might in C. For example, the object handles all the memory allocation issues. To add a carriage return-linefeed combination to the end of an existing CString called command, you need only write:

```
command += "\r\n";
```

CString's += operator handles the rest.

If you've ever programmed in BASIC, you might recognize the CString function being called here:

```
first = command.Right(5);
```

Chances are, any string manipulation that is part of the standard C library or the BASIC language is implemented in CString.

Collection Classes

If your application needs to keep a number of strings, or numbers, or any other kind of object, the MFC collection classes make it easy. There are collection classes to keep strings, unsigned integers, double words, and CObject objects.

Array collections are accessed just like conventional arrays. For example, use `CStringArray` to keep an array of `CStrings` accessed by a zero-based integer index. List collections are doubly-linked lists, which can be traversed in forward or reverse sequence. Maps are lookup tables. Here's an example:

```
CStrngArray Words;
Words.Add("hello");
Words.Add("world");
CString word = Words[1];
```

This code declares a `CStringArray`, adds two elements to it without any concern for memory allocation, and puts the second element, `hello`, into a `CString` variable for further manipulation.

Besides saving you a great deal of time writing `operator[]`, `Add`, and `Delete` functions, these collection classes have other helper functions you may not have even thought of. You use collection classes wherever possible in your applications.

CTime

`CTime` encapsulates everything you'd ever want in a date and time class, and lots more. It has a companion class, `CTimeSpan`, which represents the difference between two `CTime` objects. Here are some examples of how easy some fairly tricky work becomes:

```
CTime date_time = CTime::GetCurrentTime()-CTimeSpan(2,0,0,0);
```

This code gets the current date and time, subtracts two full days from it (the particular `CTimeSpan` constructor being called here takes four numbers which are days, hours, minutes, and seconds) and puts the result into a `CTime` object called `date_time`. All in one line of code! Or try this:

```
CTime time = CTime::GetCurrentTime();

text += CString(time.Format("%a, %d %b %Y %H:%M:%S "));
```

This gets the current time, formats it into a string of the form `Mon, 17 Jan 1994 11:14:55` and adds it to a `CString` called `text`, declared and initialized earlier in the program. The codes passed to `Format` function much like the format codes for `printf`. They are exactly the codes used by the ANSI C function `strftime`.

Each of these operations (subtracting some amount of time from a date, formatting a date for output) typically takes pages of code, but by using `CTime` you can do it in one line. Not bad at all.

AppWizard

AppWizard makes applications for you. It handles creating the subfolder, creating the "project file," setting up the makefile to handle compiling and linking, even creating some .CPP and .H files with boilerplate code in them. How much boilerplate? Your first Internet application, developed in the next chapter, has about 1000 lines in the .CPP, .H, .RC, and .MAK files. Over 900 of those lines came from AppWizard.

You see just how to use AppWizard in the next chapter, with step-by-step instructions and diagrams. For now, here is a list of the features AppWizard asks you to include or exclude before your application is created:

- Multiple document interface (several files open at once)

- OLE support: none, container only, mini-server, full server, container and server, automation

- Database support: none, headers only, file only, database and file support

- A toolbar (also called ribbon bar)

- A status bar at the bottom of your main window

- Printing (and print preview)

- Support for Visual Basic controls

- Context-sensitive help

- 3-D controls

- MAPI support

- Sockets support, which all your applications will want

NOTE   A *Multiple Document Interface* (*MDI*) application enables the user to have more than one file open at a time; a *Single Document Interface* (*SDI*) application does not. In an MDI application there may be more than one type of document open at once (for example, a spreadsheet and a chart) and the framework will arrange for different menus to be displayed when the different views have focus.

If you're using Visual C++ version 1.51 or 1.52, you are not asked about the status bar, 3-D controls, MAPI support, or socket support. You can add the socket support by hand as described in Chapter 3, "Windows Sockets (WINSOCK.DLL)." You will also be asked whether to use the Medium or Large memory model. Choosing Large will make your eventual port to 32 bits much easier.

You also specify whether you want AppWizard to sprinkle your source with explanatory comments—you do, trust me.

Finally you check the classes AppWizard is about to generate and the file names it will use. In some cases you'll make small changes: choosing to have your View class inherit from CFormView rather than CView, for example. Then AppWizard sets to work generating code. It generates entire functions and files that you may never even touch, and other functions that look like this:

```
CFingerDoc::CFingerDoc()
{
    // TODO: add one-time construction code here
}
```

You are expected to write these functions, but AppWizard has at least saved you a few lines of typing and made sure you remember to write the function.

Interface Features You Can Get "Free"

Windows applications are interface-centric, meaning they are built around the interface instead of the interface being built around the program. When you're building a text-based program in DOS or UNIX, you typically start by making the program do the *task* that it's designed to do, and then add a crude interface after you're sure you can get it to work. But in Windows you start by creating the crude interface. After you create at least some portion of the interface, then you add the functionality and tie interface elements to functions.

After you run AppWizard you can compile and link your new application (by choosing Project, Build) and then run it (Project, Execute) right away, even though you haven't written a single line of code. Up comes a window like the one in figure 4.1 with your application name in the title bar, and menus for File, Edit, and Help. Depending on the options you selected as you went through the wizard process, there may be View and Window options as well. It behaves as you expect a Windows application to—you can minimize it (down to a fairly boring icon), close it in the usual ways, resize, move it around the screen, and so on.

Fig. 4.1

This "nothing" application was generated entirely by AppWizard. It does the usual things you'd expect any Windows application to do.

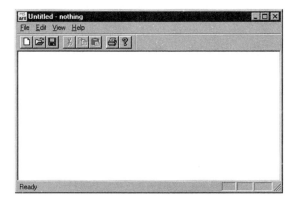

The File menu contains New, Open, Save, Save As, a list of recently opened files, and Exit as a bare minimum. (You have absolutely no work to do to make that list of recent files either—the framework takes care of it.) If you chose to have support for Print and Print Preview, these appear on the menu, and if you have a Multiple Document Interface then Close will appear too.

The Edit menu has Undo, Cut, Copy, and Paste. If you have OLE support there are OLE-related options on this menu as well. The Help menu has at least an About option, and if you chose to support context sensitive help, the usual Index and Using Help items are added.

The Document/View Paradigm

AppWizard assumes that every application has something it wants to store in a file, something the user can save by choosing File, Save and retrieve by choosing File, Open. This collection of "information that will be saved" is called a *document*. In most applications, some (but not all) of the information in the document is displayed in the windows of the application. A window that is displaying information that "belongs" to the document is called a *view*.

For example, if you use a spreadsheet, your formulas and numbers are kept in the document and displayed in a view. Some of your option settings may also be kept in the document, but they are not directly displayed in the view. And the view displays some information (like the location of soft page breaks) that is calculated on the fly, not stored with the document.

There can be more than one view on a document: for example, a spreadsheet table and a graph of the same numbers. When you change the numbers in the spreadsheet table, the changes are actually made in the underlying document, and that's why they are reflected immediately in the chart. In the mail application you develop in Chapter 11, "Building an Internet Electronic Mail Application," the document contains the information needed to access a remote mailbox. One view of that document's data is a list of the mail messages in that remote mailbox; another is the contents of a specified mail message.

It's easy enough to think of applications that don't appear to need a document; what could you save from a Calculator application, for example? But if you realize that not everything stored is displayed, you could imagine that the calculator might save your options settings in the document, or even the number in the memory.

Assuming you're writing an application that will store information in the document, you'll really like what AppWizard generates for you. You are given a document class that inherits from the MFC class CDocument, which comes with functions to open, save, new, and close a file. AppWizard generates code to ask the document if it has been modified, and prompt the user to save before closing a modified file. You need only write a Serialize function for your document, which can be as short as a single line!

Using views can save you a great deal of effort too. CScrollView, for example, is a scrollable view. If you choose to have your application's view inherit from CScrollView instead of CView, you will not have to do anything else at all to implement scrolling. When the amount of data in the view grows, scroll bars appear. When the user sizes the application larger, the scroll bars disappear again. When the user clicks above the elevator, the view pages up. The framework handles all of this and you do nothing. To see this in action, look at figure 4.2, which shows a fairly small view with both horizontal and vertical scrollbars, and figure 4.3, which shows the same view resized so that all the data fits. The scrollbars have been removed automatically. This view, which inherits from CSrollView, is part of the newsreader application developed in Chapter 12, "Building an Internet Newsreader Application."

Fig. 4.2

This view in the newsreader application built for this book has scrollbars generated automatically.

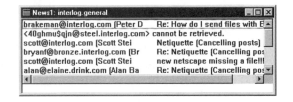

Fig. 4.3

The same view as shown in figure 4.2, when the user resizes it so that all the data fits, does not have scrollbars.

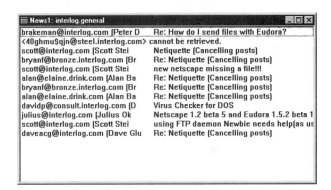

CEditView is both a view and an edit box at the same time. The user can type, select text, cut, copy, or paste to or from the Clipboard, and all the other things users can do in simple word-processing environments like Notepad. Your effort: a single line of code that fills the view with its initial data, perhaps another that extracts the text the user entered. You see how powerful edit controls are throughout this book.

Edit boxes don't just have to be for text the user can edit. You can set a "read only" flag and use an edit box as a handy output box.

One of the applications that uses a view inheriting from CEditView is Gopher. Figure 4.4 shows one of Gopher's output views, filled with pages of information. The code to add incoming text onto the end of the edit view is just three lines long, and it looks like this:

```
int nLen = GetEditCtrl().GetWindowTextLength();
GetEditCtrl().SetSel(nLen, nLen, TRUE);
GetEditCtrl().ReplaceSel((char *)buffer);
```

This uses three edit box functions, GetWindowTextLength(), SetSel(), and ReplaceSel() to add the characters in buffer to the end of the data already in the output view. And since CEditView inherits from CScrollView, scrollbars are taken care of automatically. This code is discussed in more detail in Chapter 10, "Building an Internet Gopher Application."

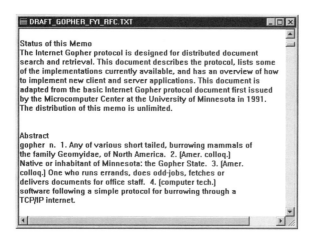

Fig. 4.4
This Gopher output view inherits from CEditView. It takes only three lines of code to fill and use this view.

Messages

To truly understand Windows programming, you must understand messages. Everything that happens in a Windows program is mediated by messages. Messages are sent to application windows when the user presses a key, or clicks, releases, or moves the mouse. They are also sent from elsewhere in the application to request a resource, or report that it is available, or tell another part of the application to do something.

A message has three parts: a message number, a word parameter, and a long parameter. The message number is usually disguised through the use of #define. For example, the message generally referred to as WM_COMMAND has a numeric value, defined in WINUSER.H:

```
#define WM_COMMAND      0x0111
```

Of course, no one ever refers to this command by its hexadecimal number. It is always called WM_COMMAND. The parameters are passed to the code that "catches," or deals with, the message. Often the word parameter is a pointer to a structure, window, or buffer, while the long parameter is a simple number such as a status code, or the number of bytes in the buffer.

In Windows 3.1, messages also mediate multi-tasking, and your application should remember to give control to Windows by dispatching messages while it's waiting for a message.

Often a single event triggers a sequence of messages, with each one caught by a higher and higher level of the operating system or your application. For example, when a user clicks a button, the operating system catches messages like "the mouse button is down" and a moment later "the mouse button is back up." It decides what window (if any) is under the mouse co-ordinates, and a new message that means "the OK button was clicked in this dialog" is generated and sent to the window that "owns" the dialog. That window processes the information on the dialog and may generate more messages to other parts of the application. Your application does not receive low-level messages, but is notified of events like button-clicking or menu-item-selecting.

Three very important messages are WM_PAINT, WM_COMMAND, and WM_DESTROY. WM_PAINT is sent to a message procedure when the window's contents should be repainted; for example, when it's being restored from a minimized state. WM_COMMAND is sent to a message procedure to indicate that a menu item or control has been selected. The word parameter that's passed in with the WM_COMMAND message contains the identifier for the control selected. Typically an enum is used so that the parameter is an understandable word like ID_FILE_OPEN rather than a number. The names of the enum elements are the resource IDs of the controls (menu item, button, and the like) in your application. WM_DESTROY is sent to a window that is about to be destroyed. This gives you a chance to run a cleanup routine, freeing memory or other resources. In the simple cases you start with, the framework can handle these messages.

You will arrange code to "catch" WM_COMMAND messages like button-clicking or menu-option-selecting with the ClassWizard, described in the ClassWizard section of this chapter, in the Buttons and Menus subsections.

AppStudio

AppStudio enables you to build interface components quickly and easily. Dialogs, menus, and bitmaps are arranged for easy editing. Again, the step-by-step instructions are in the next chapter, and you'll concentrate here on the advantages of AppStudio for developers.

Menus

Menu items can easily be added, changed, or deleted. In one dialog box, as shown in figure 4.5, you can set the menu option (for example, File, Save), arrange for a letter in the menu option to be underlined and act as a shortcut key, provide the text that appears in the Status bar to explain the menu item (for example, the prompt for most Save items is something like "save the active document"), and set the resource ID, used to connect the control to your code.

Fig. 4.5
Here is the menu
generated for
the "nothing"
application of
figure 4.1 in
AppStudio. The
Properties sheet
enables you to
change the
appearance and
behavior of the
menu item.

If you have a menu item such as Options, Preferences, and you decide it should be Options, Settings, you can change the name while leaving everything else about it intact. If you decide it shouldn't be under Options after all, you can cut-and-paste it to the menu you prefer. You can copy menu items, too, to save repetitive typing.

Dialogs

Dialogs are built and changed with a very visual WYSIWYG interface. If you need a button on your dialog box, you grab one from the control palette, drop it where you want it, and change the caption from Button1 to Lookup or Connect or whatever you want the button to read. All the familiar Windows controls are available for your dialogs, as shown in the following table:

Control	Description
Static text	Not really a control, this labels other controls such as edit boxes
Edit box	Single line or multiline, place for users to type strings or numbers as input to the program
Button	Every dialog starts with OK and Cancel buttons, but you can add as many of your own as you want
Check box	Sets options on or off; each option can be set or unset independently

(continues)

Control	Description
Radio button	Selects only one of a number of related options. Selecting one button unselects the rest
Combo box	A combination of an edit box and a list box, this control enables users to select from a list, or type their response if the one they want isn't on the list
List box	Selects one item from a list hardcoded into the dialog or filled in by the program as the dialog is created. The user cannot type in the selection area
Scroll bar	Rarely needed for scrolling output, since it should be put into a control that will scroll itself, it is still useful as a simple slider control
Tab Control	Used to build Windows 95 "tabbed dialogs" and property sheets
Tree View	A list box organized into a tree, whose branches can be collapsed or expanded
List View	A list presented as both icons and text, the way the list of files is presented in Windows 95 Explorer
Hot Key	Enables the user to set custom hot keys
Track Bar	Also called a slider, sets values that can be arranged as numbers on a line
Progress Bar	A rectangle that is filled in as a long operation progresses
Up/Down	An "up" and "down" button used to increment or decrement a value
Custom control	Developed for Visual Basic or similar applications, this third-party control may resemble a circular dial, slider, calendar, or other imaginative interface items. They can all be incorporated into your application as easily as if they came with the compiler

Some of these controls (Tab Control, Tree View, List View, Hot Key, Track Bar, Progress Bar, and Up/Down) will only be available under Windows 95. Microsoft plans to support them in a future release of NT.

In case you're not used to calling these controls by name, figure 4.6 shows a sample dialog that contains examples of each standard control.

Any control on a dialog box can be moved or resized simply and intuitively with the mouse. If your button needs to move down a little, click and hold the mouse, move the button to the new location, then release the mouse. AppStudio takes care of the rest.

Fig. 4.6
A sample Windows dialog illustrates the names of the various controls. The empty square is a list box that currently has no choices in it. Note that the user has typed "hello" in the combo box rather than choosing from the list offered.

Before you set to work trying to imitate the standard File, Open dialog, you should know that it and many other common dialogs are available for you to use as though they were your own. How's that for saving time?

Bitmaps and Icons

In a Windows application, bitmaps are used in icons, on toolbars, and for more specialized controls. AppStudio provides a rudimentary bitmap editor that looks a lot like the "zoom" mode of Paintbrush, the drawing program that has shipped with Windows for years. You can see it in action in figure 4.7. While you won't become another Rembrandt with this tool, you should be able to create simple icons and toolbar buttons that will help your users remember their way around your application.

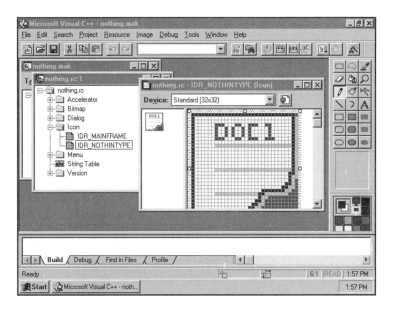

Fig. 4.7
The bitmap editor is used to edit bitmaps and icons. This icon is a default one provided by AppWizard for your "nothing" application.

II

Developing Applications

ClassWizard

ClassWizard connects interface items (menus, dialogs, and controls) to objects and variables in your code. AppStudio only helps you lay out these interface items: until you connect them to code with ClassWizard, they cannot do anything.

Dialogs

After you create a dialog in AppStudio, calling up ClassWizard from within AppStudio creates a class that usually inherits from the MFC CDialog class. To make the dialog appear on the screen, declare an instance of this class. Call its Create function to bring it up as a modeless dialog, or DoModal to bring it up as a modal dialog. The functions Create, DoModal, and many more are all part of the MFC class CDialog—you don't need to write code to bring up the dialog, other than the function call.

Modal dialogs have the input focus and you can't do any other task in the application while the dialog has focus; modeless dialogs float over the application and allow you to keep working while they're up. Each has its own uses.

Within ClassWizard, the Member Variables tab lets you connect controls (using their resource ID) to member variables of the class. ClassWizard takes care of the declaration in the header, initialization in the constructor, and everything else needed to bind the control to the variable. If you want to restrict the input in any way (for example, accepting only numbers between 0 and 100, or strings up to 25 characters long) you can do that on the Member Variables tab too, and ClassWizard handles the data validation.

ClassWizard makes intelligent suggestions about the data types to use for your member variables. For example, most of the time you will want to store the contents of an edit box in a CString variable, but the contents of a check box (on or off) in a BOOL (true or false) variable. You can also assign the control itself (rather than its contents) to a member variable.

Buttons

When you add a button to a dialog box, you need to give it a meaningful resource ID. It should start with IDC to indicate it's a control, then the dialog name, then the button name. If you only have one dialog you can skip the dialog name. So the Lookup button on your only dialog might be IDC_LOOKUP, while in a many dialog application the Refresh button on the Group Subscribe dialog might be IDC_GROUPSUB_REFRESH.

Assign a meaningful name to each control. Whatever you do, don't stick with the default `IDC_BUTTON1` provided by AppStudio.

There are times when you need to access the button as a button—primarily to gray or ungray it depending on what's going on with the rest of the dialog. You can do that on the Member Variables tab along with the other controls. Connect the button's resource ID to a member variable in your class as usual, but rather than `CString` or `BOOL`, this variable will be a `CButton`. You can then call `CButton` functions on this member variable that will affect the button the user sees on-screen, including graying and ungraying it.

One thing you always want to know is when the button is clicked. You don't arrange this with the Member Variables tab; clicking a button generates a message, and you use the Message Maps tab to tell ClassWizard you want this class to catch the message. ClassWizard creates a function that is called whenever the button is clicked. Such message-handling functions should always have names that start with `On`.

Menus

The standard menu items that were added by AppWizard are generally handled by code AppWizard generates, and require no intervention from you. As soon as you write a `Serialize` member function for your document, for example, your application will handle File, Save; File, Save As; and File, Open automatically. But useful as AppWizard is, once it has run it doesn't generate any more code, and it doesn't read minds. That means if you add items to your menus (and you probably will), you're going to have to arrange for code to do whatever should be done when the user selects the menu item.

When you add a new menu item with AppStudio, make a note of the resource ID assigned by AppStudio. Though you can change it, you probably shouldn't—AppStudio uses a sensible naming scheme, and most applications have too many menu items to remember all their IDs without a scheme. If you add the menu item Options, Preferences, it has the resource ID `ID_OPTIONS_PREFERENCES`. When a user clicks a menu item, a special type of Windows message called a command is sent and the resource ID is a parameter of the message.

Next, ask yourself which class in your application should handle the menu message. That is, when the user chooses Options, Preferences, will they be changing variables that belong to the view, the document, or the entire application? This is not always a simple question for new Windows programmers to answer. As the book progresses you will see situations where a view object catches menu messages, others where a document object does, and a few where the main application catches them. These help you learn how to decide which class should catch the message.

Once you know the resource ID of the message, and the class that will catch it, you run ClassWizard and select the Message Map tab to make the arrangements. You'll cover the step-by-step in Chapter 10, "Building an Internet Gopher Application"; you select the class, select the message, and ask ClassWizard to add a function that should be called when the message is received. It's very similar to connecting dialog box buttons. You will also see how to gray a menu item if the user should not be able to select it.

Beyond ClassWizard

Message maps are the key to the way that MFC programs actually work. You can think of them as lookup tables that connect the resource ID of a Windows message with the name of one of your functions. ClassWizard generates them for you, but there are times you need to add your own entries; for example, to handle a message sent from elsewhere in your code. Your socket class communicates by sending messages, so in your very first application you add your own message map entries to handle socket messages.

The Visual C++ Environment

MFC and the wizards do save you a lot of coding, but eventually you have to type in code, compile it, and execute it. You do that from the Visual C++ environment, which Microsoft calls the *Workbench*. It is a multiwindow editor with "hooks" to the compiler, linker, debugger, and tools like AppWizard, AppStudio, and ClassWizard. Figure 4.8 shows the environment in action, with two windows open. The one on the left is the project, or MAK, file. To open any file in the project, double-click its name to open an editing window like the one on the right. The Window, Cascade menu item arranges all your open windows into a neat cascade.

There are a number of toolbars you can use to speed your work, but the one you'll use the most is the Standard toolbar, shown across the top of figure 4.8. You're going to be using the standard toolbar a lot, so let's work through it from left to right:

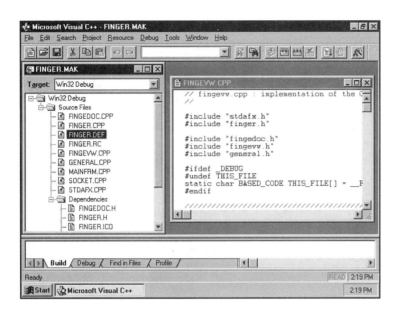

Fig. 4.8
The Visual C++
Workbench is
used to edit and
compile code,
menus, and dialog
boxes.

Button or Feature	Function
New Source File button	Brings up an empty text or code file. Equivalent to choosing File, New and then selecting Code/Text
Open button	Brings up the usual File, Open dialog box and is handy when you want a file from another project
Save button	Saves the file that has focus at the moment (the current file). It's gray if the file has not been changed yet
Cut button	Cuts the current selection to the Clipboard
Copy button	Copies the current selection to the Clipboard
Paste button	Pastes the clipboard contents to the insertion point
Undo button	Reverses your most recent action
Redo button	Reverses an Undo
Find box	Makes searching for a text string simple— type the text and click on the binoculars to the right of it. The box drops down a list of strings you searched for recently if you click the down arrow
Find in Files button	Brings up a dialog box to direct a search through your files

The next four buttons handle compiling and building. The leftmost one compiles only the current file, the second one compiles all files that have changed since they were last compiled, and then links them into an executable, and the third one compiles all the files in the project and then links them. The rightmost button interrupts a build in progress.

The next two buttons on the bar relate to debugging. The Visual C++ debugger is a powerful way to see what's going on when your programs run. You control the execution by placing breakpoints in your program: when control reaches a statement tagged with a breakpoint, execution stops temporarily so that you can examine variables or just wonder how on earth you got there. Knowing that, you cover those two buttons:

Button	Function
Run	Causes the program to run to the next breakpoint
Toggle BreakPoint	Turns a breakpoint on or off at the current cursor location (insertion point)

Finally, there's the magic wand waving a trail of stars over a collection of boxes (they are supposed to represent a class hierarchy) brings up ClassWizard. If all these buttons seem a lot to remember, don't worry; if you hold the cursor over any toolbar button and linger a few seconds, a *Tool Tip* will appear to remind you of the name of the button.

From Here...

You're going to be seeing a lot of AppWizard, AppStudio, and ClassWizard through the rest of this book, so get used to them. And starting with the very next chapter, you'll be using them to make an Internet application.

Chapter 5

Building an Internet Finger Application

Just who is **mabjg@trentu.ca**, anyway? Some e-mail addresses, like **president@whitehouse.gov** or **kate@gregcons.com**, can be read quickly and easily. But sites that use student numbers, employee numbers, or cryptic abbreviations make it hard for you to know who you're meeting on the Internet. Even if you know a name, there's really so much more to know, isn't there? In this chapter you build your first Internet application: Finger. It can help you find out just who people are. You learn:

■ What Finger can help you learn about other users

■ How the Finger protocol works

■ How to build a Finger client of your own

■ How to use Finger

■ How to improve your client once it's working

What Does Finger Do?

Born of the UNIX/TCP world and adopted by the Internet community at large, Finger is used to look up users in the databases of mainframes all over the world. It's a simple application that provides access to information about users of specific host systems. They don't even have to be real users, as you'll see in "Using Finger," later in this chapter, where you discover vending machines connected to the Internet.

A Finger client is provided with most UNIX implementations. The command to invoke it is finger, and the output typically looks like Figure 5.1.

Fig. 5.1

The UNIX finger command prepares and submits a finger query, then displays the response.

```
% finger kgregory@interlog.com
[interlog.com]
Login: kgregory                          Name: Kate Gregory
Directory: /usr/u/kgregory              Shell: /bin/csh
Last login Fri Apr 28 23:08 (EDT) on ttyp0 from BLAZE.TRENTU.CA
Mail forwarded to: kate@gregcons.com
No Plan.
%
```

Just like all other Internet applications, Finger follows the client/server model. As described in RFC 1288, a Finger application connects to a host system, sends the host an Internet user's name, and displays the information returned by that host system to the user that's requesting the information. The RFC is on the CD-ROM that comes with this book, and you really should read it as you go through this chapter. Most RFCs are rather dry and boring, but this one made me laugh out loud, in the section about vending machines:

> Vending machines SHOULD respond to a {C} request with a list of all items currently available for purchase and possible consumption. Vending machines SHOULD respond to a {U}{C} request with a detailed count or list of the particular product or product slot. Vending machines should NEVER NEVER EVER eat money.

Of course, as you probably guessed by now, giving out information about users poses something of a security problem. Users may not want their telephone numbers, addresses, or even real names at the fingertips of anyone with a Finger. For this reason, the RFC doesn't specify a format for the data returned by Finger servers. One host may give out less detailed information than others, and with an entirely different appearance. It does *suggest* that Finger servers return at least the following information about their corporate users:

- User's full name

- Address or location at the office

- Office telephone number and extension

- ID of the user's terminal

Many servers also return the date and time of the last login, and whether or not there is unread mail for the user. Some systems enable their users to leave a "plan" file to be shown to everyone who fingers them. Vending machines typically return what products they contain, to save you from walking all the way down the hall to discover there's no more Coke. Some go so far as to report whether the pop is cold or warm!

Finger applications aren't just useful for getting information about users; they also provide a good chunk of information about host systems. If you send a Finger query to a host without specifying a user, the host is supposed to return a list of its users. Optionally, though, the host can return a list of users that are currently signed onto the system.

How Does Finger Work?

Now that you know what a Finger application does, let's talk about how it works. As stated before, Finger is based on the client/server model. For Finger to work, there must be a client that asks the questions and a server that answers them. If you look at the client/server model graphically, it looks something like the picture shown in figure 5.2. The client is responsible for making a connection to the host, sending queries, and receiving information. It's the server's job to listen for incoming connections, respond to queries, and terminate connections. There are some exceptions to this simple description, but this will do for now.

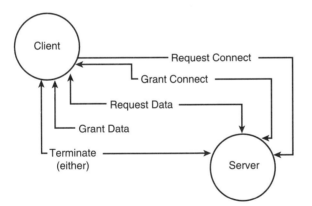

Fig. 5.2
This is a simple example of the client/server model that Finger fits into.

A Finger query starts by establishing a connection. All Internet communications involve a "port," which is a software identifier rather than a real hardware port. The standard Internet applications have standard port numbers; 79 is set aside for Finger. When a machine on the Internet receives a request to connect to port 79, it runs the Finger server program and passes subsequent port 79 messages to that program.

If this isn't making sense, refer to Chapter 2, "Understanding Internet Protocols."

Once the connection is established, the Finger client sends a command (sometimes referred to as a *selector*) indicating the information it wants to retrieve. A command is always an ASCII string that's terminated by a carriage return and linefeed pair. In this case, the command is simply the name of the user for which the client wants information. Upon receiving the command, the Finger server (sometimes referred to as *RUIP—Remote User Information Program*) returns the requested information. Bear in mind that the information returned does not have to be in a specific format. The server can return one or more lines containing any variation of user data. After the server has spilled its guts, so to speak, it terminates the session by closing the connection.

Figure 5.3 shows what happens during a typical Finger session. Notice how the connection is initiated by the client and terminated by the host. In your application, you'll watch for all incoming data and display the incoming data on a window. How will you know, though, when you can stop watching for the incoming data and possibly perform another request? That's easy; you'll just keep watching for incoming data until the connection is closed by the host.

Fig. 5.3

In a Finger session, the connection and request for information are initiated by the client. The server responds by returning the requested information and terminating the connection.

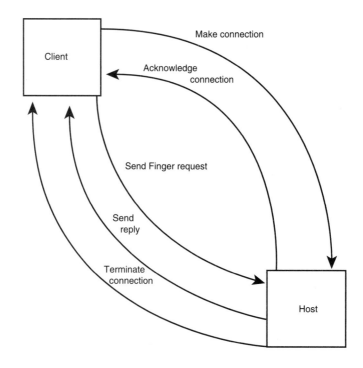

Building Your Own Finger Client

Before you so much as touch a keyboard, you need to start with design. What menu options and commands will your application have? What dialog boxes will it use to ask questions of the user? How will it provide information to the user?

You need to ask the user for a user name and host name or host address, then after sending the query you need to tell the user what response you got from the remote Finger server. You can make a dialog box with two edit boxes (one labeled Host, the other User) and a button that, when clicked, causes the query to be sent.

How will the user make this dialog appear? The usual approach is to add a menu option called Specify (or some similar name) that makes the dialog box appear. But why? Anyone who starts this program is going to want to use this dialog right away. That's what the application is for, after all. There's a simple solution, built right into MFC. Remember in Chapter 4, "Building a Windows Application Framework," you learned about views and how the framework brings the main view up automatically when the application starts. MFC has several types of views, and the one you're going to use is CFormView. This is a view that can contain dialog box controls—just what you want. It will be brought up right away when the user runs the application.

What about the response from the Finger query, the output? The easiest approach is to use an edit box, and let the framework take care of scrolling and other user interface details. Watch how quickly this comes together, or better still, follow along yourself!

You start by asking AppWizard to make a framework application for you. Start Visual C++, and choose File, New, then select Project and click OK. All the applications for this book are in their own subfolders under a folder called INTAPPS, as shown in figure 5.4. You'll probably want to put the applications you build under your existing source folder. Click Create after filling in the dialog box.

In Visual C++ 1.51 or 1.5x, the AppWizard process does not look quite like that described here. The essential questions being asked are the same (MDI versus SDI, do you want OLE support and so on) but the way you get those answers to AppWizard is a little different. Fill in the project name and then click each of the buttons along the right edge in turn, filling out the subdialog boxes those buttons bring up.

Fig. 5.4
AppWizard creates
a new folder for
your application,
\INTAPPS\FINGER,
and fills it with
starter files.

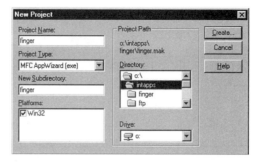

Step 1 of AppWizard asks how many documents you want your users to be able to open at once. Select Single Document—you'll see examples of multiple document and dialog-based applications in later chapters. The sample screen on the left side of the dialog box changes to remind you what a single document interface looks like. Click Next.

You don't need database support, so in step 2 make sure None is selected and click Next. You don't need OLE either, so in step 3 make sure None and No automation are selected, then click Next.

Step 4 is next. You don't need a toolbar, status bar, printing, or help. 3-D controls are a nice touch, so select them. Make sure to turn on support for sockets if you have Visual C++ version 2.1 or later—if not, see Chapter 3, "Windows Sockets (WINSOCK.DLL)," for instructions on socket support. Before you click Next on step 4, the dialog box should resemble figure 5.5. Click Next.

Fig. 5.5
AppWizard gives
you a great deal of
control over the
appearance of
your application.
Make sure you
request support for
sockets.

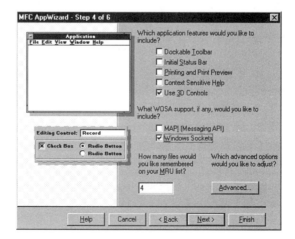

In step 5, select including comments, Visual C++ makefile, and static library, then click Next. Finally, a list appears, showing the four classes that AppWizard plans to create for you: CFingerApp, CMainFrame, CFingerDoc, and CFingerView. (Microsoft likes to start all class names with C.) Click CFingerView and then the drop-down list box labeled Base Class. Change the base class to CFormView.

Click Finish, and AppWizard confirms the settings, summarized on one page. Click OK and wait while the classes, menus, and connections are all prepared for you automatically.

Now, you need to place those controls into the view: your two input edit boxes, a button, and an output edit box. You do this with AppStudio just as though you were creating an everyday dialog box.

Start AppStudio by double-clicking FINGER.RC in the file list, and click the + next to Dialog. Surprisingly, there are two dialog boxes to choose from already: one has the resource ID IDD_ABOUTBOX and the other is IDD_FINGER_FORM. You need to edit the form template, IDD_FINGER_FORM—double-click it. (You can also right-click it and then choose Open.) AppWizard has created an almost-empty dialog box with one control: a piece of static text reminding you to edit the dialog box (see fig. 5.6).

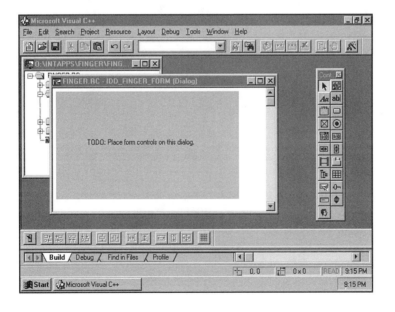

Fig. 5.6
AppWizard has created a form template for your application. You lay out the dialog box with AppStudio.

Now get to work with AppStudio. If the control palette is not on-screen as it is in figure 5.6, display it by choosing Tools, Toolbars and checking Controls. To make it float over the dialog box being edited, as it does in Figure 5.6, grab it with the mouse and drag it out of the status bar. If the Properties box is not on-screen, display it by choosing Edit, Properties. Add controls to your dialog box by single-clicking the desired control in the palette, then again where you want it on the dialog box. If you prefer, you can click and hold the palette, drag to where you want the control, and release. Place two edit boxes and two pieces of static text on the dialog box, and use the properties box to change the static text captions to Host Name or Address: and User:. Change the resource IDs of the edit boxes to IDC_HOST and IDC_USER, and lengthen them—make them as long as possible within the confines of the dialog box. Figure 5.7 shows how your AppStudio session should look by now.

Fig. 5.7

Your Finger dialog box is under construction. At this point you have two edit boxes and their static captions. Remember to change the ID in the Properties sheet from IDC_EDIT1 to IDC_HOST.

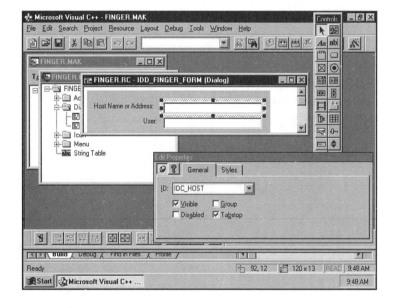

Add a button under the two edit boxes and their associated text. Change its resource ID to IDC_LOOKUP and its caption to &Look up. The & will underline the L on the button, and create a mnemonic entry so that typing **l** is the same as clicking the button. Now add another edit box under the button, and change its Resource ID to IDC_OUTPUT. Enlarge the child window in which you are creating the dialog box, and then enlarge the dialog box as much as you can. Finally make the edit box at the bottom as wide and as high as possible. Now, in the properties box, click the drop-down list box that reads General and select Styles instead. You need to change the style of this edit box from the default settings. First, and most important, select the Multiline check box.

Then check the Horiz scroll and Vert scroll—see how the scroll bars appear on the edit box as you do so? Leave the Border box checked and finally check Read Only—this prevents the user from typing in the box and is a sensible choice for an output box. Figure 5.8 shows the final styles for our output edit box.

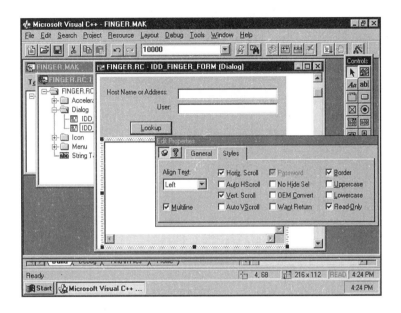

Fig. 5.8
Here is your finished Finger dialog box. You have added a button and a large edit box—note the Style settings for this box.

Now, close the IDD_FINGER_FORM dialog and FINGER.RC. Although you have yet to type a line of code, you have a sizable application already, and it's time to compile it and try a run. Press the Build button on the toolbar or choose Project, Build. After the compile is complete (all my programs compile first time, don't yours?), run the application by choosing Project, Execute FINGER.EXE. You should see something a lot like figure 5.9—the working shell of an application with your dialog brought up as the first view.

Believe it or not, you're still not ready to write any code. The next few steps in the process involve giving your program access to the controls in the dialog box and are handled with ClassWizard.

Open ClassWizard by choosing Project, Class Wizard, and click the Member Variables tab. If the topmost drop-down list box is not showing CFingerView, drop the box down and select CFingerView. Select IDC_HOST from the list box in the middle of the dialog by clicking it, and then click the Add Variable button. As you see in figure 5.10, you connect this edit box to a member variable called m_host, and the member variable will be a CString containing the value of the edit box contents. As you see if you click the drop-down list

II

Developing Applications

box now set to `Value`, you can declare member variables that let you access the controls as controls, but in this case you only want to know what the user typed in the host box, so you use `Value`. Connect `IDC_USER` to `m_user` and `IDC_OUTPUT` to `m_output` in the same way.

Fig. 5.9
Your Finger application actually runs. It doesn't do anything, but it comes up and displays the dialog.

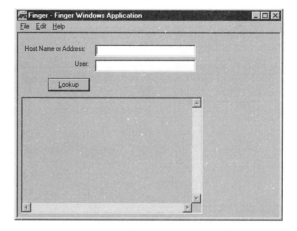

Fig. 5.10
You can connect dialog controls to member variables in the class `CFingerView` by using ClassWizard.

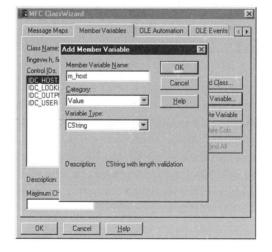

Now, click the Message Maps tab. You want to connect the Windows message "the user has clicked the Lookup button on this dialog" to a piece of code. Class Manager automates this for you, too. Select `IDC_LOOKUP` from the left-hand list box by clicking it. The right-hand list box immediately changes to only two entries: `BN_CLICKED` and `BN_DOUBLECLICKED`. Select `BN_CLICKED` and then click the Add Function button. ClassWizard calls a member function of

CFingerView whenever this button is clicked, and you are being prompted to name it. Only in highly unusual circumstances should you choose a name other than the one ClassWizard suggested. OnLookup is a perfectly sensible name for this member function (see fig. 5.11), and so you click OK.

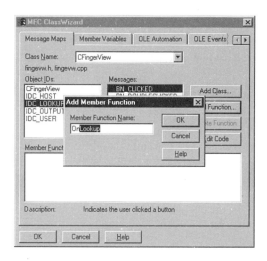

Fig. 5.11
Adding a function to handle the Windows message generated when the user clicks the Lookup button. ClassWizard suggests OnLookup for the function name.

Well, you've done a lot of work, but not a speck of code so far. You have a working application shell, with menus and a dialog view, that opens and closes nicely, but it doesn't actually do anything. Now it's time to change that.

The first thing you'll need is a socket. As discussed in Chapter 3, "Windows Sockets (WINSOCK.DLL)," the QSocket class encapsulates most of the socket code for you. This class needs a QSocket object to handle connecting, sending commands, receiving responses, and disconnecting. You need to add a member variable to the class CFingerView. Should it be a QSocket or a pointer to a QSocket? A pointer enables you to create and destroy the object according to your needs, so it's a better choice.

In FINGEVW.H, in the Attributes section, add:

```
private:


QSocket* pSocket;
```

You are following the Microsoft programming convention of using a lower-case p as the first letter of a variable name if it's a pointer to something. Now, In FINGEVW.CPP, right after the AFX_DATA block in the constructor add:

```
pSocket = NULL;
```

In the destructor add:

```
delete pSocket;
```

Now you need to write that OnLookup function. As you can see, ClassWizard added a declaration to FINGEVW.H and a skeleton definition to FINGEVW.CPP. You're going to fill out that skeleton, which starts out looking like this:

```
void CFingerView::OnLookup()
{
    UpdateData(TRUE);
    if (m_host != "" || m_user != "")
    {
        if (pSocket != 0)
            delete pSocket;
        pSocket = new QSocket();
        pSocket->SetReceiveTarget(this, WM_SOCKET_RESPONSE);
        if (!pSocket->Connect(m_host, 79))
        {
            AfxMessageBox("Host is unreachable.");
            delete pSocket;
            pSocket = 0;
            return;
        }

    }
    else
    {
        AfxMessageBox("Please fill in host or user, or both.");
        return;
    }
}
```

The call to UpdateData fills your member variables with the current contents of the controls. Next, you make sure the user has filled in at least one edit box—look at the bottom of the function for a minute. If they haven't filled in at least one box, your else clause calls AfxMessageBox. This function puts up a little message box with an OK button on it and some text, passed as an argument. There are other arguments to AfxMessageBox that cause it to display a stop sign, exclamation mark, question mark, or other icon, or to have other buttons besides just an OK. You'll leave those aside for now.

Next, you check pSocket; if it's not NULL you delete it, and then you allocate a new QSocket.

Now you need to tell the QSocket object what to do when it has a response to deliver. The call to SetReceiveTarget tells the socket what window to send a message to (this, the pointer to your instance of CFingerView) and what message to send (WM_SOCKET_RESPONSE). You'll come back to that message in a bit.

The `if` on the next line is a classic C idiom, calling a function and testing its return all at once. You pass the `Connect` method of the socket class two parameters: the name or address of the host, and the port number to use. The socket class figures out whether you passed a name or address, performs name resolution, and makes the connection. You get the port number, 79, from the RFC.

> Right here you may notice a problem. If the user leaves the Host edit box blank, you'll try to connect to "", which will probably fail. You'll address this once you have it working with remote hosts, since most of the people using this application are programmers like you and me, connected by a dialup SLIP connection, with no other users on the machine. Who would you finger on your own machine? Nonetheless, the application should either insist on a nonblank host or handle a blank one gracefully, so keep this in mind for later.

If the connection attempt fails you put up another handy `AfxMessageBox`, delete the `QSocket` that you allocated with `new`, and set the pointer to NULL to prevent future deletions, then return. What do you do if the attempt succeeds? Nothing. Just because the function returned TRUE doesn't mean you've actually connected to the remote system, only that you've started to try. The socket sends you a message when it has made the connection.

If you recall, while you were writing `OnLookup` you told the socket to send a `WM_SOCKET_RESPONSE` message when it had a response to deliver. How do I know that's the message name? I made it up. I tell Windows that I've made it up by adding a line at the top of FINGEVW.H:

```
#define WM_SOCKET_RESPONSE WM_USER+201
```

I just added an arbitrary amount to `WM_USER`, the number that starts the block of Windows messages set aside for the user to define. If your application is going to have more than one custom message, do take care not to set two of them to `WM_USER+201`!

When the socket has a response for you, it sends the message `WM_SOCKET_RESPONSE` to this instance of the `CFingerView` class. How will the message be caught? Your other message, that the user clicked the Lookup button, is caught because of an entry in the Message Map for the function. Well, you can add entries to that map—not between the lines marked `AFX_MSG`, but just after them. In FINGEVW.H you add one line declaring the function that will handle the message, `OnSocket`. The message map in FINGEVW.H now looks like this:

```
// Generated message map functions.
protected:
    //{{AFX_MSG(CFingerView)
    afx_msg void OnLookup();
    //}}AFX_MSG
    afx_msg LRESULT OnSocket(WPARAM wParam, LPARAM lParam);
    DECLARE_MESSAGE_MAP()
```

If a function handles a message, it should have a name that begins with On.

How do you know that you should use those two parameter types? All Windows messages have those two types to pass along. Now, in FINGEVW.CPP you change the message map to read:

```
BEGIN_MESSAGE_MAP(CFingerView, CFormView)
    //{{AFX_MSG_MAP(CFingerView)
    ON_BN_CLICKED(IDC_LOOKUP, OnLookup)
    //}}AFX_MSG_MAP
    ON_MESSAGE(WM_SOCKET_RESPONSE, OnSocket)
END_MESSAGE_MAP()
```

This line actually tells the system to call OnSocket when this window gets the WM_SOCKET_RESPONSE message.

Now, write OnSocket. It gets two parameters: the number of characters in the response and a char* to the characters in the response, a null-terminated string. You need to cast these parameters to use them, because Windows passes them around as WPARAM and LPARAM variables. If the socket wants to tell your application about a change in its state, it sends the message with a negative amount. Here's the function:

```
LRESULT CFingerView::OnSocket(WPARAM amount, LPARAM buffer)
{
    if ((int)amount > 0)
    {
        if (buffer != 0)
        {
            // Don't have to use amount as your data will
            // not contain NULLS and the socket class
            // NULL terminates the buffer.
            m_output += (char*) buffer;
            UpdateData(FALSE); // Fills output area on-screen
        }
    }
    else
    {
        // If amount < 0 it is a receive command
        switch ( (SocketReceiveCmd)amount )
        {
            case SocketStatusChanged:
                switch (pSocket->GetStatus())
                {
```

```
                        case CONNECTED:
                            m_output = "";
                            UpdateData(FALSE);
                            // Clears output area on-screen
                            // Send the finger request
                            pSocket->Send(m_user + "\r\n");
                            break;

                        case DISCONNECTED:
                            break;

                        default:
                            // All other status states
                            // represent an error.
                            break;
                    }
                    break;
                }
            }
        return 0;
    }
```

If amount is positive, as it usually is, and buffer is not NULL, this routine is incredibly simple: it adds the string in buffer to m_output, and then calls UpdateData(FALSE) to set the edit box value to that in m_output.

> The MFC class CString has a lot of very intuitive operators defined. The += operator adds one string onto the end of another.

But what if the socket is trying to tell you something? First, you confirm that the negative amount actually matches SocketStatusChanged. Then you ask the socket what its current status is by calling GetStatus.

If the status is CONNECTED you have just made the connection and need to send your finger command. First, you set m_output to "" and set the edit box value to that by calling UpdateData(FALSE). Finally you send the command, which is simply the user name followed by a carriage return and linefeed. You don't even need to test if the user is nonblank.

The last two cases handle the times when the socket is telling you about a dropped line or other problem. At the moment you don't do anything at all in these cases, but you may add some post-processing later, so the skeleton is here.

Believe it or not, you're done! You added a member variable to the class, some code to handle that member in the constructor and destructor, wrote two functions (OnLookup and OnSocket), invented a message and added message map entries for it, and everything else you let MFC and the wizards handle for you. And this application really works—just look at figure 5.12.

Fig. 5.12
Don't underestimate a simple interface. This is the first Windows Finger utility I've seen that actually lets you type the host name and the user name without first opening a dialog box (usually from a menu option).

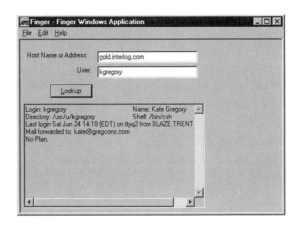

Using Finger

Using the Finger application is very simple. Your machine has to be connected to the Internet, so make your SLIP or PPP connection first. Compile your Finger application and run it from within Visual C++ by choosing Project, Run, or copy the FINGER.EXE file from the CD-ROM included with this book to your local hard disk and execute the program by choosing Start, Run (choose File, Run from the Program Manager in Windows or NT), then typing the path and name of the Finger application into the text box in the Run dialog box and pressing Enter.

Once you have the Finger application up and running, type the desired host name or IP address into the Host Name or Address field. Now, type the name of the user about whom you want information into the User's name field. Press the Lookup button to start the query. It's that easy! The Finger utility resolves the name that you typed into the host field, connects to the host, and sends the user name you've specified. When the host responds, Finger puts all of the information that's returned by the host in the area just below the input fields.

Remember, if you don't know the user's ID, but do know their name, most systems will accept that as finger input and find their ID for you. And if you want some fun, try fingering the user **coke** on the host **g.gp.cs.cmu.edu**. It's one of many vending machines connected to the Internet and accessible with Finger.

A Few Little Improvements

The application you've just created is a working Finger client, but there are things it doesn't do. Most of these shortcomings are things you should take care of in any Windows application; some are specific to this program. You'll learn about a few right now, and leave the rest for another chapter.

Blank Host

Let's start with that "blank host" problem. If the user has left the host name blank you should connect to a Finger server on your own machine. There's a trick here: the address 127.0.0.1 is always your own machine (it's called a *loopback*). Before the Connect you add an if block that sets the host to the loopback address if it is blank:

```
if (m_host == "")
{
    m_host = "127.0.0.1";
}
```

This works beautifully, but when OnSocket calls UpdateData(FALSE) after filling m_output, this new value of m_host will appear in the dialog box, which could confuse an inexperienced user. Another if, after the Connect, takes care of that:

```
if (m_host == "127.0.0.1")
{
    m_host = "";
}
```

Now if a user types in 127.0.0.1 as an address, it disappears, but who would ever type such an address? If it worries you, you can try a different approach.

```
BOOL blankhost = FALSE;
if (m_host == "")
{
    m_host = "127.0.0.1";
    blankhost = TRUE;
}
... the Connect block...
if (blankhost)
{
    m_host = "";
}
```

This involves an extra variable and a little more code, but only blanks the host if the user left it blank to begin with.

II

Developing Applications

Default Button

In the testing of this program you have done so far, has it annoyed you at all to lift your hands from the keyboard to the mouse so you can click the Lookup button? You can also make Lookup the default button, so that pressing Enter automatically clicks the button. This could hardly be simpler. Open FINGER.RC from within the Visual C++ environment (by double-clicking it), then click the + next to Dialog. Double-click IDD_FINGER_FORM, and when that dialog box is open, select the Lookup button by clicking it. If the Properties box is not displayed, open it by choosing Edit, Properties. Check the box next to Default Button.

Graying a Button

Let's not leave that button just yet. As you may have noticed, some of these Finger queries take a few seconds to process, and you really can't be sure when they are finished. What if you could gray the button as soon as it was clicked, and ungray the button after the socket disconnected? You can.

First, open ClassWizard (choose Project, ClassWizard), and select CFingerView if it's not already selected. Click the Member Variables tab. Only one control is not connected to a variable: the Lookup button. Click it, then click the Add Variable button. ClassWizard suggests that you map it to a CButton—simply fill in a variable name like m_lookup and click OK. ClassWizard adds the member to the class and handles construction and so on. You need only to add some calls to EnableWindow.

```
m_lookup.EnableWindow(FALSE);
```

grays the button and prevent the user from clicking it. You add this line at the very top of OnLookup.

```
m_lookup.EnableWindow(TRUE);
```

ungrays the button again. You add this line twice in OnSocket, once in the DISCONNECTED case and again in the default case. Now the user is getting visual feedback on the status of the request—a gray button means it's not finished yet. And you don't have to worry about sending the same request many times, or socket collisions, because the user can't click again until you're finished.

 You should try to do something like this in all your applications—whenever you add a button or a menu item, consider graying it while it does its work.

Dealing with Noncompliant Sites

The RFC makes it clear that sites do not have to run a Finger server and do not have to return any specific information in response to a query. But it makes it just as clear that what they do send should be broken into lines and that each line should end in a carriage-return-linefeed pair. What if some sites don't follow the rules?

Try fingering the user **president** on the site **whitehouse.gov**, for example. As you see in figure 5.13, all the output appears on a single line, and there are some strange vertical bars embedded in it. Setting a breakpoint in OnSocket and looking at the content of buffer explains the mystery: those vertical bars are linefeed characters. The carriage returns are missing.

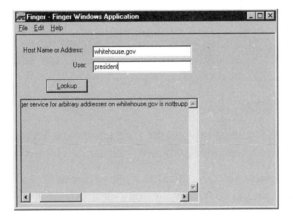

Fig. 5.13

Your application expects carriage returns and linefeeds at the end of each line, and when only linefeeds are sent, the output is misformatted. Use the scroll bar to see all of it.

You can modify the program a little so that if it gets a linefeed that is not preceded by a carriage return, it inserts one. This fixes the behavior of this badly behaved site. Unfortunately you give up the simplicity of the single line in OnSocket:

```
m_output += (char*) buffer;
```

You replace it with this:

```
for (unsigned int i = 0; i < amount; i++)
    {
        if ( ((char *)buffer)[i] == '\n' &&
            (i == 0 || ((char *)buffer)[i-1] != '\r') )
        {
            m_output += '\r';
        }
        m_output += ((char *)buffer)[i];
    }
```

This code copies the characters in buffer over one at a time, checking each against \n (a linefeed) and inserting a \r character if necessary. As you see in figure 5.14, the White House finger response looks much better now.

Fig. 5.14
The modified program works even when the response from the remote site doesn't quite follow the RFC.

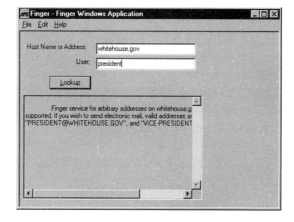

From Here...

This application is getting nicer all the time, but there is yet more that can be done. These are concepts you'll cover in later chapters of this book:

■ The framework has created a whole pile of menus for you: File, Save; File, New, and so on, that really don't mean anything in this application. You can get rid of them in AppStudio by editing the menu. There will be some useless code left behind in your application, but that's harmless enough.

■ Some of the other menu items, specifically Edit, Cut, Copy, and Paste would be very useful. If you typed someone's name and their system told you their ID, wouldn't you want to copy that ID to the Clipboard to paste into your mail client? Or if you got mail from someone you didn't know, you might copy their ID into the Clipboard to paste into Finger. You'll cover the implementation of these features in the next chapter for a very similar application, Whois.

■ Would you ever want to print the results of a Finger query? As it stands, your application has no printing support.

■ Sometimes a site may connect but not respond. The only a way a user can drop the connection is to close the application. You could add a

Cancel button to the dialog that would disconnect the socket and
ungray the Lookup button. This would enable the user to cancel requests that are taking too long.

■ Isn't it a little annoying that you can't resize the output edit box?
Resizing the application's main window doesn't have any effect on the
dialog at the moment, but it could. Whenever the main window
changes size it sends a message to its child windows, which you can
catch and use to resize the output edit box. This too is saved for the
Whois chapter, coming up next.

In the next chapter you build on the concepts you've covered here to create
your second Internet application, Whois, and demonstrate some useful approaches to Windows programming in general. Whois is very much like Finger, with a focus on telling you about sites rather than users.

II

Developing Applications

Chapter 6

Building an Internet Whois Application

Before you pop the hood on another Internet program, think about what you're getting yourself into. Whois is a protocol that's very similar to the Finger protocol that you learned about in the last chapter—it's used to get information about users. Unlike Finger, though, Whois is used with a specific server, or set of servers, known as the *NIC*, or *Network Information Center*—but, it's designed in such a way that it can be used with any server that wants to support it (like all other Internet protocols). NIC servers are remnants of the Internet when it existed as ARPANET back in the 1970s.

NIC servers provide large databases of users and hosts from all around the world. Don't get scared! They don't know you exist until you tell them. NIC gives you information about users or host systems that are registered with its databases. Hosts and users register by sending e-mail messages to the NIC mail server at **REGISTRAR@NIC.DDN.MIL**. If you buy access through a commercial Internet Service Provider they will usually register your site with NIC on your behalf.

So what's the difference between the information provided by Whois and that provided by Finger? Not much. Whois tends to give you more in-depth data on whatever, or whoever, you're querying about. Other than that and the fact that Whois is used only with NIC servers, Whois is more like Finger than it is different. Whois fits the client/server model, as you'll find with all the other applications you learn about in this book, and you can't rely on the format of the data you receive in answer to a query. Even the way your Whois application talks to the NIC server is the same as the Finger application!

You're probably wondering what this chapter's going to teach you, considering that Finger and Whois are basically the same, right? There's a lot to learn about Internet programs and programming in general, so hang on! With that in mind, this chapter:

- Examines what's in a Whois program—an overview of how a Whois program works

- Tidies up the interface that carries over from the Finger application—shows you how to add keyboard accelerators, add cut, copy, and paste capability, change the font for the output box, and load a default value from the string table

- Wraps things up by showing you how to use the Whois application included on the CD-ROM and telling you where to go from here

What's in a Whois?

You'll start things off by learning about how the Whois protocol works. As stated earlier, the mechanics of Whois are just like those of Finger. To get information about a user or a host, the Whois application builds a command. Recall from Chapter 5, "Building an Internet Finger Application," that a *command*, in this case, is just a string that's terminated by a carriage return and linefeed pair. In this case, a command is the name of a user, group of users, host, group of hosts, or help information.

After building a command, the Whois application makes a connection to a NIC server. It makes the connection using TCP port 43. Once the connection is established, the Whois program sends the command, which contains the name of the entity that you want to obtain information about. NIC looks the name up in its databases. NIC then returns the data requested by the Whois program and disconnects. Pretty simple, isn't it?

It looks really similar to the Finger protocol, and for the most part it's the same, but there are some extra features supported by the NIC server that aren't supported by Finger servers. Those features are discussed under the "Using the Whois Application" section in this chapter. Right now, let's concentrate on what it takes to build a Whois program.

Building the Whois Application

Since a Whois program is basically a Finger program, except that it talks to a specific group of servers, you can reuse almost all of the code from the Finger application. In fact, you get a quick start by just copying your Finger source files into a new folder and doing a little bit of renaming. (Be sure to change all references to Finger in the program, like the title, class names, and window titles, to Whois. Change the filenames, too.) Most of the improvements you're going to make to the Whois applications are in the user interface, although you'll also need to change some of the network stuff too.

The Whois port is 43, so the first change you need to make is to the `Con-nect()` call in `CWhoisView::OnLookup()`. As you saw in Chapter 5, "Building an Internet Finger Application," this function is called when the user clicks the Lookup button on your main view. The `OnLookup` function ends up looking like this:

```
void CWhoisView::OnLookup()
{
        m_lookup.EnableWindow(FALSE);
        UpdateData(TRUE);
        if (m_host != "" || m_user != "")
        {
                m_output = "";
                UpdateData(FALSE); //clears output area on-screen
                delete pSocket;
                pSocket = new QSocket();
                pSocket->SetReceiveTarget(this, WM_SOCKET_RESPONSE);
                if (!pSocket->Connect(m_host, 43))
                {
                        AfxMessageBox("Host is unreachable.");
                        delete pSocket;
                        pSocket = 0;
                        m_lookup.EnableWindow(TRUE);
                }
        }
        else
        {
                AfxMessageBox("Please fill in host or user, or both.");
                m_lookup.EnableWindow(TRUE);
        }
        UpdateData(FALSE);
}
```

II

Developing Applications

This is a two-character change (just the port number) from the working Finger program you built in the previous chapter. But with this simple change, you have transformed your working Finger client into a working Whois client! Figure 6.1 shows the application in action. The "host" box is really the "where to look up the WHOIS information" box now, and the "user" box is really "user or site about which information is requested."

Fig. 6.1
WHOIS finds contact information for Macmillan Computer Publishing, Que's parent company. **DS.INTERNIC.NET** is a good choice for the host.

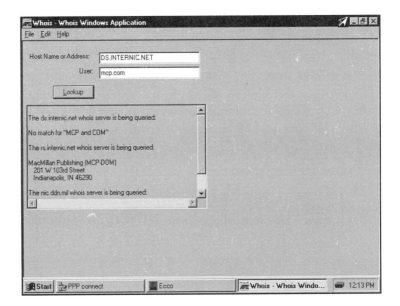

The remainder of this chapter will be concerned with making this program easier to use, and adding features that are useful in any Windows program. First, you'll automatically load the Host text box with a hostname from the string table so the user doesn't have to type it in every time. Then you'll add cut, copy, and paste capability to the text fields and output box. Next, you'll add keyboard accelerators so that the user can scroll the output box using the Page Up and Page Down keys. Finally, to make the Whois responses better formatted, you'll change the font of the output box to a monospaced font.

Preloading the Host Address Box

In Finger, the host edit box describes the machine on which the user you're looking for has an account. But in Whois, it describes the host where you want the search performed, and that's almost always going to be **DS.INTERNIC.NET**. So why not enter that as a default value for the box, while still allowing the user to specify a different host if that's appropriate?

Adding a default server is quite simple. You simply need to tell the Whois application to put a server name in the host edit box when the application is first opened. Do you recall the input dialog box you learned about in the last chapter? The input dialog box is the window that contains the host and user edit boxes and the Lookup pushbutton. In the source for your Whois application, you simply initialize the m_host edit box with a value from the string table.

The goal here is to change the text of the host edit box to the name of a default server when the input dialog box is created, and only then. When the input dialog box is created, the constructor for CWhoisView gets called. You simply add a call to LoadString() to this constructor, like this:

```
m_host.LoadString(IDS_WHOIS_SERVER);
```

Make sure you add this line outside the AFX_DATA block. LoadString() is a member function of the MFC class CString, and it causes the CString to fill itself from the string table, using the resource ID IDS_WHOIS_SERVER to find the string. IDS_WHOIS_SERVER is an identifier that points to the string **DS.INTERNIC.NET**, or whatever you want the default server to be. Why do you use string resources instead of hard-coding this stuff into your code? Well, for one thing, it's easier to localize your code for foreign versions if your strings are in resources instead of in your code. For a second thing, you can change the default server without recompiling your C/C++ source files. Sure, you may have to recompile and relink your resources, but resource files are typically much smaller than your source files (it's usually faster to change a resource, compile, and relink, than it is to compile and relink C/C++ source files).

The next task is to get the string **DS.INTERNIC.NET** into the string table, with a resource ID of IDS_WHOIS_SERVER. The string table is part of the resource file, so double-click FINGER.RC and then String Table. (In version 1.52 or earlier, choose Tools, AppStudio, and then String Table.) Select the string with resource ID IDR_MAINFRAME, and choose Edit, Copy, and then Edit, Paste. This puts a copy of the string into the string table. Change the ID to IDS_WHOIS_SERVER and the caption to **DS.INTERNIC.NET** using the Properties box. (If the Properties box is not on the screen, pressing Enter will bring it up.) Close the string table and the RC file.

Now when the input dialog box is created, the constructor logic for CWhoisView is executed and the server name is set to **DS.INTERNIC.NET**— you've just saved the user some typing time and made your program easier to use! (See fig. 6.2.)

Fig. 6.2

AppStudio makes editing the string table for your program simple and visual.

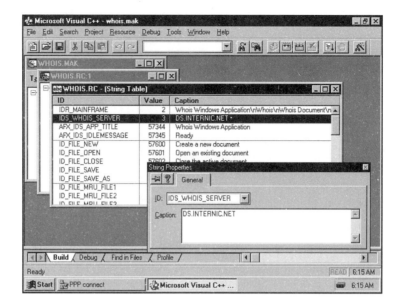

Adding Accelerators

To make it easier to scroll the output box using the keyboard, you'll add accelerator support. At the moment, if the user clicks in the edit box and presses Page Down, the framework will scroll the edit box automatically. However, if some other control has focus, Page Up and Page Down won't affect the output edit box at all. You can make them work no matter which control has focus by setting them up as *accelerator keys*.

MFC makes accelerators very easy to add. Since you used AppWizard to create the base code, an accelerator table already exists, complete with keyboard equivalents for cut, copy, and paste, as well as many other keys. You just need to add accelerators for the Page-up, page-down, arrow-up, and arrow-down keys.

Open WHOIS.RC, click Accelerator, and double-click IDR_MAINFRAME. This is the accelerator table for Whois (some applications may have different tables for different circumstances). Click the blank entry at the bottom of the screen and press Enter to bring up the Properties box. Fill in the ID as ID_SCROLL_PAGE_DOWN. You want this accelerator to use the Page Down key, but perhaps you didn't know that key is called VK_NEXT. Luckily you don't need to memorize the key names. Click the Next Key Typed button, then press Page Down. The key name, VK_NEXT, is filled in for you automatically. In the same way, connect ID_SCROLL_PAGE_UP to VK_PRIOR (type Page Up instead of Page Down), ID_SCROLL_LINE_UP to VK_UP (type the up arrow key) and ID_SCROLL_LINE_DOWN to VK_DOWN (type the down arrow key.) The final accelerator table should like like figure 6.3.

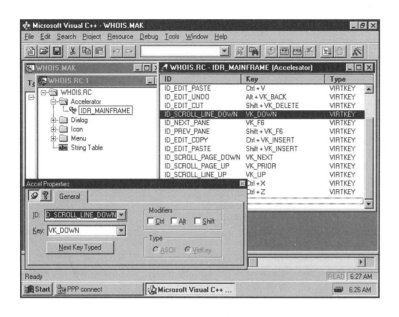

Fig. 6.3
Accelerator tables
make it simple to
connect keys to
code.

II

Developing Applications

While still in the accelerator edit dialog box, invoke ClassWizard. In
ClassWizard, choose the CWhoisView class and attach functions to each
accelerator. Create and attach the function names OnScrollPageUp,
OnScrollPageDown, OnScrollLineUp, and OnScrollLineDown. When the user
presses an accelerator, the CWhoisView receives a WM_COMMAND message with the
accelerator's ID. ClassWizard automatically maps these messages to the right
functions, adding entries to the message map for CWhoisView like this:

```
.
ON_COMMAND(ID_SCROLL_LINE_DOWN, OnScrollLineDown)
ON_COMMAND(ID_SCROLL_LINE_UP, OnScrollLineUp)
ON_COMMAND(ID_SCROLL_PAGE_DOWN, OnScrollPageDown)
ON_COMMAND(ID_SCROLL_PAGE_UP, OnScrollPageUp)
.
```

All you need to do is write the functions to scroll the output box up or down
a line or page. To do that, you need to access the edit box as an edit box,
rather than through the CString it contains as you have been doing. Use the
Member Variables tab in Class Wizard to connect the edit box, IDC_OUTPUT
(as a control rather than a variable) to the member variable m_output_box.
Then you can use the convenient CEdit method LineScroll, as shown in the
following section of code.

```
void CWhoisView::OnScrollLineDown()
{
    // Scroll down a line using the builtin edit box method.
    m_output_box.LineScroll(1, 0);
}
```

```
void CWhoisView::OnScrollLineUp()
{
    // Scroll up a line using the builtin edit box method.
    m_output_box.LineScroll(-1, 0);
}

void CWhoisView::OnScrollPageDown()
{
    // Scroll down a page.
    m_output_box.LineScroll(10, 0);
}

void CWhoisView::OnScrollPageUp()
{
    // Scroll up a page.
    m_output_box.LineScroll(-10, 0);
}
```

These all call LineScroll(), which scrolls the output box. The first parameter is the number of lines (negative means up, positive means down), and the second is the number of characters (negative means left, positive means right.) None of these calls will scroll the box horizontally. Ideally OnScrollPageDown() and OnScrollPageUp() would calculate how many lines make up a page at the moment (it depends on the font size being used and the size of the window) but the simple approach is just to hard code a ten-line page.

Changing the Font

Since the Whois server responses often depend on monospaced output to make certain columns line up, you change the font of the output box to Courier, a monospace font. (Unlike proportionally spaced fonts, which use a different width for each character, monospaced fonts use the same width for every letter.) That makes it easier to line up character-based output, a common requirement on the Internet, which grew up as a character-based system.

To change the font, you'll need to define the font structure you want and then assign the font to the output box. Since you need to do this only once, you can do it in the OnInitialUpdate method, which is called when the view is first opened. Before you define a new font, you need a member variable of type CFont to hold it. Allocating a CFont object on the stack will not work, as the CFont object must persist after the routine returns. As shown in the following sections of code, you define the m_TerminalFont member variable in WHOISVW.H. Then, in WHOISVW.CPP, you use the CreateFont and SetFont methods to assign the new font to the output box.

```
// In WHOISVW.H:
    public:
    //{{AFX_DATA(CWhoisView)
        .
    CFont      m_TerminalFont;
    //}}AFX_DATA
    // Overrides
    // ClassWizard generated virtual function overrides
    //{{AFX_VIRTUAL(CWhoisView)
    public:
    virtual void OnInitialUpdate();
    //}}AFX_VIRTUAL

// In WHOISVW.CPP:
void CWhoisView::OnInitialUpdate()
{
m_TerminalFont.CreateFont((GetDC()->GetDeviceCaps(
        ➥LOGPIXELSY) * 8) / 72,
        0, 0, 0, FW_NORMAL, 0, 0, 0, ANSI_CHARSET,
        OUT_DEFAULT_PRECIS, CLIP_DEFAULT_PRECIS,
        DEFAULT_QUALITY,FF_DONTCARE, (LPSTR)"Courier");
    GetDlgItem(IDC_OUTPUT)->SetFont(&m_TerminalFont);
    ResizeParentToFit(FALSE);        // Shrink parent frame
                                     // to dialog size.

    CFormView::OnInitialUpdate();
}
```

That call to CreateFont() is quite complex, with fourteen parameters. The
first is the height of the font, in *logical units*. This is calculated by calling
GetDC() to determine the current *device context*—probably a screen for output.
The call to GetDeviceCaps() asks about the capabilities of the device; passing
the LOGPIXELSY parameter asks how many pixels per logical inch in the y direction (vertically) the device can display. You want an 8-point font. Divide
that 8 by 72 because there are 72 points per inch—the final result is in the
logical units that CreateFont() wants.

The second parameter is the width of the font; by leaving it zero you are
asking the framework to choose a width that goes with the height you calculated. The third parameter is the escapement, used when writing text along
an angled line, and the fourth is the orientation, used to write angled text
along a flat line. Leave these both zero to write normal text. The fifth parameter is line weight (thin, bold, and so on) and FW_NORMAL is a sensible choice.
The sixth, seventh, and eighth parameters specify whether the font is italic,
underline, or struck-through, and in all three cases zero means it is not.

The ninth parameter sets the character set—you want the ANSI character set,
so use ANSI_CHARSET for this parameter. The tenth parameter is the output
precision; the default, OUT_DEFAULT_PRECIS, is fine for simple text output. The

eleventh parameter, clipping precision, governs the clipping of characters on the border of a region. The default value, CLIP_DEFAULT_PRECIS, is fine. The twelfth parameter governs the quality. For an 8 point Courier font it probably doesn't matter what value you choose: DEFAULT_QUALITY will be fine. The thirteenth parameter is the font family: set it to FF_DONTCARE because you will set the face in the final parameter. If you didn't know what font you wanted, the Font dialog box available under the control panel has a long list of font names and samples of the way they appear. "Courier" is a simple and familiar monospaced font, perfect for our purposes.

Having created the font, the call to SetFont() actually sets the font for the edit box (whose resource ID is IDC_OUTPUT) to this font. ResizeParentToFit() takes care of any resizing of IDC_OUTPUT as a result of the font change. Finally a call to CFormView::OnInitialUpdate() does the rest of the work associated with getting the view onto the screen.

While that's a lot of work, it accomplishes a very nice effect. Keep it in mind for all your Internet applications—in fact for any Windows program that may need to change fonts.

Adding Cut, Copy, Paste, and Undo Support

Now, to allow copying text from the output box, you need to add handlers for the clipboard copy event. But why stop there? You can add cut, paste, and undo as well for the other text boxes in the Whois view—the host and user fields. These events should be handled by CWhoisView, but unfortunately ClassWizard doesn't present these events as possible ones for CWhoisView to catch. That doesn't mean you can't catch them, though—you just follow the same procedure as you did in Chapter 5, "Building an Internet Finger Application," when you added the socket message. In WHOISVW.H, change the message map so that it has four extra entries:

```
// Generated message map functions
protected:
        //{{AFX_MSG(CWhoisView)
        afx_msg void OnLookup();
        afx_msg void OnScrollLineDown();
        afx_msg void OnScrollLineUp();
        afx_msg void OnScrollPageDown();
        afx_msg void OnScrollPageUp();
        //}}AFX_MSG
        afx_msg LRESULT OnSocket(WPARAM wParam, LPARAM lParam);
        afx_msg void OnEditCut();
        afx_msg void OnEditCopy();
        afx_msg void OnEditPaste();
        afx_msg void OnEditUndo();
        DECLARE_MESSAGE_MAP()
```

Be sure to use the names that ClassWizard would suggest: `OnEditCut()` for example, rather than just `Cut()`. Then in WHOISVW.CPP, add the message map entries to connect the Windows messages to these functions, so that the message map looks like this:

```
BEGIN_MESSAGE_MAP(CWhoisView, CFormView)
    //{{AFX_MSG_MAP(CWhoisView)
    ON_BN_CLICKED(IDC_LOOKUP, OnLookup)
    ON_COMMAND(ID_SCROLL_LINE_DOWN, OnScrollLineDown)
    ON_COMMAND(ID_SCROLL_LINE_UP, OnScrollLineUp)
    ON_COMMAND(ID_SCROLL_PAGE_DOWN, OnScrollPageDown)
    ON_COMMAND(ID_SCROLL_PAGE_UP, OnScrollPageUp)
    //}}AFX_MSG_MAP
    ON_MESSAGE(WM_SOCKET_RESPONSE, OnSocket)
    ON_COMMAND(ID_EDIT_CUT, OnEditCut)
    ON_COMMAND(ID_EDIT_COPY, OnEditCopy)
    ON_COMMAND(ID_EDIT_PASTE, OnEditPaste)
    ON_COMMAND(ID_EDIT_UNDO, OnEditUndo)
END_MESSAGE_MAP()
```

The code for these functions couldn't be simpler. Here's `OnEditCut()`:

```
void CWhoisView:: OnEditCut()
{
    ((CEdit*)GetFocus())->Cut();
}
```

You call `GetFocus()` to determine which control has focus, then call the `Cut()` method for that control. `OnEditCopy()` calls `Copy()`, `OnEditPaste()` calls `Paste()`, and `OnEditUndo()` calls `Undo()`. There's no work for you to do!

A side effect of adding support for paste and undo is that you need to add update handlers to automatically enable or disable the paste and undo menu commands. After all, the user cannot paste if there's nothing in the clipboard, or undo if nothing's been done. You do this by hand as well. As well as connecting a function to COMMAND for the messages ID_EDIT_PASTE and ID_EDIT_UNDO, connect functions to UPDATE_COMMAND_UI. Add these lines to the message map in WHOISVW.H:

```
afx_msg void OnUpdateEditUndo(CCmdUI* pCmdUI);
afx_msg void OnUpdateEditPaste(CCmdUI* pCmdUI);
```

Again, use the names, `OnUpdateEditPaste()` and `OnUpdateEditUndo()`, that ClassWizard would suggest for these functions. Add these lines to the message map in WHOISVW.CPP:

```
ON_UPDATE_COMMAND_UI(ID_EDIT_UNDO, OnUpdateEditUndo)
ON_UPDATE_COMMAND_UI(ID_EDIT_PASTE, OnUpdateEditPaste)
```

II

Developing Applications

These functions are called just before the menu is drawn and used to determine whether the items are enabled or grayed. Here's the code for OnUpdateEditPaste():

```
void CWhoisView::OnUpdateEditPaste(CCmdUI* pCmdUI)
{
    pCmdUI->Enable(::IsClipboardFormatAvailable(CF_TEXT));
}
```

The SDK function ::IsClipboardFormatAvailable() returns TRUE if the clipboard contains some data in the specified format (text, in this case) and FALSE if it is empty or contains some other format (perhaps a graphic). Update handlers should be as fast as possible, typically one line long, because they are executed every time the menu is displayed. OnUpdateEditUndo() is also short and sweet:

```
void CWhoisView::CanUndo(CCmdUI* pCmdUI)
{
    pCmdUI->Enable(((CEdit*)GetFocus())->CanUndo());
}
```

Like the other methods, this one determines which control has focus with a call to GetFocus(). It then calls the CanUndo() method, which, not surprisingly, returns TRUE if there is something that can be undone and FALSE if there is not.

So now your rudimentary Whois program is looking pretty good. In fact, you might want to add some these changes to the Finger program you built in the previous chapter.

Using the Whois Application

Using a Whois program is just as easy as using a Finger program. Copy the WHOIS.EXE file from the CD-ROM included with this book or compile the one you've written. You can find WHOIS.EXE on the CD-ROM in the \WHOIS folder. Execute the program by choosing File, Run from the Desktop. Type the path and name of the Whois application in the edit box of the Run dialog box and press Enter.

Using Whois: The Basics

Figure 6.4 shows the main window of the Whois program after a query is answered by the NIC servers. (By the way, compare the font in the output edit box in figure 6.1 with that of figure 6.4.)

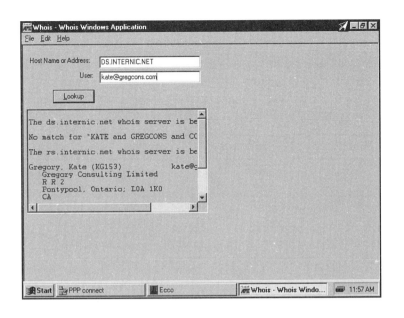

Fig. 6.4
The Whois main
window is shown
after a query. You
can use the scroll
bar to scroll up
and down through
the data, or you
can use the arrow/
page keys.

To make a query, you enter the name of the host you want to query in the
host edit box. Enter a NIC-server address—probably **NIC.DDN.MIL** or
DS.INTERNIC.NET—it defaults to **DS.INTERNIC.NET**. There are three
main Whois hosts to choose from. The **DS.INTERNIC.NET** host acts as a
central query host which will return responses from the other hosts. Use the
following table as a guide:

Whois Host	Name	Description
NIC.DDN.MIL	DISA NIC	MILNET information
RS.INTERNIC.NET	InterNIC Registration Services	Registration information
DS.INTERNIC.NET	InterNIC Directory and Database Service	Person information that does not fit into either of the above categories

You can retrieve an updated list of Whois hosts from the following URL:
ftp://sipb.mit.edu/pub/whois/whois-servers.list.

Once you have entered the name of a Whois host, enter the name of the
Internet user about whom you want information by typing the full e-mail
address in the User box. When you're done typing the host and user names,
select the Lookup button to initiate the query.

II

Developing Applications

Using Whois: Advanced Requests

When you enter a name in the user field, you're actually entering a search key. If you enter **gregcons.com**, for example, you're going to get all info that corresponds to **gregcons.com**. If you want to get information about a specific record in the NIC databases, you can precede the record name with specific keywords or symbols, as described in the following table:

Symbol/Keyword	Example	Action
?	?	Return the WHOIS host's query syntax.
!	!NET-INGR	Search for a specific reference by handle. *Handles* are record specifiers that appear in parenthesis in summary listings.
@	drjarmon@ingr.com	Search for entries that match the given email address.
.	.brady	Search for information from the record with the specified name.
Help	help	Return a page of help for the WHOIS host.
Domain	Domain ingr.com	Search for Internet domain name entries.
Host	Host ingr.ingr.com	Search for host entries.
Network	Network 129.135	Search for specific Internet network address entries.

For more information on advanced Whois queries, take a look at RFC 954 available on the CD-ROM in the \RFC folder.

From Here...

During the course of this chapter you took the Finger framework and, with a two-character change, made it into a Whois application, because Internet protocols and port numbers took care of the rest of the effort. Then you learned how to add accelerators to your application, add support for cut, copy, paste, and undo, and change the font of the output box. You can get the source for the Whois program written for the book from the enclosed CD-ROM. This Whois application has the basic functionality of an Internet program, but lacks polishing here and there. Things you can do on your own include:

- Create a capture feature that writes all incoming data into files. Add some items to the File menu to start a capture, stop a capture, and re-play a capture. Hints: Use the same routines for replay that you use to put incoming data on the screen, and account for recursive situations.

- Add a status bar and report each phase of the connection, such as "Re-solving hostname...," "Connecting...," "Sending Request...," "Receiving Response...," and "Ready."

- Replace the Host edit box with a combo box that is pre-loaded with several NIC host servers, such as **DS.INTERNIC.NET**, and **NIC.DDN.MIL**.

- Allow users to print out data that's received from the NIC servers. You'll need both Print and Print Setup menu items.

Chapter 7

Building an Internet FTP Application

Perhaps you've heard that it's possible to get files over the Internet—to download drivers or patches or shareware programs from sites all over the world. *FTP*, or *File Transfer Protocol*, is the Internet service used to bring files from remote sites to your desk, or to send your files to a faraway vendor. In this chapter you'll learn:

- What FTP does

- What anonymous FTP is

- How FTP works

- How to build an FTP client

- How to use your FTP client

What Does FTP Do?

When you use FTP, you can explore the files on another Internet site, and copy its files to or from your computer. Most FTP clients provide commands that enable you to:

- connect to a remote site

- focus your attention on a specific directory—called the current remote directory—on the remote site

- change your current remote directory

- list the files in the current remote directory

- get a file from the current remote directory

- put a file into the current remote directory

- disconnect from the remote site

In addition, most clients enable the user to specify whether transfers should be binary (machine language) or ASCII (readable text). The vast majority of FTP clients, even for Windows, look like UNIX sessions and use UNIX-style commands such as ls (which stands for "list"), as you can see in figure 7.1.

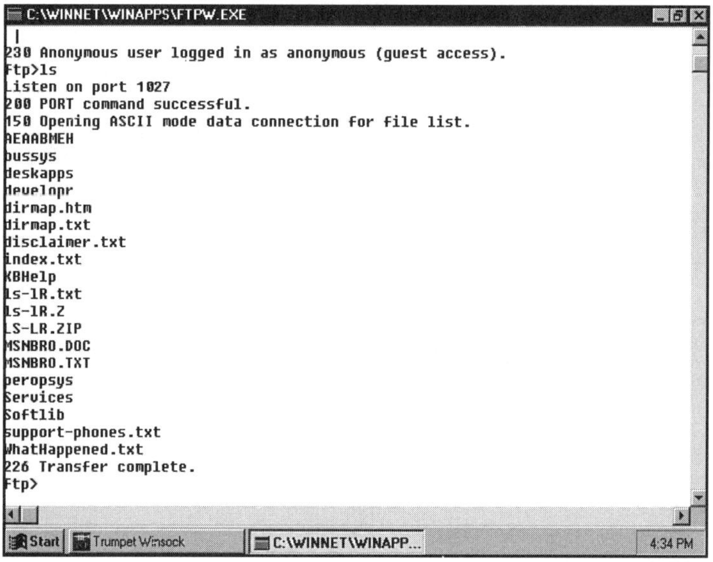

Fig. 7.1
This FTP client, called ftpw, comes with the Trumpet Winsock. It behaves exactly like the UNIX ftp command and has a command-line interface, not a typical Windows interface.

```
C:\WINNET\WINAPPS\FTPW.EXE

230 Anonymous user logged in as anonymous (guest access).
Ftp>ls
Listen on port 1027
200 PORT command successful.
150 Opening ASCII mode data connection for file list.
REAABMEH
bussys
deskapps
develapr
dirmap.htm
dirmap.txt
disclaimer.txt
index.txt
KBHelp
ls-lR.txt
ls-lR.Z
LS-LR.ZIP
MSNBRO.DOC
MSNBRO.TXT
peropsys
Services
Softlib
support-phones.txt
WhatHappened.txt
226 Transfer complete.
Ftp>
```

What Is Anonymous FTP?

Anonymous FTP is primarily a convention or agreement among the various sites on the Internet. The user must normally supply a user ID and password to gain access to files on a remote site, but many sites have some directories that they will allow anyone to access.

Obviously, if you are writing an FTP server you need to concern yourself with prompting for a password and user ID, checking against registered users of the site, and checking access privileges for each directory and file. As the author of a client program you need only supply these to the server as part of the connection process. A user-friendly client makes it easy to supply the agreed-on user ID (anonymous) and password (the user's full e-mail address in the form **user@somesite.com**) during connection. Since there will be times when the user actually has an account on the remote machine, the client should make it possible for other user IDs or passwords to be used.

How Does FTP Work?

As you learned in Chapter 2, "Understanding Internet Protocols," an FTP session takes place over two connections between sites. One is used for commands and the other for data. Still, the basic pattern of sending a command and waiting for a response is the same as it is for Finger and Whois. The complete FTP specification is in RFC 959, which is included on the CD-ROM that comes with this book. Be sure to read it as you read this chapter. The FTP commands you will implement are listed below. Each is followed by the parameters, if any, they require, and explained more fully in a moment.

- USER—user ID

- PASS—password

- CWDhr.—new directory name

- CDUP—parent directory

- LIST—directory name

- TYPE—A or I

- RETR—file name to retrieve

- STOR—file name to store

These commands are not entirely intuitive, unfortunately. CWD changes the working directory; CDUP changes to the "parent" directory—useful if the remote system doesn't use the special directory name [..] to mean the parent directory. LIST returns a list of the names of the files in the specified directory, or the current one if none is specified.

TYPE is either A for ASCII or I for Image (also called binary). ASCII works for text files, PostScript files, and uuencoded files; binary should be used for ZIP files, executables, graphics files (GIF, JPEG, and so on), and any other files that contain non-printable characters.

Finally, the commands that actually do the work: RETR transfers a file from the remote site to the user's machine, and STOR transfers from the user to the remote site.

These commands are sent over the control connection, and a simple reply, usually a success or failure indicator, comes back over the control connection. The remote server makes the data connection (a third "listening" connection is used only to find out where the data connection has been made) and the list of files, or the contents of the file itself, come back over the data connection. When the transfer is complete another response comes over the control connection and indicates this.

Building Your FTP Client

As always, before you start to develop, you design. Then you use AppWizard and the other tools of Visual C++ to make an application for yourself, before you finally fill in the last few touches by actually writing code. As you'll see, this more complicated application requires a lot more code, but far less than it would writing it from scratch without the MFC classes to handle routine tasks.

Design

The design for Finger and Whois was pretty straightforward; there were only two pieces of information the user could fill in, and one action the user could request. But FTP is a more complex application and you will need a more complex interface. One useful technique in interface design is simply to list everything that the user could tell the application, be told by the application, or ask the application to do—input, output, and commands.

The inputs from the user include:

- Site name

- user ID

- password

- directory to change to on a remote site

- file name to get (receive) or put (send)—remote name

- directory and file name (local site)

The outputs to the user are:

- list of directories and files on a remote site

- status messages from a remote server

The commands the user might select are:

- `connect`

- `disconnect`

- `change remote directory`

- `get remote file`

- `put local file to remote site`

- `set transmission mode` (ASCII or binary)

In addition, you might want your interface to remind the user what the local directory is, and provide a way to change it. You are going to need a lot of interface elements, probably too many to fit on a single form view like those you used for Finger and Whois. There are some things you can do to reduce the number of controls in your main view:

- Have the user provide a user ID and password in a separate dialog box that appears when the user clicks Connect. These don't need to be on-screen once a successful connection has been made.

- Don't provide any controls on the main view to change the local file name or directory name, just edit boxes for the user to type them into.

- Don't repeat the name of the selected file or directory in an edit box of its own, but let the user simply see which file or directory name is highlighted in the list box.

What controls will you use? Use single-line edit boxes for site name, user ID, password, local file name and directory; a multiline edit box for messages from the remote site; a list box for the list of files and directories. List boxes are controls that contain several text strings, displayed one per line. The user can select one or more items from a list box with the mouse.

AppWizard

To build your skeletal FTP application, follow these steps:

1. Start Visual C++.

2. Choose File, New.

3. Select Project from the list of possible new things, and click OK. Type in the project name (**ftp** seems a natural choice), and click Create.

4. Choose <u>S</u>ingle Document (not a <u>D</u>ialog-based interface—they have no menus and you're going to use your menus eventually) and click <u>N</u>ext.

5. Choose N<u>o</u>ne for database support and click <u>N</u>ext.

6. Choose N<u>o</u>ne for OLE support and <u>N</u>ext.

7. Uncheck the check boxes for <u>T</u>oolbar, <u>S</u>tatus bar, and <u>P</u>rint support.

   If you're using version 2.1 or greater, check <u>W</u>indows Sockets support. If you're not, you'll add it in by hand as described in Chapter 3, "Windows Sockets (WINSOCK.DLL.)"

8. Click the <u>A</u>dvanced button and type **ftp** as the file extension.

9. Click Close, then <u>N</u>ext.

10. Select a <u>s</u>tatic library so that users don't need the MFC DLLs to run your application and click <u>N</u>ext.

11. Select CFtpView from the list of classes and change its base class to CFormView by dropping down the list and selecting it.

12. Click <u>F</u>inish, look over the summary of what will be created, and click OK.

If these steps seem a little rushed, read Chapter 4, "Building a Windows Application Framework," and the early part of Chapter 5, "Building an Internet Finger Application" for clarification.

If you're using version 1.5x, you run AppWizard a little differently, though the basic questions you're answering are the same:

1. Choose <u>P</u>roject, App<u>W</u>izard, and fill in the directory and project name.

2. Click the Options button and turn off MDI, toolbar, and Print support. Click OK.

3. Click the Classes button back on the AppWizard dialog box. Have CFtpView inherit from CFormView.

4. Click OK on the Classes dialog box, OK on the AppWizard dialog box, and Create on the confirmation dialog box.

AppWizard creates the project and opens the project file. If you're using a version prior to 2.1, you can't ask AppWizard to give you socket support automatically, as discussed in Chapter 3, "Windows Sockets (WINSOCK.DLL)." Follow the instructions there to get socket support for your application.

AppStudio

Now you need to build dialog boxes and menus in AppStudio. The main dialog box is already stubbed for you; AppWizard has given it the name IDD_FTP_FORM. Even with the steps previously outlined to unclutter this main view, there are still going to be a lot of controls on it.

Open the dialog box with AppStudio and size it as large as you can. Next, start placing controls. Each edit or list box will need a piece of static text above it that I'll call its label, and a resource ID I'll just call ID. Each button will have a resource ID and a caption. Add these controls:

Control	Resource ID	Label
Edit box	IDC_SITE_NAME	Remote Site
Button	IDC_CONNECT	Connect
Button	IDC_DISCONNECT	Disconnect
List box	IDC_FILES	Files and Directories On the Styles panel of the Properties box, select the Horiz Scroll and Vert Scroll check boxes.
Button	IDC_CHANGE_REMOTE_DIRECTORY	Selected
Button	IDC_CHANGE_DIRECTORY_UP	Up
Button	IDC_GET	Get
Button	IDC_PUT	Put
Check box	IDC_BINARY	Binary
Edit box	IDC_MESSAGES	No label On the Styles panel of the Properties box, select the Multiline, Horiz Scroll, Vert Scroll, and Read Only check boxes.
Edit box	IDC_LOCAL_DIRECTORY	Local Directory
Edit box	IDC_LOCAL_FILE	Local File

One possible arrangement of these controls is shown in figure 7.2. The boxes around the groups of buttons are strictly decorative and don't connect the buttons to each other in any way. They do, however, make this crowded dialog box easier to understand and allow much shorter button captions.

II

Developing Applications

Groupbox is in the third row of the control palette, on the left. As with the static text control, you enter the text by editing the Caption of the control. Resize it by dragging the sizing handles until it fits around the buttons you want to surround.

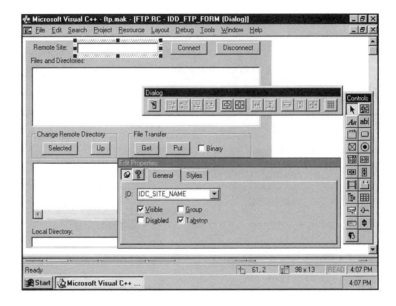

You can save yourself a great deal of work in trying to create your own version of this dialog if you use the toolbar buttons in AppStudio that make a group of controls the same size, align a group of controls, and so on. To select a group of controls, click one, then shift+click the remainder. The last one clicked is the controlling selection: the other controls will be resized or moved to match the controlling selection.

For example, the four buttons across the middle of the dialog box should all be aligned horizontally. After creating them all, click Selected, then shift+click Up, Get, and Put. When all four are selected, click the last toolbar button in the leftmost group, whose icon shows a group of controls moving down to a thick horizontal line. This will align the bottoms of the four buttons. Similarly, align the left edges of the site name, file and directory list, messages, and local directory edit boxes, as well as the Change Remote Directory group box. These tools help you create a professional appearance for your application without sweating each pixel.

Once the dialog box is complete, close it. Next, you can build that little dialog box for the user ID and password. Open a new dialog box, bring up the Properties box if it is not already open, and change the ID of the new dialog box to IDD_CONNECT and the caption to Connect.

The new dialog box already contains an OK button and a Cancel button. Add two edit boxes and their static text labels, giving one the ID IDC_USER and the label User and the other the ID IDC_PASSWORD and the label Password. You will probably find the dialog box is a little big for these few controls, so size it a bit smaller. The Connect dialog box I put together for this application is shown in figure 7.3.

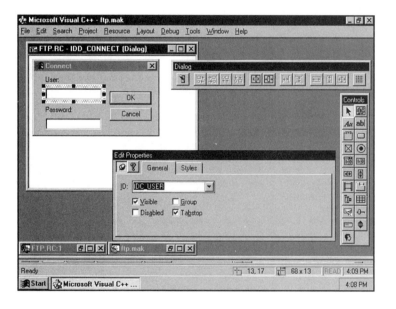

Fig. 7.3
Your Connect dialog box under construction in AppStudio.

Let's leave it at that for now, declaring that you expect the user to type in a valid directory and file name for local files. You'll revisit this decision later in the chapter.

ClassWizard

Now you have an application and a lot of resources. You need to connect the resources to code by using ClassWizard. The main dialog box, IDD_FTP_FORM, is already connected to the class CFtpView, but your new dialog box is still floating free. Open IDD_CONNECT and bring up ClassWizard by choosing Project, ClassWizard. You are prompted for information about the class you will add. Fill in the class name as **CConnectDialog**, and accept the default file names of CONNECTD.CPP and CONNECTD.H. Click the Create

Class button. ClassWizard generates code for you; then you can connect dialog controls to member variables in this new class.

You connect the edit box IDD_USER to a member variable called m_user, a CString, and IDD_PASSWORD to another CString called m_password. First, click the Member Variables tab, click IDD_USER to select it, and click the Add Variable button. Fill in the variable name m_user as shown in figure 7.4, then click OK. Repeat the process for IDD_PASSWORD. Click OK on ClassWizard, because your work with IDD_CONNECT is done for now.

Fig. 7.4

Adding a member variable, m_user, that will be linked to the edit box control IDC_USER on the connect view.

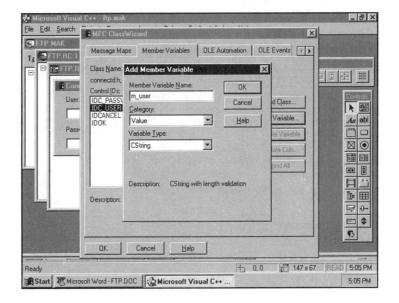

Close IDD_CONNECT and open IDD_FTP_FORM, then bring up ClassWizard again. Connect the controls as follows: first, the variable name should be m_ followed by the part of the resource ID after the IDC, converted to lower case. For example, IDC_SITE_NAME is connected to m_site_name. Second, connect edit boxes to CStrings (Values), but the list box IDC_FILES, to a CListBox item (Control). Connect the check box, IDC_BINARY, to a BOOL variable. Figure 7.5 shows the Member Variables tab after all the controls have been connected.

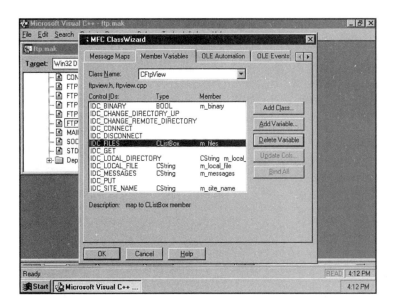

Fig. 7.5
The controls on your main view are connected to member variables as shown on Class Wizard's Member Variables tab.

Click the Message Maps tab and for each button, connect it to code as you did for the Lookup button in Chapter 5, "Building an Internet Finger Application," by following these steps:

1. Click the button ID (such as, IDC_CONNECT) in the Object IDs drop-down list box.

2. Select BN_CLICKED in the Messages list.

3. Click the Add Function button.

4. Accept the suggested function name; ClassWizard generates a skeleton function.

Figure 7.6 shows the Message Maps tab after all the buttons have been connected to functions.

Click OK on ClassWizard, then close AppStudio to return to Visual C++. Are you ready to write code yet? Yes, you are.

II

Developing Applications

Fig. 7.6
The messages
generated by
clicking buttons
on your main view
are connected to
member functions
as shown on Class
Wizard's Message
Maps tab.

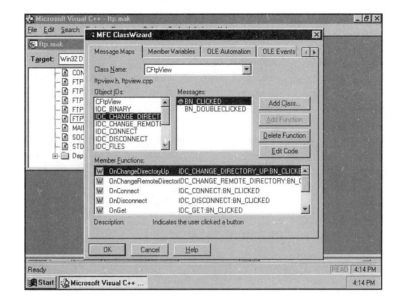

Initial Connection and Directory List

You'll start with OnConnect, since clicking the Connect button is the first command the user will send to you. Much like the OnLookup function in Finger,
this routine needs to start by making the connection to the remote host.
Then it will get a list of the files and directories available to the user to make
the Get and Change Directory buttons meaningful. Figure 7.7 illustrates these
steps.

You'll need to get a socket and instruct it to connect. Since you know there
will be multiple connections in this application, call this socket
pControlSocket rather than just pSocket as before.

Add pControlSocket as a private member of the class, and add a
pControlSocket = NULL to the constructor and a deletepControlSocket to the
destructor. Now all the member functions of CFtpView can access the socket
which will be dynamically allocated.

OnConnect starts off like this:

```
delete pControlSocket;
pControlSocket = new QSocket();
pControlSocket->SetReceiveTarget(this, WM_SOCKET_RESPONSE);
```

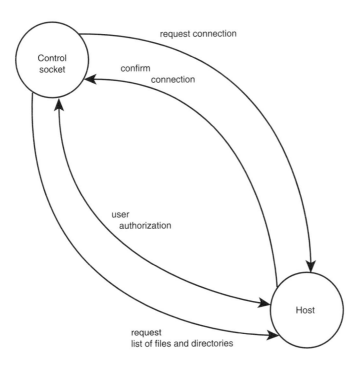

Fig. 7.7
When the user
clicks Connect,
your client does far
more than just
send a connect
command.

This gets rid of any existing socket, finds a new one, and arranges for its messages to come to this window with a WM_SOCKET_RESPONSE message. As with Finger, you add a #define to FTPVIEW.H that defines this message:

```
#define WM_SOCKET_RESPONSE WM_USER+201
```

You also add an entry to the message map in FTPVIEW.H and FTPVIEW.CPP calling a function OnControlSocket when this message is received, so that the message map in FTPVIEW.H looks like this (I've deleted most of the entries between the AFX_MSG flags):

```
// Generated message map functions.
protected:
    //{{AFX_MSG(CFtpView)
    afx_msg void OnConnect();
    ...
    //}}AFX_MSG
  afx_msg LRESULT OnControlSocket(WPARAM wParam, LPARAM lParam);
    DECLARE_MESSAGE_MAP()
```

and the FTPVIEW.CPP message map looks like this:

```
BEGIN_MESSAGE_MAP(CFtpView, CFormView)
    //{{AFX_MSG_MAP(CFtpView)
    ON_BN_CLICKED(IDC_CONNECT, OnConnect)
    ...
```

```
//}}AFX_MSG_MAP
ON_MESSAGE(WM_SOCKET_RESPONSE, OnControlSocket)
END_MESSAGE_MAP()
```

OnConnect continues, once the socket has been set up:

```
// Get host name from edit box.
UpdateData(TRUE);
// Blank files box.
m_files.ResetContent();
UpdateData(FALSE);
```

The first call to UpdateData fills the member variables with the control contents, so that m_site_name now holds the string the user typed in the edit box labeled Remote Site. ResetContent wipes out anything that may be in the file list m_files, and the second call to UpdateData fills the controls from the member variables, so that the on-screen list box is now empty.

Finally, you connect the socket to the host on port 21 (the standard port for FTP control connections). If Connect returns FALSE, you inform the user and clean up your socket. Otherwise, you are finished; the socket will generate a WM_SOCKET_RESPONSE message when its status changes to CONNECTED:

```
if (!pControlSocket->Connect(m_site_name, 21))
{
    AfxMessageBox("Host is unreachable.");
    delete pControlSocket;
    pControlSocket = 0;
    return;
}
```

Your next step must be to write OnControlSocket, since you have delegated most of the work there. What will happen when the socket becomes connected?

As you saw in Finger, the first parameter tells the routine what the socket has to say. If it's positive, it's the number of characters of reply in buffer, the second parameter. If it's negative, it's a status code. In the case of a control connection, you don't expect any real replies to come to this routine, so you don't process them:

```
if ((int)amount > 0)
{
}
```

It's what happens in the else of that if that matters here. You cast amount to a SocketReceiveCmd and make sure you've been told SocketStatusChanged. Then you switch on the socket's current status, though you're only adding code right now to handle becoming CONNECTED:

```
        else
        {
            // If amount < 0 it is a receive command.
            CString response;

            switch ( (SocketReceiveCmd)amount )
            {
                case SocketStatusChanged:
                    switch (pControlSocket->GetStatus())
                    {
                        case CONNECTED:
```

What will you do when the socket becomes connected? First, you'll switch
the socket back to getline mode rather than have it send messages to this
window when it has a response. This keeps you more tightly sequenced and
makes sure you have each response before you send the next command.
That's why you don't need code to process real replies: they won't be coming
through this way.

```
            // Switch to getline.
            pControlSocket->SetReceiveTarget(NULL,0);
```

Many FTP servers send responses to connection, saying something like Enter
your userid, for example. You need to handle these responses, and put them
into the multiline edit box you set aside for messages from the server. The
RFC explains that all control connection responses start with a three digit
response code. Multiline responses follow the response code with a "-," while
single line responses do not. After the first line, multiline responses can start
with any characters, except that the last line starts with the response code
again, so that a multiline response might look like this:

```
123- Welcome to FTP.GREGCONS.COM
Please check the file README.TXT for instructions.
123 All transactions are logged.
```

Unfortunately, some very popular servers implement a variation of this where
the response code appears on every line, like this:

```
230-                          Welcome to
230-                  THE OAK SOFTWARE REPOSITORY
230-         A service of Oakland University, Rochester Michigan
230-
230- If you have trouble using OAK with your ftp client,
230- please try using a dash (-) as the first character
230- of your password — this will turn off the continuation
230- messages that may be confusing your ftp client.
230- OAK is a UNIX machine, and file names are case sensitive.
230-
230- Guest login ok, access restrictions apply.
```

II

Developing Applications

Notice how this message acknowledges that repeating the response code on every line may confuse some clients. Not yours! Here's the code to handle multiline responses and put them into the message box:

```
HandleResponse();
```

Yes, you're going to put it into a method of the CFtpView object, since it will be a common activity. That function looks like this:

```
BOOL CFtpView::HandleResponse()
{
    CString response = pControlSocket->GetLine();
    CString responsecode = response.Left(3);
    m_messages += response;
    if ( response[3] == '-')
    {
        // Multiline response.
        response = pControlSocket->GetLine();
        m_messages += response;
        while ( response.Left(3) != responsecode
                || response[3] == '-')
        {
            response = pControlSocket->GetLine();
            m_messages += response;
        }
    }
    UpdateData(FALSE);

    if (responsecode[0] == '1' || responsecode[0] == '2')
    {
        return TRUE;
    }
    else
    {
        return FALSE;
    }
}
```

The function returns a BOOL because it's a simple enough matter to do and some of your other work will be easier if you can get the response code analyzed easily.

The call to GetLine asks the socket for the first line (terminated with \r\n) of the response it has so far. The first three characters are the response code, which you save. You then add the whole response onto the end of whatever's in the message edit box at the moment. If the fourth character is a "-," you need to loop through all the lines of the response until you reach one that starts with the response code but does not have a "-" in the fourth position. This code will handle both kinds of continuation message styles.

Finally, `UpdateData(FALSE)` puts the contents of `m_messages` into the control `IDC_MESSAGES`, and the function returns TRUE if the response code started with 1 or 2, FALSE otherwise.

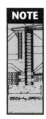

> The RFC explains response codes in detail, and you'll cover the relevant ones as you progress. For now, you need to know that the 100 and 200 level codes are all success indicators, while 300, 400, and 500 level responses are error indicators. Response codes starting with 3 "provide more information before the command can be completed," codes starting with 4 "cannot be completed at the moment," and codes starting with 5 "could never be completed;" for example, a request to retrieve a file that does not exist.

Back in `OnControlSocket`, after you call `HandleResponse` to deal with the "hello and welcome to our FTP server" messages, you need to sign on, and to do that you need to get the user ID and password from the user. You created a dialog for this already, `IDD_CONNECT`, and linked it to a class called `CConnectDlg` in the files CONNECTD.H and CONNECTD.CPP. Getting a dialog like this onto the screen is a simple matter: declare an instance of the class, then call its `DoModal` method. If the method returns IDOK, the user clicked OK; process the member variables of the dialog box. Otherwise, the user clicked Cancel and the sign on should not proceed. Here's what that looks like in code:

```
CConnectDialog dlg;
if (dlg.DoModal() == IDOK)
{
    pControlSocket->Send("USER "
        + dlg.m_user + "\r\n");
    HandleResponse();
    pControlSocket->Send("PASS "
        + dlg.m_password + "\r\n");
    HandleResponse();
```

In the file FTPVIEW.CPP you'll actually see the declaration outside the large switch statement. That's a peculiarity of the switch statement in C++: it balks at declaring objects in only one case statement of the switch, and to get around it you simply move the declaration to before the switch statement.

So if the user clicks OK, you send a `USER` command with the contents of `dlg.m_user`, what the user typed in `IDC_USER`, handle the response, and send a `PASS` command with the password. Assuming the user didn't make any typos, you're signed on and ready to go. You need to fill that list box so that the user can select a directory to change to or a file to get. That was the last step in figure 7.7.

The command to list files is LIST, and the reply comes back over the data connection, so before you send the LIST command you have to be ready to get replies from the data connection. As mentioned above, you do this with a listening socket. The steps are illustrated in figure 7.8. The control socket sends the actual commands, the listening socket waits for transmission to begin and then sets up the data socket, and the data socket actually receives the reply.

Fig 7.8

Requesting and handling a list of files and directories involves three sockets.

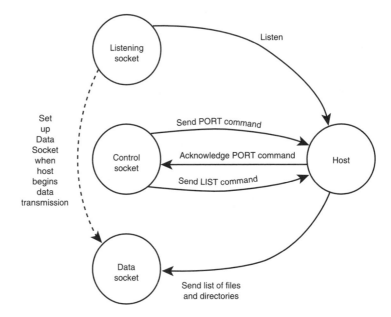

Here's the block of code that gets this file and directory list together: it's going to take a fair bit of explaining:

```
delete pListeningSocket;
pListeningSocket = new QSocket;
pListeningSocket->SetReceiveTarget(this,
                WM_SOCKET_LISTEN);
SOCKADDR_IN sock_address;
SOCKADDR_IN cont_address;
int addr_size = sizeof(sock_address);
sock_address.sin_family = AF_INET;
sock_address.sin_addr.s_addr = htonl(INADDR_ANY);
sock_address.sin_port = 0;
pListeningSocket->Bind((SOCKADDR*)&sock_address,
                    addr_size);
pListeningSocket->Listen();

pListeningSocket->GetSockName((SOCKADDR*)&sock_address,
                    &addr_size);
```

```
pControlSocket->GetSockName((SOCKADDR*)&cont_address,
                            &addr_size);

unsigned char *port =
  ➡(unsigned char *)&(sock_address.sin_port);
unsigned char *host =
  ➡(unsigned char *)&(cont_address.sin_addr);

char command[512];
sprintf(command, "PORT %i,%i,%i,%i,%i,%i\r\n",
        host[0], host[1],host[2], host[3],
        port[0], port[1]);
pControlSocket->Send(command);
```

To start with, you get rid of any old listening socket (by the way, remember to add pListeningSocket to FTPVIEW.H, and to set it to NULL in the constructor and delete it in the destructor) and get a new one, then ask it to send its responses to this window using a WM_SOCKET_LISTEN message. Define the message in FTPVIEW.H and add message map entries as you did for WM_SOCKET_RESPONSE above, with the function named OnListeningSocket.

The next few lines of code, it might be argued, should be hidden away in the socket class. FTP is the only application that needs this at the moment, so here it is.

You need two socket address structures, one for the listening socket (sock_address) and one for the control socket (cont_address). You then start to fill in the elements of sock_address. First, the address family. WINSOCK.H includes a list of the codes for address families: AF_INET means that you are specifying an Internet address. You don't care what the actual address is so you use INADDR_ANY, and pass it through htonl, which converts an address from host byte order to network byte order, as discussed in Chapter 3, "Windows Sockets (WINSOCK.DLL)." Finally you set the port to zero. Then you bind pListeningSocket to the address structure you have filled in, and put it into Listen mode.

After binding the socket, you need to know what actual address was assigned, so you call GetSockName to fill sock_address with the assigned address so you can extract the port. You also need to know the host address, but binding doesn't set the port on an unconnected socket. You know that both the control and listening sockets are attached to the same host, though, so you can ask the control connection for a host address.

Finally, you use sprintf to build a PORT command, breaking the host address up into four 8-bit words and the port number into two, and send this command over the control connection. This tells the server what port to use when setting up the data connection.

This listening socket is not where the replies come back. Instead, what the listening socket will provide is a pointer to yet another socket, the actual data socket. You'll see this in just a moment.

You handle the response from the PORT command (which is almost certainly "200 PORT command successful"), clear out the file list box, and then actually send the LIST command:

```
HandleResponse();

m_files.ResetContent();
UpdateData(FALSE);
State = ReceivingList;
pControlSocket->Send("LIST\r\n");

HandleResponse();
    }
    break;
```

The LIST command will return a list of files in the remote directory over the data connection. The function that handles responses over the data connection needs to know if it is receiving a file or a list of files, and so you use the variable State. In FTPVIEW.H, add an enum definition before the class and add State as a private variable within the class:

```
enum DataChannelState {Idle,ReceivingFile,ReceivingList};
...
DataChannelState State;
```

You set State to Idle in the constructor, and will check it before handling responses over the data connection.

The rest of OnControlSocket is just closing all the open switch statements and returning zero.

So, OnControlSocket is complete. When it is told you are connected it puts up the dialog box for user ID and password, sends them, arranges a listening socket, sends a PORT command and then a LIST command. Now you need to write OnListeningSocket. It's much shorter:

```
LRESULT CFtpView::OnListeningSocket(WPARAM amount, LPARAM buffer)
{
    if ((int)amount > 0)
    {
    }
    else
    {
        // If amount < 0 it is a receive command.
        switch ( (SocketReceiveCmd)amount )
```

```
        {
            case SocketStatusChanged:
                break;
            case NewSocketAccepted:
                // The only function of this listening
                // socket is to tell you where to find the
                // data socket that the server connected to.
                // After that, you work with the data socket.
                pDataSocket = (QSocket*) buffer;
                pDataSocket->SetReceiveTarget(this,
                    WM_SOCKET_DATA);
                break;
        }
    }
    return 0;
}
```

As with OnControlSocket, this routine isn't expecting to get any real replies back. It is expecting a SocketReceiveCmd of NewSocketAccepted, and if that's what was sent, the second parameter is a pointer to the new socket. You set pDataSocket to this pointer and arrange for responses on the data socket to generate a WM_SOCKET_DATA message. Once again you'll need to add pDataSocket to the class, NULL it in the constructor and delete it in the destructor, add the #define of the message WM_SOCKET_DATA to FTPVIEW.H and add entries to each message map. Call the function OnDataSocket. That's what you have to write next.

OnDataSocket actually has to process responses, so it starts with the usual test of amount, but actually does something when amount is positive:

```
if ((int)amount > 0)
{
    if (State == ReceivingList)
    {
        unsigned int leftoverlength = leftovers.GetLength();
        char* fullbuffer = new char[amount+leftoverlength+1];

        strcpy(fullbuffer,leftovers);
        strcat(fullbuffer, (char*) buffer);

        char* cur = fullbuffer;
        char* cr_lf = strstr(cur, "\r\n");
                // Location of the CR LF pair.
        while (cr_lf)
        {
            *cr_lf = 0;
            m_files.AddString(cur);
                // Will go from cur to the null you just put in
            cur = cr_lf + 2;            // Skip over the null.
            cr_lf = strstr(cur, "\r\n"); // Search again.
```

II

Developing Applications

```
            }
            leftovers = cur;
        }
    UpdateData(FALSE);
    }
```

If you're receiving a list, you need to parse it into lines that end with \r\n. If there is a partial line at the end of the response, you will keep it in a member variable called leftovers for the next time we come into this routine. So this routine must start by handling any leftovers that already exist. (Don't forget to add the CString variable leftovers to the class. It doesn't need any initialization.)

You take the leftovers plus the buffer the socket has for you now and put them both into fullbuffer, then make an extra pointer, cur, to hold your place in fullbuffer. You search for \r\n starting from cur, and if you find it, control passes into the while loop. Setting the contents of cr_lf to 0 puts a NULL into the array of characters, so that AddString and other string-oriented functions will copy only up to the NULL. This is far quicker than copying (cur to cur + cr_lf) into a temporary string and then calling AddString. You advance cur, your pointer into fullbuffer, past the null and the \n that follows it, and execute the search again. When you finally leave the while loop, cur is pointing to the fragment of a reply that needs to be saved for next time, so you put it into leftovers.

A call to UpdateData(FALSE) ensures that the member variables are used to update the controls on-screen, and your processing of the data connection reply is complete. Your client now handles all the transactions illustrated in figures 7.7 and 7.8.

But what if amount was negative? What else could the data socket have to tell you? It could tell you it has been closed by the server, because the transmission is over. Here's how to handle that:

```
    else
    {
        // If amount < 0 it is a receive command.
        switch ( (SocketReceiveCmd)amount )
        {
        case SocketStatusChanged:
        HandleResponse();  // 226 Transfer complete
        State = Idle;
        break;
        }
    }
```

That's right; you just handle the final response and set State to Idle.

That's a lot of code just to sign on, isn't it? But the bulk of the work is done now. Figure 7.9 shows your application connected to **ftp.microsoft.com** and the result of the LIST command.

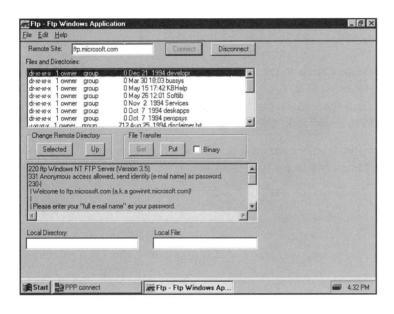

Fig. 7.9
Your application in action, listing some of the directories on the Microsoft FTP site.

If you're building and testing along, remember you must be connected to the Internet before running this application.

Using the File List Information

The format of responses to the LIST command is not specified in the RFC. The information is designed to be read by a person, not a program, and so may vary from site to site. However, most UNIX sites, and many non-UNIX sites also (**ftp.microsoft.com** runs NT) use the format you see in figure 7.9. I did a quick survey of the big, well-known FTP sites and didn't find any that didn't return their detailed list in this format. You're going to develop this application assuming this format, which means there are some sites for which this client won't work, even if I haven't found them yet.

The amount of information returned in each line of the response is rather staggering, but only two pieces of it really matter: the first character of the line, which is "d" for a directory, "-" for a file, and "l" for a link, and the file name at the end of the line. You should gray and ungray the Get and Selected buttons according to that first character: if the user has clicked a list box entry that starts with "d," the Selected button should be ungrayed and Get should be grayed, and if the user has clicked a list box entry that starts with "-," Selected should be grayed and Get ungrayed. Links are rare, but if a user clicks one you can just gray both buttons.

You gray and ungray buttons by connecting the control to a CButton member variable and calling the EnableWindow method of the button. You really should handle all the buttons while you're doing this. At first, all the buttons should be gray except Connect. Once the user is connected, Connect should be gray and Disconnect ungrayed, and Put and Up can be ungrayed too. Get and Selected will follow the rules laid out above.

First, go into ClassWizard and connect each button to a member variable with a name constructed the same way the other member variable names have been; for example, IDC_CONNECT should be connected to m_connect. ClassWizard guesses so much of what I want automatically, knowing that I want the member variable to be a CButton and so on, that I find myself wishing it would guess these names too. Still, the drudgery of typing the names out is nothing, compared to the old way of connecting controls and code.

To set the initial states of the buttons, you can't use the constructor, because at the time the C++ object is being constructed there is no connection to a screen window. Instead, you override the CView function OnInitialUpdate. This method is called the first time a view (including a CFormView) is created on-screen.

```
void CFtpView::OnInitialUpdate()
{
    CFormView::OnInitialUpdate();

    // Gray all buttons except Connect.
    m_put.EnableWindow(FALSE);
    m_get.EnableWindow(FALSE);
    m_disconnect.EnableWindow(FALSE);
    m_change_remote_directory.EnableWindow(FALSE);
    m_change_directory_up.EnableWindow(FALSE);

    m_connect.EnableWindow(TRUE);

}
```

Don't forget to declare OnInitialUpdate in FTPVIEW.H. I put it with the other override, DoDataExchange.

What happens when the user clicks in the list box? Will one of your methods be called? Not at the moment. Will a message be generated? Absolutely. How can you arrange for your view to catch the message? By using ClassWizard, of course.

Open ClassWizard and select IDC_FILES in the Object IDs list. The list of messages is different from those you've seen before, isn't it? LBN_SELCHANGE means
List Box Notify Selection Changed—in other words, the user has clicked an
item in the list box or moved the highlight with the cursor keys. You add a
function to handle this message, and ClassWizard suggests you call it
OnSelchangeFiles. Here's the code:

```
void CFtpView::OnSelchangeFiles()
{
    UpdateData(TRUE);
    CString selectedline;
    m_files.GetText(m_files.GetCurSel(),selectedline);
    switch (selectedline[0])
    {
        case  'd':
        m_get.EnableWindow(FALSE);
        m_change_remote_directory.EnableWindow(TRUE);
        break;

        case '-':
        m_get.EnableWindow(TRUE);
        m_change_remote_directory.EnableWindow(FALSE);
        break;

        default:
        m_get.EnableWindow(FALSE);
        m_change_remote_directory.EnableWindow(FALSE);
    }
}
```

The only tricky part here is getting the text from the list box into CString
selectedline. The CListBox method GetText needs an index to say which
string to return: you call GetCurSel to get this. GetText doesn't return the
CString; instead, you pass it your CString and it fills it for you. Technically,
the function takes a reference to a CString object, which is how it is able to
change one of its own arguments.

The rest of OnSelchangeFiles just grays and ungrays buttons depending on
the first character of selectedline. If you're coding along, compile and test
this—it really works!

Changing the Remote Directory

What command will you send when the user clicks the Selected button to
change the remote directory to the one selected in the file list? CWD, as described in the RFC. You need only to extract the directory name from the end
of the long string in the list box.

The empty function, OnChangeRemoteDirectory, has already been created by ClassWizard and is just waiting for some code. It ends up looking like this:

```
void CFtpView::OnChangeRemoteDirectory()
{
    UpdateData(TRUE);
    CString selectedline;
    m_files.GetText(m_files.GetCurSel(),selectedline);

    int namestart = selectedline.ReverseFind(' ');
    CString directory = selectedline.Right(selectedline.GetLength
                                - namestart - 1);
    // Don't want the space at position namestart              ()
    // included in directory.

    pControlSocket->Send("CWD " + directory + "\r\n");
    HandleResponse();

    ListFiles();
}
```

This code extracts the string between the last space and the end of the string, which for almost all sites is the file or directory name, and passes it as an argument to the CWD command. After handling the response (which should be "150 CWD successful," since the user doesn't get a chance to type the directory name or get confused about which names are files and which are directories), you call ListFiles.

ListFiles is a new function with the old code from OnControlSocket, from delete pListeningSocket through to sending the LIST command and handling the response. As a nice touch I added two lines at the top to gray both the Selected and Get buttons, since there will no longer be anything selected in the list box. I also went back into OnControlSocket and had it call ListFiles rather than duplicating the code.

Changing to the parent directory is even simpler because there's no parameter to pass—you just send the command CDUP:

```
void CFtpView::OnChangeDirectoryUp()
{
    pControlSocket->Send("CDUP\r\n");
    HandleResponse();

    ListFiles();
}
```

Is it just me, or are these functions getting simpler and simpler? If you're building along, compile and test the client now. Even though you can't get files yet, just moving around the directories of an unfamiliar site is so much easier this way than in the usual command line-oriented FTP clients. Just wait until it can get files!

Retrieving Files

Getting a file from the server is not very different from getting a file list: you ask for it, listen for the data connection, and get what you asked for over the data connection. Instead of adding entries to a list box, you'll be writing to a file, and you'll have to open it first and close it afterwards, but the concepts are the same.

Your first attempt at this has absolutely no error checking. The user must remember to type a file name into the edit box, and if it isn't a valid file name, the program will probably blow up. You'll just make a note of those things for later. Probably the nicest behavior, if the local file edit box is left blank, would be to build a legal file name on the user's behalf.

FTP transfers can be binary or ASCII. Similarly, MFC includes two useful file classes: CFile for binary I/O and CStdioFile (which inherits from CFile) for ASCII or plain text I/O. These objects are nicely designed: the constructor takes a file name, and opens the file. You don't know whether you need a CFile or CStdioFile object until you know what transmission type the user has selected, but there's a way around this.

Add a member variable called userfile that is a pointer to a CFile object by adding this line in FTPVIEW.H:

```
CFile* userfile;
```

As usual, this pointer should be set to NULL in the constructor and the destructor should delete it.

You construct the object by calling new. If you invoke the CStdioFile constructor in your new call, the compiler makes you a CStdioFile object and casts the pointer to a CFile*.. If you invoke the CFile constructor, the compiler makes us a CFile object and no cast is necessary. Then, because the Write function you'll be using later is virtual, when you execute a line of code like:

```
userfile->Write((char*) buffer,amount);
```

either CFile::Write or CStdioFile::Write is called depending on the constructor you originally invoked.

If ever you need a real-life example of the use of polymorphism in C++, now you have one!

So how does OnGet start? Like this:

```
void CFtpView::OnGet()
{
    // Open the file specified by the user for now,
    // ignoring the local directory edit box and putting
    // the file in the working directory. Also, this needs
    // exceptions in case the file doesn't open.

    UpdateData(TRUE);
    if (m_binary)
    {
        userfile = new CFile(m_local_file,
            CFile::modeWrite¦ CFile::typeBinary
            ¦ CFile::modeCreate);
    }
    else
    {
        userfile = new CStdioFile(m_local_file,
            CFile::modeWrite¦ CFile::typeText
            ¦ CFile::modeCreate);
    }
```

The next few lines are very much like those in ListFiles, setting up the listening socket:

```
delete pListeningSocket;
pListeningSocket = new QSocket;
pListeningSocket->SetReceiveTarget(this, WM_SOCKET_LISTEN);
SOCKADDR_IN sock_address;
SOCKADDR_IN cont_address;
int addr_size = sizeof(sock_address);
sock_address.sin_family = AF_INET;
sock_address.sin_addr.s_addr = htonl(INADDR_ANY);
sock_address.sin_port = 0;
pListeningSocket->Bind((SOCKADDR*)&sock_address, addr_size);
pListeningSocket->Listen();

pListeningSocket->GetSockName(
    (SOCKADDR*)&sock_address, &addr_size);
pControlSocket->GetSockName(
    (SOCKADDR*)&cont_address, &addr_size);

unsigned char *port =
➡(unsigned char *)&(sock_address.sin_port);
unsigned char *host =
➡(unsigned char *)&(cont_address.sin_addr);

char command[512];
sprintf(command, "PORT %i,%i,%i,%i,%i,%i\r\n",
```

```
            host[0], host[1],host[2], host[3],
            port[0], port[1]);
pControlSocket->Send(command);

HandleResponse();
```

Now, instead of sending a LIST command you need to build a RETR command, which takes a file name as its parameter. You also send a TYPE command to set the transmission type to ASCII (A) or Image (I), which most people call binary. You trust the user to set this correctly with the check box. The parsing of the file name is just like the way you extracted the directory name in OnChangeRemoteDirectory.

```
            CString selectedline;
            m_files.GetText(m_files.GetCurSel(),selectedline);

            int namestart = selectedline.ReverseFind(' ');
            CString file = selectedline.Right(selectedline.GetLength()
                            - namestart - 1);
            // Don't want the space at position
            // namestart included in directory.

            if (m_binary)
            {
                pControlSocket->Send("TYPE I\r\n");
            }
            else
            {
                pControlSocket->Send("TYPE A\r\n");
            }
            HandleResponse();

            State = ReceivingFile;
            pControlSocket->Send("RETR " + file + "\r\n");
            HandleResponse();  // 150 Opening connection...
```

That takes care of OnGet, but you'll need to change OnDataSocket a little to handle the cases where State is ReceivingFile. Add another if, right after testing if State is ReceivingList:

```
            if (State == ReceivingFile)
            {
                if (m_binary)
                {
                    userfile->Write((char*) buffer,amount);
                }
```

Binary transfers are simple—just write out whatever the server has sent with no processing whatsoever. ASCII transfers are a little more difficult: you have to strip out any carriage returns the server may have added, because the ASCII write function expands all linefeed characters into carriage-return-linefeed pairs. This looks a lot like the preceding code that parses into lines, except you don't need a leftovers variable: you just write out whatever's left over.

```
else
{
    char* cur = (char*)buffer;
    char* cr = strchr(cur, '\r'); //location of the CR
    while (cr)
    {
        *cr++ = 0;
        userfile->Write((char*) cur,strlen(cur));
        // Will go from cur to the null
        // termination you just put in.
        cur = cr;                  // Skip over the null.
        cr = strchr(cur, '\r');    // Search again.
    }
    userfile->Write((char*) cur,strlen(cur));
        // Write out any leftover amount.
}
```

Your changes to `OnDataSocket` aren't quite complete. When the server closes the data connection, you need to close the file. The `case` statement for status change now looks like this:

```
case SocketStatusChanged:
    HandleResponse();  // 226 Transfer complete
    if (State == ReceivingFile)
    {
        delete userfile;
        userfile = NULL;
    }
    State = Idle;
    break;
```

When `userfile` is deleted the file will be closed. Try it out—this is an FTP client that does what FTP clients do, but with a true Windows interface.

Disconnecting

Other than the complete and utter absence of any error checking at all, have you implemented all your functionality yet? The six buttons on the dialog box are Connect, Disconnect, and change remote directory to Selected or Up, Get, and Put. You've completed all except Disconnect and Put. I'm going to leave Put for you to work through yourself, but Disconnect is far simpler.

One way to keep the Disconnect code simple is by keeping the button gray whenever a transfer is in process. That way you don't have to worry about cleaning up a working socket. So insert the line

```
m_disconnect.EnableWindow(FALSE);
```

at the start of `OnGet`, `OnChangeRemoteDirectory`, and `OnChangeDirectoryUp`.

In OnDataSocket, when the socket status changes, just before State = Idle, enable the button again.

This gives you a nice short OnDisconnnect:

```
void CFtpView::OnDisconnect()
{
    // Gray all buttons except connect.
    m_put.EnableWindow(FALSE);
    m_get.EnableWindow(FALSE);
    m_disconnect.EnableWindow(FALSE);
    m_change_remote_directory.EnableWindow(FALSE);
    m_change_directory_up.EnableWindow(FALSE);

    m_connect.EnableWindow(TRUE);

    // Wipe out any ongoing work.
    delete pControlSocket;
    pControlSocket = NULL;
    delete pListeningSocket;
    pListeningSocket = NULL;
    delete pDataSocket;
    pDataSocket = NULL;

    delete userfile;
    userfile = NULL;
}
```

This grays and ungrays buttons as in OnInitialUpdate, and deletes and sets to NULL the three sockets and the userfile. That's all there is to it.

Saving a Little Typing

There's one thing you're sure to have noticed if you've been testing as we go. Typing **anonymous** and your e-mail address over and over again gets boring fast. Let's have this application save the host name, your ID (which will probably be "anonymous") and your password (which will probably be your e-mail address) in a document.

You need to open the file FTPDOC.H and add three CString variables to the class: call them Host, User, and Password. The easiest way to let the view access these variables is to make them public:

```
// Attributes
public:
    CString Host;
    CString User;
    CString Password;
```

The framework handles saving and opening files automatically as long as you override the Serialize function for the document. After all, the framework is good, but it can't guess what you actually want to save in a file and what you don't. There's a skeletal Serialize already in place, and you need only to add six lines to it.

```
void CFtpDoc::Serialize(CArchive& ar)
{
    if (ar.IsStoring())
    {
        // TODO: add storing code here.
    }
    else
    {
        // TODO: add loading code here.
    }
}
```

Typically Serialize functions save and load objects by calling their Serialize functions or by using the << and >> operators to send them to the CArchive or retrieve them from it. These operators are used for stream I/O in C++ and the Visual C++ framework provides implementations of these operators that allows them to be used for saving a document to a file or restoring one. Variables which are instances of objects such as CString can be written to the CArchive object with a single line of code:

```
ar << StringVariable;
```

and retrieved with the other operator:

```
ar >> StringVariable;
```

So your implementation of Serialize is:

```
void CFtpDoc::Serialize(CArchive& ar)
{
    if (ar.IsStoring())
    {
        ar << Host;
        ar << User;
        ar << Password;
    }
    else
    {
        ar >> Host;
        ar >> User;
        ar >> Password;
    }
}
```

There. Now whatever is in those variables will be saved into a file and the user can load from the file back into those variables. That doesn't do you any good, though, unless you actually use those variables for something.

You can use `Host` in your `OnInitialUpdate` to initialize `m_host`, like this:

```
// Use host from document.
m_site_name = GetDocument()->Host;
```

Add these lines at the very start of `OnInitialUpdate`, before the call to `CFormView::OnInitialUpdate`.

To save the host name that the user typed, add one line to `OnConnect`. Right after the `UpdateData(TRUE)`, which fills in `m_site_name` with what the user typed in the edit box, add:

```
GetDocument()->Host = m_site_name;
GetDocument()->SetModifiedFlag();
```

Both of these fragments call `GetDocument()`. This function, added to `CFtpView` by AppWizard, returns a pointer to the `CFtpDoc` associated with this view. That gives us access to the member variable `Host`. The function `SetModifiedFlag` tells the framework that you've changed the contents of the document. Once a document is marked as changed, the user will be prompted about saving it when closing the application.

Using and saving the user ID and password is done in `OnControlSocket`. Right before you close the dialog box, you fill in the variables, and after the user clicks OK you save them. The `CONNECTED` case now looks like this:

```
case CONNECTED:
    // Switch to getline.
    pControlSocket->SetReceiveTarget(NULL,0);
    HandleResponse();
    dlg.m_user = GetDocument()->User;
    dlg.m_password = GetDocument()->Password;
    if (dlg.DoModal() == IDOK)
    {
        GetDocument()->User = dlg.m_user;
        GetDocument()->Password = dlg.m_password;
        GetDocument()->SetModifiedFlag();
        pControlSocket->Send("USER "
        + dlg.m_user + "\r\n");
        HandleResponse();
        pControlSocket->Send("PASS "
        + dlg.m_password + "\r\n");
        HandleResponse();

        ListFiles();
    }
    break;
```

II

Developing Applications

This works, but there's one problem. Because you call `SetModifiedFlag` every time, the user will be prompted to save the file every time. It would be better to do it this way in `OnConnect`:

```
// Get host name from edit box.
UpdateData(TRUE);

if (GetDocument()->Host != m_site_name)
{
    GetDocument()->Host = m_site_name;
    GetDocument()->SetModifiedFlag();
}
```

Now the flag will only be set if the user actually changed anything. You build similar `if` statements in `OnControlSocket`. To reduce the number of calls to `GetDocument()`, you set up a local variable called `doc`, a `CFtpDoc*`, to hold the result of the function call. Remember that the declaration of `doc` needs to be outside the big switch statement in `OnControlSocket`.

There! Now you don't need to keep typing over and over again. Some users will really save a lot of time with this feature, creating a file called, say, MS.FTP with the host **ftp.microsoft.com**, user anonymous, and password their e-mail address, another file called OAK.FTP to get to **oak.oakland.edu** as anonymous, and so on for the popular FTP sites. This was a very simple feature to add, but if you actually use this product (and I hope you do—there's lots of great software out on the net and you have to retrieve it somehow) you'll soon find out how the simple touches can be the nicest ones.

Using Your FTP Client

This application is really nice to use because so much of the information you need is there for you whenever you want it. You don't have to request a directory list whenever you change to a new directory; it's done for you automatically.

Connect your computer to the Internet and run the application by clicking the Run button on the Visual C++ standard toolbar, or choose Project, Execute. Fill in the site name, say **oak.oakland.edu**, and click the Connect button. When the Connect dialog box appears, fill in **anonymous** for the user and your e-mail address for the password, then click OK.

A list of files and directories appears in the upper list box, and messages from the server appear in the lower one. Both of these list boxes scroll. It's a good idea to read the messages from the server at first, until you learn your way around. They typically point you to useful files with names like README or README.TXT, and remind you of the policies of the site.

Click a directory and then Selected to change to that directory. The file list clears and a new one appears. More messages are added to the bottom of the message window. Click a file. (Remember, the first character on each line is "d" for a directory and "-" for a file. If there are no files in the directory you selected, only more directories, change to one of the directories until you finally reach one with files in it. The number just before the file name is the size, and while you're testing you do better to choose small files over large ones.) If the file has a name that suggests plain text (for example, README.TXT), leave the "binary" check box unchecked. If it has a name that implies it's a binary file (for example, UTILITY.ZIP), check the "binary" box. Fill in a local file name and then click Get. When the message 226 transfer complete appears at the bottom of the message window, shrink this application and look for the file—you'll see the transfer worked correctly.

From Here...

This application is very fragile. It can't handle any typing mistakes or forgetting. Some of the error checking procedures that should be added are:

- When the control socket is first being connected, if the host name is wrong the socket class will put up an error message saying Error getting host name, but the Connect button will stay gray and only Disconnect will be ungrayed. This is sure to confuse a user who realizes the connection was never made. To handle this, add another case to the switch on socket status in OnControlSocket. If the socket status is ERRORSTATE, delete all three sockets and the file, and set them to null, then gray Disconnect and ungray Connect. A handy shortcut to accomplish all that is to call the function OnDisconnect, which does all those things already.

- If the user presses Cancel on the Connect dialog box the Connect button is grayed on the main menu. To fix this, add an else to the if that tests the dlg.DoModal() return value. This else clause should not call OnDisconnect but should just adjust the button graying.

- If the user makes a typing error on the user name or password, a 500 level message will appear in the message box, but it could be missed if the server normally sends long responses and the user doesn't scroll the box. In OnControlSocket, after sending the PASS command, test the return value of HandleResponse and if it is false, put up an AfxMessageBox warning the user that the logon failed, then call OnDisconnect.

- Do something graceful if the user accidentally clicks Get before filling in a local file name. It might be as simple as testing to see if `m_local_file == ""` and putting up a message box reminding the user to provide it, then skipping the rest of the `OnGet` function. Or you could provide some more sophisticated code that builds a valid Windows file name from the local file name.

- Use the local directory name as provided by the user, if it's nonblank. The file name passed to the `CFile` or `CStdioFile` constructor can be a path-and-file name like C:\INTAPPS\FTP\FTPVIEW.CPP. Before the `if` that calls the constructors, build a `CString` file name that may or may not include the path, and use this file name rather than `m_local_file` in the constructor calls.

- If that sounds intimidating, consider that most applications have to check the response from every `LIST` or `RETR` command to be sure the user has typed the file or directory name correctly. Because your user never gets a chance to type file or directory names, there can't be any errors introduced. This saves you a lot of checking.

The other large item that is not handled here is `Put`. Far fewer people place files on remote FTP sites than retrieve them, so I left this part of the application for you to finish if you think you might need it someday. It works much like `Get` except that you `Read` rather than `Write`, you send a `STOR` command rather than a `RETR` command, and so on.

If you really get hooked on this application and its visual interface, you'll probably tire of typing the directory and file names by hand, and start thinking of attaching a dialog box to let you point and click to show where to store the files you're retrieving. Be sure to look up the class `CFileDialog` in your online or paper Visual C++ documentation before you start—this framework class lets you create a dialog box that looks just like the standard Open dialog box used throughout Windows (for example, when you choose File, Open in most applications), and it will handle getting file lists, scrolling, changing directories and more, all automatically. But I have to leave something for you to discover yourself, so I'll say no more about that.

Chapter 8

Building an Internet HTTP Server

The World Wide Web is one of the most popular applications on today's Internet. In the two years since its start at CERN (also known as the European Laboratory for Particle Physics), the Web has grown until it accounts for a large percentage of all Internet traffic. The Web is implemented using the *HyperText Transfer Protocol*, or *HTTP*. HTTP enables clients (called *browsers*) to fetch pages from HTTP servers and to return data to the servers.

Until now, you've focused on building client applications. In this chapter, you're going to do something a bit different: you're going to build a usable HTTP server. Here's what you'll cover:

- What does the HTTP protocol do, and how do applications use it?

- What features of HTTP do you have to support in a server?

- How to build an HTTP server using MFC and our QSocket class

- How to use your HTTP server to serve images, text, and documents right from your desktop

What Does HTTP Do?

When you use a Web browser like Mosaic or Netscape to view a Web page, your browser actually sends HTTP requests to a Web server, then displays the data returned by the server. The file that comes back may be of almost any type, including *HyperText Markup Language (HTML)*—the language used to build Web pages. Like Finger and Whois, HTTP browsers send a command and listen for a response; instead of just simple text data, though, HTTP can return richly formatted text, graphics, sounds, movies... practically anything you can store in a file. HTTP contains commands to send *and* receive data and files, including commands that:

- get header information for a Web document, including its modification time and length

- get the body content of a Web document, including the text of the document and flags which indicate what kind of data it contains

- send data collected with a fill-in form on the browser back to the server for processing

NOTE HTML is such a rich language that it deserves more space than can be devoted here. A complete copy of the HTML specification is available from the World Wide Web Organization (W3O)'s Web server at **http://www.w3.org/hypertext/WWW/ MarkUp/MarkUp.html**, and the National Center for Supercomputing Applications maintains an excellent HTML tutorial at **http://www.ncsa.uiuc.edu/General/ Internet/WWW/HTMLPrimer.html**. Also, you can find additional information in *Special Edition Using HTML*, published by Que.

One difference between FTP and HTTP is that HTTP requires a new connection for each request. You process only one request at a time, but each request comes over its own individual socket.

HTTP is a very young protocol, and by comparison with FTP, SMTP, and NNTP, an uncomplicated one. It should evolve and grow over the next few years as users and developers find new ways to extend the Web. For example, pending proposals would add other request and data types, as well as an FTP-like feature to send multiple requests over a single socket. In addition, there are several proposals and a few implementations which add better security, logging, and negotiation features to HTTP.

How Does HTTP Work?

Like Finger and Whois, HTTP is a simple protocol: you open a connection to the server, send a request, and read the answer. HTTP is a little unusual for two reasons: you use *Uniform Resource Locators* (*URLs*) to specify the target of the request, and the returned document has content-type markers that tell the browser whether it's a graphic, a sound, plain text, or whatever else. You're going to look at HTTP a little differently, though, because you're building a server.

In your case, the server needs to accept requests, process them, and send the results back to the client. Before plunging into the details of how you build the server, look at the types of requests HTTP supports. All requests share a common structure: the request type is followed by the path and name of the requested document. A protocol identifier brings up the rear; this identifier tells the server what protocol the client is using. Following is a summary of the most common request types.

HEAD

The HEAD request asks the server to send back the named document's header. At a minimum, this header should include the document's length, its modification date, and an indicator of its content type. If the author's provided a title or other summary information, HEAD should return it too.

> Format: HEAD document-URL protocol-ID

> Example: HEAD /htdocs/index.html HTTP/1.0

GET

The GET request asks the server to fetch the named document and send it back. If the server finds the document, and if there aren't any access restrictions, the server sends back the same information returned by HEAD, followed by the document itself—all in one big chunk (subject, of course, to packetizing by TCP/IP itself.) GET can also be used to send data back to scripts for processing, but it's largely been replaced by POST in that role.

> Format: GET document-URL protocol-ID

> Example: GET /htdocs/books/building-vc.html HTTP/1.0

POST

The POST request type sends data from the browser to the server. You most often see this request type as the action for an HTML form. POST enables the user to fill out a form and click a button to make the browser send the form's contents to the server for processing. Some servers also use POST to enable users to add annotations to documents or post messages on bulletin board-like systems.

Format: POST document-URL protocol-ID

Example: POST /htdocs/forms/question.html HTTP/1.0

Handling Errors

If you're a programmer, you already know that we live in an imperfect world. Programs break, bugs creep in, and requests sometimes fail. HTTP requests might fail because the requested document doesn't exist, has been moved, or has access restrictions that exceed the client's permissions. The table below shows a list of the most common HTTP error conditions and the proper response for each. You learn more about error handling when you test and use your HTTP server.

Error Code	Message	What It Means
200	Ok	OK. Successful transmission. Browsers usually don't display this one, but they need to see it to know that a document's following.
302	Redirect	The specified document's been moved somewhere else. This code must include a pointer to the document's new home.
403	Access denied	Forbidden. The browser's asked for a document when either the server or the document has an access control that denies access. You won't use this one, because you're not implementing access controls.
404	Not found	URL not found. Your server returns this when the user asks for a nonexistent document.
500	Server error	Server error. You return this in case something goes drastically wrong while you're serving a document.

Building Your HTTP Server

Rather than firing up AppWizard and diving into the resulting code, let's pause for a minute to lay out a skeleton design for your server. MFC and Winsock together can save you a lot of work, and you don't want to waste that advantage by sloppy preparation.

First of all, bear in mind that there are a number of commercial Web servers that took several man-years each to develop. Your effort will be somewhat more modest. You won't support POST requests, which usually pass data to external programs called *CGI scripts* for processing, and you won't support logging or access control. You ignore the protocol type header altogether, and you only support one connection at a time, although you allow the user to select how many pending connections the server should permit.

Naturally, you use AppWizard and MFC to handle the user interface as much as possible—after all, that's what they're for! Your server's simple. It doesn't have, or need, documents or menus like the FTP client described in Chapter 7, "Building an Internet FTP Application," so you build it as a dialog-based application.

Of course, you don't want to reinvent the wheel, so you use your own QSocket class for socket communications. You also make maximum use of AppWizard to get your dialog boxes built and coded.

Architecture 101

In previous chapters, you've built applications that opened a socket to send a request, then displayed the data that came back. Your server's different, though; it needs to *accept* connections and requests instead of sending them. To make this work, you have to do things a little differently.

What Should the Server Do?

The purpose of your program is to serve up Web pages, so you must be able to take requests over the network and either answer them or return meaningful errors. You limit yourself to answering GET and HEAD requests (although you can always add support for POST if you're interested in a challenge).

You want to accurately return document type data so that the browser will know whether it's getting a picture, text, or whatnot. You won't provide a super-spiffy interface for configuring those types, though, and you only support a few of the most common ones.

II

Developing Applications

Speaking of user interfaces, the server needs some kind of user interface, because the server administrator will probably want to be able to start, stop, and kill off the server process. You'll add some configurable options, so you need an interface to allow the administrator to view and set them. Finally, it's always nice to see a record of who's connected and what files they requested, so you should display that.

How Should the Server Do It?

All the applications in this book have one common requirement: they all have to initialize Winsock before doing any socket I/O. Fortunately, AppWizard adds code to do this if you use Visual C++ 1.52 or 2.1.

 If you're not using one of these compilers, see Chapter 3, "Windows Sockets (WINSOCK.DLL)," for more details on the socket initialization code.

Your server departs from normalcy right after initializing Winsock, because you need to create a *listening socket* to listen for connections. The listening socket acts like a doorman; all it does is wait for someone to try to connect, then signals you that another machine wants to establish a connection. Once your listener socket hears a connection request, you'll do the actual work of serving the request, as outlined in the following steps:

1. Accept the connection.

When you accept the connection, Winsock actually creates a second socket (called the *request socket*) and establishes a real live connection between your server and the client on the net. Your listener socket is still there, listening for another connection. When you call `QSocket::Listen()`, the socket class automatically accepts connections for you. You don't have to do anything extra.

2. Read the request from the request socket.

When you read the request data, it all comes to you in one block, so you can parse it easily.

3. Parse the request.

If it isn't one of the types you can handle, you'll return an error and disconnect. If it's a valid request type, you parse it to find out which file it's asking for.

4. Open the requested file as read-only.

This avoids conflicts with multiple concurrent requests for the same file, and sends back the header information, including the file's modification date and its length.

If the request is for a nonexistent file, or if the file's permissions make it unreadable, you'll return an error to the client.

If the request was a GET, you'll also send the file itself. You let the socket class and TCP/IP take care of checking for time-outs and buffering. Of course, you also have to handle special cases for various things; you'll see more about those in a bit.

In all cases, you'll send back a set of standard response headers: the date of the response, a response code (see the earlier table for a brief list), and strings to identify your server. You'll cover the code for all these steps in more detail. First, you learn about building the application and its user interface.

AppWizard

Launch AppWizard by running Visual C++ and choosing File, New. Select Project from the file type dialog and pick a name for the project, then choose Create to start the AppWizard question-and-answer session. When the first AppWizard dialog box appears, select a Dialog-based application, because you don't need document windows or a menu bar, then click Next.

If you're used to creating SDI or MDI applications, the next AppWizard dialog box will look strange to you. The completed dialog box is shown in figure 8.1. This example has an About box and 3D controls; you can make different choices if you prefer. You also need to name your dialog window.

The most important item in this dialog box is the check box for Windows Sockets support. Make sure you check it so that you can be lazy and let the MFC do some of the socket work for you.

You can accept the default settings for the next two AppWizard dialog boxes, although you may want to specify that MFC be linked as a library so that you don't need additional DLLs. When you've completed all four dialog boxes, choose Finish and you see the familiar summary dialog box shown in figure 8.2.

II

Developing Applications

Fig. 8.1
Turn on Windows
Sockets support
by setting the
<u>W</u>indows Sockets
check box, then
set the other
options as you
please.

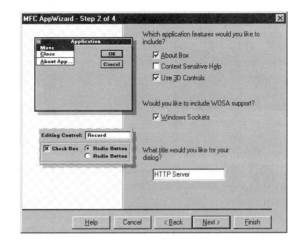

If the previous instructions don't make any sense, go back and skim over Chapters 4, "Building a Windows Application Framework," and 5, "Building an Internet Finger Application," again.

As you saw in Chapter 5, "Building an Internet Finger Application," you have to run AppWizard by choosing <u>P</u>roject, App<u>W</u>izard if you're using Visual C++ 1.5x. See the section "Building Your Own Finger Client" in Chapter 5 for more details.

Fig. 8.2
This AppWizard
summary shows
that your new
application will
have an applica-
tion class and a
dialog class. You'll
modify these
classes to make
this a real server.

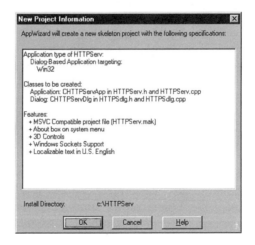

When you choose OK to close the summary dialog box, AppWizard creates the application skeleton. Remember that if you're not using Visual C++ 2.1, you'll need to manually add socket support to your application by following the instructions in Chapter 3, "Windows Sockets (WINSOCK.DLL)."

AppStudio

Now that you have an application skeleton, let's build your dialog box. Since you told AppWizard to build a dialog-based application, you don't have any menus, toolbars, or other items to fool around with, and the only window you need to work with is the server's dialog box, named `IDC_HTTPSERV_DIALOG` throughout the chapter.

Open AppStudio by opening your project file and double-clicking the resource file. The resource file displays as a tree view, so double-click `Dialogs` to open that branch of the tree, then double-click `IDC_HTTPSERV_DIALOG` to open it. AppWizard's already created a bare-bones version of your dialog box with OK and Cancel buttons, plus a to-do reminder telling you to add other controls. Figure 8.3 shows this humble beginning.

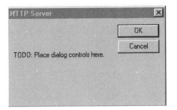

Fig. 8.3
This mostly-empty dialog box will be the centerpiece of your server after you add the needed controls with AppStudio.

You've already learned what the server needs to do: let the user start, stop, and quit; let the user set options; and let the user see who's been connected and what requests they sent. You'll rename the OK and Cancel buttons, then add buttons for stopping the server and setting options. Finally, you'll create a list box for displaying the activity log.

To rename the buttons, you need to edit their properties. Either double-click the button you want to edit or select it by single-clicking, then choosing Edit, Properties or pressing Alt+Enter to display the Properties palette. Change the OK button's name to `&Start` and the Cancel button's name to `&Quit`—but be sure to leave their resource IDs alone. Why the ampersand? AppStudio builds the keyboard shortcut table by using the ampersand to indicate which letter triggers the shortcut. When you see the dialog box itself, the trigger letter is underlined.

You also need to create two more buttons and a list box. Make sure the Tools palette is visible (if not, show it by choosing Tools, Toolbars and checking Controls). Add the buttons and list box by clicking the control type you want on the Tools palette, then clicking where you want the control placed. Once you've placed the controls, use the Properties palette to change their resource IDs; use IDC_STOP and IDC_OPTIONS for the buttons and IDC_HISTORY_LIST for the list box.

When you first run your application, the server is dormant, and you have to start it with Start before it'll do anything. Since it's not started yet, it makes no sense to try to stop it, so you disable the Stop button. Use the Properties palette to check Disabled for that button.

Once all that's done, you can experiment with grouping and moving the controls into an arrangement that suits you. You might also want to add static text labels for the history list, since you'll have several columns. Figure 8.4 shows the dialog box supplied with the source on the CD-ROM.

Fig. 8.4
This is how the HTTP server's main dialog window looks after you've edited, tweaked, aligned, and rearranged the controls for the most pleasing results.

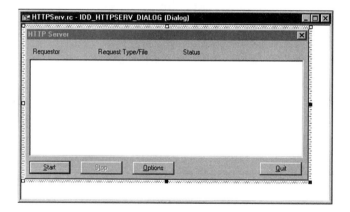

ClassWizard

Whew! Now you have a user interface, and AppStudio and AppWizard have already written much of the code to make it work. Before you start adding your own code, though, go ahead and add member functions for the two new buttons you added to your dialog box. AppWizard's already written functions for the Start and Quit buttons; you learn more about modifying them later in this section.

First, you need to add a function that is called when the user clicks Stop. As you've seen in previous chapters, you can easily link your function and your button with ClassWizard, so you do that now.

Bring up ClassWizard by choosing Project, ClassWizard (or pressing Ctrl+W). Click the Message Maps tab, then select CHTTPServDlg from the drop-down list box and IDC_STOP from the left-hand list box. The right-hand list box shows that IDC_STOP understands two messages: BN_CLICKED and BN_DOUBLECLICKED. Since you want single clicks on the button to call your function, select BN_CLICKED and then choose the Add Function button. ClassWizard selects a name for your new function; in your case, it'll be OnStop, which is a perfectly good name. Click OK. If you have HTTPSDLG.CPP open, you can scroll to the bottom and see that ClassWizard's added a skeleton function named CHTTPServDlg::OnStop() for you.

Once you've finished inspecting OnStop (it shouldn't take long since it's such a small function!), repeat the above steps for the Options button.

Now you need to add functions for your Start and Quit buttons. Since you renamed the default OK and Cancel buttons, ClassWizard thinks that your buttons have the same ID as those defaults, but with different names. That's no problem; in fact, keeping IDOK and IDCANCEL as the button IDs means that MFC can handle them without any work on your part.

Well, *almost*—you still have to use ClassWizard to add functions to handle clicks in those buttons. After all, you need to be able to start and quit your server! To add these functions, just follow the steps above. Name the Start button's function OnStart, and call the Quit button's function OnQuit. As with the Start and Options buttons, you add more code to those functions in a bit.

> Until you're an AppWizard wizard, you can search AppWizard-created files for the string TODO if you want to quickly find places where you need to add code.

Writing the Server

> As in other chapters, you're following the Microsoft convention for naming your variables. The first letter indicates the type: p for pointer, f for flag, and so on.

The very first thing you have to do is get set up to use Winsock. If you're using Visual C++ 2.1 or 1.52, and you selected the check box for adding Winsock support in AppWizard, then this is already done. If you're using an earlier version of Visual C++, see Chapter 3, "Windows Sockets (WINSOCK.DLL)," for details on what you need to do.

Before your server can do anything interesting, you need to prepare to accept requests, but in order to do *that* you need a listener socket. So that you can start and stop appropriately, you should also have a flag to tell you whether you're running or not. Let's add the sockets and flag as member variables in your dialog class. Open HTTPSDLG.H and, in the Implementation section, add:

```
private:
      BOOL fIsRunning;
      int numBacklogConns;
      QSocket *pRequestSocket;
      QSocket *pListeningSocket;
```

You want your sockets to be pointers so you can create and delete them at will. You create the listening socket when you start the server, and you destroy it when you stop the server. The request socket is created for you by `QSocket::Listen()`. It's always good practice to initialize your variables, so be sure to set the `fIsRunning` flag to FALSE, null out the pointers, and set `numBacklogConns` to a reasonable value in the dialog class's constructor.

Starting, Stopping, and Quitting

It was mentioned earlier that it would be nice to let the server administrator start, stop, and quit your server, but how will you know if the server's running or not? That's what the `fIsRunning` flag that you added above is for! You need to be able to tell whether you're already running or not so that you can toggle the Start and Stop buttons in your dialog box.

You begin by adding code so that your server can start up. Remember just a few pages ago when you learned about modifying the functions ClassWizard wrote for your dialog buttons? You're going to do that now by adding code to `CHTTPServDlg::OnStart`, shown in the code below. You go over the changes line-by-line, but look at them first.

```
void CHTTPServDlg::OnStart()
{
    BOOL status = TRUE;

    // Create your new socket and bind it to this window.
    pListeningSocket = new QSocket();
    if (pListeningSocket)
    {

        pListeningSocket->SetReceiveTarget(this,
                    WM_LISTEN_SOCKET_RESPONSE);

        // Initialize your socket: set the port number you
        // want to listen on, then bind the socket to the port.
        SOCKADDR theAddr;
```

```
theAddr.sa_family = AF_INET;
memset(theAddr.sa_data, 0, sizeof(theAddr.sa_data));
// Clear out the structure.
*(u_short *)(&theAddr.sa_data[0]) = htons(HTTP_PORT_NUM);

if (pListeningSocket->Bind(&theAddr, sizeof(theAddr)))
{
    if (pListeningSocket->Listen(numBacklogConns))
    {
        // Turn the "Start" button off
        // and the "Stop" button on.
        fIsRunning = TRUE;
        GetDlgItem(IDC_STOP)->EnableWindow(TRUE);
        GetDlgItem(IDOK)->EnableWindow(FALSE);
    }
}
}
}
```

What was *that* all about? You know that the user can't click Start again once the server's started, so you can create your listening socket without checking for an old one.

If your socket creation succeeded, you call `SetReceiveTarget(this, WM_LISTEN_SOCKET_RESPONSE)` to make your socket send its events to your dialog window. The `this` parameter is a pointer to your dialog object, and the `WM_LISTEN_SOCKET_RESPONSE` message is a code that you defined to represent socket messages. As with Finger and FTP, you add a `#define` to HTTPSERV.H that defines this message:

```
#define WM_LISTEN_SOCKET_RESPONSE WM_USER+201
```

After creating the socket, you need to make it into a listening socket. To do so, you need to use the socket's `Bind()` function. `Bind()` expects that you'll tell it what port to bind on, and you do so by filling in a `SOCKADDR` structure with a valid family and port number. Because host and network data can be in different byte order, you need to use `htons()` to convert your port number to network ordering, then you can call `Bind()`. Don't forget to add a `#define` for the port number to HTTPSERV.H, either:

```
#define HTTP_PORT_NUM 80  // 80 is the Internet-standard WWW port
```

If your call to `Bind()` succeeded, then you open for business by calling the `Listen()` method of your socket class. `Listen()` waits for an incoming connection event; the parameter specifies the number of backlogged connections that are allowed before connections are refused. When `Listen()` hears a connection request, it opens a new socket and sends a message to the target specified by `SetReceiveTarget`. In your case, your dialog window is equipped to deal with connections caught by `Listen()`.

Finally, you set the "is the server running?" flag to TRUE and enable/disable the Start and Stop buttons to indicate that the server's running. Now that you can start, you move on to stopping.

The code for your OnStop() function is shown in the code that follows. It's a bit simpler than the OnStart() function, because all you have to do is destroy the listening socket, update the fIsRunning flag, and enable the controls as appropriate.

```
void CHTTPServDlg::OnStop()
{
    // Turn the "Start" button on and the "Stop" button off.
    fIsRunning = FALSE;
    GetDlgItem(IDC_STOP)->EnableWindow(FALSE);
    GetDlgItem(IDOK)->EnableWindow(TRUE);

    // Destroy the listening socket.
    if (pListeningSocket)
    {
        delete pListeningSocket;
        pListeningSocket = NULL;
    }
}
```

Of course, you still need a way to let the user quit your server. For now, you implement a quick and dirty OnQuit() function. Open HTTPSRVD.CPP and find the CHTTPServDlg::OnQuit() function. In the middle (where it says TODO: now), add this code:

```
OnStop();
CDialog::OnCancel();
```

That will call the cleanup code in OnStop(), and then call the inherited CDialog::OnCancel() routine to clean up the dialog and user interface objects before quitting your application.

Accepting Requests

For your next trick, let's make your server actually do what it was designed for. (Pretty neat trick, isn't it?) The code you added for OnStart() causes you to get a notification message every time the listening socket hears a connection request. You still need a way to act on that message and do something useful when you receive it. You also must have a way to handle the new socket that Listen() created.

In the FTP and Finger examples, you added the WM_SOCKET_MESSAGE message to the application's message map. You need to do exactly the same thing, but twice: once for the listening socket, and once for the request socket. In

HTTPSDLG.H, add these lines just before the line that says
`DECLARE_MESSAGE_MAP():`

```
afx_msg LONG OnListeningSocket(WPARAM amount, LPARAM buffer);
afx_msg LONG OnRequestSocket(WPARAM amount, LPARAM buffer);
```

Remember that, by convention, functions in message maps start with `On`.　　　■ TIP ■

These lines tell the compiler that you're declaring two functions:
`OnListeningSocket` and `OnRequestSocket`. Next, add the message map entries
themselves in HTTPSDLG.CPP, just before the `END_MESSAGE_MAP()` line:

```
ON_MESSAGE(WM_LISTEN_SOCKET_RESPONSE, OnListeningSocket)
ON_MESSAGE(WM_REQUEST_SOCKET_RESPONSE, OnRequestSocket)
```

Now the system knows that you want it to call `OnListeningSocket` when your
dialog box window receives a `WM_LISTEN_SOCKET_RESPONSE` message from the
message pump. You also want it to make a similar call to `OnRequestSocket`
when an event occurs on the newly-created request socket. But, you still have
to write these routines, right? No problem—you've already used the core of it
in several of the previous chapters. Your routines will be a bit different from
the `OnSocket()` routines in previous chapters. Why? Everyone together,
now—"because this is a server!" Actually, `OnListeningSocket` is *very* similar to
the `OnListeningSocket` routine from the FTP client described in Chapter 7,
"Building an Internet FTP Application." Yours is shown in the following
code:

```
afx_msg LONG CHTTPServDlg::OnListeningSocket(WPARAM amount,
                            LPARAM buffer)
{
    if ((int)amount > 0)
    {
    }
    else
    {
        switch((SocketReceiveCmd)amount)
        {
            case NewSocketAccepted:
            {
                sRequest = "";
                pRequestSocket = (QSocket *)buffer;
                fGotRequest = FALSE;
                pRequestSocket->SetReceiveTarget(this,
                        WM_REQUEST_SOCKET_RESPONSE);
                pRequestSocket->Linger();
                break;
            }
        }
```

```
                              case SocketStatusChanged:
                              default:
                                    break;
                        }
                  }
                  return 0;
            }
```

Look at what this code does. As you've seen in previous chapters, the first parameter, amount, is positive when the socket has data, and negative when the socket's trying to tell you about a status change. Since this routine handles your listening socket, you don't care if there's data on it, and there actually never should be any.

When amount is negative, you check its value (after casting it to SocketReceiveCmd, naturally) and see whether it's an event you're interested in. As it happens, the only thing you really care about is the message you get when a new socket connection is accepted.

When that connection's accepted, the buffer parameter points to the newly minted socket. This socket, your *request socket*, is where you get the request and send the response. You call SetReceiveTarget() to notify your OnRequestSocket() routine of socket events on the request socket, then you call a new routine: Linger().

The default for socket operations is to unceremoniously drop all pending read and write data when the socket's closed. As you'll see in a short while, that would cause your browser to starve, because you can close the connection before all the data's delivered. Linger() makes the socket stay open until all data's delivered.

Did you notice the fGotRequest flag? (You should add it as a global in HTTPSDLG.CPP if you're coding from scratch.) You set it to FALSE here to indicate that you haven't read a request from the new socket. More on that later.

Processing Requests

Okay, you've created a request socket and set up a routine to be called when something happens. That routine, OnRequestSocket, is shown in the following listing, along with a new member variable you need to add in HTTPSDLG.H:

```
            CString sRequest;

      afx_msg LONG CHTTPServDlg::OnRequestSocket(WPARAM amount,
                                    LPARAM buffer)
      {
            if ((int)amount > 0)
```

```
        {
            sRequest = (char *)buffer;
            if (fGotRequest == FALSE)
            {
                fGotRequest = TRUE;
                pRequestSocket->SetReceiveTarget(NULL, 0);
                ProcessRequest();

                delete pRequestSocket;
                pRequestSocket=NULL;
            }
        }
        return 0;
    }
```

This probably looks familiar—it's very much like the previous incarnations of OnSocket() you've seen in other chapters. When amount is positive, your socket has data, so you read it into your request string. You ignore the case where amount is negative, because you don't care about status change messages on the socket. If fGotRequest is false, then you need to treat this as a real request, so you flip the flag, then use SetReceiveTarget() to turn off further calls to OnRequestSocket().

Why do that? You don't want to be bothered by any other data, or new requests, which may arrive until *after* you've completed this one. Once you've turned off notifications, you call ProcessRequest() to actually handle the request, then you delete the request socket.

ProcessRequest() is where the rubber meets the road; without it, you don't have a server. Before you look at what it does, review the assumptions from your design: you only allow HEAD and GET requests, you'll ignore the protocol ID field, and you won't support any kind of access controls. Both HEAD and GET requests specify that you need to pass some information about the document back to the client. You'll support three of the most common information objects:

- *Content-Length: N*, where *N* is the size in bytes of the documents. The browser can use this to display progress indicators or "time remaining" displays.

- *Content-Type: type*, where *type* is a MIME-type specifier. You support HTML (text/html), plain text (text/plain), GIF images (image/gif), and JPEG images (image/jpeg). You also learn about how you could add other supported types.

- *Last-Modified: date*, where *date* is a string in the form "Weekday, DD-Mon-YY HH:MM:SS TZ." What's all that mean? Well, "Friday, 10-Nov-95 00:00:01 GMT" is the 220th birthday of the U.S. Marine

II

Developing Applications

Corps: November 10, 1995 at one second past midnight, Greenwich Standard Time (GMT). HTTP specifies that the time zone is *always* GMT, so you need to convert from your local time to GMT before sending this string.

NOTE All of these objects conform to the *Multimedia Internet Mail Extensions* (*MIME*) standards as documented in RFCs 1521 and 1522. The HTTP protocol definitions at **http://www.w3o.org** have a lot more detail on other information objects that servers and clients can exchange. (See the RFC directory on the CD-ROM.)

So, what do you need to do? By the time the `ProcessRequest()` function is called, you have the request string from the request socket, and you have the request socket itself for returning data. All you need to do is parse the request, see if it's legal, figure out whether the file exists, and send back its header data (along with the file if it's a GET request).

Now for one more brief detour—it'll be worthwhile. For all requests, you have a specific set of optional-but-nice-to-have headers that *you* really should return. `EmitStandardHeaders()` does just that. And what if the request you get is invalid? You need a way to return errors to the browser in the right format. You write a function to do that, too. Your two new status-reporting functions are shown in listing 8.1. Don't forget to add their prototypes to HTTPSDLG.H!

Listing 8.1   Status-Reporting Functions

```
#define FORBIDDEN      403
#define NOT_FOUND      404
#define SERVER_ERROR    500

void CHTTPServDlg::EmitStandardHeaders(void)
{
    CString outString = "";
     // use strftime format with CTime
     const char *timeFmt = "%A, %d-%b-%y %H:%M:%S GMT";
CTime currTime = CTime::GetCurrentTime();

    // Your server name & version.
    outString = "Server: BIAVCServ 1.0\015\012";
pRequestSocket->Send(outString);

    outString = "Date: " + currTime.FormatGmt(timeFmt)
                        + "\015\012";
    pRequestSocket->Send(outString);
}
```

```
void CHTTPServDlg::EmitError(const int errorType)
{
    CString errStr;
    switch(errorType)
    {
        case FORBIDDEN:
            errStr = "HTTP/1.0 403 Forbidden\015\012";
            break;
        case NOT_FOUND:
            errStr = "HTTP/1.0 404 Not Found\015\012";
            break;
        case SERVER_ERROR:
        default:
            errStr = "HTTP/1.0 500 Server Error\015\012";
            break;
    }
    pRequestSocket->Send(errStr);
    EmitStandardHeaders();
}
```

EmitStandardHeaders() just gets the current time and formats it to match the
HTTP protocol's requirements, then sends that time along with a string to
identify your server ("BIAVCServ 1.0"). You use MFC's CTime object because it
provides an easy way to format the time the way the protocol's expecting it,
and it handles the required GMT conversion with no extra work on your part.

All EmitError() does is spit out an error code as shown in the table in the
"Handling Errors" section of this chapter. The browser takes care of displaying human-readable text to tell the user what went wrong. Notice that you
still put out the standard headers as part of your error response.

Now that you have a way to report the status of a request back to the
browser, take a look at ProcessRequest(), the kernel of your actual server.
Instead of presenting the code in one big chunk, you show it in several
smaller blocks with discussion intermixed.

First, you have some new global variables that you use to hold the request
and some configuration parameters. Add this code to HTTPSDLG.H, where
you previously added pRequestSocket and pListeningSocket:

```
CString sDocRoot;
CString sDefaultIndex;
```

Since sDefaultIndex and sDocRoot need to have certain values (at least until
you add code to let the user set them!), add this code to the dialog box's constructor function:

```
sRequest = "";
sDocRoot = "c:";
sDefaultIndex = "\\index.htm";
```

Finally! On to ProcessRequest() itself. You need to define the variables you'll be using. Notice that you're using the MFC CFile classes to handle your file I/O.

```
void CHTTPServDlg::ProcessRequest(void)
{
    const char cSpace = ' ';
    const char cReturn = '\r';
    const char cFwdSlash = '/';
    const char cRevSlash = '\\';
    int firstSpace=0, lastSpace=0;

    CString status = "";
    CString requestType = "";
    CString requestedFile = "";
    const char *kOKCode = "HTTP/1.0 200 OK\015\012";

    const LPCTSTR pGetType = "get";
    const LPCTSTR pHeadType = "head";
    BOOL fIsGetRequest = FALSE;
    BOOL fStatus = FALSE;

    CFile *pTheFile = NULL;
    CFileException fileExcept;
    CFileStatus theStatus;
```

The next thing to do is to check the request type and see if it's one that you support. Remember that HTTP describes several other request types that you may want to support later.

```
    firstSpace = sRequest.Find(cSpace);
    requestType = sRequest.Left(firstSpace);
    requestType.MakeLower();

    if (requestType == pGetType)
        fIsGetRequest = TRUE;
    else if (requestType != pHeadType)
    {
        EmitError(SERVER_ERROR);
        goto cleanup;
    }
```

You search your request string, sRequest, for a space, then copy the leftmost part of sRequest and force it to be all lowercase. You then compare it with your predefined tokens for GET and HEAD requests. If it's a GET, you set a flag so that you later know to copy the requested file to the socket. If it's not a type you recognize, you emit a SERVER_ERROR response and jump to a cleanup routine.

```
    lastSpace = sRequest.Find(cReturn);
    requestedFile = sRequest.Mid(firstSpace+1,
                    (lastSpace-firstSpace)-1);
    lastSpace = requestedFile.Find(cSpace);
```

```
requestedFile = requestedFile.Left(lastSpace);
requestedFile.MakeLower();

if (requestedFile.GetLength() == 1)
    requestedFile = sDefaultIndex;
else
    for (firstSpace=0,lastSpace = requestedFile.GetLength();
            firstSpace < lastSpace; firstSpace++)
        if (requestedFile[firstSpace]== cFwdSlash)
            requestedFile.SetAt(firstSpace, cRevSlash);
```

More of the same: you pick apart the request string to get the name of the requested file, then you force it to be all lowercase. Browsers can request the top-most document on the server by asking for "/" as the document name. If the request you got is for "/", you'll substitute the name of your default index document, which is stored in sDefaultIndex. Since HTTP specifies the use of the forward slash (/) for separating folder names, and Windows uses the opposite, the loop above converts all the forward slashes into reverse slashes.

Now, you open the file. To make sure you find it, you prepend the name of the document folder, sDocRoot, to the file name and force it to all lowercase, then open it.

```
requestedFile = sDocRoot + requestedFile;
requestedFile.MakeLower();
status += requestedFile + "\t";

pTheFile = new CFile();
fStatus = pTheFile->Open(requestedFile,
                    CFile::modeRead, &fileExcept);
if (fStatus == FALSE)
{
    EmitError(NOT_FOUND);
    delete pTheFile;
    pTheFile = NULL;
}
```

If the open attempt fails, you tell the browser. If it succeeds, then you're in for some *real* work. This snippet uses the CFile::GetStatus() method to get a structure containing the file size, modification time, and other useful goodies:

```
else
{
    char resultString[128];
    int statResult = 0;

    statResult = pTheFile->GetStatus(theStatus);
```

If you were able to get the file information you need, you need to send an OK code to let the browser know that you're sending valid data, then you'll emit the headers: first the standard headers, then modification time, content length, and content type of the requested file. (You learn about the EmitContent() routine after you wrap up ProcessRequest().) You conclude the header data by sending a CR/LF.

If you could *not* get the file status date, you emit an error to the browser and clean up after yourself.

```
if (statResult)
{
    const char *timeFmt =
            "%A, %d-%b-%y %H:%M:%S GMT";
     CString modTime =
            theStatus.m_mtime.FormatGmt(timeFmt);

    // Whether it's a GET or a HEAD, you
    // still need to return some fields.
    pRequestSocket->Send(kOKCode);
    EmitStandardHeaders();

    sprintf(&resultString[0], "Last-modified:
➡%s\015\012",
            (LPCTSTR)modTime);
    pRequestSocket->Send(resultString);

    sprintf(&resultString[0], "Content-length:
➡%d\015\012",
            theStatus.m_size);
    pRequestSocket->Send(resultString);

    EmitContent(requestedFile);
    pRequestSocket->Send("\015\012");
}
else
{
    EmitError(NOT_FOUND);
    pTheFile->Close();
    delete pTheFile;
    pTheFile = NULL;
}
```

If the request was a HEAD request, you're done, but if it was a GET then you have more work to do—you actually have to send the file itself! You allocate a buffer large enough to hold the file. If your buffer allocation succeeds, you read it with CFile::ReadHuge(). If you knew the file would always be smaller than 64k-1 bytes long, you could use CFile::Read() instead, but you can't make that assumption. Your next step is to use QSocket::SendRaw(). The ordinary Send() method requires that you send one CString at a time; it's great for text-oriented I/O, but you don't know what kind of data is in the files you're returning. SendRaw() just blasts the data out the socket without regard for its type. When done, you set your "success" flag to TRUE and free the buffer you just allocated.

CFile::ReadHuge() won't work with Win16, so you'll need to either make sure that the file requested is shorter than 32K or read and serve the file in 32K chunks.

If you *can't* allocate the buffer, it's a server error, so you tell the browser. If your request was a HEAD request, you don't have anything else to do, so you just set our "success" flag to TRUE.

```
if (fIsGetRequest == TRUE)
{
    char *pFileBuf = NULL;
    pFileBuf = (char *)malloc(theStatus.m_size);
    if (pFileBuf)
    {
        UINT bufSize = theStatus.m_size;
        bufSize = pTheFile->ReadHuge((void *)pFileBuf,
                                            bufSize);
        pRequestSocket->SendRaw((char *)pFileBuf,
                                            bufSize);
        fStatus = TRUE;
        free(pFileBuf);
    }
    else
        EmitError(SERVER_ERROR);
}
else
        fStatus = TRUE;
}
```

You've been jumping to a label called "cleanup" throughout this routine. Although the often-maligned goto is usually both unneeded and harmful, in this case it's just perfect: it gives you an easy way to make a clean exit from your function. If your CFile object is still around, you close it and delete it, then you're done.

```
cleanup:
    if (pTheFile)
    {
        pTheFile->Close();
        delete pTheFile;
    }
}
```

There's only one more thing to discuss—the EmitContent() routine that you called above to spit out the right document type. The following listing shows the code for EmitContent():

```
void CHTTPServDlg::EmitContent(CString &theFile)
{
    const int numTypes = 5;
    const char *extensions[5] = {"txt", "html", "htm",
                                    "gif", "jpg"};
```

```
            const char *types[5] = {"text/plain", "text/html",
                                    "text/html","image/gif",
                                    "image/jpeg"};
            const char cPeriod = '.';
            char result[128];

            CString fileExt = "";
            int periodPos = 0, typeIndex = 0;

            periodPos = theFile.ReverseFind(cPeriod);
            fileExt = theFile.Right((theFile.GetLength()-periodPos)-1);

            while ((typeIndex < numTypes) &&
               (extensions[typeIndex] != fileExt))
                  typeIndex++;

            if (typeIndex > numTypes-1)
                  typeIndex = 0;

            sprintf(&result[0], "Content-type: %s\015\012",
            types[typeIndex]);
            pRequestSocket->Send(result);
       }
```

As promised in your design section, you only handle the minimum useful number of file types. To decide what kind of file you have, you strip off the extension and loop through your predefined array of types you support. If you don't find a match, then you default to "text/plain" as the document type; if you *do* find a match, then you send back the correct content type.

That's it for processing requests! There are plenty of enhancements you could make, but for now you have a stable core. You learn about some simple changes you can make to produce a more finished and professional program.

A Few Finishing Touches

The server you've written does a perfectly good job, within the limits you set in the initial design. There are some things you can do that will make it easier to use, though, so you try to improve on what you've done up until now.

Many ordinary users are a little frightened of SERVERS, which they picture as being horribly complex and fragile resource hogs. One of the best ways to calm such users is to give them an easy interface for changing server settings.

Adding an Options Dialog Box

Throughout the chapter, you've been promising here and there to add user-configurable parameters. Now that you've got the server pretty much finished, you add an Options dialog box, attach it to your main dialog box, and write code to use the options set by the user.

Using AppStudio, create a new dialog box. Name it "Server Options" or something similar and give it an ID of IDD_OPTIONS_DIALOG. Add these items to it. Your finished dialog box should look something like Figure 8.5.

Item Type	Item ID	Label
Edit box	ID IDC_DOC_ROOT	Document Root Directory
Edit box	ID IDC_DEFAULT_INDEX	Default Index File
Edit box	ID IDC_NUM_CONNS	Max # of Connections

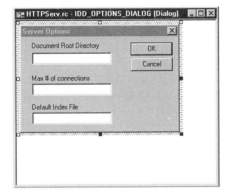

Fig. 8.5
The Server Options dialog box enables the user to exert some control over how the server works.

Now, you use ClassWizard to create a new class for your dialog box. In the process, it also writes a bunch of useful code without any real work on your part. Open ClassWizard (choose Project, ClassWizard, or just press Ctrl+W) and click the Add Class button. When the Add Class dialog box appears, type in a class name (use CHTTPOptionsDlg) and ClassWizard fills in reasonable file names for you. Select CDialog from the Class Type drop-down list box, then select your new dialog (IDD_OPTIONS_DIALOG, or whatever you named it) from the Dialog drop-down list box. Click OK; ClassWizard creates new header and body files for your class and puts them in your project file.

Before writing any more code, you still need to add some member variables to your new class. In the ClassWizard dialog box, select the Member Variables tab and add new member variables for the new dialog box as shown here.

Item ID	Member type	Variable type	Length
IDC_DOC_ROOT	value	type CString	maximum length 255
IDC_DEFAULT_INDEX	value	type CString	maximum length 255
IDC_NUM_CONNS	value	type int	minimum value 1, maximum value 255

Now, you're almost done. You still need a function to bring up the Options dialog when the user clicks your dialog box's Options button. Use Class-Wizard to add a function for OnOptions(): bring up ClassWizard, click the Message Maps tab, select CHTTPServDlg from the drop-down list box and click IDC_OPTIONS in the left-hand pane. Use the Add Function button to add a function triggered by the BN_CLICKED message; name the function OnOptions.

Now, you see what goes into OnOptions(), as shown in the following listing. Don't forget to add an #include directive to HTTPSDLG.CPP so that you can declare an object of the options dialog class.

```
void CHTTPServDlg::OnOptions()
{
    CHTTPOptsDialog theDlg;
    theDlg.m_DocRoot = sDocRoot;
    theDlg.m_NumConns = numBacklogConns;
    theDlg.m_IndexFile = sDefaultIndex;

    if (theDlg.DoModal()==IDOK)
    {
        sDocRoot = theDlg.m_DocRoot;
        numBacklogConns = theDlg.m_NumConns = 1;
        sDefaultIndex = theDlg.m_IndexFile;
    }
}
```

If you take advantage of its features, MFC makes it really easy to create and use dialog boxes like this one. You don't have any property sheets, custom controls, or other unusual items—just plain edit controls. All you have to do is follow three easy steps:

1. Create the dialog box object, either on the stack (as you did here) or by using the new operator. Don't forget to dispose of objects you create with new when you're done with them!

2. Set the dialog object's member variables to the values you want displayed in the dialog. MFC automatically calls UpdateData(TRUE) to fill in your dialog fields when it displays the dialog.

3. Call DoModal(); if the response indicates that the user confirmed his choice (usually that means he clicked OK, hence your test for IDOK), set your application's variables to whatever the dialog object's member variables contain.

If you wanted to add more features to your server, it would be easy to build the user interface by adding more dialog boxes in the manner described here. There's always a danger of having too many dialogs, since users usually don't like having to trudge through dialog after dialog when they could be using menus and keyboard commands instead. One possible solution is to add property sheets.

Keeping the User Informed

Remember that list box in the middle of your dialog box? It would be nice to let the user see who's been connected and what files they requested, so let's put that list box to use (either that or delete it, because it looks funny sitting there blank!).

First, use ClassWizard to add a member variable for the list box. All the member variables you've added before have been values; in this case, you want a variable that points to a control so that you can call the control's methods directly. To do this, launch ClassWizard, select CHTTPServDlg from the drop-down list box, and click the Member Variables tab. Add a variable named m_histList for the IDC_HIST_LIST control, and make sure to specify that it's a control, not a value.

Now use AppStudio to open up the server's main dialog, select the list box, and make sure that its property sheet has the Use Tabstops option checked. You need to use tab stops to align the fields of your list. To actually take advantage of tab stops in a list box, you need to add a few lines of code to CHTTPServDlg::OnInitDialog():

```
const int kFirstTab = 25;
int tabStops[2] = {kFirstTab, kFirstTab+80};
m_histList.SetTabStops(2, &tabStops[0]);
```

All this does is use CListBox::SetTabStops() to set a pair of tab stops for you. You could determine the settings for the tab stops by trial and error, but you might find a better way!

Now that the list box can display neatly formatted columns, you need to put something into it. At a minimum, you should display the TCP/IP address of the requester, the request type, the requested file, and whether the request succeeded or not. To accomplish this, you'll need to add some code in various places. First off, you need to add this block to `ProcessRequest()`; it needs to go at the very beginning.

```
CString status = "";
BOOL fStatus = FALSE;
{
    SOCKADDR_IN req_address;
    int addr_size = sizeof(req_address);
    pRequestSocket->GetSockName((SOCKADDR*)&req_address,
                                 &addr_size);
    unsigned char *host = (unsigned char *)
                             &(req_address.sin_addr);

    char address[128];
    sprintf(address, "%i.%i.%i.%i\t", host[0],
                host[1], host[2], host[3]);
    status = address;
}
```

`QSocket::GetSockName()` fetches the address of the remote end of the socket, but it comes to you as a set of four octets, so you have to copy it to a string and add it to your status string. Notice that the `sprintf()` includes a tab character at the end; that forces the next item added to your status `CString` to appear in the second column of the list box. Now, you need to add one line to add the request type itself. Add this line right after `requestType.MakeLower()`:

```
status += requestType + " ";
```

Now your status string has the TCP/IP address and the request type, so you're halfway there. Right before the block of code that creates your `CFile` object, add this line:

```
status += requestedFile + "\t";
```

You're almost finished; adding the file and the second tab means the only thing left to add is the request status itself. You won't know that until after your cleanup block is executed. After the code under the `cleanup:` label, add this:

```
if (fStatus)
    status += "Succeeded";
else
    status += "Failed";
m_histList.InsertString(-1, LPCTSTR(status));
```

The only remaining task to complete is adding code to set `fStatus` to TRUE when a `HEAD` or `GET` request succeeds, but that's an exercise for you to test how well you understand `ProcessRequest()`. You can always see the source on the CD-ROM if you need hints.

Using Your HTTP Server

As with most server applications, there's not a lot to *do*. Connect your computer to the Internet and run the application by clicking the Run button on the Visual C++ toolbar. Click the Start button. Voilà! Congratulations are in order, as you're now a World Wide Web server.

Some sample HTML documents are on the CD so that you can get a head start on testing the server. You also need a client. For serious Internet surfing, you want a full-featured client like NCSA Mosaic or the wildly popular Netscape Navigator.

Extending the Server

As mentioned before, most of the popular Web servers for Windows, Windows NT, and UNIX have long lists of features. This version only scratches the surface of what your server *could* do. Of course, yours runs under Win32s, Windows NT, and Windows 95, and its memory requirements are small. Here are some improvements you might consider making, grouped by relative difficulty:

Easy Improvements

The items listed here are all easy to do, especially if you've read all the preceding chapters. Try them first to flex your MFC and Internet muscles!

- Better error handling. Although the server is pretty robust, no program ever has too much error handling. Make sure that the server handles errors returned by the socket classes, and make sure that abnormal network events don't keep the server from fulfilling its mission.

- Provide a way to write the connection log to disk. Not only does this provide a permanent record of connection activity, but there are many log file analyzers which can produce useful statistics from WWW server logs. Make sure to use the same format as the NCSA and Apache WWW servers, since they're most common.

- Add a Browse button to the Options dialog so that users can easily select their default document directory. See the MFC documentation on `CFileDialog` for a quick guide on how to do this easily.

- Add more user preferences and options. Give the user control over whether the TCP/IP address or the full hostname is shown in the connection log, whether the log is written to disk, and even which fields are included. Let the user specify custom messages to be returned along with the error codes. Whatever else you do, save the user's preferences to disk so they don't have to reset them each time!

Somewhat More Challenging

These feature enhancements require a bit more time and energy, but they reward your investment of time by teaching you more about the internals of MFC and the socket underworld. Completing these puts you squarely on the front slope of the learning curve:

- Add support for more content types, and give the user a way to add new types with a dialog box or (at the least) a text file read in when the server starts. Make EmitContent() work with a runtime table instead of a hardcoded array.

- Make ProcessRequest() understand the If-Modified-Since header. Browsers use that header to ask the server to only send a document if the server's copy is newer than the browser's cached copy. This caching cuts down on network traffic and keeps users happy.

- Support HTTP redirections. When a browser asks for a particular object, a redirection from the server tells that browser that the object's moved, and where it's located, so that it can refetch the document from its new home.

- Give the user access controls. Let the user choose whether to accept or deny connections based on the requester's TCP/IP address or hostname.

- Clickable imagemaps are a nifty feature of the Web. Servers usually implement them by keeping a list of links and polygon, circle, or rectangle that triggers each one. Make the server understand the common query addition to the GET request type.

- Rewrite the Options dialog box as a tabbed dialog box. Use the MFC CPropertySheet and CPropertyPage classes to do the dirty work.

Not for the Faint of Heart

If you're looking for a challenge, try these additions. To complete them, you need a good understanding of the HTTP protocol specification and a willingness to get under the hood of MFC and Win32. Successfully implementing these features mark you as a true Windows Internet master.

■ Rewrite the server core as a Windows NT service or a Windows 95 VxD. That way users can run the server as a faceless background process, without always seeing it on their desktop. Don't forget to provide a full interface to the NT service control manager if you take that route. (This one really isn't that hard, although it sounds quite daunting.)

■ Support username and password authentication so that server users can set access controls that force browsers to give a valid username and password.

■ Support CGI (Common Gateway Interface) programs and the POST method. This enables the server to accept input from HTML forms and process it by way of an external program. For more details on CGI, see the NCSA CGI pages at **http://hoohoo.ncsa.uiuc.edu/cgi/**.

■ Make the server multithreaded. Multithreaded programs take full advantage of multiple-CPU systems, and they provide a quick way to support many simultaneous connections. See the online or paper MFC documentation for a discussion of the CWinThread class and the AfxBeginThread() function. ProcessRequest() is almost ready to be used as a thread's worker function, but you need to make some changes to QSocket, or abandon it in favor of the less-sophisticated CAsyncSocket.

From Here...

Now that you've successfully built a Web server, the next chapter will return you to the by-now-familiar client world. You'll implement an Internet Relay Chat (IRC) client using QSocket, MFC, and the Windows Multiple Document Interface (MDI).

Chapter 9

Building an Internet IRC Application

II

Developing Applications

Imagine that you could use a tool that would let you converse in real time with a large number of people, no matter what their geographic location. Wouldn't it be neat to get together with others who share your interest in roses, or home-brewed beer, or auto racing, or Windows programming?

Internet Relay Chat, usually called IRC for short, is an Internet-based service that lets you carry on typed conversations with dozens or even hundreds of people all over the world—in real time! It's the Internet equivalent of a party line or CB radio, and it provides the immediate conversational give-and-take that many people find lacking in other Internet services.

One common complaint heard from new Internet users is that it's not interactive enough. Sure, you send e-mail all over the world, and although it's faster and cheaper than faxes and paper mail, it's no more intimate or interactive. FTP and the Web, while immensely useful for *broadcasting*, aren't very good for actually *communicating* with other people either.

> **NOTE** Most Internet dwellers are generally friendly, but they usually have very little patience for people who don't follow community standards. Just like with UseNet, it pays to do some cultural research on IRC before using it. There's a terrific introduction to IRC hosted at **http://urth.acsu.buffalo.edu/irc/WWW/ircdocs.html**. You should read and heed it before you join your first channel. It's time well spent.

This chapter will introduce the IRC protocol and server network and explain how to build a multiple-window IRC client. Here's what it covers:

- What can you do with an IRC application?

- How does the IRC protocol work?

- Building an MFC-based IRC client using the Windows Multiple Document Interface (MDI)

- Using your IRC client to chat on the Internet

What Does IRC Do?

If you're interested in more technical detail, you might want to consult the exhaustive description of IRC in RFC 1459, which is on the CD enclosed with this book.

At its most basic, IRC allows you to talk with other IRC users by typing text on your computer. An IRC channel is just a group of people. When the first client joins a new channel, it's created; others can join it at will. When the last user leaves the channel, it disappears. IRC supports many channels, and you can join one or several channels at a time. Whatever you type on a channel goes to an IRC server, which rebroadcasts your comments to everyone on that channel.

IRC links servers together in a server tree to extend the number of people who can participate on a channel. For example, it's not uncommon for there to be 200 people on a popular channel like #jeopardy (IRC channel names begin with # by convention). Users on any server can see what users on their channel are saying, no matter what server those users are on.

You can also send IRC commands to the server. These commands let you join and leave channels, create new channels, see who's on a channel, send private comments to other users, and do all sorts of other interesting things. Besides the commands that are part of the IRC protocol, many clients implement their own useful commands and features, like the ctcp protocol for communicating directly between clients.

As previously mentioned, IRC conversations aren't limited to the server world; a feature called Direct Client Chat (DCC) lets a user talk directly with another user. It's like dropping off the party line to talk with one person, with this one difference: IRC doesn't require users to leave the channels they're on.

IRC clients range in sophistication from the simple command-line clients found on many UNIX systems to elaborate multiwindow Windows clients that support the full range of IRC commands with each channel in its own window. The client described in this chapter strikes a middle ground.

How Does IRC Work?

The server tree is the essence of IRC. The worldwide network of IRC servers consists of machines that communicate among themselves to share the load caused by messages passing among thousands of users. The standard IRC port number is 6667, although other port numbers are commonly used also. In fact, some busy servers run more than one server process, each with its own port. Server operators generally publish the port number if they aren't using the default.

When you start an IRC session, you're really opening a socket to the server (sound familiar?) and passing commands and data back and forth. The server you connect to communicates with other servers so that your messages get routed to people on your channel, no matter what server they're on.

All of the messages on IRC are plain 8-bit ASCII. Also, IRC is *line-oriented*: each command has a maximum length of 512 characters and must end with an ASCII linefeed and carriage return pair. As you'll see later, this line orientation simplifies the process of building an application because data from the server arrives in neatly delimited chunks.

The basic flow of commands and data is like that in the other applications we've talked about: the client sends commands to the server, and the server sends back responses. The server's responses are like FTP's: a three-digit numeric response followed by the actual message parameters. The client must decode and pay attention to the status messages. Another type of server message transmits messages typed by other users on your channel(s), so the client needs to be able to pick out these channel messages and display them in the appropriate pane.

A message typed by the user into the client goes to the server, swaddled as a command. The server takes care of rebroadcasting it to other servers that carry the selected channel. That way, it should reach everyone on the channel. The server also sends you the message text that other users have typed. Fortunately, communication between servers is transparent to the client.

At the start of each connection to a server, the client has to *register* the connection by sending messages to tell the server who's connecting. Registration consists of identifying the user with a unique *nickname* and a string identifying the login name and host of the user. If the registration succeeds, the server will allow the client to join one or more channels and communicate with other users; if not, the client can't talk to any channel until it successfully registers.

Channels have *modes* that control whether other users can see or join the channel. For example, setting the mode of a channel to +I makes that channel available by invitation only, while setting it to -I removes that restriction. You can join invitation-only channels only if someone already on the channel invites you. Other modes make channels secret, moderate channels so that only a moderator can allow messages to pass, and restrict other channel users from changing the channel's topic. (This is done by a string that briefly explains the channel's purpose.) Users have modes too, and they're set the same way as channel modes.

Each channel also has an *operator*, or *op*, who can change the channel's mode, bar disruptive users from the channel, and perform other useful maintenance functions. If you're the first person to join a channel, the server creates the new channel for you, and you become the operator for that channel as long as the channel exists—even if you leave the channel! You can't take operator privileges away from another user, but you can give up your op status to another user.

Building an IRC Client

As previously, before building an IRC client, it's a good idea to decide what features and functions are important. In this project you'll continue to use your own QSocket class for socket I/O, because you probably understand it pretty well by now. You'll also use MFC, but you'll branch out and add some new classes to spice things up a bit.

What does an IRC client need to be able to do? Like the HTTP servers in Chapter 8, "Building an Internet HTTP Server," there are some IRC programs out there with very nice features that have been developed by their authors over a period of years. But for the purposes of this chapter some more modest requirements will do:

- Let the user specify which server and port to connect to

- Let the user specify—and change—a nickname

- Let the user join one or more channels, and change from one channel to another at will

- Let the user send private messages to other users

- Let the user save the contents of channel windows as text files

- Provide useful error messages when things go wrong

Because IRC allows you to join multiple channels, it's a natural use for Windows' multiple-document interface (MDI). Fortunately, MFC provides very good support for MDI applications. The following discussion will show you first how to produce an interface with one child window per server, and then how to provide one child window per individual channel.

If you're not already generally familiar with MDI, you might want to look at an application that uses it, like any program in the Microsoft Office suite. The client in this chapter doesn't have fancy elements such as toolbars, but the basic paradigm is the same: a "parent" frame window containing one or more "child" document windows.

You will use the `CSplitterWnd` class to provide two views within each child window. (Multipane windows that allow resizing of each pane are called *splitter* windows.) The upper view will display text (but not error messages) received from the server, and the lower view will allow users to compose their messages in a multiline edit control before sending them. Don't worry. Although all this talk of splitter windows, panes, and MDI may sound a bit daunting, you'll soon see that it's simpler than it seems. Figure 9.1 shows an example of using multiple MDI windows, each with multiple split views.

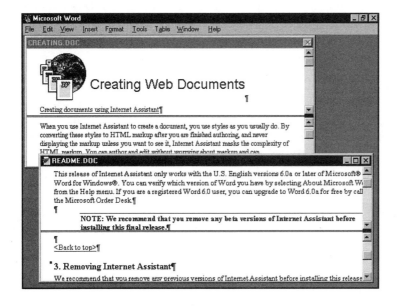

Fig. 9.1
Microsoft Word supports the full Windows multiple-document interface and the splitting of one document window into more than one view. Each view can scroll independently.

Here's the plan of attack: after building the IRC client with AppWizard, you'll add the dialog boxes and menus with AppStudio and ClassWizard. The next step is to provide first an MDI child window so that multiple windows can be open at once, and next the CIRClientDoc class required to actually connect with servers.

After all that, you'll link in the dialog boxes and menus you've already created. At that point you'll have a fully functional user interface, so you'll add the underpinnings that actually send commands to, and handle responses from, the server.

AppWizard

Launch the AppWizard by running Visual C++ and choosing File, New. Select Project from the file type dialog box and pick a name for the project (you'll see IRClient as the name throughout the chapter). Then select Create to start the AppWizard question-and-answer session. When the first AppWizard dialog box appears, select a Multiple-document interface application, and then click Next.

You should accept the default settings for AppWizard steps 2 and 3. There is no database connectivity or OLE in this application. Step 4 is important, though. Turn off the toolbar, status bar, and printing/print preview check boxes (and set Use 3D Controls to match your personal tastes). The key item in this dialog box is the check box for Windows Sockets support. Click the Advanced button and type TXT as the file extension. Click Close and then Next. Select a static library so that users won't need the MFC DLLs to run your application. Next, click CIRClientView and change its base class to CEditView by dropping down the list and selecting it. This provides the ability to edit text with no extra work—always a bargain.

Finally, click Finish and review the list of what AppWizard will create. When you're done, click OK. AppWizard will then build the project and open the new project file. If you're using a version prior to 2.1, you can't ask App-Wizard to give you socket support automatically, as discussed in Chapter 3, "Windows Sockets (WINSOCK.DLL)." Follow the instructions there to get socket support for your application.

Implementing the Interface

To build dialog boxes and menus for the client, you'll use AppStudio, as before. Unlike the CFormView and dialog-box-based applications in other chapters, this IRClient app doesn't have any views or dialog boxes (except the About box) defined at the start. Not to worry, because you'll remedy that problem shortly. You'll also continue to get as much work out of the ClassWizard as possible. In this section, though, you'll get to get your hands dirty and write some of your own code. One nice feature of wizards is that they take over much of the drudgery and leave the programmer free to do more exciting coding.

Creating Menus. Creating menus is the first step. An MDI application has two sets of menus: one set that's active when only the main frame window is visible and there are no child windows, and another set that appears when at least one child window is active. In this application, the menus are named IDR_MAINFRAME (for the main frame-only menus) and IDR_IRCLIETYPE (for the full set). Here are the changes you need to make. Figure 9.2 shows the completed IDR_IRCLIETYPE menu bar.

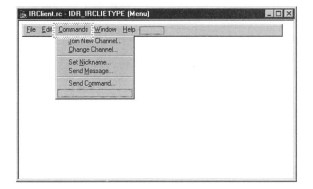

Fig. 9.2
A new item, Commands, has been added to IDR_IRCLIETYPE menu bar. Later, those commands will be tied to individual dialog boxes and actions.

II

Developing Applications

1. Rename the File, New item in the IDR_MAINFRAME and IDR_IRCLIETYPE menus to File, Connect. Remove the File, Open and Recent Files List items from both menus too.

2. Rename the File, Close item in IDR_IRCLIETYPE to File, Disconnect.

3. Add a File, Disconnect item in IDR_MAINFRAME and assign it an ID of ID_FILE_CLOSE.

4. Add a new menu called "Commands" to the IDR_IRCLIETYPE menu. Drag the menu items around so that Commands appears between Edit and Window. Add four items to your new menu: Join New Channel (command ID of ID_COMMAND_JOIN), Change Channel (command ID of ID_COMMAND_CHANGE), Change Nickname (command ID ID_COMMAND_NICK), and Send Private Message (command ID ID_COMMAND_MESSAGE).

When you're finished, save your changes. You might want to take a short break, or maybe a quick walk out in the yard. Building the dialog boxes and views is going to take a bit of time, so this is a good time to stop and rest before you press onward.

Creating Dialog Boxes. You'll need several dialog boxes to meet the goals of this application: one to let the user connect to a server, one for each of the commands in the Commands menu, and the standard set of file save dialog boxes (which MFC provides.) The dialog boxes all gather information that you'll need later, so you'll use ClassWizard to add member variables for them, too. Finally, you need a class for the MDI child windows, and that class will have to do some fancy footwork to support a splitter and multiple panes.

You'll need a total of four dialog boxes. To build the dialog box classes for these new dialogs, create the dialog box and start ClassWizard (choose Project, ClassWizard, or just Ctrl+W). Then use the New Class button to create a new CDialog-based class with the given name. After doing that, select the Member Variables tab and use Add Variable to add the necessary variables.

First, create the Connect... dialog box; name it CConnDialog and fill it with the items in the table below. The OK and Cancel buttons are added to the new dialog box for you, so don't delete them! The completed dialog box should look something like figure 9.3.

ID	Label	Variable Name	Type	Length
IDC_SERVER	Server To Connect	m_Server	CString	max 64
IDC_PORT_NUM	Port Number	m_PortNum	int	min 1, max 32766
IDC_NICKNAME	Your Nickname	m_Nickname	CString	max 9
IDC_CHANNEL	Start on Channel	m_Channel	CString	max 200

Fig. 9.3
The Connect To Server dialog box allows you to collect the data needed for connecting to the server and registering the client.

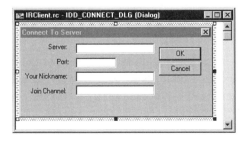

These length restrictions may seem arbitrary, but they're in the RFC. Because MFC does length validation for you, you can use it to make sure you stay legal with the IRC protocol.

The change channel and set nickname dialog boxes have only one edit control each, so they're somewhat simpler. Name the channel dialog box CIRCJoinDialog and give it an edit field with ID IDC_NEW_CHANNEL and a CString member variable named m_Channel with a maximum length of 200. Create the nickname dialog box, call it CIRCNicknameDialog, and add an edit field with ID IDC_NEW_NICKNAME, plus a CString member variable named m_Channel with a maximum length of 9.

The send private message dialog box is easy, too. Give it a class name of CIRCMessageDialog. It needs two edit controls. The first is for specifying who gets the message; give that control ID IDC_RECIPIENT and a CString member variable of maximum length 128. The second should be a multiline field, because it's where the user actually types a message (use the Styles tab of the Properties palette to change the edit control to multiline). Give it an ID of IDC_MESSAGE and a member variable of m_Message.

In all the hustle and bustle of building these dialog boxes, please don't forget to add labels, align the controls, and tweak the layout to achieve a pleasing appearance. After all, one of the best things about Windows Internet tools is that they offer the familiar Windows interface.

Now's a good time to pause and build the application. Choose Project, Build, or press Ctrl+F8. Visual C++ will compile each of the individual files and build an executable. Run the executable by choosing Debug, Go or pressing F5. Notice how File, Connect doesn't do anything yet? You're about to tackle that problem.

Building the Frame Window. You've already seen several SDI applications in this book, so you're already well on the way to understanding how MDI applications work. Now it's time to look at which objects create what in an SDI or MDI application:

1. The CWinApp application object class creates a new document template object (based on CSingleDocTemplate or CMultiDocTemplate).

2. The document template takes a document class, a frame window class, and a view class as parameters; it creates a document object for the application to use. For SDI applications, the template reuses the same document object over and over, but for MDI programs a new object is created.

3. When the document object is created, it makes a frame window to display the document. In this project, that frame window is derived from CMDIChildWnd. Each document that is open in an MDI app will have its own MDI child window, no matter what class it's based on.

4. The frame window can (and should) create as many views as it needs to display the document. Views can be plain CView objects, or they can use the CView derivatives like CFormView (like the FTP client) or CEditView (which you'll use here.)

Don't get discouraged if this doesn't all make sense at first. After you see the code, it will be much clearer. Microsoft includes several samples on the VC++ CD that illustrate MDI and splitter windows in great detail. See the Scribble example for a good starting point.

As you can see, you really do need to build your frame window class before you worry about the details of managing documents. Until your document class can create a window, and until that window has views, there's not much point in creating a document!

As mentioned above, the application will provide two panes in the window: one to read what others have said, and one to compose messages before sending them out. File Manager and the Windows 95 Explorer both use them heavily, and Microsoft provides splitter windows in Word and Excel as well.

To provide splitter windows in the program, all you have to do is create your own frame window class (based on CMDIChildWnd) and use CSplitterWnd instead of CWnd. The frame window class will create and attach however many views you want to use (two, in this case) to the splitter. At runtime, MFC will handle all the sizing and scrolling (that is, if you use CEditView!).

Thanks to ClassWizard, this whole process turns out to be easy to do. First, use ClassWizard to create a new class based on CMDIChildWnd; call it CIRCMDIWnd. ClassWizard will generate a new header and source file for that class. By default, MFC assumes that you don't want splitter windows, so you'll need to override that assumption. The specific hook you need to change is the OnCreateClient() message function. Use ClassWizard to add your own override of CMDIChildWnd's OnCreateClient(). This process will be described in a few paragraphs.

You'll need three new member variables in CIRCMDIWnd: pointers to the two views discussed above, and a pointer to the splitter window. Add them in the Attributes section of ircmdiwn.h:

```
#include "irclivw.h"                 // Makes your CIRCLientView
                                      // visible.
 public:
     CIRClientView *pServerView, *pClientView;
 private:
     CSplitterWnd *pSplitWnd;
```

You still need to add code to initialize these three pointers in CIRCMDIWnd's constructor, and to free them in its destructor; this code should be old hat by now, so I won't show it.

Now, on to OnCreateClient(). This function is called by MFC when you create a new client window. ClassWizard generated a function that calls the parent class' OnCreateClient. Its default action will create a simple single-pane window with no splitter—none of that here! Listing 9.1 shows a spiffy replacement for OnCreateClient().

Listing 9.1   The OnCreateClient () Replacement

```
BOOL CIRCMDIWnd::OnCreateClient(LPCREATESTRUCT lpcs,
                 CCreateContext* pContext)
{
    CDocument *pTheDoc = NULL;
    BOOL status = FALSE;
    SIZE aSize;

    pSplitWnd = new CSplitterWnd;
    pSplitWnd->CreateStatic(this, 2, 1,
            WS_CHILD¦WS_HSCROLL¦WS_VSCROLL);

    // Pane #1 is our text-from-server
    aSize.cx=80; aSize.cy=170;
    status = pSplitWnd->CreateView(0, 0,
            RUNTIME_CLASS(CIRClientView),
                 aSize, pContext);
    pServerView = (CIRClientView *)pSplitWnd->GetPane(0, 0);
    ((CEdit *)pServerView)->SetReadOnly(TRUE);

    // Pane #2 is where we type
    aSize.cx=80; aSize.cy=40;
    status = pSplitWnd->CreateView(1, 0,
            RUNTIME_CLASS(CIRClientView),
                 aSize, pContext);
    pClientView = (CIRClientView *)pSplitWnd->GetPane(1, 0);
    SetActiveView(pClientView, TRUE);
```

(continues)

II

Developing Applications

Listing 9.1 Continued

```
        pSplitWnd->ShowWindow(SW_SHOWNORMAL);
        pSplitWnd->UpdateWindow();
        return TRUE;
    }
```

CSplitterWnd is like CWnd: first you construct it with a constructor, then you call a creation method to attach the C++ object to a window. Start off by creating a new CSplitterWnd object, then calling its CreateStatic() function to create a splitter window with two rows and one column. The views get scroll bars by default.

Next, create the two view panes. They're both based on CIRClientView, which is in turn based on CEditView. Create each pane by specifying its row and column position within the splitter window, its size, and the view class on which it's based.

The upper pane, pointed to by pServerView, is a read-only pane; it shows what messages have come from the server. Because you don't want the user to edit it, call CEdit::SetReadOnly() to make it read-only. The lower pane, pointed to by pClientView, is where users can type their messages. Because it doesn't make sense for the focus to be in a read-only pane, use SetActiveView() to make the client view get the focus; then display the splitter window.

There's one other minor change you need to make for this to work. In CIRClientApp, the code in InitInstance() is going to create a new CMultiDocTemplate based on CMDIChildWnd, which you've just eliminated. Edit the code that creates the document template so that it looks like this:

```
    pDocTemplate = new CMultiDocTemplate(
        IDR_IRCLIETYPE,
        RUNTIME_CLASS(CIRClientDoc),
        RUNTIME_CLASS(CIRCMDIWnd),
        RUNTIME_CLASS(CIRClientView));
```

The fruit of your labor is shown in figure 9.4: a resizable client window with two panes and a splitter. It won't look that way in the client right now, though; first, you'll have to work on the code that actually talks with the server.

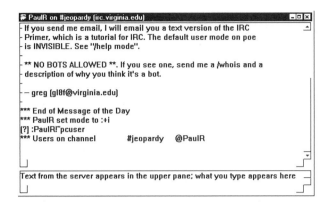

Fig. 9.4
Create splitter
windows by
overriding the
`OnCreateClient()`
method of
`CMDIChildWnd` and
then adding your
own views.

Connecting to the Server. If you want to require the user to be connected
before you allow any documents to be created, it would probably be a good
idea to give the user a way to connect! You've already built the connection
dialog box that gathers all the data needed to make a connection, so the next
step is to tie that into the `CIRClientApp` class. Add these member variables to
`irclient.h`:

```
BOOL fIsConnected;
 QSocket     *pAppSocket;
CString sServerName;
CString sNickname;
CString sInitialChannel;
int nPortNum;
```

The program will use only one socket to talk to the server, so you need a
socket variable, the server's name and port number, and the user's nickname.
The application also needs a flag to signal whether the user's already connected to a server or not. Make sure to set these to reasonable values in the
class constructor.

You need to override `CWinApp`'s default `OnFileNew action()`, so use
ClassWizard to add a function to the `CIRClientApp` class and call it
`OnFileNew()` too. Listing 9.2 shows what that routine looks like.

II

Developing Applications

Listing 9.2 Adding OnFileNew () to the CIRClientApp Class

```
void CIRClientApp::OnFileNew()
{
    if (!fIsConnected)
    {
        CConnDialog theDialog;
        theDialog.m_PortNum = 6667;
        if (theDialog.DoModal()==IDOK)
        {
            nPortNum = theDialog.m_PortNum;
            sServerName = theDialog.m_Server;
            sNickname = theDialog.m_Nickname;
             if (!theDialog.m_Channel.IsEmpty())
                  sInitialChannel = theDialog.m_Channel;
            pAppSocket = new QSocket();
            pAppSocket->SetReceiveTarget(m_pMainWnd,
                     WM_SOCKET_MESSAGE);

            if (pAppSocket->Connect(sServerName, nPortNum))
            {
                fIsConnected = TRUE;
                CWinApp::OnFileNew();
            }
            else
            {
                AfxMessageBox("Host is unreachable.");
                delete pAppSocket;
                pAppSocket = 0;
            }
        }
    }
}
```

This function is much simpler than it looks. Start by putting up the connection dialog box; if the user fills it out, copy its member variables. Then create and connect a new QSocket. The initial channel chosen by the user gets stashed away for later use, too; finally, call CWinApp::OnFileNew(), which actually does the work of creating a new document. When the connection is complete, the socket action function will catch it—more on that in a bit. CIRClientApp will be discussed later in more detail also, but the next step is to learn how you can create a new document for each channel.

Joining Channels. Even though MFC works with documents, a document is just a container for a channel, so this chapter will continue to use "channels" and "documents" interchangeably from now on. Now that you have code to connect to a server, you'll want to join channels at will. MFC provides convenient hooks to use whenever the user wants a new document created, so use that mechanism to do your bidding.

Before learning how you create a new document object, it's important to see what each document needs to know. Since each document is a channel to a server, you need the name of that channel. You'll also need a pointer to the application class, since you'll be calling several methods to work with messages you want to exchange with the server. You can stash all this data as part of the document class by adding these declarations in the Attributes section of `irclidoc.h`:

```
public:
    CView *pServerView;

private:
    CString sChannel;
    CIRClientApp *pApp;

// Operations
public:
    CString CIRClientDoc::GetChannelName(void);
```

Having done that, you can go about writing code to handle the channel connections. Because you'll allow the user to specify an initial channel to join in the connection dialog box, you need to capture the channel selection in the constructor so you can use it later. Here's what the constructor will look like when you're done:

```
CIRClientDoc::CIRClientDoc()
{ .
    pApp = (CIRClientApp *)AfxGetApp();
    sChannel="";
    if (!pApp->sInitialChannel.IsEmpty())
        sChannel = pApp->sInitialChannel;
}
```

Get a pointer to the application instance and copy the initial channel selection if it exists. That's it! You'll use that initial channel selection later.

Now override `CDocument`'s default `OnNewDocument()` method to make a connection to the server. Use ClassWizard to add a new method to `CIRClientDoc` for `ID_FILE_NEW`'s `COMMAND`. Listing 9.3 shows the code for the `OnNewDocument()`.

Listing 9.3 Overriding CDocument's Default OnNewDocument ()

```
BOOL CIRClientDoc::OnNewDocument()
{
    if (pApp->fIsConnected)
    {
        CIRCJoinDlg theDialog;
```

(continues)

Listing 9.3 Continued

```
            if (sChannel.IsEmpty())
            {
                if (theDialog.DoModal()==IDOK)
                {
                    if (theDialog.m_NewChannel.IsEmpty())
                        return FALSE;
                    sChannel = theDialog.m_NewChannel;
                }
                else
                    return FALSE;
            }

            if (!CDocument::OnNewDocument())
                    return FALSE;

            if (pApp->pAppSocket->GetStatus()==CONNECTED)
            {
                CString sJoinCmd = "JOIN ";
                sJoinCmd += sChannel + "\n\r";
                pApp->pAppSocket->Send(sJoinCmd);
            }

            {
                char sTitle[128];
                sprintf(&sTitle[0], "%s on %s (%s)",
                ((LPCTSTR)pApp->sNickname),
                        (LPCTSTR)sChannel,
((LPCTSTR)pApp->sServerName));
                SetTitle(&sTitle[0]);
            }
                return TRUE;
        }
        else
            return FALSE;
    }
```

If you've already connected to the server, begin by checking to see if the sChannel is already set; it will be if this is your first new document since connecting to the server, and it's a good idea to honor that initial channel. If this is an ordinary "new channel" action, you'll post the join new channel dialog box you've already coded and created, and then use its data. If the user completes that dialog box with the OK button, have the application check for a nonblank channel name before proceeding.

Most of the actual work is done by the call to CDocument::OnNewDocument(), which actually creates the new document (which in turn creates the new frame window, and so on). If the socket's already connected, then you know that it's OK to send a JOIN command for this channel, so do so. The last thing you need to do is set the title of the new window to display the server, channel, and nickname you're using. If any of these steps fails, FALSE will be returned to the caller, and no document will be created.

Remember when you added a command called Join New Channel to the Commands menu? The code above will work just fine for that same purpose, but you need to tie it in via a message map. Use ClassWizard to add a function to CIRClientApp for the ID_COMMAND_JOIN message; then put this in the middle of your new function:

```
CWinApp::OnFileNew();
```

That's all it takes to make Join New Channel work. In the span of just a few pages, you've created a multiwindow client that lets users join an arbitrary number of channels. Each channel has its own independent window. Pretty amazing, isn't it? Imagine how much work would be required to do this without ClassWizard and MFC—not a pleasant thought, is it?

Keeping Track of Channels. You're going to need a way to keep track of what channels are open. Why? For one reason, you'll want to put each channel's messages directly into the channel's window. When the user closes a channel window, the program should tell the server that you're leaving the channel by sending a PART command. Having a list of channels also provides lots of flexibility for adding more features later.

MFC provides several "dictionary" classes which map a WORD or CString to a pointer, a string, or a CObject pointer. You'll use the CMapStringToOb class to keep a list of the channels and windows, and you'll provide some methods for registering, renaming, and deleting channels. Start by adding a member variable to the public section of IRClient.h:

```
CMapStringToOb *pChanList;
```

Don't forget to allocate a CMapStringToOb object in the application's constructor and to free it in the destructor. Now you need methods to add and remove channels from the list. Throw in one for changing the name of an existing channel, because you'll need that for the change channel command on the following page. Listing 9.4 shows these functions, which you should add to IRClient.cpp. Be sure to add them as public methods in IRClient.h.

Listing 9.4   Methods to Add and Remove Channels from a List

```
void CIRClientApp::AddChanWindow(const CView *pNewView,
                    const CString &sChannel)
{
    pChanList->SetAt((LPCTSTR)sChannel, (CObject *)pNewView);
}

void CIRClientApp::RemoveChanWindow(const CString &sChannel)
{
    BOOL status = pChanList->RemoveKey((LPCTSTR)sChannel);
}

void CIRClientApp::ChangeChanWindow(const CString &sOldChannel,
                    const CString &sNewChannel)
{
    CView *pChild = NULL;
    if (pChanList->Lookup((LPCTSTR)sOldChannel,
            (CObject *&)pChild))
    {
        BOOL status = pChanList->RemoveKey((LPCTSTR)sOldChannel);
        AddChanWindow(pChild, sNewChannel);
    }
}
```

These functions all use methods of CMapStringToOb. To add a new channel
window to the list, you use SetAt(), which accepts a string as the key that
references the object you want to store. SetAt() will replace an object if one
already exists with the specified key. To remove a channel from the list, use
RemoveKey(). The key you supply is used to look up and remove the entry in
the list. Changing the channel name requires that you find the old channel,
save the view object, and create a new channel with the same view but a new
name.

MFC's collection and utility classes, like CMapStringToOb and CObList, can save you a
lot of work when you need to keep a list or array of objects or pointers. As you can
see, they're easy to use.

Now that you have a way to manipulate the channel list, you still have to
register each new channel with the list when you create or delete it. The
problem is that CDocument objects keep pointers to their views, not their windows, so you can't register the window directly. You'll also use a slightly
different scheme for creating the initial channel if the user specified one.

Whatever way you use for registering channels should let you easily re-register windows when the user uses change channel. The solution is to override CIRClientDoc::SetTitle(), because every time you create a channel you also set its title. Here's the code:

```
void CIRClientDoc::SetTitle(LPCTSTR lpszTitle)
{
    pApp->AddChanWindow(pServerView, GetChannelName());
    CDocument::SetTitle(lpszTitle);
}
```

This code registers the server view for each document. In this case, that's the view that should display the messages coming back from the server. How do you know which of the two views in each window is the server view? Well, that's a good question. The code CIRCMDIWnd::OnCreateClient() creates two views, and the server view is always created first. That view isn't guaranteed to be first in the window's view list, though, so you've cheated. How? By overriding CIRClientDoc::OnChangedViewList(), which is called every time you add a view to the document. Check this code out:

```
void CIRClientDoc::OnChangedViewList()
{
    static BOOL fFirst = TRUE;

    if (fFirst)
    {
        POSITION pos = GetFirstViewPosition();
        pServerView = GetNextView(pos);
         fFirst = FALSE;
    }
    CDocument::OnChangedViewList();
}
```

The first time the view list changes—when the server view is added—you store a pointer to it. It couldn't be any simpler.

Back to SetTitle(). Now that you have a pointer to the view stored, you can call AddChanWindow() to register it and then call the default SetTitle() method so the title actually gets set. The GetChannelName() function is an accessor method of CIRClientDoc that just returns the channel's name.

To deregister a channel when you change channels or close a window, you'll override the document class' OnCloseDocument() method. The new version needs to send a PART command to tell the server you're dropping the channel. Then it should call RemoveChanWindow() with the channel's name. Here's what the code looks like:

```
void CIRClientDoc::OnCloseDocument()
{
    CString sPartCmd = "PART ";
    sPartCmd += sChannel + "\n";
    pApp->pAppSocket->Send(sPartCmd);
    pApp->RemoveChanWindow(sChannel);
    CDocument::OnCloseDocument();
}
```

Congratulations! The hardest, and least familiar, part of the application is behind you. Build your application by using Project, Build (or Ctrl+F8) and practice joining and deleting channels for a bit. After that, why not take a short break? You still have plenty more work to do before you're finished.

Changing Nicknames and Channels. You've built all the user interface needed for changing channels and nicknames and for sending private messages, but you haven't tied it into the framework. Now is a good time to do that.

You've seen how to use ClassWizard to link a function or method with a dialog box control or button. It probably won't surprise you to know that MFC gives you a similar way to link a menu command to a function or method. The main difference is that the message you use to do the triggering will have a command name of ID_<menu>_<item>. For example, ID_FILE_NEW corresponds to File, New, and ID_COMMAND_JOIN is the same as Commands, Join Channel.

Linking menus is easy; just bring up ClassWizard, choose the class whose messages you want linked, click the Message Maps tab, and choose the messages from the left-hand list. In fact, the process is identical to the way you link buttons and methods; the only difference is the actual message.

Use ClassWizard to add functions to CIRClientDoc for the ID_COMMAND_CHANGE and ID_COMMAND_MESSAGE commands; name them OnCommandChange and OnCommandMessage. Then add functions to CIRClientApp for ID_COMMAND_JOIN and ID_COMMAND_NICK. Name these functions OnCommandJoin and OnCommandNick. Figure 9.5 shows the ClassWizard message maps property page for the CIRClientApp class.

Why add these functions to different classes? The user can have only one nickname per server connection, and the application class handles the details of the server connection. Because you can have only one nickname and one server connection, it makes sense to put them in the application. Joining a new channel means creating a new document... also a function of the application class. Conversely, change channel operates on an existing channel document, so it belongs in the document. Send private message could go in either, but you've included it in the document class.

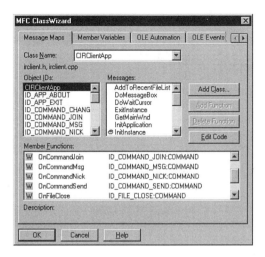

Fig. 9.5
ClassWizard makes
it easy to add
handlers for all
these messages to
the application
class.

A look at each of those functions follows, starting with `OnCommandJoin()`. It's
very simple:

```
void CIRClientApp::OnCommandJoin()
{
        CWinApp::OnFileNew();
}
```

Joining a channel is equivalent to creating a new document, so that's all you
have to do! As you just saw, the document class will handle asking the user
which channel to join. Changing the nickname is only slightly more complicated; the `OnCommandNick` function is shown in Listing 9.5.

Listing 9.5   The OnCommandNick Function

```
void CIRClientApp::SetNickname(CString &newNick)
{
     CString sNickCmd = "NICK ";
     sNickCmd += newNick + "\n\r";
     theApp.pAppSocket->Send(sNickCmd);
     sNickname = newNick;
}

void CIRClientApp::OnCommandNick()
{
     CIRCNicknameDialog theDialog;
     theDialog.m_NewNickname = sNickname;
     if (theDialog.DoModal()==IDOK)
          SetNickname(theDialog.m_NewNickname);
}
```

In what's probably become a very familiar sequence by now, this code brings up a modal dialog box and, if the user selects OK, proceeds to do something. In this case, the user has asked that we change her nickname, so we should change the nickname by calling SetNickname(). SetNickname() sends a NICK command to the server; it also updates the sNickname global to keep track of the change.

OnCommandChange() is a bit trickier. When the user changes channels, the channel window is kept but the user drops out of the original channel and joins a new one instead. Listing 9.6 shows how this function works.

Listing 9.6   The OnCommandChange() Function

```
void CIRClientDoc::OnCommandChange()
{
    CIRCJoinDlg theDialog;
    theDialog.m_NewChannel = sChannel;
    if (theDialog.DoModal()==IDOK)
    {
        CString sJoinCmd = "";
        sJoinCmd = "PART " + sChannel + "\n\r";
        pApp->pAppSocket->Send(sJoinCmd);

        sJoinCmd = "JOIN " + theDialog.m_NewChannel + "\n\r";
        pApp->pAppSocket->Send(sJoinCmd);

        pApp->ChangeChanWindow(sChannel, theDialog.m_NewChannel);

        sChannel = theDialog.m_NewChannel;
        {
            char sTitle[128];
            sprintf(&sTitle[0], "%s on %s (%s)",
            ((LPCTSTR)pApp->sNickname),
                    (LPCTSTR)sChannel,
((LPCTSTR)pApp->sServerName));
            SetTitle(&sTitle[0]);
        }
    }
}
```

After the user confirms the change channel dialog box, all you need to do is send a PART command to tell the server you're leaving the existing channel, followed by a JOIN command to join the new channel. When you're done, you capture the new channel's name and retitle the window. Changing the window's title also retitles its entry in the channel list.

OnCommandMsg() is almost the same, except that it has to get the message text from the dialog box. In a mildly interesting twist, you'll have to preface the message text itself with a colon to tell the server that it may contain whitespace. The actual string you send is `PRIVMSG <recipient> :<message>`, where recipient and message come from the `IDD_MESSAGE` dialog box's controls. Here's what it looks like:

```
void CIRClientApp::OnCommandMsg()
{
    CIRCMessageDialog theDialog;
    if (theDialog.DoModal()==IDOK)
    {
        if (!theDialog.m_Recipient.IsEmpty())
        {
            CString sMsg = "PRIVMSG " + theDialog.m_Recipient;
                sMsg += " :";
            sMsg += theDialog.m_Message;
            sMsg += "\n";
            pAppSocket->Send(sMsg);
        }
    }
}
```

Talking to the Server

What do you still need to do? Since the user interface is complete, the only missing piece of the IRC client is the communications code. This code needs to do a few basic things, which will be discussed in detail shortly:

- Send what the user types to the server

- Send commands generated through the dialog boxes to the server

- Receive messages from other clients

- Receive and interpret status messages from the server

- Report errors that occur during the above steps

Sending What the User Types. Your goal is to let the user type a message, edit it, and then send it by pressing Enter. IRC clients send messages out to the world with the `PRIVMSG` command. The only difference between using `PRIVMSG` to send a message to a channel and using it to send a private message to one user is the argument you give it to specify the recipient.

It would be nice to support cut, copy, and paste in the message pane, too. Because the document uses `CEditView` for its view class, much of this is already done. All you have to do is find a way to know when the user has pressed Enter so you can send the message. The good news is that there's already a way to do just that: by overriding the view's `OnChar()` method. Use ClassWizard to add a new function to handle the view's `WM_CHAR` messages, and then see the code in Listing 9.7.

II

Developing Applications

Listing 9.7   Overriding the View's OnChar() Method

```
void CIRClientView::OnChar(UINT nChar, UINT nRepCnt, UINT nFlags)
{
    if (nChar == 13)
    {
        CString sNewText = "PRIVMSG ";
        CDocument *pDoc = GetDocument();
        CString sEmpty = "";

        sNewText += ((CIRClientDoc *)pDoc)->GetChannelName() + " :";

        ((CWnd *)this)->GetWindowText(sEmpty);
        sNewText += sEmpty;
        sEmpty = "";
        ((CWnd *)this)->SetWindowText(sEmpty);

        sNewText += "\n";
        pTheApp->pAppSocket->Send(sNewText);

    }
    else
        CEditView::OnChar(nChar, nRepCnt, nFlags);
}
```

OnChar() will be called every time the user enters a keystroke in this view. The only key you care about is ASCII CR, or decimal 13. If the user hits any other key, you just call the inherited OnChar(). When the user does hit Enter, you copy the window text, wrap it up as a PRIVMSG command, and clear out the view's text. After adding the required CR to the command, you send it to the server for delivery.

Sending Commands. You've already seen which functions need to send commands, since those functions were covered a few pages ago. To actually send these commands, you're using plain old QSocket::Send(). IRC is a line-oriented protocol, and every command must be a single line of less than 512 characters. The existing Send method works very well under these circumstances, so just use it without modification.

Receiving Messages. As mentioned earlier, every message you get from the server is guaranteed to be a line of no more than 512 characters, and it will always end with a CR/LF pair. These truths make it a great candidate for using QSocket's GetLine() method, which is designed to operate on a socket that gets data line-by-line. Since there's only one socket, you should put it in the application class, but in this case it makes more sense to have the MDI main frame window own the socket function. Why? Well, mostly because that function will cause things to be displayed in various child windows owned or pointed to by the CMainFrame object. Here's how to make the client hear incoming messages:

1. In `mainfrm.h`, define the message for the socket actions by adding this line:

```
#define WM_SOCKET_MESSAGE WM_USER+201
```

2. Add this line to the message map section in `mainfrm.h`, just before the line that says `DECLARE_MESSAGE_MAP()`:

```
afx_msg LONG CMainFrame::OnSocket(WPARAM amount, LPARAM
    buffer);
```

3. Link the message to the function by adding an entry in the `AFX_MSG_MAP` section of `mainfrm.cpp`:

```
ON_MESSAGE(WM_SOCKET_MESSAGE, OnSocket)
```

4. Add a call to `SetReceiveTarget()` so that incoming socket events will cause `QSocket` to send the application a message. Put it in `CIRClientApp::OnFileNew()`, right after the brace following the call to `pAppSocket->Connect()`:

```
pAppSocket->SetReceiveTarget(pMainFrame, WM_SOCKET_MESSAGE);
```

Socket events will now trigger the socket handler, which will parcel out replies, as you'll see below. Listing 9.8 shows the `OnSocket()` method. You'll probably find that it looks familiar, with good reason—it's very similar to the ones you used for Finger and Whois.

Listing 9.8 The OnSocket() Method

```
afx_msg LONG CMainFrame::OnSocket(WPARAM amount, LPARAM buffer)
{
    char *p = (char *)buffer;

    if ((int)amount > 0)
    {
        p[amount] = '\0';
        AddToReceive(p, amount);
        ParseResponse();
    }
    else
    {
        // if amount < 0 it is a receive command
        switch ( (SocketReceiveCmd)amount )
        {
            case SocketStatusChanged:
                switch (pApp->pAppSocket->GetStatus())
                {
                    case CONNECTED:
                    {
```

(continues)

Listing 9.8 Continued

```
                                        CString tempCmd = "";
                                        char hostname[128];
                                        int s = 0;

                                        pApp->SetNickname(pApp->sNickname);

                                        tempCmd = "USER pcuser ";
                                        s=gethostname (&hostname[0], 128);
                                        tempCmd += hostname;
                                        tempCmd += " ignore :BIAVC User\n\r";
                                        pApp->pAppSocket->Send(tempCmd);

                                        tempCmd = "JOIN " + pApp->
                                          ⮕sInitialChannel + "\n\r";
                                        pApp->pAppSocket->Send(tempCmd);
                                        pApp->sInitialChannel = "";
                                        break;
                                }

                        case DISCONNECTED:
                                break;

                        default:
                                // all other status states represent
                                // an error
                                break;
                        }
                        break;
                }
        }
        return 0;
}
```

If the message parameter indicates that a socket event has occurred, check to see whether the socket has completed its connection process. If it has, you can register the connection by sending NICK and USER commands, and then join the specified initial channel, if any.

If data has arrived, you'll call CMainFrame::AddToReceive() to put it into the line-oriented buffer, followed by a call to ParseResponse() to actually process what comes back. You might be wondering why you're duplicating AddToReceive() instead of just calling QSocket::GetLine(). You want to be as asynchronous as possible, and short of messy solutions involving setting a timer in CMainFrame and then having it call GetLine() and ParseResponse() if data's arrived, duplicating the code so it can execute in parallel is the best solution.

Displaying Messages. All kinds of messages will arrive at the client. Some will be comments sent by other users, while others will be status or error messages from the server. These messages will indicate things like `PaulR has joined channel #hornet`, or `BillyBob has changed his nickname to William`. Of course, these are paraphrases; the server will actually say things like:

```
:BillyBob!bob@netcom.com NICK :William
```

It's up to you to parse these messages and figure out how to display them. The first step is to create the display methods, because they're pretty simple. Some messages, like the server's message of the day, should go in the active window so the user can see them immediately. Others, like user messages, belong to a particular channel and should appear only in the channel's window. You can do both—the code for `PutInActive()` and `PutInChanWindow()` is shown in Listing 9.9.

Listing 9.9   Code for PutInActive() and PutInChanWindow()

```cpp
void CMainFrame::PutInChanWindow(const CString &sChannel,
                                 CString &sMessage)
{
    char nl = '\n';
    CIRClientView *pChild = NULL;
    CString tempR = sMessage;
    if (tempR.Find(nl) == -1)
        tempR += "\r\n";

    if (pApp->pChanList->Lookup((LPCTSTR)sChannel, (CObject *&)pChild))
    {
        int tLen = ((CWnd *)pChild)->GetWindowTextLength();
        ((CEdit *)pChild)->SetSel(tLen, tLen);
         ((CEdit *)pChild)->ReplaceSel(tempR);
    }
}


void CMainFrame::PutInActive(CString &response)
{
    char nl = '\n';
    CIRCMDIWnd *pChild = NULL;
    CString tempR = response;
    if (tempR.Find(nl) == -1)
        tempR += "\r\n";

    pChild = (CIRCMDIWnd *)MDIGetActive();
    int tLen = ((CWnd *)pChild)->GetWindowTextLength();
    ((CEdit *)pChild)->SetSel(tLen, tLen);
    ((CEdit *)pChild->pServerView)->ReplaceSel(tempR);
}
```

These two functions are very similar; the primary difference is in how they determine which view to put text into. Both start by adding a linefeed to the outgoing message if it needs one. PutInChanWindow() uses the channel list to get a pointer to its target view, while PutInActive() uses MDIGetActive() to get its pointer. In either case, you force the text to the end of the view by getting the current length of the view's text, setting the selection range to be exactly that length and then calling ReplaceSel() to actually append the text.

 Remember the get length, set selection, ReplaceSel() trick, because it's the only way to append text to an edit control, CEditView, or descendant.

Some messages consist of a three-digit status code, plus parameters that supply useful data. You can ignore some messages because they don't pertain to you, and you can ignore others because the application won't be able to handle them. The code should either display messages in a useful format or silently ignore them, whichever is most appropriate.

Parsing Messages. You may be wondering why I told you how to display messages before talking about how to parse and recognize different kinds of messages. The real reason is that many people find themselves less interested in the parser than in other things. The parser, which is rather sizable, looks at the lines in the CMainFrame's ReceiveLines buffer and picks each one apart, looking for nuggets of data. By itself, the parser code takes up about 300 lines of code, mostly for tokenizing and other kinds of string manipulation. If you're interested in how it works, consult the RFC for a complete description of the command format. The parser code is included on the CD also, so we won't take up space for it here.

Finishing Touches

A few tasks remain to be done. You still need to save chat sessions into text files, and since the application doesn't support every IRC command defined in the protocol, you really should give the user a way to send arbitrary commands.

Saving Files. To save files, you need to implement the Serialize() method of the document class. Normally, the Serialize() method would have to extract data from the view and document objects and write it out, either as binary data or text. In this case, there is a plain CEditView, which holds only text. How can you get the text out into a file on disk?

Once again, MFC rescues you from drudgery! Since the view is a plain CEditView, you can use CEditView::SerializeRaw() to dump the text.

`SerializeRaw()` differs from the standard `CView::Serialize()`, which normally writes object reference information out into the stream. The only thing `SerializeRaw()` writes out is the actual text. Here's what the code looks like when it's done:

```
void CIRClientDoc::Serialize(CArchive& ar)
{
    if (ar.IsStoring())
        ((CEditView *)pServerView)->SerializeRaw(ar);
}
```

Sending Arbitrary Commands. The IRC protocol offers so many commands that it's difficult to pack them all into one program, much less to have a clear and useful user interface when you do that. To help solve that problem, add a command to the client to enable users to send any arbitrary command string to the IRC server. This is a useful stopgap measure that keeps users happy without requiring you to add dozens of buttons, dialog boxes, and gadgets to support rarely used or obscure IRC commands.

To do this, create a new dialog box with ID `IDC_CMD_DIALOG`; add one text field called `IDC_COMMAND`, plus the usual OK and Cancel buttons. Name the resulting class `CIRCSendCmdDialog` and give it a `CString` member variable named `m_Cmd`. Then use the menu editor in AppStudio to add a new menu item to the Commands menu; call it "Send Command" (or something similar) and give it command ID `ID_COMMAND_SEND`. Finally, use the ClassWizard to tie `ID_COMMAND_SEND` to `CIRClientApp`'s `OnCommandSend()` method. Here it is:

```
void CIRClientApp::OnCommandSend()
{
    CIRCSendCmdDialog theDialog;
    if (theDialog.DoModal()==IDOK)
    {
        if (!theDialog.m_Cmd.IsEmpty())
            pAppSocket->Send(theDialog.m_Cmd);
    }
}
```

Using the IRC Client

To use the client, just run it and choose File, Connect To Server; you can also press Ctrl+N. When the Connect To Server dialog box appears, choose a server, a port (the dialog box fills in a default for you), a nickname, and a starting channel. Remember that nicknames are limited to nine characters or fewer, and that channel names usually start with #.

You'll see a blank window for a short time, until the server on the other end accepts your connection registration. After that's done, you'll start seeing messages appear in the upper pane of your window. Each message will start with the nickname of the sender, so that the following represents three messages, each from a different user:

Doc: This new IRC client is pretty neat!

Dopey: Yeah, I don't like the client I'm using now.

Sneezy: Which one is it?

You can change the channel you're on by using <u>C</u>ommands, <u>C</u>hange Channel and entering the channel you want to change to. You can also join additional channels, with each appearing in its own window, with the <u>C</u>ommands, <u>J</u>oin New Channel command. To leave a channel, either change to another one or close the channel's window.

You can change your nickname at any time with <u>C</u>ommands, Set <u>N</u>ickname, and you can send private messages to other users with <u>C</u>ommands, Send <u>M</u>essage. Finally, if you know what you're doing, use <u>C</u>ommands, Send Co<u>m</u>mand to send any legal IRC command to the server.

Because you used MFC, the Edit and Window menus behave just like they should, and you can cut, copy, and paste to your heart's content. Of course, the File menu works too. Save transcripts of your conversations by using <u>F</u>ile, <u>S</u>ave or <u>F</u>ile, Save <u>A</u>s. In short, you've written a full-fledged Windows application. Good job!

Extending the Client

If you read over the 65-page RFC that covers IRC, or if you look at a well-implemented shareware or commercial IRC client, you'll see that the IRC protocol supports a lot of options and features that this client doesn't. The good news is that the minimalist approach used here gives you a framework to build on, so you can add more features as you wish.

Easy Additions

This client has an impressive amount of functionality, but there are still some rough edges and missing features. All of the improvements discussed below should be easy to add and will help make the program more polished.

- The application doesn't do much error handling or input validation. This is partly because MFC does so much. However, you certainly can add more. The existing client doesn't handle sudden disconnections from the server very well, but it should. IRC servers get so busy that it's not uncommon for a user to get accidentally disconnected in the middle of a chat.

■ The window title for each child window contains the server name, the channel name, and your nickname. When you change your nickname, the window's title doesn't change to reflect this fact. It would be nice if it did.

■ Right now, there's no way for users of the client to see a list of active channels. The IRC protocol specifies that the LIST command will return a list of channels, each on its own line. You might try adding support for this command to the parser. Here's a hint: LIST works very much like the RPL_NAMREPLY handler that's already in the parser.

■ One neat feature of some IRC clients is a way to set an Away message. People who send you messages while your Away flag is set to get a message like Paul just stepped over to the fridge… be right back! instead of dead air. The RFC has complete documentation for the AWAY command if you're interested.

A Bit More Challenging

If you think the above suggestions are rather easy, that's a good sign: it means you've gained a good understanding of how MFC and the IRC protocol work. For more of a challenge, try these enhancements:

■ Enable and disable menu items when appropriate. For example, after the user has connected to a server, Connect To Server should be disabled until he or she disconnects again. Check out the CCmdUI object and the ON_COMMAND_UI message in the MFC documentation.

■ Add a dialog box to let a user change his or her MODE setting. While you're at it, wouldn't it be nice to support the operator privileges that IRC users can have? The MODE command has several options that work in various combinations; you'll probably need to refer to the RFC to complete this task.

■ It won't take long before you find a favorite IRC server and channel. It would be nice to be able to jump to a server or channel that you visit often. Why not modify the Connect To Server and Join Channel dialog boxes to use CComboBoxes instead of CEdit controls? You may also want to store a list of servers and channels in a configuration file so that users can edit their list of favorites.

Developing Applications

■ Add an MFC `CStatusBar` to the application. In addition to the usual panes (such as the ones that display whether Caps Lock and Num Lock are enabled), try adding a clock (so you can see how many hours you've whiled away on IRC!) or a counter of the total number of messages you've sent. It would also be nice to provide status messages to inform the user what's going on at certain times—for instance, when the application's waiting for the server to answer.

For the Adventurous Only

As with the HTTP server, there are some interesting challenges tucked away in the protocol definition, just waiting to help you to *carpe cryptem* (seize the code). The most popular UNIX IRC client, IRC-II, implements many of these features—hence its popularity. Bringing these features to the Windows world would be a worthy accomplishment indeed.

■ Add printing support. MFC offers quite a bit of printing support built into the framework, but you'll need to implement a way to paginate the text and format it in a pleasing way.

■ Support the client-to-client protocol (`ctcp`) and the direct client chat (`dcc`) protocol. These two protocols allow clients to talk directly to one another without passing traffic through a server.

■ IRC-II has one particularly attractive feature: it can fall back from one server to another. If the server you're connected to goes down, IRC-II is smart enough to connect you to another server and join you to your original channel. Because IRC servers often fall prey to overloading, this would be a welcome capability.

From Here...

This chapter introduced you to some high-powered features of MFC, and you spent quite a bit of time customizing the program to handle the intricacies of the IRC protocol. In the next chapter, you'll learn how to write a Gopher client that can navigate through hierarchies and webs of information.

Chapter 10

Building an Internet Gopher Application

What Is a Gopher?

Similar to the way its furry eponymous cousin burrows through your garden, Gopher applications burrow through the network looking for information. Gopher applications connect to servers and ask for lists of documents. Servers provide lists of document titles and information about how to retrieve them. Using the latter information, Gopher applications retrieve documents on requested subjects.

In this chapter, you learn the following:

- How the Gopher protocol operates

- How to use MFC to create an application that handles multiple document types

- How to build and use the Gopher application included on the CD-ROM

In this chapter, first you'll view a simple Gopher session from a user's perspective. Then the discussion will take you back for a look at the Gopher protocol from the client server perspective, to see what is happening "under the covers."

A user will normally start a Gopher client with the intention of connecting to a Gopher server. This is done by typing a command line (for example, `gopher gopher.micro.umn.edu`) or by choosing from a list of well-known Gopher servers. Once the user connects to the server, a list appears of the different topics available from that server. The user selects one of the items from the list and then sees either a new list to choose from or a document to look over. Because all Gopher sites are interconnected, the Gopher may actually retrieve a file from another Gopher server, but to the user it appears that all files are available from the original Gopher server. When done searching for information or looking at lists, the user quits the Gopher client. Gopher pages are text-based. Here's a sample one:

```
Internet Gopher Information Client v2.1.1
   Home Gopher server: tc.umn.edu

 —> 1.  Search U of MN Directory <?>
      2.  University of Minnesota, US
      3.  Academic Retirees/
      4.  Alumni Association/
      5.  Application Services/
      6.  Validation Utilities and Services/ <??>
      7.  Student E-mail Account Initiation <??>
      8.  Duluth Campus Gopher Server/
      9.  Morris Campus Gopher Server/
     10.  Twin Cities Campus Gopher Server/
     11.  Crookston Campus/
     12.  Duluth Campus/
     13.  Morris Campus/
     14.  Other Campuses and Stations/
     15.  Twin Cities Campus/

 Press ? for Help, q to QuitPage: 1/1
```

This text-based interface is the most obvious difference between Gopher and the World Wide Web, although there are text-based Web browsers on the Internet. The most important difference between the two protocols is one of authority. Administrators control Gopher pages. A page is either information or a list of links. Information and links are not mixed on the same page as they are on the Web. On the Web, if a user has added links to a page, anyone can follow them, but with Gopher, links are added only to pages of links, and only administrators can add them. This administrative control makes Gopher a more organized protocol than the Web, and often a more useful one.

How Does the Gopher Protocol Work?

The Gopher protocol at its roots is very simple. RFC 1438, which is available in the \RFC folder on the CD accompanying this book, describes it fully. It basically consists of a client sending a request to a server and the server returning the information requested. The connection between the client and server is limited to that one transaction. The connection does not stay around for more requests from the client. Upon receiving a request from a client, the server will return either a directory list or an actual document.

A directory list consists of links to other directory lists or documents. A document can be anything from a simple line of text to a full binary file or anything the users and developers of Gopher have come up with. Since Gopher is extendible, there is plenty of room for it to grow as new technologies become available.

When a user makes a selection from the initial list, the client will open a connection. The host and port used for the connection are actually specified on the list item that the user selected. Sometimes the connection is to the host that holds the list of links; other times it's to another host. The Gopher protocol reestablishes the connection every time. Once that connection is established, the client will send the selector string followed by a CRLF to the server. The server then returns the list or document associated with that selector in the same manner that the first list was returned. This process continues until the user quits the Gopher application.

Connecting to the Server

When a user first chooses to open a connection to a Gopher server, the local client establishes a TCP connection to a Gopher server on TCP port 70. The server accepts the connection but does not acknowledge it in any way. The client then sends a forward slash (/) as the selector, followed by a CRLF, telling the host to list what it has available. The server then sends a series of lines that each end with a CRLF. These lines are the first list from the server that the user sees. Once these lines have been transmitted, the server sends a period on a line by itself followed by a CRLF. The lone period marks the end of the transmission. The server then terminates the connection and goes back to waiting for another connection.

Parsing the Document Listing Returned by the Server

Before going any further, it's important to understand the lines that the server returns. Each line contains five fields. The first field is a single character indicating what the item is (for example, a directory, a document, or a file). A complete list of the more common types of items is given below. Client applications often place little indicators (such as icons, words, or letters) next to the lines they display telling the user telling what the line represents. The second field starts in the second column and contains the text that the user should actually see on the screen. This is the only field that should be displayed to the user. The third field is separated from the second by a tab and contains a unique selector for the particular item. The server will recognize this selector and return the appropriate item. A tab also separates the third field from the fourth, which contains the host where the item is located. Likewise, a tab separates the fourth field from the fifth and final field, which contains the port number on the host that the client should connect to in order to retrieve the item. The last two fields allow a server to provide access to items not physically stored on itself.

A service listing contains the following information:

- Type of service: 0 for file, 1 for directory, or 7 for search (the most commonly used)

- Title of service

- Service selector string

- Server location used to retrieve the service

- Port number

Service listings have their components separated by a tab and are terminated with a CRLF.

If the application is returned a type of document that your client does not understand (check the first character of the line), it should either not show that line to the user, or display it as an unknown type and explain that accessing that item could cause unpredictable results.

Here are some of the more common document types defined for Gopher. To keep things simple, the application explained in this chapter will provide support for documents of type 0 and 1.

0 - A file

1 - A directory listing

2 - A CSO phone-book server

3 - Error

4 - A BinHexed Macintosh file

5 - A DOS binary archive of some kind

6 - A UNIX unencoded file

7 - An Index-Search server

8 - Pointer to a text-based Telnet session

9 - A binary file

g - A GIF format graphics file

I - Some kind of image file

The characters from 0 to Z are reserved for future document types. If you want to implement a server with a unique document type, be sure not to use any of these reserved characters.

Retrieving Services from the Host

When burrowing for information using Gopher, the user typically makes use of three basic types of requests: directory listing, document, or information search.

Sending a Request to Get the Contents of a Directory

To request the contents of a directory, the client sends the selector string for the directory specified in the services listing. Upon receiving a directory request, the Gopher server provides a listing of services in the specified directory in the same format as the initial list: CRLF-separated entries terminated by a line containing a period.

Requesting the contents of a directory is different from actually changing the current directory on a host. In the world of Gopher, the client keeps track of this type of information when it's required to do so by the interface design.

Sending a Request for a Document or File

To request a document, the client sends the selector string for the document to the specified server at the specified port. The server responds by sending the specified document. As with service listings, documents are terminated by a line containing only a period.

Sending a Request for a Search Service

An Index-Search server is a special server that has the ability to search various Gopher documents for text matching a supplied text string. To request a list of documents or files containing specific text strings, the client sends the selector string for a search service (entries in the service listing preceded with 7), a tab, and the search string.

Like most PC-based database searching utilities, spaces between words in search strings are almost always treated as AND conditions—that is, all documents returned by the server contain all the words in the search strings.

Developing a Gopher Application

As you'll see, developing a Gopher application is quite easy using Visual C++ and MFC. Before jumping into the implementation details though, it's a good idea to know about the design elements.

Design

At a minimum, the Gopher application should be able to display Gopher menu listings and simple text documents. Each menu listing should appear in a list box within a window of its own. When the information listing appears, the user should be able to double-click documents and additional sublistings to transfer and view them. Also, since the user should be able to view several documents and menus at the same time, the application should use a Multiple-Document Interface, or MDI.

NOTE   The list of links and documents on a Gopher page is commonly called a *menu*. Don't confuse it with a Windows menu like the one that appears when you choose <u>F</u>ile or <u>E</u>dit.

MDI applications can have several documents open at once. For example, in Microsoft Word you can have several .DOC files open at the same time, and in Microsoft Excel you can have several .XLS files open at once. This makes it easy to switch back and forth between documents. Notepad, which comes with Windows, is a Single Document Interface, or SDI, application: when you open a second file, the first is automatically closed. Luckily AppWizard and MFC make creating and coding an MDI application simple and straightforward, as you'll see.

Gopher users typically want to open connections directly to a specific server, so the application should provide a dialog box that enables them to specify the host system, port, selector, and title. The application will use the title as the window title above documents and Gopher listings.

When viewing documents, the user should be able to copy and scroll the text. Fortunately, MFC provides a convenient document view class called CEditView that handles all of this.

Since the application will use two different document types, you might think that adding support for multiple types will be your biggest challenge. Actually, the process is quite simple—you can use the MFC document template class to handle the details.

With the basic Gopher application design in mind, it's time to create the initial Gopher framework using AppWizard.

AppWizard

To start AppWizard, choose File, New Project within Visual C++. Enter Gopher as the project name and click Create. In the subsequent AppWizard menus, choose Multi-Document, no database support, no OLE support, no Toolbar, no Status bar, and no Print support. With Visual C++ versions 2.1 and later, AppWizard can add Windows Sockets support. Otherwise, you can add socket support manually, as described in Chapter 3, "Windows Sockets (WINSOCK.DLL)." Finally, make CGopherView derive from CFormView, and create the project. AppWizard opens the project file in Visual C++.

For step-by-step examples and illustrations using AppWizard, see Chapter 5, "Building an Internet Finger Application."

Once you have created the initial framework for the Gopher application, you can begin to tailor it and add dialog boxes, accelerators, and string table entries in AppStudio.

AppStudio

Double-click the GOPHER.RC resource file from within the project window to start AppStudio. Within AppStudio, you'll create the dialog box and form elements, modify the menu, and add necessary string table entries.

Gopher Menu

Click MENU under GOPHER.RC and you'll see that AppWizard has created two menus for you, one called IDR_MAINFRAME and one called IDR_GOPHERTYPE. The first is used when no files are open and the second is used when a Gopher document is open. Work on IDR_GOPHERTYPE first—double-click it to open it. Since Gopher references remote files and directories, the application doesn't need the File Open, File Save, and File Save As menu selections. Remove them by clicking once on the item to select it and then pressing Delete. The File menu should contain only New, Close, and Exit. Use the Properties box to rename the New item Open Gopher Connection.... Do not change the resource ID. The menu should resemble figure 10.1 at this point.

II

Developing Applications

Fig. 10.1

The File menu for the Gopher application.

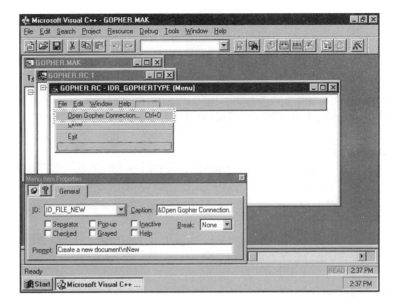

The Edit, Window and Help menus should be fine as provided by AppWizard, so there's no need to change them. Close IDR_GOPHERTYPE and open IDR_MAINFRAME. Make the same changes to it as you did to IDR_GOPHERTYPE. Notice that it doesn't have a File, Close item—you cannot close a file if there isn't one open.

Dialog Boxes

This Gopher application needs three dialog box elements. Two of them are already provided by AppWizard, namely, the About box and a simple Gopher view. Feel free to modify the About box with more pertinent information about yourself or the application, including the version number and copyright information.

In the Gopher view dialog box, change the ID to IDD_GOPHER_LIST, remove all the controls provided by AppWizard, and add a single list box control. Set the ID of the listbox to IDC_LISTBOX and give it the caption of Gopher List. You'll build your Gopher listing view around this control later.

Create a third dialog box with the ID of IDD_GOPHER_DIALOG. This dialog box will be used to prompt the user for a new Gopher server connection. Since this dialog box will be displayed as modal, select the modal frame.

In the dialog box, create four Edit boxes and two buttons. Each edit box will need a piece of static text above it that I'll call its label, and a resource ID that I'll just call ID. Each button will have a resource ID and a caption. Add these controls:

Control	Resource ID	Label
Edit box	IDC_HOST	Host or Address
Edit box	IDC_SELECTOR	Selector
Edit box	IDC_PORT	Port
Edit box	IDC_TITLE	Gopher Title
Button	IDOK	OK
Button	IDCANCEL	Cancel

Define the OK button as the default button, so that pressing Return is the same as clicking OK. Finally, define the caption for the dialog box as Open Gopher Connection. The completed dialog box should resemble figure 10.2.

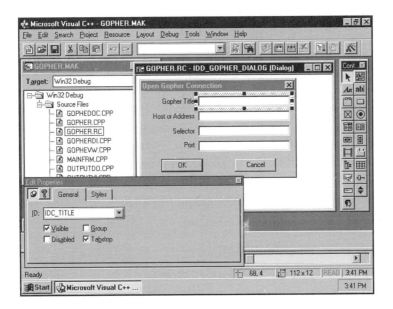

Fig. 10.2

The dialog box for opening a Gopher connection.

Filling in the Code

Once you have created the initial framework and added the necessary resources, you use ClassWizard to connect the dialog boxes and controls to
code. While still in AppStudio, start up ClassWizard to create a CGopherDialog
class for this dialog box. Connect the controls to member variables, as
follows:

```
Cstring    m_selector;     //Attached to the IDC_SELECTOR control
Cstring    m_host; //Attached to the IDC_HOST control
UINT       m_port; //Attached to the IDC_PORT control
Cstring    m_title;        //Attached to the IDC_TITLE control
```

In Chapter 6, "Building an Internet Whois Application," you used default
values kept in the string table. There are default values that make sense in
this application, too. The Gopher Home page at the University of Minnesota
is a sensible default page to open. Add entries to the string table for its selector and title:

```
IDS_GOPHER_SERVER     "gopher.micro.umn.edu"
IDS_GOPHER_TITLE      "Gopher Home"
```

As before, use LoadString to fill member variables from the string table. Here's
the constructor for CGopherDialog:

```
CGopherDialog::CGopherDialog(CWnd* pParent /*=NULL*/)
    : CDialog(CGopherDialog::IDD, pParent)
{
    m_host.LoadString(IDS_GOPHER_SERVER);
    m_title.LoadString(IDS_GOPHER_TITLE);
    //{{AFX_DATA_INIT(CGopherDialog)
    m_selector = _T("/");
    m_port = 70;
    //}}AFX_DATA_INIT
}
```

The default selector is just a /, meaning the root directory, and the default
port is 70.

To set the keyboard focus on the Title control, override OnInitDialog like this:

```
BOOL CGopherDialog::OnInitDialog()
{
    CDialog::OnInitDialog();

    GetDlgItem(IDC_TITLE)->SetFocus();

    return FALSE;       // return TRUE unless you set the focus
                        // to a control
                        // EXCEPTION: OCX Property Pages
                        // should return FALSE
}
```

Two Types of Documents

Unlike the other applications you developed earlier, this Gopher application uses two kinds of documents: the Gopher menu listing and an actual text document. In order to implement support for two document types, and their related views, use *document templates*. Add these lines to GOPHER.H:

```
CMultiDocTemplate* pMenuTemplate;
CMultiDocTemplate* pDocTemplate;
```

In CGopherApp::InitInstance() in GOPHER.CPP, define the two document templates using the CMultiDocTemplate constructor, like this:

```
pMenuTemplate = new CMultiDocTemplate(
    IDR_GOPHERMENU,
    RUNTIME_CLASS(CGopherDoc),
    RUNTIME_CLASS(CMDIChildWnd),
    RUNTIME_CLASS(CGopherView));
AddDocTemplate(pMenuTemplate);

pDocTemplate = new CMultiDocTemplate(
    IDR_GOPHERDOCUMENT,
    RUNTIME_CLASS(COutputDoc),
    RUNTIME_CLASS(CMDIChildWnd),
    RUNTIME_CLASS(COutputView));
AddDocTemplate(pDocTemplate);
```

The pMenuTemplate template holds the relationship of a Gopher menu listing, the frame window, and the associated listbox view. Similarly, the pDocTemplate template is used for the text output document.

Finally, use AppStudio to add entries to the string table. Use Edit, Copy and Edit, Paste to duplicate one of the existing entries, and edit it. The resource IDs and captions to add are:

```
IDR_GOPHERMENU        "\nGopher Menu\nGopher Menu\n\n\
    ➥nGopher.Menu\nGopher Menu"
IDR_GOPHERDOCUMENT    "\nGopher Document\nGopher Document\n\n\
    ➥nGopher.Document\nGopher Document"
```

These resource IDs appeared in the calls to CMultiDocTemplate above.

Now you need to handle menu events. The only real menu item at the moment is Open Gopher Connection... which is ID_FILE_NEW on all the menus. Use ClassWizard to arrange for CGopherApp to catch this message, and name the function NewGopherMenu. The code for that function looks like this:

```
void CGopherApp::NewGopherMenu()
{
    pMenuTemplate->OpenDocumentFile(NULL);
}
```

II

Developing Applications

This uses the template to determine the document and open an empty Gopher menu document. Later, you'll write some other simple functions that call OpenDocumentFile() with a parameter: the Gopher selector, host, and port that describe the location of a menu or Gopher document. The template will end up calling the document's OnOpenDocument() method and passing the parameter along.

Before you leave GOPHER.CPP, add a call in the InitInstance method to call NewGopherMenu. Now, when the user starts the application, the Open Gopher Connection dialog box will display, and the user won't have to select the menu entry or type Ctrl-O first. Just add this line to the end of InitInstance():

```
NewGopherMenu();
```

By now the application should be ready to compile and build. When you run it, you should see something like figure 10.3, with the default values filled in. Nothing will happen if you press OK, so press Cancel and close it down for now.

Fig. 10.3
The Gopher application's Open Gopher Connection dialog box.

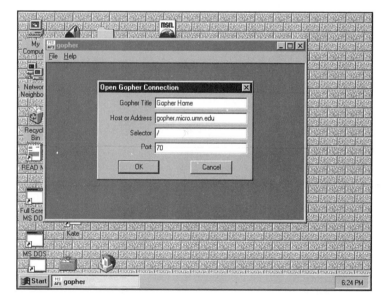

CGopherDoc
Now to make something happen. The CGopherDoc class defines Gopher menu listings. The member variables are Host, Selector, Title, and Port. The Host variable is the fully qualified domain name of a Gopher host, such as

gopher.intergraph.com. The Port variable is the port where the remote
Gopher server is available. Usually the Port is 70, but some Gopher servers are
established on other ports. The Selector is the location of the document on
the Gopher server, and finally the Title is the name of the Gopher document.
In the Gopher menu listing, you'll display the titles, and use them as the
name of the window.

The first step is to write OnOpenDocument() method, which is called whenever a
new menu listing is opened. You are overriding the OnOpenDocument method
from CDocument, which takes a char*, a pointer to a null-terminated string.
Following Microsoft's naming convention, call the parameter lpszSelector.
This defines the Gopher selector, as it appears in a menu listing from the
server. If lpszSelector is NULL, then OnOpenDocument should display the
Open Gopher Connection dialog box and then, if the user clicks OK, transfer
the dialog box values to the member variables. If lpszSelector is not NULL,
then it must be parsed into the four member variables. The C string manipulation function strtok provides a convenient way to do this.
OnOpenDocument ends up looking like this:

```
BOOL CGopherDoc::OnOpenDocument(LPCTSTR lpszSelector)
{
    char *s = (char *)lpszSelector;
    if ( s == NULL )
    {
        CGopherDialog theDialog;
        if (theDialog.DoModal()==IDOK)
        {
            if (theDialog.m_host.IsEmpty())
                return FALSE;
            Host = theDialog.m_host;
            Selector = theDialog.m_selector;
            Port = theDialog.m_port;
            Title = theDialog.m_title;
        }
        else
            return FALSE;
    }
    else
    {
        char    type = *s;                  // type of gopher item
        Title = strtok(&s[1], "\t");        // title
        Selector = strtok(NULL, "\t");      // selector
        Host = strtok(NULL, "\t");          // host
        Port = atoi(strtok(NULL, "\t"));    // port number
    }
    return TRUE;
}
```

Now, when the user clicks Open Gopher Connection, the dialog box will display and the member variables of `CGopherDoc` will be set to the values entered in the box. When the user wants to follow a link, the code will be already in place to parse the selector into those four variables. But how will the user follow a link?

CGopherView: Displaying Gopher Menus

The `CGopherView` class is perhaps the most complex of all the Gopher classes. It is responsible for handling the fetch and display of the Gopher menu listing, as well as the user selections. Since it actually connects to other machines, it is going to need a socket. Add to `GOPHEVW.H`:

```
private:
    QSocket* pSocket;
```

Remember to set this pointer to `NULL` in the `CGopherView` constructor and to delete it in the destructor.

Next, add some entries to the `CGopherView` message map:

```
BEGIN_MESSAGE_MAP(CGopherView, CFormView)
    //{{AFX_MSG_MAP(CGopherView)
    ON_WM_SIZE()
    ON_WM_CLOSE()
    ON_LBN_DBLCLK(IDC_LISTBOX, OnDblclkListbox)
    //}}AFX_MSG_MAP
    ON_MESSAGE(GET_GOPHER_MENU, ShowGopherMenu)
END_MESSAGE_MAP()
```

The `ON_WM_SIZE` entry tells MFC that the application is interested in receiving notification when the window size changes. If that occurs, you want to resize the listbox accordingly. The `ON_WM_CLOSE` entry indicates that you want to know when the view is closed, so you can perform some cleanup. When a user double-clicks an item in the listbox, the `ON_LBN_DBLCLK` message occurs. Here you'll call your own `OnDblclkListbox` to process the request and open a new Gopher document. Finally, you define your own message called `GET_GOPHER_MENU`. This message is posted during the initial update of the view. If the application posts the message instead of making a direct call, the regular queue of events can take place first, and you can return from the posting routine without waiting for the menu items to come back over the socket.

When the Gopher menu view is first opened, the application framework calls the `OnInitialUpdate` method to get things rolling. It is in this method that you will use the four member variables of the document to fill the view.

Here's the code:

```
void CGopherView::OnInitialUpdate()
{
    CGopherDoc* doc = GetDocument();

    doc->SetTitle(doc->Title);

    if (doc->Host != "")
    {
        m_listbox.ResetContent;
        delete pSocket;
        pSocket = new QSocket();
        if (!pSocket->Connect(doc->Host, doc->Port))
        {
            AfxMessageBox("Host is unreachable.");
            delete pSocket;
            pSocket = 0;
        }
        else
        {
            PostMessage(GET_GOPHER_MENU, 0, 0);
        }
    }
    else
    {
        AfxMessageBox("Please fill in host name.");
    }

    // Initially, resize the parent window to fit the listbox
    ResizeParentToFit(FALSE);

    CFormView::OnInitialUpdate();
}
```

To give your view a meaningful title, use SetTitle() to change the title of the window to the title of the Gopher menu.

If Host is not empty, clear the listbox that will contain the menu listing, create a new pSocket object, and connect the socket to the Gopher host at the specific port. If all goes okay, queue a GET_GOPHER_MENU event to yourself. This enables the view to continue filling while the socket connection completes. If Host is empty, or if the Connect() fails immediately, display an error message.

Toward the end of the method, use ResizeParentToFit()to shrink the parent MDI window to the size of the listbox. Call CFormView::OnInitialUpdate(), to let the framework finish displaying the view.

II

Developing Applications

The ShowGopherMenu() method appears in response to the GET_GOPHER_MENU message that was posted in OnInitialUpdate(). ShowGopherMenu is responsible for sending the Gopher selector to the host and processing the response. It looks like this:

```
LRESULT CGopherView::ShowGopherMenu(WPARAM wParam, LPARAM lParam)
{
    // Wait until we're connected
    for (;;)
    {
        SocketStatus status = pSocket->GetStatus();
        if (status == CONNECTED)
            break;
        else if (status != CONNECTING)
        {
            AfxMessageBox("Error making connection.");
            return NULL;
        }
        else
        {
            // Not connected yet, so process events to allow the
            // socket events to occur
            for(;;)
            {
                MSG msg;
                if (PeekMessage(&msg, NULL, 0, 0, PM_REMOVE))
                {
                    TranslateMessage(&msg);
                    DispatchMessage(&msg);
                }
                else
                    break;
            }
        }
    }

    // Send the Whois request
    pSocket->Send(GetDocument()->Selector + "\r\n");

    // Get the server responses, line by line, and add them
    // to our Gopher menu list box.
    for (;;)
    {
        CString s = pSocket->GetLine();
        if ( s.IsEmpty() )      // Empty string indicates
                                // close of connection
            break;
        if (s[0] == '.' && s[1] == '\r')
            continue;

        // Get title to appear in the menu and assign
        // the selector to the listbox item
        char    *string = new char[s.GetLength() + 1];
        strcpy(string, s);
        char *title = strtok(&string[1], "\t");
```

```
            int item = m_listbox.AddString(title);
            delete string;
            m_listbox.SetItemDataPtr(item, strdup(s));
        }
        UpdateData(TRUE); //fills output area on-screen
        return NULL;
    }
```

Since you're using line-mode processing from the socket, you aren't notified when the connection is ready. So start ShowGopherMenu with a message pump as long as the status is still CONNECTING. If the socket moves from the CONNECTING status to some other status, display an error message and return.

Once CONNECTED, request the Gopher listing from the server by sending Selector. The server responds with the Gopher menu, with each item on a separate line. This is where QSocket::GetLine() method comes in handy—you don't have to worry about parsing the responses into lines because GetLine does it.

For each line that the server returns, parse it for a title and add the title to the listbox. Use SetItemDataPtr() to connect the full Gopher line to the listbox item. Then, when the user double-clicks the item, you can get the selector string easily and open the new menu or document.

At this point, the application can display a menu, although it can't follow links. If you run it and accept the default Gopher Home page, you should see something like figure 10.4.

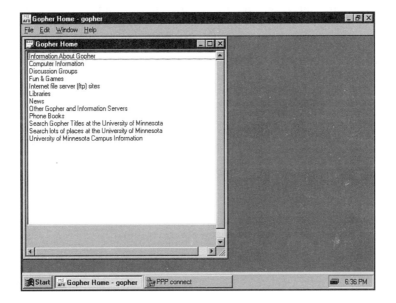

Fig. 10.4
The Gopher Home page at the University of Minnesota.

Your application is almost finished. All you need to do is to add code to follow links, and to display documents as well as menus.

Here's how to follow links. When the user double-clicks an item in the Gopher menu listbox, the application sends the ON_LBN_DBLCLK message and calls the OnDblclkListbox method. It looks like this:

```
void CGopherView::OnDblclkListbox()
{
    char    *s = (char
*)m_listbox.GetItemDataPtr(m_listbox.GetCurSel());

    if ( s == (char *)-1)
        return;

    // Check the type of gopher item
    switch ( *s )
    {
    case '0':
        theApp.OpenGopherDocument(s);
        break;
    case '1':
        theApp.OpenGopherMenu(s);
        break;
    default:
        AfxMessageBox("Sorry, support for this type
    ➥ of Gopher document is not implemented.");
        break;
    }
}
```

The first thing you do is to get the data associated with the selected item, the full menu string as sent from the server. If the string starts with the character 1, then the user asked to open a new Gopher menu. Otherwise, it must be a document. Since the application doesn't support the other Gopher document types, it should display an error message for those types.

You need to add two little functions to CGopherApp. They both pass a selector down to OpenDocumentFile:

```
void CGopherApp::OpenGopherMenu(LPSTR selector)
{
    pMenuTemplate->OpenDocumentFile(selector);
}

void CGopherApp::OpenGopherDocument(LPSTR selector)
{
    pDocTemplate->OpenDocumentFile(selector);
}
```

When the user closes a Gopher view, some cleanup is necessary. When you populated the listbox with the Gopher menu titles, you allocated storage for the associated data. To free that storage, walk through the listbox and free each data pointer, like this:

```
void CGopherView::OnClose()
{
    // Free the memory we've allocated for each menu item
    void*    p;
    for (int i = 0; i < m_listbox.GetCount(); ++i)
        if ( (p = m_listbox.GetItemDataPtr(i)) != (void *)-1 )
            free(p);
    CFormView::OnClose();
}
```

Why free and not delete? Because this memory was allocated with strdup. Calling CFormView::OnClose() makes sure the remainder of the cleanup goes on normally after your special processing is finished.

Users can use the scrollbars to see long or wide menus in the listbox. However, that isn't as useful as the ability to resize the window and have the listbox grow too. Catching the WM_SIZE method enables you to arrange that. Unfortunately, the application calls the OnSize method before it even creates the listbox, so you have to make sure that it is a valid window before you change it. Here's one way to do it:

```
void CGopherView::OnSize(UINT nType, int cx, int cy)
{
    CFormView::OnSize(nType, cx, cy);

    // Whenever the parent window is resized,
    // resize the enclosed listbox too
    if (!IsWindow(m_listbox.m_hWnd))
        return;
    RECT    r;
    GetClientRect(&r);
    m_listbox.MoveWindow(&r);
}
```

There are many ways to check whether the listbox has been created yet, but this call to IsWindow is one of the nicest. The m_hWnd member of m_listbox is NULL until it's created; after that it's a window handle, and it doesn't matter what the value is, as long as it isn't NULL.

II

Developing Applications

COutputDoc: **Displaying Gopher Documents**

COutputDoc holds the Host, Port, Title, and Selector of Gopher documents.This class needs an OnOpenDocument function that takes a selector. It looks very much like CGopherDoc::OnOpenDocument, but it can't handle NULL selectors and it doesn't put up a dialog box. Here's the code:

```
BOOL COutputDoc::OnOpenDocument(LPCTSTR lpszSelector)
{
    char *s = (char *)lpszSelector;
    if ( s == NULL )
        return FALSE;
    else
    {
        char    type = *s;                    // type of gopher item
        Title = strtok(&s[1], "\t");          // title
        Selector = strtok(NULL, "\t");        // selector
        Host = strtok(NULL, "\t");            // host
        Port = atoi(strtok(NULL, "\t"));      // port number
    }
    return TRUE;
}
```

The COutputView class is a simple text viewer used to display Gopher documents. Because it's derived from CEditView, it comes complete with methods for Cut, Copy, Paste, Undo, Save, and Save As. Unlike CGopherView, COutputView doesn't use line-oriented socket input. Instead, define the method OnSocket and connect it to the WM_SOCKET_RESPONSE message by adding an entry to the message map for COutputView:

```
BEGIN_MESSAGE_MAP(COutputView, CEditView)
    //{{AFX_MSG_MAP(COutputView)
    //}}AFX_MSG_MAP
    ON_MESSAGE(WM_SOCKET_RESPONSE, OnSocket)
END_MESSAGE_MAP()
```

 Don't forget to set up a #define for this message and change the message map entries in OUTPUTVI.H as well.

This view needs a socket, too. Add pSocket to the class, set it to NULL in the constructor, and delete it in the destructor.

When the document view first appears, `OnInitialUpdate()`is called to fetch the document. Here's how `OnInitialUpdate()` works:

```
void COutputView::OnInitialUpdate()
{
    COutputDoc* doc = (COutputDoc*)GetDocument();

    doc->SetTitle(doc->Title);
    doc->SetPathName(doc->Title);
    if (doc->Host != "")
    {
        delete pSocket;
        pSocket = new QSocket();
        pSocket->SetReceiveTarget(this, WM_SOCKET_RESPONSE);
        if (!pSocket->Connect(doc->Host, doc->Port))
        {
            AfxMessageBox("Host is unreachable.");
            delete pSocket;
            pSocket = 0;
        }
    }
    else
    {
        AfxMessageBox("Please fill in host name.");
    }

    CEditView::OnInitialUpdate();
}
```

First, set the window title and `pathname` of the document. (The pathname is used if the user saves the document to a file.) Since Windows 95 and Windows NT support long filenames, set the pathname to the document title.

> If you can't use long filenames, you'll need to create a sensible filename based on the document title.

The remainder of the code is very similar to `CGopherView::OnInitialUpdate()`, except that it uses the `QSocket::SetReceiveTarget()` method to define the window so that it will receive socket messages. `OnSocket():` processes these messages:

```
LRESULT COutputView::OnSocket(WPARAM amount, LPARAM buffer)
{
    COutputDoc* doc = (COutputDoc*)GetDocument();

    if ((int)amount > 0)
    {
```

```
                              ((char *)buffer)[amount] = '\0';
                              int nLen = GetEditCtrl().GetWindowTextLength();
                              GetEditCtrl().SetSel(nLen, nLen, TRUE);
                              GetEditCtrl().ReplaceSel((char *)buffer);
                              doc->SetModifiedFlag(FALSE);     // Avoid prompt to
                              // save when closing the document
                  }
                  else
                  {
                       // if amount < 0 it is a receive command
                       switch ( (SocketReceiveCmd)amount )
                       {
                            case SocketStatusChanged:
                                switch (pSocket->GetStatus())
                                {
                                    case CONNECTED:
                                        // send the Gopher request
                                        pSocket->Send(doc->Selector +
        "\r\n");

                                        break;

                                    default:
                                        // all other status states
                                        // represent an error
                                        break;
                                }
                                break;
                       }
                  }
                  return 0;
        }
```

When data is available to read, amount is greater than zero. In that case, you need to append the text to the end of the edit control in the CEditView. Insert a NULL at the end of buffer, find the end of the edit control with GetWindowTextLength, and insert the text with SetSel and ReplaceSel. All these edit control methods are available through GetEditCtrl, which allows classes derived from CeditView to use edit control functions.

When amount is negative, the socket status has changed. If it has become CONNECTED, send Selector. Otherwise there is an error.

There! You now have a functional Gopher application. Figure 10.5 shows a document that explains a bit about Gopher itself: what it's for and how it got its name. Each window in the figure is a separate document.

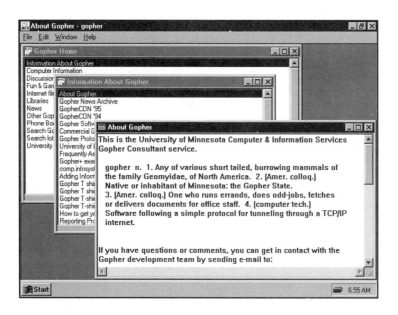

Fig. 10.5
A definition of the word *gopher*, displayed using Gopher.

Using the Internet Gopher Application

If you haven't built the Gopher application, you can use the one provided on the CD-ROM enclosed with this book. It's easy to use, and since the popular Gopher server **gopher.micro.umn.edu** is the default host, it will give you plenty to burrow through.

In Explorer or File Manager, double-click the Gopher application icon to invoke it. The first thing that should appear is a large Gopher window with the Open Gopher Connection dialog box displayed, as in figure 10.3. Accept the default values or provide your own; then click OK. Right away, the Gopher application should display a window and begin to fill it in with a menu of additional choices. Now choose an interesting topic. Continue to dig deep until you find what you're looking for, or perhaps something you didn't even know you were looking for. Like the Web, Gopher can take you to some strange places.

If you have several windows open, you can use the Window menu to tile or minimize them. To close a Gopher menu, simply double-click the close box. Close document views the same way. Also, if you want to save document information, select the text and choose Edit, Copy, or press Ctrl+C. Choose File, Open Gopher Connection to jump directly to another host.

From Here...

As you've seen, Gopher is a relatively simple protocol, and Visual C++ and MFC make building a Gopher application a fairly straightforward process. If you want to read more technical details about the Gopher protocol, read RFC 1438 or search **gopher.micro.umn.edu**.

If you would like to enhance the capabilities of your Gopher application, consider the following suggestions:

- Add an "Up" or "Back" selection. When the user selects it, display the previous menu. If the prior menu is still available in a window, make it the active view instead of reconnecting to create another.

- Add search capability. When the user double-clicks a Gopher document of type 7, display a dialog box for a search string. Then send the request to the server and display a menu of the search results.

- Add icons for each document type and display them in the Gopher menu. If the item is another menu, display an arrow or a folder. If the item is a file of type 1, display a simple document icon.

Chapter 11

Building An Internet Electronic Mail Application

E-mail is the heart of the Internet as far as most users are concerned. No matter what Internet service you use, it seems that mail is tied in there somewhere. Finger and Whois help you understand e-mail addresses or find them if you have only a name to work with. Your e-mail address is the string that identifies you when you use anonymous FTP. Most Web pages end with an URL to send mail to the person who maintains the page. Most replies to news articles are e-mail messages rather than follow-up messages. Mail was placed so late in the book only because a mail application is pretty heavy going, and the background had to be covered before you could get here. In this chapter you'll learn about:

- The SMTP protocol for sending mail messages

- The POP3 protocol for receiving messages kept in a remote mailbox

- The format of an Internet mail message

- Design issues for an Internet mail client

- Building your SMTP and POP3 mail client

- Using your mail client

The SMTP Protocol

The *Simple Mail Transfer Protocol* (*SMTP*) is one of the oldest and most stable protocols on the Net. It's described in RFC 821, last updated in 1982. SMTP is the way that two sites on the Internet exchange mail messages. It follows the familiar (it should be familiar by now!) pattern of command-response. There is only one connection between the sites, used for both commands and data.

The commands are:

- HELO *domain*
- MAIL FROM:*username*
- RCPT TO:*username*
- DATA
- QUIT

As always, each command is terminated with a CR-LF pair. Replies start with a three-digit response code and continue with text designed to be read by users.

The HELO command begins each session. Once the connection is made, the sending site sends the HELO command with its own domain name. In effect, it says "Hello, I am **gregcons.com**" (or whatever the site name is). The receiving site replies with a code of 220. Typically the text is the receiving site's name.

The MAIL FROM: command has a single parameter, which is the full e-mail address of the sender. The receiving site answers 250 OK. The RCPT TO: command identifies the recipient of the message. If the message has several recipients at the site, there will be several RCPT TO: commands, each of which gets a separate response from the receiving site. There are four possible responses to the RCPT TO: command:

- 250 OK
- 251 Forwarding to *username*
- 550 No such user
- 551 User not local; try *username*

The first two responses are successes, though a sender that gets a 251 response might want to tell the user to adjust the mailing address being used. 550 is clearly a failure, and the mail will not be sent. 551 is also a failure but the receiving site knows a similar username (on another machine) that might work; the sender might want to pass this address on to the user. In practice, few, if any, mail clients process this response code any differently from a 550, and few servers ever respond 551. It's an obscure feature many designers ignore.

Once the sending site has identified all the recipients and knows which will actually be receiving this mail message and which will not, it is time to send the actual mail message. The SMTP protocol doesn't care what format the message is in, but the program it is going to next certainly does. That format is discussed later in this chapter, in the section "Format of a Mail Message."

The DATA command announces that the mail message (headers and body) follows. After the entire message has been sent, the sender should add a "." on a line by itself. Since each line ends with CRLF, the termination code is <CR><LF>.<CR><LF>—five characters in all. It's unlikely that a user would include this as part of the message text, but not impossible. To avoid difficulties with this, the sender must change any "." characters at the start of a line to ".."—the receiver will change them back again.

The QUIT command simply closes the connection between the sites.

Here is an example SMTP session between **gregcons.com** and **somesite.com**, an imaginary Internet site where you might want to send mail. In this example, Elaine and Bill have accounts at **somesite**, but Steve does not. Messages from your sender are identified with S:, while replies from the server at **somesite.com** are identified with R:. The session goes like this (imagine a CR-LF at the end of each line):

```
[connection opens]
R: 220 SOMESITE.COM Simple Mail Transfer Service Ready
S: HELO GREGCONS.COM
R: 250 SOMESITE.COM
S: MAIL FROM:<kate@gregcons.com>
R: 250 OK
S: RCPT TO:<elaine@somesite.com>
R: 250 OK
S: RCPT TO:<bill@somesite.com>
R:251 user not local; forwarding to <bill@sub.somesite.com>
S: RCPT TO:<steve@somesite.com>
R: 550 No such user
S:DATA
R: 354 Start mail input: end with <CRLF>.<CRLF>
S: Date: 09 June 95 11:22:33
S: From: kate@gregcons.com
S: To: elaine@somesite.com, bill@somesite.com, steve@somesite.com
S: Elaine, Bill, and Steve,
S:
S: Hi, it's Kate -- I'm just testing this mail program
S: .
R: 250 OK
S: QUIT
R: 250 SOMESITE.COM closing transmission channel
```

The mail to Elaine and Bill was accepted (Bill's will be forwarded) but Steve's was not. It's up to the sending program to tell the user about this.

The POP3 Protocol

POP3 is the *Post Office Protocol*, version 3. If your site were always on the Internet, then you would receive mail with an SMTP-receiver and send it with an SMTP-sender, as previously described. But most of us are not always on the Internet, and even some who are don't have the disk space or spare cycles to run a mail server. For us, the Post Office Protocol was developed. It allows mail to be stored on another machine, one that is always on the Internet and has disk space and cycles to spare. The receiving host connects to the sending host and asks if there is any mail, then retrieves it, if necessary.

POP3 sessions consist of commands and responses as usual. There is only one channel open between the sites. Unlike FTP, which needs to go to some trouble to decide if a response is part of a multiline response, POP3 responses are classified in advance as single line or multiline. Multiline responses are terminated with a "." alone, like the body of SMTP messages. Anything within the response that actually starts with a "." will have an extra "." inserted, just as the SMTP section described earlier. Replies start with "+OK" or "-ERR" for successful and failed commands respectively. Replies about specific messages usually list both a message number and the length of the message in octets, as shown in the following table.

An *octet* is essentially a character. It's a more precise term than byte for use in network communication, and popular in RFCs. Not all machines on the Internet have 8-bit bytes, odd as that seems. Octet counts in messages always include the CR-LF pairs that end each line.

Command	Parameters	Function	Returns
USER	*username*	Identify the user whose mail is being retrieved	
PASS	*password*	Prove this program is authorized to retrieve mail	
STAT		How many messages are waiting for this user	Number of messages

Command	Parameters	Function	Returns
LIST	*[optional message number]*	How many messages are waiting for this user	Number of messages
RETR	*message-number*	Retrieves a message, sent as a multi-line response	A message
DELE	*message-number*	Deletes a message from the remote mailbox	
LAST		How many messages	The highest message number
QUIT		Ends the session	

Some servers can also support the TOP command, which retrieves the headers and a specified number of lines of the body. This allows the program to show the user something about the mail, and enables the user to decide whether to retrieve it or not. In practice, few users need these first few lines to make this decision, because the header alone (who sent it and the subject) is enough information. Since not all servers support the command, you won't be using it in your server.

A sample POP3 session might look like this (where C: is the client program and S: is the server):

```
[connection opens]
S: +OK POP3 server ready
C: USER kate
S: +OK kate valid
C: PASS secret
S: +OK kate's milbox has 3 messages
C: STAT
S: +OK 3 460
C: LIST
S: +OK 3 message (460 octets)
S: 1 120
S: 2 240
S: 3 100
S: .
C: LIST 2
S: OK 2 240
C:RETR 1
S: +OK 120 octets
S: Date: 09 June 95 11:22:33
S: From: bill@somesite.com
S: To: kate@gregcons.com
S: Kate,
```

```
S:
S: Your message got through fine -Bill.
S: .
C: DELE 1
S: +OK message 1 deleted
C: QUIT
S: +OK interlog POP3 server signing off (2 messages left)
[connection closes]
```

Note that the server keeps the client informed about how many messages are in the mailbox and how many are left behind when leaving.

Format of a Mail Message

Mail messages are formatted according to RFC 822 (it's no coincidence that the SMTP and mail RFCs have consecutive numbers). This 44-page RFC is exceptionally hard to read (and that's saying something, isn't it? Very few RFCs read smoothly) so it's summarized here.

A mail message consists of lines of text. The first few lines are called *headers* and have a defined format. The lines after the headers are called the *body* and are not specified in any way. In fact, in some cases a message may not even have a body. The headers and body are separated by an empty line—a line with no characters on it.

A header starts with a *field name* (there are a number of standard header names you'll see listed in a moment), followed by a colon and the field body. The contents of the field body may be rigidly defined or free form, as you'll see.

The following headers are mandatory; that is, there must be a header with each of these names:

- Date

- From, or Sender and From

- To, or CC (carbon copy), or BCC (blind carbon copy) (can have several of each)

NOTE All the recipients from To and CC fields are listed in the message and everyone who receives it knows who else got a copy. Recipients from the BCC fields are not listed in the message, and no one knows they got a copy.

The following headers are optional:

- Return-path
- Received
- Reply-To
- Message-ID
- In-Reply-To
- References
- Keywords
- Subject
- Comments
- Encrypted

Some of these headers are obscure and rarely used. You'll learn about the important ones as you need them.

In addition, some mail clients generate their own extra headers. Many such extra headers start with the characters "X-," because if extra mail headers are added to the RFC they will never start with these characters.

A header may be split over two lines according to the following rules:

- The split must be at a place where whitespace (blanks or tabs) would normally occur; for example, not in the middle of a username or similar field.
- The continuation line must start with a space or a tab.

So, an example header would be:

```
From: kate@gregcons.com (Kate Gregory)
```

This header could be "folded" into two lines like this:

```
From: kate@gregcons.com
      (Kate Gregory)
```

Similarly, a header can have extra spaces almost anywhere except in the middle of a field. One very nice place to put extra spaces is after each colon in the header. The reason why this is nice will become more clear in the next chapter, which describes a newsreader—news articles are almost identical to mail messages but they need a space after the colon in the header.

II

Developing Applications

Designing a Mail Client

The design task here is far greater than for the applications you've already completed, but luckily almost everyone has used e-mail, so there's some common ground in creating a simple interface. Let's do functionality before interface.

There's no point writing a mail client that uses SMTP for both send and receive. Such a client is useful only for sites that are always connected to the Internet. SMTP is fine for sending messages, because the user will make a SLIP or PPP connection before running the program, but you will need to use POP3 to retrieve the messages. You don't even need a mailbox on the user's machine: the POP3 protocol gives you complete access to the remote mailbox.

So the user will connect to the Internet and then start this application. You'll connect to the POP3 host, find out what mail is there, retrieve some of it if the user asks for it, delete anything that should be deleted, and then close the connection when the user is finished. If the user wants to compose and submit replies, you send them using SMTP to the SMTP host, which may be the same as the POP3 host, or may not.

Now, back to the interface. You're going to need to show the user a list of some sort indicating the messages that are available to be read. You'll need to display individual messages on request, and to compose replies. You need to know the Internet addresses of the POP3 and SMTP hosts, the user's e-mail address, and the user's real name. You could use your by-now familiar main view inherited from CFormView, with a list box for the message list and a small edit box for the message being read or the new one being composed, but this application really needs more screen space than that. You need a variety of different views open at once, in windows that can be tiled, overlapped, minimized, or maximized.

The Document/View Paradigm

You may recall that in Chapter 4, "Building a Windows Application Framework," you covered documents and views. It is possible to have two views on the same document; for example, a table of numbers and a graph as two views on the same file of numbers.

One way of designing this mail application is to say that the document will save the host names, user names, and so on, and that there will be several views onto each document. One view lists the messages in the POP3 remote mailbox. Another view lists the contents of a specific message. A third view is used to compose a new message that will be delivered by SMTP. You call these three views the Message Selection View, Message View, and Compose View respectively.

Because these views won't be full of controls, their design is simpler, but you do need to decide how they will present the information to the user. Since you want to show a list of messages in the Message Selection View, you want the view to contain a list box. Does this mean it has to be a form view, after all? No, a regular view can contain a list box, as you'll see.

The other two views are natural choices to inherit from CEditView. An edit view is both a view (with all the functions and data members of every view) and an edit box. The Message View can be a Read Only edit view, and the Compose View will allow the users to edit the message they are writing.

Menus

If you leave behind your CFormView view, you also leave behind buttons sitting right in the view for the user to click. You have to add to your menu system to give the user commands that can be issued. However, the framework gives you a toolbar to make access to your menus as easy as ever, as long as you put in the small amount of work that's needed to connect menu items to toolbar buttons.

What menu items will this application need? Something to call up a Setup dialog box for the hosts and user information, something to check the POP3 mailbox for mail, to open a particular message for viewing, to start composing a reply, to start composing a message that is not a reply, to send a message once it has been composed, and to delete a message that has been read. Add two items to the File menu, Setup and Check Mail, and add a new menu called Message with the items Display, Reply, New, Send, and Delete.

Building a Mail Client

You'll start your building process as usual with AppWizard, then get to work with AppStudio to build the interface. Because you're adding new views you'll start adding your own code sooner than usual, but once they are in place you'll do some ClassWizard work and then add the code to handle each menu item in turn. Then you'll go back and add a few nice touches.

AppWizard

The AppWizard process goes much as it always has, with two important exceptions: this must be an MDI application, and you want a toolbar.

MDI stands for multiple document interface, and it may seem wrong at first to have to use MDI when all you want is multiple views on a single document. However, that's the way it is, and who knows? Perhaps some users will find it useful to have several mailboxes open at once. The process of creating this MDI application is quite similar to that in Chapter 10, "Building an Internet Gopher Application." That chapter covers the concepts of MDI.

So, bring up AppWizard and follow these steps:

1. Choose File, New Project, OK. Use `mail` for the project's name.

2. Click Create, and choose `Multiple Document Interface`, `Next`, `None` for database, `Next`, `None` for OLE, `Next`.

3. Leave `Status Bar` and `Toolbar` checked, but uncheck `Print support`. Check `Sockets support` if you're using 2.1 or greater (the rest of you can add it by hand as discussed in Chapter 3, "Windows Sockets (WINSOCK.DLL)").

4. Click the `Advanced` button and type **mail** as the file extension, click `Close`, then finally `Next`, static library, `Next`, `Finish`, `OK`.

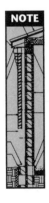

NOTE If you're using version 1.5x, you run AppWizard a little differently, though the basic questions you're answering are the same. Follow these steps:

1. Choose Project, AppWizard, and fill in the directory and project name.

2. Click the Options button and turn on MDI, and toolbar, and turn off Print support.

3. Click OK, then click the Classes button back on the AppWizard dialog.

4. Click `CMailDoc` and change the extension.

5. Click OK on the Classes dialog, OK on the AppWizard dialog, and Create on the confirmation dialog.

Phew! But hey, imagine doing all the real work involved in that. It's not surprising that these wizards can take awhile to complete.

AppStudio

This time around, AppStudio is going to be used for menus. Double-click MAIL.RC in the project list, then `Menu`. You'll see there are two menus already: `IDR_MAINFRAME` and `IDR_MAILTYPE`.

If you're using version 1.5x, bring up AppStudio by choosing Tools, AppStudio. Click Menu in the Type list, and you too will see these two menus.

Have you ever used an MDI application and noticed how the menus changed? With no file open at all, typically there are very few menu items—perhaps only File and Help. If you're using a spreadsheet program like Excel, the Chart menus are not the same as the Sheet menus. This application can do that too—when you write the menus you can write a different menu for each view.

IDR_MAINFRAME is the menu that is used when no file is open. There's no point in expanding this menu—without a document you have nowhere to save the options they might set on a Setup dialog box, for example, so you shouldn't add Setup to the File menu on IDR_MAINFRAME. None of the other menu options you're planning to add make any sense when there's no document open.

IDR_MAILTYPE is the menu that is used when a file is open and a CMailView view has focus. This is where you will add your extra menu items.

Click File, so that the existing File menu drops down. There is a blank item at the bottom—click it to select it. Use the Properties box to change the caption to Se&tup and the prompt to "Set up hosts, user id, name, etc." The & before the t in Setup makes it a keyboard shortcut—it appears underlined when the menu is displayed. Figure 11.1 shows the creation of this new menu item. Now click this new menu item and drag it up above the Exit item.

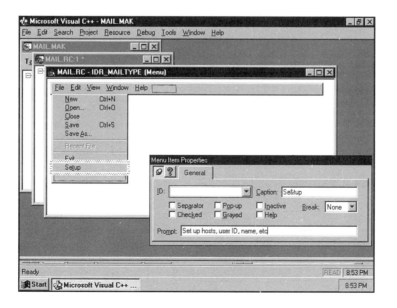

Fig. 11.1
Adding File, Setup to the main menu, IDR_MAILTYPE, shared by all three views.

II

Developing Applications

When you started typing a caption for the blank menu item, another blank one was created. Click that new blank one, set the caption to Check &Mail and the prompt to "Contact the POP3 host to get new mail." Drag this item up between Setup and Exit. Now drag the latest blank item up between Check Mail and Exit, and click the Separator check box in the Properties box. This changes the potential menu item into a thin line that is used to group related items together. Figure 11.2 shows the final File menu.

Fig. 11.2
The File menu now has two new items and a separator.

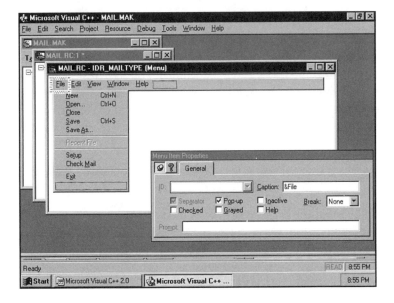

That completes your changes to the File menu. Now you need a whole new menu, Message. There's a blank box to the right of Help—click it and change the caption to &Message. A blank item appears under it. Add five menu items, as shown in figure 11.3, with the following captions and prompts:

Caption	Prompt
&Display	Display the highlighted message
&Reply	Compose a reply to this message
&New	Compose a new mail message
&Send	Send the composed message to the SMTP host
D&elete	Delete the highlighted message

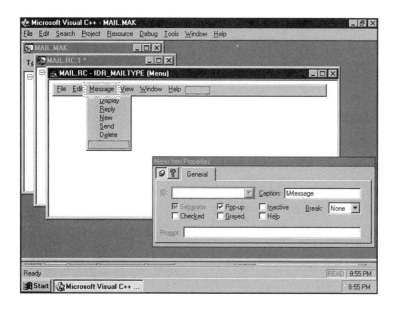

Fig. 11.3
The Message menu
is being added to
your application.

Of course, some of these menu items only make sense if there is a highlighted
message, or if the user is composing a message at the moment. You'll deal
with that later when you gray certain menu items. The framework will do
most of it for you, as you'll see.

Adding New Views

The framework keeps track of views in the string table for the application. To
add new views, the first thing you do is add new entries in the string table.
Bring up AppStudio and select String Table. (If you're using 1.52 or lower,
double-click Segment 0.) There is an entry for IDR_MAINFRAME and for
IDR_MAILTYPE. These are the views that AppWizard has already defined for
you.

The entries in the string tell the framework what kind of document is associated with these views, what prompt to use to describe that document, and
more. You will be able to copy most of the entries for MAILTYPE. Make sure
the Properties box is up and pinned to the screen, then click IDR_MAILTYPE to
select it. Choose Edit, Copy to put this entry into the Clipboard. Choose
Edit, Paste to paste in a copy, and change the name (using the properties
box) from IDR_MAILTYPE2 to IDR_MESSAGE. Paste again and change that to
IDR_COMPOSE. Now you have three string table entries, identical except for
their names.

Now, a trick. When the user chooses File, New, and there are several views available, the system puts up a dialog box to enable the user to choose the type of file they require. It does so even if all the views involve the same kind of file. This is annoying, and you are going to prevent it. Click one of the three strings and look in the properties box. Notice that, three times, it says Mail Document. The first time is a prompt for this File, New routine, and if you remove it, so that the string starts \nMail\n\n, then this dialog box will not appear as part of File, New. Remove the first Mail Document from IDR_MESSAGE and IDR_COMPOSE, but leave it in IDR_MAILTYPE.

Close MAIL.RC (close AppStudio in version 1.52 or lower) and open MAIL.CPP, which contains your Application object, CMailApp. In the function InitInstance, you can find the following code fragment:

```
// Register the application's document templates.
// Document templates
// Serve as the connection between documents,
// frame windows and views.

CMultiDocTemplate* pDocTemplate;
pDocTemplate = new CMultiDocTemplate(
    IDR_MAILTYPE,
    RUNTIME_CLASS(CMailDoc),
    RUNTIME_CLASS(CMDIChildWnd),
    // Standard MDI child frame
    RUNTIME_CLASS(CMailView));
AddDocTemplate(pDocTemplate);
```

This declares a *template* that gathers together the resource string IDR_MAILTYPE (which as you've seen contains the file extension .MAI and is the name of a menu) and three C++ object classes: CMailDoc, CMDIChildWnd, and CMailView. Microsoft should probably have avoided the word "template" for this document-view gathering object, since template already means something in the C++ language, but confusing or not, that's the word they use. By creating this template you enable all the behind-the-scenes work that connects real files to CMailDoc objects, and CMailDoc objects to CMailView objects.

You need two more templates, one for each of the views you are adding. You also need all three of your templates to be members of the CMailApp class rather than stack variables as pDocTemplate is here. Add to MAIL.H:

```
CMultiDocTemplate* pDocTemplate;
CMultiDocTemplate* pMessageTemplate;
CMultiDocTemplate* pComposeTemplate;
```

For now you will simply make up names for the frame and view objects associated with each view. You'll write the code for them later. IDR_MESSAGE is still associated with a CMailDoc and CMDIChildWnd, but the view will be

CMessageView. IDR_COMPOSE will have the view CComposeView. Change the
names of the template pointers in the new blocks of code to pMessageTemplate
and pComposeTemplate. The code should look like this:

```
// Register the application's document templates.
// Document templates serve as the connection
// between documents, frame windows and views.

pDocTemplate = new CMultiDocTemplate(
    IDR_MAILTYPE,
    RUNTIME_CLASS(CMailDoc),
    RUNTIME_CLASS(CMDIChildWnd),
    // Standard MDI child frame
    RUNTIME_CLASS(CMailView));
AddDocTemplate(pDocTemplate);

pMessageTemplate = new CMultiDocTemplate(
    IDR_MESSAGE,
    RUNTIME_CLASS(CMailDoc),
    RUNTIME_CLASS(CMDIChildWnd),
    // Standard MDI child frame
    RUNTIME_CLASS(CMessageView));
AddDocTemplate(pMessageTemplate);

pComposeTemplate = new CMultiDocTemplate(
    IDR_COMPOSE,
    RUNTIME_CLASS(CMailDoc),
    RUNTIME_CLASS(CMDIChildWnd),
    // Standard MDI child frame
    RUNTIME_CLASS(CComposeView));
AddDocTemplate(pComposeTemplate);
```

Use ClassWizard to create the new classes and add them to the project. Bring
up ClassWizard, click Add Class and fill in the class names and file names.
You can use MESSAGE.CPP and MESSAGE.H for CMessageView, COMPOSE.CPP
and COMPOSE.H for CComposeView. Both classes should inherit from
CEditView.

If you're using version 1.5x, ClassWizard doesn't present CEditView as an option for
the base class. Use CView, and then edit MESSAGE.H, MESSAGE.CPP, COMPOSE.H,
and COMPOSE.CPP. Change CView to CEditView—it occurs twice in the .CPP files
and once in the .H files. Now your new classes inherit from CEditView.

Don't forget to add #includes to MAIL.CPP for MESSAGE.H and COMPOSE.H so
that this new code will compile.

Now there is the matter of menus. Everything is set up right now so that
the IDR_MAINFRAME menu will be shown when there is no file open, the

IDR_MAILTYPE menu will be shown when a file is open and a CMailView has focus, the IDR_MESSAGE menu when a CMessageView has focus, and the IDR_COMPOSE menu when a CComposeView has focus.

 A window has focus if it is the one receiving input. It is on top and visible and the title bar (if any) is active. Only one view can have focus at a time.

There are two approaches you can take at this point. You can make up two new menus (IDR_MESSAGE and IDR_COMPOSE) which may be exactly like the IDR_MAILTYPE message, or you can outsmart the framework. Since the differences between the menus would be so small, you can outsmart the framework. One reason for this choice is that these extra menus tie up system resources and can slow down your application. If you really need them, they're great, but you don't really need them.

Each document template gathers up a bundle of information about documents, views, frame windows, and menus. The name of the menu defaults to the name of the resource string, but it doesn't have to. The following lines of code arrange for all three views to use the same menu and accelerator table:

```
pMessageTemplate->m_hMenuShared  =  pDocTemplate->m_hMenuShared;
pMessageTemplate->m_hAccelTable  =  pDocTemplate->m_hAccelTable;
pComposeTemplate->m_hMenuShared  =  pDocTemplate->m_hMenuShared;
pComposeTemplate->m_hAccelTable  =  pDocTemplate->m_hAccelTable;
```

Put the pair that affect pMessageTemplate before the call to AddDocTemplate for pMessageTemplate, and the pComposeTemplate pair before the pComposeTemplate call to AddDocTemplate.

ClassWizard

In your previous applications the user commanded the application primarily by clicking buttons on a view. This time around you're using menus, and ClassWizard helps you connect menu options to code just as you connected buttons to code.

When the user selects a menu item, a Windows message is generated. One of your objects can "catch" the message and call on its own functions as a result. It's not a mad scramble, though; Windows actually offers the message to a series of objects in turn. First, the view with focus, then if that doesn't catch it the document associated with that view, then finally the application itself, get a chance to process the message.

What menu options did you add? Setup and Check Mail under File, and Display, Reply, New, Send, and Delete under Message. When deciding what view or views should catch these commands, you ask yourself which objects know what must be known in order to process the command, and which object has the responsibility for telling the user the result.

File, Setup changes the user information that you will keep in the document. The document object, `CMailDoc`, should handle this. File, Check Mail needs that user information from the document, but it changes the contents of the list in `CMailView`, the list of messages in the mailbox. `CMailView` handles this message and asks the document for the required information.

Message, Display is only meaningful if a `CMailView` has a focus and a message is highlighted. It makes no sense to select this message item when already viewing a message (`CMessageView` has focus) or composing one (`ComposeView` has focus.) If `CMailDoc` or `CMailApp` were to catch this message, they could do so when `CMessageView` or `CComposeView` had focus, which is not right. So the menu item Message, Display should be caught by the `CMailView` object.

Applying the same thinking to Message, Reply, it makes sense from a `CMessageView` only. Message, New makes sense from both `CMailView` and `CMessageView`—this is not a problem, both views can catch the message. However, to simplify this application you will only have `CMailView` catch this message at the moment. Message, Send obviously belongs with `CComposeView`, and Message, Delete with `CMailView`, which manages the list of messages.

Having made these decisions you are ready to use ClassWizard to make the connections. Bring up ClassWizard and select `CMailDoc` from the drop-down list box. The Object IDs box now contains a number of resource IDs—the ones that AppStudio assigned to menu items. Select `ID_FILE_SETUP`, then choose `COMMAND` in the messages box. Click the Add Function button, and accept the suggested name, `OnFileSetup`, by clicking OK.

Now change the selection in the drop-down list box to `CMailView` (save your `CMailDoc` changes when prompted) and catch the messages `ID_FILE_CHECKMAIL`, `ID_MESSAGE_DISPLAY`, and `ID_MESSAGE_NEW`. Change the selection to `CMessageView` and add functions to catch `ID_MESSAGE_REPLY` and `ID_MESSAGE_DELETE`. Finally, have `CComposeView` catch `ID_MESSAGE_SEND`.

ClassWizard will add these functions to your .H files, and add skeletons to your .CPP files. In the next section you'll make these do something, but first, let's compile this skeletal application. When you bring it up, an empty `CMailView` is there because this is your main window. Click the File menu and you'll see that Setup and Check Mail are there and enabled. Under the Message menu, only Display and New are enabled; Reply, Send, and Delete are all grayed. This is done automatically because the kinds of views that catch those menu items don't have focus at the moment. This saves you the work of graying and ungraying menu items, very nicely.

Your view, though, leaves a lot to be desired. It has no list, indeed no list box. How do we make your CMailView contain a list box? It's simple. You add a line to MAILVIEW.H saying that the view has a list box called MessageList:

```
CListBox MessageList;
```

This box is empty until the user selects Check Mail to fill it, but you need to create the box when you create the view. You add an override of the OnInitialUpdate method for your view, and have it call the list box Create method, which causes the list box to appear in the window:

```
void CMailView::OnInitialUpdate()
{
    CRect rectangle;
    GetClientRect(rectangle);
    MessageList.Create(LBS_NOTIFY |LBS_USETABSTOPS|
                    WS_CHILD|WS_VISIBLE|WS_VSCROLL|WS_HSCROLL,
                    rectangle, this,IDC_MESSAGELISTBOX);
}
```

This code declares a rectangle and fills it by calling GetClientRect for the view. By passing this rectangle down to the list box's Create function, you arrange for the list box to completely fill the view.

The first parameter to the Create call is the style flags, ored together. LBS_NOTIFY means that if anyone clicks in the list box, this view should be notified. LBS_USETABSTOPS turns on tabs in the list box; if a string is added with a \t character embedded it will be expanded. You'll set those tab stops after the Create call.

WS_CHILD, WS_VISIBLE, WS_VSCROLL, and WS_HSCROLL are fairly standard style settings for any window within another window. The second parameter is the rectangle you already declared. The third is the parent window for this list box, this view. Finally you pass a resource ID for the list box. You just make this up, and add a #define at the top of MAILVIEW.H defining it:

```
#define IDC_MESSAGE_LISTBOX 200
```

200 is a safe number to use: look at the IDs in the string table to get an idea of what ranges are available. You'll be using this ID later on.

Back to those tab stops, now. Here's the code to set them:

```
#define tabwidth 60
    MessageList.SetTabStops(tabwidth*4); //dialog units
    MessageList.SetHorizontalExtent(LOWORD(GetDialogBaseUnits())
                            *tabwidth*2); //pixels
```

The key here is to understand dialog base units. The SetTabStops function takes dialog units, which are one-quarter of a dialog base unit (for width; it's one-eighth for height.) You can think of a dialog base unit as the average width of a single character. The SetHorizontalExtent function takes a number of pixels: GetDialogBaseUnits returns the number of pixels in a dialog base unit. So you're setting your tab stop at about 30 characters, and the width of your list box at double that.

Code for the File, Setup Menu Item

Your list box stays empty until the user chooses File, Check Mail. But before Check Mail can work, the user must have set the host addresses and so on, either by opening a file that has saved them, or by using File, Setup. You'll do File, Setup first, then File, Check Mail.

The first thing File, Setup needs to do is put up a dialog. It needs to determine:

- SMTP host address (name or numbers)

- POP3 host address

- This site address

- User's ID

- User's real name

These just need to be six edit boxes. In AppStudio, create a dialog called IDD_SETUP with these six edit boxes, like the one shown in figure 11.4. Their IDs should all start with IDC, because the edit boxes are controls. Here's the list of resource IDs used:

- IDC_SMTP

- IDC_POP3

- IDC_SITE

- IDC_USERID

- IDC_PASSWORD

- IDC_USERNAME

Fig. 11.4
Your Setup dialog
is under
construction.

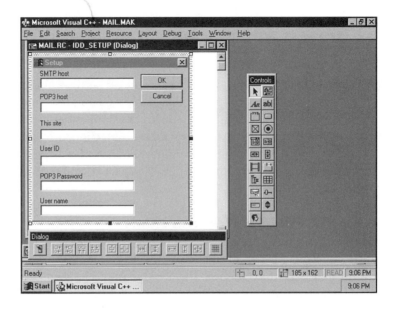

When all the boxes are in place, and neatly aligned, make sure the user can tab through them in the right order. Select Layout Tab order, then click the controls in the order the Tab key should go through them. A good order would be each of these controls, starting at the top, followed by the OK button. The Cancel and all the statics should be after that. This one small step makes all the difference to someone trying to use your dialog.

 Creating dialogs and hooking them to classes is discussed in detail in earlier chapters, like Chapter 5, "Building an Internet Finger Application."

Next, use ClassWizard to create a class for this dialog and connect these controls to six CString variables. Call the class CSetupDialog and the variables m_smtp, m_pop3, m_site, m_userid, m_password, and m_username. By now you're probably detecting a pattern. Always write as though someone else is going to have to change your code later, and they shouldn't have to bring up AppStudio to find out the name you gave your edit control, then bring up ClassWizard to find out what member variable you hooked that control to, when they want to know what member variable to use. It should be obvious and consistent.

The function that CMailDoc::OnFileSetup is called when the user chooses File, Setup. You need to add code there to bring up this dialog and then use it. To use it, you need variables in the document object that will hold the values the user sets. They are all CStrings; call them SMTP, POP3, Site, Userid,

Password, and Username. Add the appropriate lines to MAILDOC.H. Then
CMailDoc::OnFileSetup becomes:

```
void CMailDoc::OnFileSetup()
{
    CSetupDialog dialog;
    dialog.m_smtp = SMTP;
    dialog.m_pop3 = POP3;
    dialog.m_site = Site;
    dialog.m_userid = Userid;
    dialog.m_password = Password;
    dialog.m_username = Username;

    if (dialog.DoModal() == IDOK)
    {
        SMTP = dialog.m_smtp;
        POP3 = dialog.m_pop3;
        Site = dialog.m_site;
        Userid = dialog.m_userid;
        Password = dialog.m_ password;
        Username = dialog.m_username;
    }
}
```

This constructs a dialog, fills it with anything that has already been saved,
and puts it up for the users to change. To actually save these variables and
restore them, you need to write the Serialize method:

```
void CMailDoc::Serialize(CArchive& ar)
{
    if (ar.IsStoring())
    {
        ar << SMTP;
        ar << POP3;
        ar << Site;
        ar << Password;
        ar << Userid;
        ar << Username;
    }
    else
    {
        ar >> SMTP;
        ar >> POP3;
        ar >> Site;
        ar >> Password;
        ar >> Userid;
        ar >> Username;
    }
}
```

As you saw in Chapter 7, "Building an Internet FTP Application," Serialize
functions are very simple to write. Each member variable is sent to the
archive if you are storing, or filled from the archive otherwise. Since the <<
and >> operators are already defined for CString, everything else is taken care
of by the framework.

II

Developing Applications

Code for the File, Check Mail Menu Item

You now need to write CMailView::OnFileCheckmail. You need to connect to the POP3 host and ask it how many messages there are, then get each message in turn and add a string describing the message to the list box in the main view. The connection should be closed at this point; it can always be re-opened if the user wants to access the mailbox again to display or delete the message.

As with FTP though, you don't hang around waiting to get connected. You send the connection request, set up the callback, and the rest is handled after the connection comes through. So CMailView::OnFileCheckmail looks like this:

```
void CMailView::OnFileCheckmail()
{
    delete pSocket;
    pSocket = new QSocket();
    pSocket->SetReceiveTarget(this, WM_SOCKET_RESPONSE);
    // blank list box
    MessageList.ResetContent();
    State = CheckMail;
    if (!pSocket->Connect(GetDocument()->GetPop3(), 110))
    {
        AfxMessageBox("Host is unreachable.");
        delete pSocket;
        pSocket = 0;
        return;
    }
}
```

You need to add the #define for WM_SOCKET_RESPONSE to MAILVIEW.H and add the message map entries so that the WM_SOCKET_RESPONSE message triggers a call to OnSocket. This is done just as it was for FTP (refer to Chapter 7, "Building an Internet FTP Application).

The line State = CheckMail is a little bit of advance planning. If you are going to disconnect every time, then the piece of code that handles getting connected is going to need to know why you're getting connected. So, as you've done earlier, you add a member variable State that keeps track of what you're doing. Add to MAILVIEW.H, before the class declaration:

```
enum CommandState {Idle, CheckMail };
```

You'll add other elements to that enum later. Add within the class declaration, with the other private member variables:

```
CommandState State;
```

In MAILVIEW.CPP, add

```
State = Idle;
```

to the constructor. Now the line in OnFileCheckmail will work just fine.

So the work is once again delegated to OnSocket. It should look awfully familiar by now:

```
LRESULT CMailView::OnSocket(WPARAM amount, LPARAM buffer)
{
    if ((int)amount > 0)
    {
    }
    else
    {
        // if amount < 0 it is a receive command
        CString response;
        CMailDoc* doc = GetDocument();

        switch ( (SocketReceiveCmd)amount )
        {
            case SocketStatusChanged:
                switch (pSocket->GetStatus())
                {
                    case CONNECTED:
                        //switch to getline
                        pSocket->SetReceiveTarget(NULL,0);
                        response = pSocket->GetLine();
                        pSocket->Send("USER "
                         + doc->GetUserid() + "\r\n");
                        response = pSocket->GetLine();
                        pSocket->Send("PASS "
                         + doc->GetPassword() + "\r\n");
                        response = pSocket->GetLine();

                        if (State == CheckMail)
                        {
                            FillListBox();
                            State = Idle;
                        }
                        break;

                    case DISCONNECTED:
                        break;

                    default:
                        break;
                }
                break;
        }
    }
    return 0;
}
```

The actual work of getting a list of messages and putting them into the list box has been gathered up into a function called FillListBox, which you'll see in a minute. The rest of OnSocket has nothing to do if there's actual data, because you switch to getline mode as soon as the connection is made. You send the USER and PASS commands first. Note the complete absence of error checking. You'll be adding some in later, but for now type very carefully when testing.

Since you have to reconnect each time you send USER and PASS no matter what State is, but you only call FillListBox if you are, in fact, checking mail.

FillListBox needs to know first how many messages there are. The STAT command is used for this, and there's a little parsing needed to get the number out of the response:

```
CString response;
pSocket->Send("STAT \r\n");
response = pSocket->GetLine();
response = response.Right(response.GetLength()-4);
// Strip away '+OK '
int space = response.Find(' ');
response = response.Left(space);
int msgs = atoi(response);
```

The CString function Right gets the last portion of the string, from after the fourth character to the current length of response. The Find function tells you where the space is after removing the "+OK," and the Left function extracts just the part of the string before that space. Finally the atoi function (it takes a char* but there is a conversion operator between CString and char*) turns the ASCII characters into an integer. That enables you to set up a loop through all the messages, parsing out the headers.

```
CString subject, from, line ;
for (int i=1;i<=msgs;i++)
{
    char command[20];
    // Unlikely to have a 13 digit number of messages
    sprintf(command, "RETR %i \r\n",i);
    pSocket->Send(command);
    response = pSocket->GetLine();
    int length;
    if ( response.Left(3) == "+OK")
    {
        //headers follow
        subject = "";
        from = "";
        while ( (response = pSocket->GetLine()) != ".\r\n"
                    && pSocket->GetStatus() == CONNECTED)
        {
            length = response.GetLength();
            if (response.Left(9) == "Subject: ")
            {
```

```
                    subject = response.Right(length - 9);
                    length = subject.GetLength();
                    if (length >= 2
                        && subject[length-2] == '\r'
                        && subject[length-1] == '\n')
                    {
                        subject = subject.Left(length-2);
                    }
                }
                if (response.Left(6) == "From: ")
                {
                    from = response.Right(length - 6);
                    length = from.GetLength();
                    if (length >= 2
                        && from[length-2] == '\r'
                        && from[length-1] == '\n')
                    {
                        from = from.Left(length-2);
                    }
                }
            }

            line = from.Left(tabwidth);
            // So as not to overshoot tabstop.
            line += '\t'; //tab -- see Create
            line += subject;
            MessageList.AddString(line);
        } //if response = +OK
    } //for loop going through messages
```

You use GetLine in this loop so you don't have to split the headers into lines
yourself. You look at each line of each message and compare it to "Subject:"
or "From:," saving the parts of these lines after the field name in the local
CStrings subject and from. Once you have these, you put them into the list
box with AddString. Why Subject and From? They just seemed like the sorts
of things you'd like to know about a message when deciding to read it—who
sent it to you and what it is about.

You then disconnect:

```
    pSocket->Send("QUIT \r\n");
    response = pSocket->GetLine();
    delete pSocket;
    pSocket = NULL;

}
```

At this point the Check Mail process is completely coded. As figure 11.5
shows, the view presents a list of mail messages in the POP3 mailbox.

Fig. 11.5

Your mail client lists the messages in the remote mailbox for the user to select.

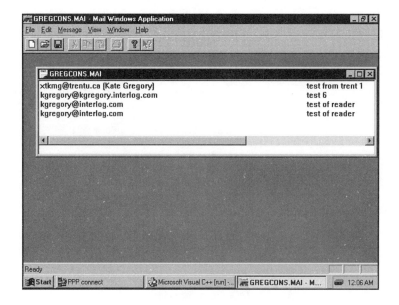

Code for the Message Display Menu Item

The next logical step is Message, Display. This function determines which message is to be displayed, creates a new view, and passes the message number to the new view.

```
void CMailView::OnMessageDisplay()
{
    int index = MessageList.GetCurSel();
    if (index < 0)
    {
        // User hasn't selected a message -- use the first one.
        index = 0;
    }

    CMailApp* App = (CMailApp*)AfxGetApp();
    CMDIChildWnd* pNewFrame = (CMDIChildWnd*)App->pMessageTemplate
        ->CreateNewFrame(m_pDocument,NULL);
    if (pNewFrame == NULL)
    {
        return;
    }
    App->pMessageTemplate->
        ➡InitialUpdateFrame(pNewFrame, m_pDocument);

    CMessageView* pMessageView =
        ➡(CMessageView*)pNewFrame->GetActiveView();
    pMessageView->SetMessageNumber(index);

}
```

On reading this code, can you tell where the new view is created? You create it indirectly, by creating a new frame through the template. The call to InitialUpdateFrame also calls the OnInitialUpdate method for the view. Once that is done, you ask the frame for a pointer to the view, and use that pointer to set the message number.

What function in CMessageView will go and get the message and put it in the view? At first it seems that OnInitialUpdate is the only choice, but unfortunately, when OnInitialUpdate is called the view does not yet know the message number. You could invent another function called Fill, and call it right after the call to SetMessageNumber, or you can add the fill code at the end of SetMessageNumber.

```
void CMessageView::SetMessageNumber(unsigned int msg)
{
    MessageNumber = msg + 1;
    // Index in list box is zero based; mailbox is 1 based.

    delete pSocket;
    pSocket = new QSocket();
    pSocket->SetReceiveTarget(this, WM_SOCKET_RESPONSE);
    if (!pSocket->Connect(GetDocument()->GetPop3(), 110))
    {
        AfxMessageBox("Host is unreachable.");
        delete pSocket;
        pSocket = 0;
        return;
    }

}
```

Doesn't this bear an uncanny resemblance to OnCheckMail? You don't need to set a State variable here, since in this view you are only ever filling the view, but other than that it's just the same. However, this is not a CMailView object, and that means you have some things to add to MESSAGE.H and MESSAGE.CPP; you need to declare this function, SetMessageNumber, you need to declare pSocket (and set it to NULL in the constructor and delete it in the destructor,) #define the WM_SOCKET_RESPONSE message, and add to the message map in both files so that OnSocket gets called when a WM_SOCKET_RESPONSE message arrives.

As usual, OnSocket is the interesting function here. It has the usual structure:

```
LRESULT CMessageView::OnSocket(WPARAM amount, LPARAM buffer)
{
    if ((int)amount > 0)
    {
        // Handle socket data.
    }
```

```
        else
        {
            // if amount < 0 it is a receive command
            CString response;
            CMailDoc* doc = GetDocument();

            switch ( (SocketReceiveCmd)amount )
            {
                case SocketStatusChanged:
                    switch (pSocket->GetStatus())
                    {
                        case CONNECTED:
                            // handle connection
                            break;

                        case DISCONNECTED:
                            break;

                        default:
                            break;
                    }
                    break;
            }
        }
        return 0;
}
```

You'll fill in "handle socket data" and "handle connection" in just a moment, but they are each quite long and they hide the fact that this is the same old familiar OnSocket you've been using all this time. Here's what you do when the status becomes CONNECTED:

```
// Switch to getline.
pSocket->SetReceiveTarget(NULL,0);
response = pSocket->GetLine();
pSocket->Send("USER " + GetDocument()->GetUserid()
        + "\r\n");
response = pSocket->GetLine();
pSocket->Send("PASS " + GetDocument()->GetPassword()
        + "\r\n");
response = pSocket->GetLine();

pSocket->SetReceiveTarget(this, WM_SOCKET_RESPONSE);
char command[20];
// Unlikely to have a 13-digit message number.
sprintf(command, "RETR %i \r\n",MessageNumber);
pSocket->Send(command);
```

As before you send the USER and PASS commands, but then you switch out of getline mode before building and sending the RETR command to retrieve the specified message number. The message will come back to the top half of this very function, the block called "handle socket data." That block works with a `CString` called `windowtext` that you add to the class. Each time `OnSocket` is called with data, it adds to `windowtext` until the <CRLF>.<CRLF> is reached. The code looks like this:

```
windowtext += (char*) buffer;
if (windowtext.Right(4) == "\n.\r\n")
// End of transmission.
{
    // Find .. at start of lines, and drop one .
    if (windowtext.Left(2) == "..")
    {
        windowtext = windowtext.Right(
            ➡windowtext.GetLength()-1);
    }
    char* position;
    char* windowbuffer = windowtext.GetBuffer(0);
    position = windowbuffer;
    while (position = strstr(position,"\n.."))
    {
        int length = windowtext.GetLength();
        strcpy(position+1,position+2);
        // Skip second dot.
        position += 2;
        // Get past the \n. left behind.
    }
    GetEditCtrl().SetWindowText(windowtext);
    // Switch to getline.
    pSocket->SetReceiveTarget(NULL,0);
    pSocket->Send("QUIT \r\n");
    CString response = pSocket->GetLine();
    delete pSocket;
    pSocket = NULL;
}
```

As you can see, this routine just tacks buffer on to the end of `windowtext`. If there's more to come, nothing else happens. The bulk of the work is done once `windowtext` contains the complete text of the mail message.

First, any "." characters at the start of a line are stripped out. Then the call to `GetEditCtrl().SetWindowText` connects our `CString` windowtext to the actual edit control that is part of your `CEditView`. At this point, you're finished, so you go back to `getline` mode, send the QUIT command, and get rid of the socket.

It's time to test again—this code really does display a message, as you can see in figure 11.6.

Fig. 11.6

A test message is
being displayed in
your application.
A few things are
ugly here—the
frame titles
are awful
(GREGCONS.MAI
is the name of the
open file) and the
first line in the
view, starting
+OK, is not really
part of the
message and
should be
trimmed away.

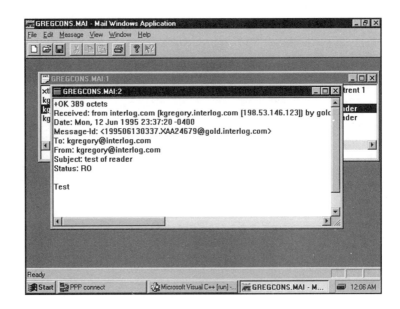

Code for the Message, Delete Menu Item

Well, this is great! You can connect to a remote mailbox, see what's in it, and
look at the messages. Before you rush off to sending messages, though, let's
take care of deleting them. You see, sending new mail is done with the SMTP
protocol, while deleting is still POP3, and it's better to finish all the POP3
code before starting SMTP.

OnMessageDelete, you may recall, is in CMessageView. It's going to do much the
same as File, Check Mail at first: make the connection, then in OnSocket send
the USER and PASS commands:

```
void CMailView::OnMessageDelete()
{
    delete pSocket;
    pSocket = new QSocket();
    pSocket->SetReceiveTarget(this, WM_SOCKET_RESPONSE);
    State = Delete;
    if (!pSocket->Connect(GetDocument()->GetPop3(), 110))
    {
        AfxMessageBox("Host is unreachable.");
        delete pSocket;
        pSocket = 0;
        return;
    }
}
```

Don't forget to add Delete to the enum in MAILVIEW.H. Now, in OnSocket,
after the block you execute if State is CheckingMail you need to add another
block:

```
if (State == Delete)
{
    int index = MessageList.GetCurSel();
    if (index >= 0)
    {
        MessageList.ResetContent();
        char command[20];
        // Unlikely to have a 13-digit message number.
        sprintf(command, "DELE %i \r\n",index+1);
        pSocket->Send(command);
        response = pSocket->GetLine();

        pSocket->Send("QUIT \r\n");
        response = pSocket->GetLine();
        delete pSocket;
        pSocket = NULL;

        OnFileCheckmail();
    }
    else
    {
        State = Idle;
    }
}
```

You first determine which message has been selected. Then you clear away the contents of MessageList, send the DELE command, and QUIT. You then call your own function OnFileCheckmail to connect again and fill the list box with the revised list. You have to do it this way because the POP3 mailbox only marks the messages for deletion—it doesn't actually delete them until the QUIT command is processed. There's no point re-inventing the wheel writing code to connect and fill the list box when OnFileCheckmail already does just that.

If for some reason the user chooses Message, Delete with no message highlighted, you just reset State and return. Later you'll make it impossible for the user to choose Message, Delete unless a message is highlighted, and then you can drop these lines.

Code for the Message New Menu Item

Now, that's all the POP3 material taken care of. Let's work on OnMessageNew now. It's in CMessageView. Like OnMessageDisplay, it needs to bring up a new view—in this case using the pComposeTemplate template.

```
void CMailView::OnMessageNew()
{
    CMailApp* App = (CMailApp*)AfxGetApp();
    CMDIChildWnd* pNewFrame = (CMDIChildWnd*)App->pComposeTemplate
        ->CreateNewFrame(m_pDocument,NULL);
    if (pNewFrame == NULL)
```

```
    {
        return;
    }
    App->pComposeTemplate->InitialUpdateFrame(pNewFrame,
                                   m_pDocument);

    CComposeView* pComposeView =
        ➥(CComposeView*)pNewFrame->GetActiveView();
    pComposeView->Fill();
}
```

There's no reason in this case why you can't initialize the view in
OnInitialUpdate—it's not waiting for any extra information this time. How-
ever, when you write OnMessageReply you need to pass some information to
a CComposeView. So planning ahead, you add a function called Fill to
CComposeView and add a call to that function here.
CComposeView::OnInitialUpdate is then very simple:

```
    void CComposeView::OnInitialUpdate()
    {
        GetEditCtrl().SetReadOnly(FALSE);
        CEditView::OnInitialUpdate();
    }
```

This just ensures that the user will be able to edit the contents of the view,
then calls the base class function to finish initializing the view.
CComposeView::Fill is a little more interesting:

```
    void CComposeView::Fill()
    {
        CString text = "";
        text += "To: \r\n";
        text += "From: " + GetDocument()->GetUserid()
                + "@" + GetDocument()->GetSite() + "\r\n";
        text += "Subject: \r\n";

        text += "\r\n";

        GetEditCtrl().SetWindowText(text);
        int selchar = GetEditCtrl().LineIndex(
            ➥GetEditCtrl().GetLineCount()-1);
        GetEditCtrl().SetSel(selchar,selchar);

    }
```

As you did when filling the CMessageView, you use a CString and just keep
adding to it. A blank To, a From using the information already provided by
the user, and a blank Subject line are all the headers you need to start. You
add an extra blank line because mail messages must include an empty line
separating headers from body. All the word-processing aspects of this view
are taken care of by the framework—your job is done until the user chooses

<u>M</u>essage, <u>S</u>end. That triggers a call to CComposeView::OnMessageSend, which must look really familiar by now:

```
void CComposeView::OnMessageSend()
{
    delete pSocket;
    pSocket = new QSocket();
    pSocket->SetReceiveTarget(this, WM_SOCKET_RESPONSE);
    if (!pSocket->Connect(GetDocument()->GetSMTP(), 25))
    {
        AfxMessageBox("Host is unreachable.");
        delete pSocket;
        pSocket = 0;
        return;
    }
}
```

Actually there are two important differences from the previous calls, both in the call to Connect. You are connecting to the SMTP host this time, and to port 25 rather than 110 for POP3. The lower port numbers, by the way, belong to the older services. The rest of the good stuff is in OnSocket as always. Remember to add pSocket and the message stuff to COMPOSE.H and COMPOSE.CPP just as you did for CMessageView. Here's OnSocket, with the "handle connection" code replaced by a comment to show the structure:

```
LRESULT CComposeView::OnSocket(WPARAM amount, LPARAM buffer)
{
    if ((int)amount > 0)
    {
    }
    else
    {
        // If amount < 0 it is a receive command.
        CString response;
        unsigned int i;
        unsigned int lines ;
        CString to;
        CMailDoc* doc = GetDocument();

        switch ( (SocketReceiveCmd)amount )
        {
            case SocketStatusChanged:
                switch (pSocket->GetStatus())
                {
                    case CONNECTED:
                        // Handle connection.
                        break;

                    case DISCONNECTED:
                        break;

                    default:
                        break;
```

```
                    }
                    break;
            }
        }
        return 0;
    }
```

So far, being SMTP instead of POP3 hasn't made any difference. But, as you might expect, the "handle connection" code varies a bit. First, instead of USER and PASS, you send the HELO command:

```
// Switch to getline.
pSocket->SetReceiveTarget(NULL,0);
response = pSocket->GetLine();
pSocket->Send("HELO "
            + GetDocument()->GetSite() + "\r\n");
response = pSocket->GetLine();
```

Next, you send the MAIL FROM command:

```
pSocket->Send("MAIL FROM: <"
            + GetDocument()->GetUserid() + "@"
            + GetDocument()->GetSite() + ">\r\n");
response = pSocket->GetLine();
```

Now you need to decide who this is to. Because this is just a demonstration, you'll take the easy way out, and assume there is only one To line, and no CC or BCC lines. Further you'll assume there's just one userid on the To line. Later you'll learn how to improve this.

```
// Determine recipient -- only one at the moment.
// Should handle cc, bcc as well and for to, cc, bcc
// should handle comma-separated names.
// Commas in the To field will probably blow this up.

char buffer[5004];
// For \r, \n, zero term, and perhaps an extra .
lines = GetEditCtrl().GetLineCount();
unsigned int linelength;
for (i = 0; i< lines; i++)
{
    linelength = GetEditCtrl().GetLine(i,buffer, 5000);
    if (strnicmp(buffer,"To: ",4)==0)
    {
        buffer[linelength] = 0;
        to = buffer+4;
        break;
    }
}
```

Here you get each line into a buffer, compare the first four characters to "To:," and if you get a match you save the rest of the line in the CString to. Next you'll actually use that variable:

```
    pSocket->Send("RCPT TO: <" + to + ">\r\n");
    response = pSocket->GetLine();
```

The RCPT TO command identifies the recipient. You should be checking here
that the SMTP host has said OK, but at this point you just plow on. You'll
add error checking later. All that remains is to send the actual message:

```
    pSocket->Send("DATA \r\n");
    response = pSocket->GetLine();

    for (i = 0; i< lines; i++)
    {
        linelength = GetEditCtrl().GetLine(i,buffer, 5000);
        buffer[linelength] = 0;
        if (buffer [0] == '.')
        {
            pSocket->Send('.' + (CString)buffer + "\r\n");
        }
        else
        {
            pSocket->Send((CString)buffer + "\r\n");
        }              }
    pSocket->Send(".\r\n");
    response = pSocket->GetLine();
```

This code goes through each line and sends it to the SMTP host. If the line
starts with a "." you send another "." first. After the loop you send a "." on a
line by itself to tell the host the message is complete. All that remains is to
QUIT:

```
    pSocket->Send("QUIT\r\n");
    response = pSocket->GetLine();
```

and the "handle connection" part of OnSocket is complete.

One thing that's a little messy here is that the view stays open after the message is sent. If you could close it automatically, the user would know the
command got through and wouldn't keep clicking Message, Send over and
over again. Luckily you can do that, in just two lines of code:

```
    CWnd *wnd = GetParent();
    wnd->DestroyWindow();
```

The call to GetParent will return the frame that created this view for you.
Calling the frame's DestroyWindow method removes the frame and this view
from the screen. Once you add error-checking, you should only remove this
view if the message was successfully sent.

Figure 11.7 shows a message (from you to you) being composed, and figure
11.8 shows that same message in the list box, proving it arrived. It was successfully transferred up to the SMTP host, over to the POP3 host, and back
down to your list box. Both halves of this application now work.

Fig. 11.7
A test message is being composed.

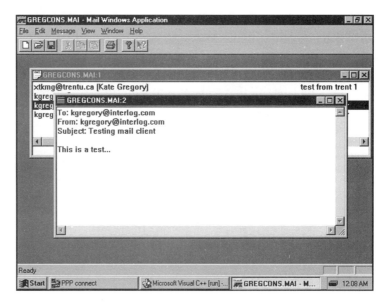

Fig. 11.8
That same test message has arrived in the POP3 mailbox, proving the SMTP send works.

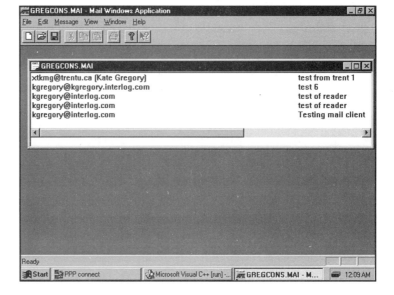

Code for the Message Reply Menu Item

Replying to a message is a lot like making a new one, but the Subject should be based on the old one, and the To of this message should be the From of the old message. The easiest thing to do is add two parameters to Fill—the subject line and the To line. You determine these before calling Fill. So, CMessageView::OnMessageReply looks like this:

```
void CMessageView::OnMessageReply()
{
    CMailApp* App = (CMailApp*)AfxGetApp();
    CMDIChildWnd* pNewFrame = (CMDIChildWnd*)App->pComposeTemplate
        ->CreateNewFrame(m_pDocument,NULL);
    if (pNewFrame == NULL)
    {
        return;
    }
    App->pComposeTemplate->InitialUpdateFrame(
        ➥pNewFrame, m_pDocument);

    CString from,subject;
    char buffer[5004];
    // For \r, \n, zero term, and perhaps an extra .
    unsigned int lines = GetEditCtrl().GetLineCount();
    unsigned int linelength;
    for (unsigned int i = 0; i< lines; i++)
    {
        linelength = GetEditCtrl().GetLine(i,buffer, 5000);
        if (strnicmp(buffer,"From: ",6)==0)
        {
            buffer[linelength] = 0;
            from = buffer+6;
            break;
        }
    }
    for (i = 0; i< lines; i++)
    {
        linelength = GetEditCtrl().GetLine(i,buffer, 5000);
        if (strnicmp(buffer,"Subject: ",9)==0)
        {
            buffer[linelength] = 0;
            subject = buffer+9;
            break;
        }
    }

    CComposeView* pComposeView =
            ➥(CComposeView*)pNewFrame->GetActiveView();
    pComposeView->Fill(from,subject);
}
```

What makes this different from CMailView::OnMessageNew? Only the code that fills the CStrings from and subject. You can choose to do two separate for loops so you can break after finding a match. Without a break, looking for both in the same loop would involve reading the entire body of the message as well, which is at best a waste of time and at worst a way to get the wrong values into from and subject. If you'd rather have a single loop, after setting either from or to, compare the other to "" and break if they are both set.

So now you want to call Fill with parameters. You could write a second Fill function, or you can choose to change it to take two parameters, then supply default values for those parameters. This is a really nice C++ feature that saves you writing the same code over and over again. In COMPOSE.H, change the declaration of `Fill` from:

```
void Fill();
```

to:

```
void Fill(CString To = "", CString Subject = "");
```

This tells the compiler that any calls to just `Fill()` should be treated as calls to `Fill("","")`—in other words leaving both To and Subject empty. Next, you need to change the implementation of `Fill` to use those parameters.

```
void CComposeView::Fill(CString To, CString Subject)
{
    CString text = "";
    text += "To: " + To + "\r\n";
    text += "From: " + GetDocument()->GetUserid()
            + "@" + GetDocument()->GetSite() + "\r\n";
    text += "Subject: " + Subject+ "\r\n";

    text += "\r\n";

    GetEditCtrl().SetWindowText(text);
    int selchar = GetEditCtrl().LineIndex(
        ➥GetEditCtrl().GetLineCount()-1);
    GetEditCtrl().SetSel(selchar,selchar);
}
```

How is this different from the old `Fill`? The two parameters are listed now, for one thing. Note that there's no indication of the default values here in COMPOSE.CPP. It's helpful to add C-style comments that remind users of the default values:

```
void CComposeView::Fill(CString To /* = "" */,
                        CString Subject /* = "" */)
```

If you look carefully at the lines that start `text +=`, you'll see that the parameters are being inserted into the To: and Subject: headers. If they are "", this will have no effect, and so `Fill()` behaves just like the old `Fill`. Now `CMailView::OnMessageNew` and `CMessageView::OnMessageReply` can both set up a `CComposeView` and call its `Fill` method to make a blank mail message.

Try sending yourself a message by using Message, New, then displaying it and replying with Message, Reply. It works!

At this point you have a working application, but there are a few nice touches that can be added.

Resizing the List Box when the Main View Resizes

At the moment the list box is a fixed size, determined in OnInitialUpdate. But the list box fills the whole view, and it's natural for the user to assume that resizing the CMailView will resize the list box, too. This is a really simple thing to add, and makes any application feel more intuitive.

Whenever a view resizes, a WM_SIZE message is sent to it, telling it the new dimensions. You simply need to catch this message and resize the list box. There is only one trick: a WM_SIZE message is also sent before OnInitialUpdate is complete. Since that's where you call Create for the list box, and you can't resize a listbox that hasn't been Created yet, you need to add a flag to the class. In MAILVIEW.H add:

```
BOOL ListCreated;
```

Set this to FALSE in the constructor. You want to set it to TRUE after a successful Create, FALSE after a failed one. Luckily Create returns a Boolean value, so you simply assign the return value to ListCreated:

```
void CMailView::OnInitialUpdate()
{
    CRect rectangle;
    GetClientRect(rectangle);
    ListCreated = MessageList.Create(LBS_NOTIFY¦LBS_USETABSTOPS
                        ¦WS_CHILD¦WS_VISIBLE
                        ¦WS_VSCROLL¦WS_HSCROLL,
                        rectangle, this,IDC_MESSAGELISTBOX);
#define tabwidth 60
    MessageList.SetTabStops(tabwidth*4); //dialog units
    MessageList.SetHorizontalExtent(LOWORD(GetDialogBaseUnits())
                        *tabwidth*2); //pixels
}
```

Now let's catch that WM_SIZE message. Bring up ClassWizard and select CMailView from the drop-down list box. Choose the Message ID of CMailView—the Messages box fills with messages staring WM_. Scroll down to WM_SIZE, select it, and click AddFunction. You get no opportunity to set the name—this function is called OnSize. ClassWizard puts in a call to the OnSize member of the base class, and you add the check of ListCreated and the resizing of the list box:

```
void CMailView::OnSize(UINT nType, int cx, int cy)
{
    CView::OnSize(nType, cx, cy);
    if (ListCreated)
    {
        MessageList.MoveWindow(0,0,cx,cy);
    }
}
```

This function is called whenever the CMailView is resized: cx and cy are the new size. CListBox doesn't have a Size function, but the MoveWindow function is effectively a size: it takes the x and y coordinates of the two corners of the box. This call makes the list box fill the view.

Graying a Menu Item

As you've already seen, the framework grays and ungrays menu items according to which view has focus. For example, only CComposeView has a message map entry for Message, Send. When a CMessageView or CMailView has focus, Message, Send is grayed, and when a CComposeView has focus it is enabled (ungrayed). This is a great start, and saves a lot of work, but you need more. OnMessageDisplay makes an intelligent choice when the user hasn't highlighted a message, but Message, Delete probably shouldn't be available unless a message is highlighted.

ClassWizard makes this easy. You have created message map entries throughout this chapter for the COMMAND message associated with each menu item. You've ignored the UPDATE_COMMAND_UI message ClassWizard offered you in the Messages: box of the Message Maps tab. You're going to use it for Message, Delete, but first, a little digression and Windows explanation.

Whenever Windows has a free moment, it updates the user interface. That means writing text to the status line, lighting or dimming indicators on the status line, and doing all sorts of things to menu items if the menu is being displayed. Some menu items may have check marks by them, they may be grayed or ungrayed, and so on. To do these user interface updates, Windows sends out UPDATE_COMMAND_UI messages. Views in a position to know what state the menu item should be in catch the messages and update the user interface. In your case the CMailView knows whether or not a message is highlighted and so whether Message, Delete should be grayed.

Bring up ClassWizard and select CMailView from the drop-down list box. Click the MessageMaps tab and select the ID_MESSAGE_DELETE from the Object IDs list and UPDATE_COMMAND_UI from the Messages: list. Add a function: ClassWizard suggests OnUpdateMessageDelete; click OK. Figure 11.9 shows the ClassWizard dialog after adding this function. Click the Edit Code button to close ClassWizard and take you straight to OnUpdateMessageDelete.

Fig. 11.9
Use ClassWizard to arrange for your own function, OnUpdateMessage Delete, to be called when the Message, Delete menu item is to be displayed.

User interface update functions should be as fast as possible, because they are called just as the menu is drawn, and slow functions will make the menus behave oddly, coming up enabled but then graying, for example. Your update function has just one line:

```
void CMailView::OnUpdateMessageDelete(CCmdUI* pCmdUI)
{
    pCmdUI->Enable(MessageList.GetCurSel()>=0);
}
```

GetCurSel returns –1 if nothing is selected. The Enable function grays the menu item if it is passed FALSE and ungrays it if passed TRUE. The pointer to the interface item, pCmdUI, is provided by the framework for you to use.

You can now remove the if in OnSocket that makes sure the user is not choosing Message, Delete with nothing highlighted. Leave the contents of the if there, and remove the else block entirely. That neatens up your code and prevents wasted cycles by not starting the delete process if it could never work.

Double-Clicking a List Box

If you've been testing this application, you may have found it a little clunky to use. Menus are great for people who aren't sure what to do, but they can be slow when you're an experienced user. You probably automatically double-clicked a message a time or two, hoping to display it that way. Well, let's make it so it does!

You want the Windows event "double-clicking the list box contained in
the CMailView class" to trigger a call to the function OnMessageDisplay of
CMailView. ClassWizard won't do that for you, but you can do it yourself, by
adding a line to the message map in MAILVIEW.CPP:

```
BEGIN_MESSAGE_MAP(CMailView, CView)
    //{{AFX_MSG_MAP(CMailView)
    ON_COMMAND(ID_FILE_CHECKMAIL, OnFileCheckmail)
    ON_COMMAND(ID_MESSAGE_DISPLAY, OnMessageDisplay)
    ON_COMMAND(ID_MESSAGE_NEW, OnMessageNew)
    ON_COMMAND(ID_MESSAGE_DELETE, OnMessageDelete)
    ON_UPDATE_COMMAND_UI(ID_MESSAGE_DELETE, OnUpdateMessageDelete)
    //}}AFX_MSG_MAP
    ON_MESSAGE(WM_SOCKET_RESPONSE, OnSocket)
    ON_LBN_DBLCLK(IDC_MESSAGELISTBOX, OnMessageDisplay)
END_MESSAGE_MAP()
```

You don't need to change the message map in MAILVIEW.H because it is
only declaring the functions that get called, and OnMessageDisplay has already
been declared.

Just like that, you've made double-clicking a list box item equivalent to
single-clicking it and then choosing Message, Display. This flexibility is made
easy by insisting on separate functions to handle every message.

Connecting a Menu Item to a New Toolbar Button

That takes care of displaying the messages without having to mouse all the
way up to the menu bar, down to Display, and so on. But what about Message, Delete? Let's add it to the toolbar.

The toolbar is another of those neat "freebie" interface items the framework
gives you. It has icons already for File, New; File, Open; and so on—you may
have even been using them during testing. You're going to add a button to
that toolbar.

Use AppStudio to edit MAIL.RC and select Bitmap. There's only one,
IDR_MAINFRAME, so select it. Scroll rightwards through the bitmap until the end
of it is visible. Select the menu item Image Grid Settings and check the Tile
Grid checkbox, then click OK to accept the default grid values. This makes it
easy to enlarge the bitmap by exactly one tile. Move the mouse over the border of the bitmap until a sizing cursor appears, then drag the end of the
bitmap right one tile to create an empty button at the end of the bitmap,
as shown in figure 11.10.

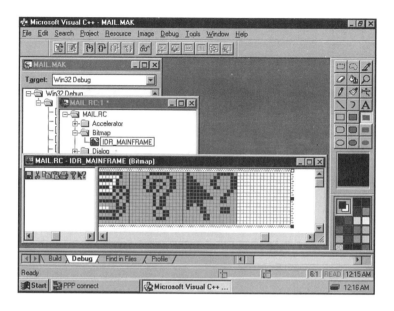

Fig. 11.10
The `IDR_MAINFRAME` bitmap is being stretched to accommodate a new button.

Click the selection tool—it's in the upper-left corner of the tools palette. Click in the upper-left corner of the second last button, then drag to the bottom-left corner of the last button. Release the mouse button, and click again somewhere in the selected region, then drag it rightwards. Now there is a plain white square in the middle of the toolbar bitmap (see fig. 11.11).

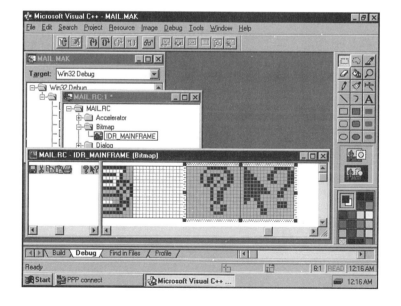

Fig. 11.11
After selecting and dragging the last two buttons one space rightward, the empty tile is now in the correct position.

This plain white square needs to be turned into a button. Your artistic abilities may well exceed mine: I simply wrote the letters DEL on the usual gray background (see fig. 11.12).

Fig. 11.12
The final toolbar includes a new button with the letters DEL, third from the right.

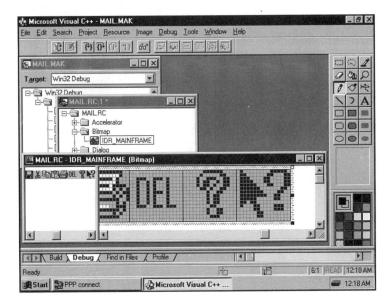

Close MAIL.RC and open the file MAINFRM.CPP. Find the definition of the buttons array. This maps the buttons on the toolbar to menu items through resource IDs. Entries in this array of ID_SEPARATOR cause a gap between buttons. You want to add ID_MESSAGE_DELETE, surrounded by separators. The array then becomes:

```
// Toolbar buttons - IDs are command buttons.
static UINT BASED_CODE buttons[] =
{
    // Same order as in the bitmap 'toolbar.bmp'.
    ID_FILE_NEW,
    ID_FILE_OPEN,
    ID_FILE_SAVE,
        ID_SEPARATOR,
    ID_EDIT_CUT,
    ID_EDIT_COPY,
    ID_EDIT_PASTE,
        ID_SEPARATOR,
    ID_FILE_PRINT,
        ID_SEPARATOR,
    ID_MESSAGE_DELETE,
        ID_SEPARATOR,
    ID_APP_ABOUT,
    ID_CONTEXT_HELP,
};
```

Just like that, Message, Delete has been added to the toolbar (see fig. 11.13), and it works! Try it yourself. And whenever the menu item is grayed, so is the toolbar button—automatically.

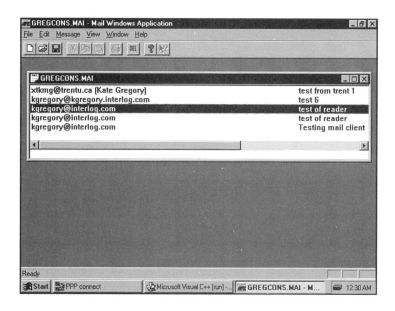

Fig. 11.13
The toolbar in your application now has the new button. The space surrounding it is generated by the ID_SEPARATOR entries in the buttons array.

Error Checking

The SMTP and POP3 hosts go to some trouble to check what you're doing, and let you know if it succeeded or not. At this point you're ignoring almost every response from these hosts; let's do something about that.

In `CMailView::OnSocket` you send a `USER` command and a `PASS` command. If the response to either of these is "-ERR", you can't access the mailbox and the user should be told to run File, Setup again. You just wrap the code after the `USER` command in an if:

```
if (response.Left(3) == "+OK")
```

and add an else clause that tells the user about the problem and closes the connection:

```
else
{
    AfxMessageBox("Userid incorrect. Enter the
        ➥correct userid with File Setup.");
    pSocket->Send("QUIT \r\n");
    response = pSocket->GetLine();
    delete pSocket;
    pSocket = NULL;
}
```

II

Developing Applications

You do the same thing after the PASS command, so that the CONNECTED case
looks like this:

```
case CONNECTED:
    // Switch to getline.
    pSocket->SetReceiveTarget(NULL,0);
    response = pSocket->GetLine();
    pSocket->Send("USER " + doc->GetUserid() + "\r\n");
    response = pSocket->GetLine();
    if (response.Left(3) == "+OK")
    {
        pSocket->Send("PASS " + doc->GetPassword() + "\r\n");
        response = pSocket->GetLine();
        if (response.Left(3) == "+OK")
        {

            if (State == CheckMail)
            {
                FillListBox();
                State = Idle;
            }
            if (State == Delete)
            {
                int index = MessageList.GetCurSel();
                MessageList.ResetContent();
                char command[20];
                // Unlikely to have a 13-digit message number.
                sprintf(command, "DELE %i \r\n",index+1);
                pSocket->Send(command);
                response = pSocket->GetLine();

                pSocket->Send("QUIT \r\n");
                response = pSocket->GetLine();
                delete pSocket;
                pSocket = NULL;

                OnFileCheckmail();

            }
        }
        else
        {
            AfxMessageBox("Password incorrect. Enter
               ➥the correct password with File Setup.");
            pSocket->Send("QUIT \r\n");
            response = pSocket->GetLine();
            delete pSocket;
            pSocket = NULL;
        }
    }
    else
    {
        AfxMessageBox("Userid incorrect. Enter
           ➥the correct userid with File Setup.");
        pSocket->Send("QUIT \r\n");
```

```
        response = pSocket->GetLine();
        delete pSocket;
        pSocket = NULL;
    }
    break;
```

You do the same thing in `CMessageView::OnSocket`. In `CComposeView::OnSocket` you are talking to the SMTP server, where `220` (for a `HELO`), `250`, and `251` are successful replies. Test `response.Left(1)` against "2" in this routine. Also, copy the block of code that sends the `QUIT` and deletes the socket to all the `else`s—you will `QUIT` no matter what. Make sure the `DestroyWindow` call is inside all the `if`s, so that if anything is wrong the compose view stays up. This enables the user to correct the error and then select Message, Send again. The `DestroyWindow` call must be after the send of `QUIT`, since `DestroyWindow` will call the `CComposeView` destructor, which deletes `pSocket`.

Using Your Mail Client

Though this client uses two different Internet protocols, you don't need to understand either of them to use it. Your Internet service provider should tell you your SMTP host, your POP3 host and ID, and your POP3 password. Some providers give your POP3 information as an account: the part before the @ is your ID and the part after it is the host. When you first run this program, select File, Setup and fill in the hosts, ID, password, and real name fields. After clicking OK, select File, Save As so you won't have to type all that again. From then on just open this file (give it the name of your service provider if you have more than one, or your own name if several people use your machine.)

To list the messages in your mailbox, choose File, Check Mail. To view a message, double-click it, or single-click it and choose Message, Display. To delete a message, from the main view click it and click the DEL button on the toolbar or choose Message, Delete. To reply to a message, display it and from that message view choose Message, Reply. To enter a new message that is not a reply to an existing one, from the main view choose Message, New. Whether composing a new message or a reply, when it is complete choose Message, Send to dispatch the message to its recipient.

From Here...

This application needs more than just simple error-checking; it needs error prevention. Just as you grayed Message, Delete to prevent the user from selecting the menu item without a highlighted message, you can keep the user out of trouble with a little thought. For example:

- In `CMailDoc::OnFileSetup`, you assume that the user has filled in all of the fields on the dialog, and filled in reasonable values. To do this, override the `OnOK` function in the `CSetupDialog` class. If a field has been left blank or fails some other test you choose to implement (for example, userids should not contain '@' characters), you put up a message box asking the user to correct the error and return from `OnOK`. If all the fields pass all the tests, call `CDialog::OnOK()` before returning. This closes the dialog and makes `DoModal` return `IDOK`.

- The user must leave an empty line between the headers and the body. Before connecting the socket, check for this blank line. It's easier said than done, because long header lines may be folded as described earlier. One quick test would be to ensure that there is at least one empty line somewhere in the edit control. It may be too far down, in which case the first half of the message body wil be folded into the last header. Warn the user with an `AfxMessageBox` and don't close the view or send the message if there's no empty line.

The product should be able to handle several recipients for a single mail message, for example a To line of:

```
To: kate@gregcons.com, elaine@somesite.com
```

You'll need to replace the single `CString` in `CComposeView::OnSocket` with a `CStringArray`, and after finding a line that starts To:, look through it for commas and parse out the individual recipients, then add each recipient to the `CStringArray`. Similarly, look for `cc` lines. If you're feeling adventurous, you can handle `bcc`, too. These lines have to be removed from the message before you send it, so that the other recipients don't know who is getting the "blind carbon copy."

You may have already caught this one: it's a bad idea to store the password in the document as you are doing in this application. Remove `IDC_PASSWORD` from `IDD_SETUP` (and `m_password` and Password from `CSetupDialog` and `CMailDoc`, too). Create a new password dialog and have it put up as part of `OnConnect` to get the password from the user. Do not save it or store it.

Finally, these views of ours have distinctly ugly window titles: the name of the setup file followed by a :1 or :2. Wouldn't it be better to have, for example, the subject line of the mail message as the window title for the Message View? The key to this change is to write your own MDI Child Window Frame classes, one for each view, that inherit from `CMDIChildWnd` but override the function that handles frame titles. You'll see this in action in the next chapter, "Building an Internet Newsreader Application."

Chapter 12

Building an Internet Newsreader Application

UseNet news is often referred to these days as "Internet news" or "Internet newsgroups," though originally UseNet operated completely independently of the Internet. The development in the mid-1980s of NNTP (Network News Transport Protocol, which allowed news to travel over the Internet) brought UseNet onto the Internet and facilitated its tremendous growth in the late 80s and early 90s. In this chapter you'll learn about:

- How news is structured

- What a newsreader does

- Using the NNTP news transport protocol to get and send news

- How to design your own newsreader

- How to build your newsreader

The Structure of News

Just what is news? It's the Internet's version of an electronic bulletin board. It's also thousands of conversations going on all at once, with people communicating by posting news messages into *newsgroups*. A news message looks a lot like a mail message, with a few important distinctions. A sample news posting is shown in figure 12.1.

Fig. 12.1

This sample UseNet posting discusses the difference between radio buttons and check buttons in MFC. The first nine lines are the header of the article, and the remainder is the body.

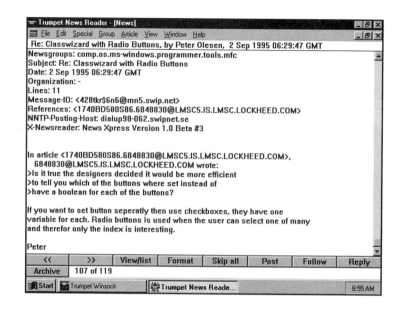

News differs from BBS systems or online conferencing systems in many important ways, including the behavior of the people who use it. The differences between the structure of a news article and some other kind of message include:

- There is no To header. News is public and never addressed to a specific individual.

- News postings are not mixed in with private messages.

- News postings that are a response to a previous message have Subject headers that start with "Re:" (without the quotes).

- There is a Message-ID header that contains a unique identifier for each message.

- There is a References header that contains the Message-IDs of any and all previous messages that inspired the posting.

- The Newsgroups header of a news posting may contain more than one newsgroup name. This is called *crossposting* and is an important news feature.

- Special headers called Reply-To and Followup-To tell users who are generating followups or replies to use a different list of newsgroups or e-mail address respectively.

- There are other headers such as Path, NNTP-Posting-Host, and Sender that track the origin and history of the posting.

Probably the most important distinction to draw is the definition of a newsgroup. Newsgroups are arranged in a topical hierarchy according to the material discussed in them. (A few groups are not for discussion, but rather for announcements or non-text postings; they are also placed according to their subject matter.) The name of the group explains the material it covers.

Newsgroup names consist of two or more components separated by dots: for example, **misc.kids**, **comp.lang.c++**, or **rec.arts.tv.soaps.abc**—the groups for discussing child-raising, the C++ programming language, or ABC television's soap operas, respectively. Some groups are *moderated*, which means only one person can submit articles to them; contributors e-mail submissions to the moderator, who posts or rejects them. Most groups are *unmoderated* and articles can be posted to them through an NNTP server. (There are other ways to post news as well, but the conversation is being restricted to NNTP since that is the protocol used to carry news over the Internet.)

> **NOTE**   If you want to learn more about UseNet news, *Using UseNet Newsgroups*, published by Que, is an introduction to the culture of news, covering how to find what you want and how to participate yourself as well as the features of a number of popular newsreaders.

Just as the format of a mail message is defined by RFC 822, the format of a news message (also called a *posting* or an *article*) is defined by RFC 1036. News is transferred between machines by a number of different transport methods; NNTP, the method you'll be using, is defined by RFC 977. By the time you've finished reading this chapter, you should also have read both these RFCs— they're on the CD that comes with this book.

Basic Functions of a Newsreader

A newsreader enables a user to read and respond to articles in selected groups. It shows the user what groups are available, what articles are available in each group, and displays selected articles. It also enables users to generate new articles or followups to existing articles, or private e-mail responses. Even a just-barely-functional newsreader is a far more complex application than finger, whois, or most of the other Internet applications you've covered so far. And what you're building here will be just that, a barely functional newsreader.

To get an idea of all the functionality that should be in any newsreader you'd actually use, point your Web browser at **http://www.mit.edu:8001/ people/rnewman/Good-Netkeeping-Seal**—this document describes the features of a newsreader that will produce well-formed articles. Some of the key points are:

- All the "essential" headers must, by default, be displayed while a user is reading an article. These are Subject, Newsgroups, Followup-To (if different from Newsgroups,) and Reply-To (if different from From).

- The commands to create a new article, a followup article, and an e-mail reply must be clearly different.

- *Crossposting*, sending the same article to more than one newsgroup (not individual copies to each group), must be implemented.

- Users must be allowed to edit the essential headers of articles they are preparing, at any time in the process.

- Followup articles must create Newsgroups, Subject, and References headers based on the original article, following a strict set of rules.

- E-mail replies must create Subject and To headers based on the original article.

- When creating followup articles and e-mail replies, users must be able to include quoted text from the original article, and the software must generate an attribution line that identifies the source of the quoted material.

- All articles must have a nonblank Subject header and a From header that includes a full e-mail address.

- The software must be able to generate cancel messages that delete one of the user's own articles from all the news servers on the net.

- When a user is preparing a posting, the software must ensure the user knows where the line breaks are. Many other people read news on text-based systems that can't handle long lines, and many users don't realize that their lines are not wrapping on other people's machines.

- Users should be warned if they prepare and send an article (followup or original) with no new material of their own.

This is a long list of features, and you won't be implementing them all in this chapter. You will create a functional newsreader and newsposter, though.

Using NNTP

You will be writing an NNTP newsreader, to access articles stored on another machine across the Internet. The NNTP protocol was discussed in Chapter 2, "Understanding Internet Protocols," and is fully described in RFC 977.

As with your other Internet applications, you will be building commands and sending them to a port on another machine, then receiving information in response. The NNTP port is 119. Commands are sometimes followed by a parameter (the command and the parameter are separated by one or more spaces or tabs) and always by a carriage return-linefeed pair. As usual, they are restricted to 512 characters in length.

NNTP responses are either text or status. The first line of any response is always a status response, which may indicate that there is text to follow. The text may be the headers for an article, the body for an article, or some other information you have requested. The end of a text response is a "." alone on a line terminated with a CR-LF pair. The status responses all start with a three digit number. (RFC 977 explains the meaning of each digit.)

Different commands will produce different status responses. Since newsreaders enable you to read articles, you'll start with the command to get an article from the NNTP server:

```
ARTICLE <message-id>
```

A successful ARTICLE command gets the response 220 *n* <a>, where *n* is the article number within the current group, which you can ignore, and <a> is the message ID. The text response that follows is the article header, a blank line, the article body, and the "." alone on a line to terminate the text response.

The HEAD command is just like the ARTICLE command except it returns only the headers of the message. Both ARTICLE and HEAD need a message ID as the sole parameter. How will you know what message ID to send? There are lots of ways, but one obvious choice is to use the NEWNEWS command, which returns a list of message IDs that reached the server after a specified time, as in:

```
NEWNEWS newsgroups date time [GMT] [<distribution>]
```

This command has three required parameters and two optional parameters (remember the entire command is limited to 512 characters):

II

Developing Applications

- The newsgroups parameter may be the name of a single group, such as **news.newusers.questions**, or it may be a list of group names separated by commas. There cannot be any spaces in the newsgroups parameter.

- The date is sent as YYMMDD with no punctuation.

- The time is sent as HHMMSS with no punctuation.

- If you have converted local time to Universal time (formerly called Greenwich Mean Time), you add the letters GMT after the time—you won't bother converting from local time.

- The fifth parameter, distribution, is obsolete; you won't be specifying it either.

The status response to a successful NEWNEWS command is 230. The text response that follows is message IDs, one per line, of new articles. The list terminates with a "." alone on a line, and if there are no new articles there will be nothing in the text response before the terminating ".".

How will you know what newsgroup names to put in the NEWNEWS command? The LIST command returns a list of all valid newsgroups. There are no parameters to a LIST command, and the only response code is 215. The text response that follows is a series of lines of the form "group last first p," where group is the name of the newsgroup (such as **news.newusers.questions**), first is the article number of the first article the server has in that group, last is the article number of the last article, and p is a single character to indicate whether users can post directly to the group: 'y' for yes and 'n' for no. Only the newsgroup name is needed for your newsreader.

After your user successfully composes an original article or a followup, you can use the POST command to deliver it to the server. And before you close down the program, the QUIT command tells the server you're finished.

These six commands (LIST, NEWNEWS, ARTICLE, HEAD, POST, and QUIT) are all that you'll need to implement your reader.

Designing a Newsreader

Your newsreader design seems pretty straightforward. It will be a multi-view design much like your mail application (refer to Chapter 11, "Building an Internet Electronic Mail Application"). You'll get the name of the NNTP server the user wants to read news from, and connect to it. Then you'll use the LIST command to get a list of newsgroups and put it into the main view, the Group Selection View. When the user indicates a group should be displayed (perhaps by double-clicking, perhaps with a menu choice), you'll use the NEWNEWS command to get a list of message IDs for new articles in that group, and put them in a new view, an Article Selection View. When the user indicates which one to read (by double-clicking, or another menu choice), you'll use the ARTICLE command to get the article and display it in an Article View. If the user wants to compose a followup or original article, that is done in a Compose View, just as in Mail. To send e-mail replies, you'll have to copy the SMTP send material from Mail.

This seems reasonably straightforward except for one thing: "the user chooses a message ID." What's in a message ID that lets a user know whether an article might be worth reading? Well, nothing. It's just a unique identifier. What can you show the user that might be useful? The header has some very useful information, like Subject and From, so you'll show those, as you did with mail. You get just the header with the HEAD command.

You'll get your message IDs into the Article Selection View with NEWNEWS, get the header for each message ID with HEAD, display a list of the Subject and From headers, and when the user chooses to display an article, you use the ARTICLE command to get the whole article into an ArticleView.

You'll need some new menus and menu items, too. File, Setup will be like File, Setup in mail (see Chapter 11, "Building an Internet Electronic Mail Application,") setting the host and user information. You'll also need Group, Display and Article, Display, plus other Group and Article commands that you'll learn about as you go. Great, now get started!

Developing a Newsreader

By now the basic steps involved in building any Internet application should be getting pretty familiar. You'll create the application, add things to the menu, build a dialog or two, and then develop the actual newsreader code to connect to the server, list newsgroups, list articles in a newsgroup, display an article, create a new article, send an article to the NNTP server, and disconnect.

Creating the Application
First, you'll use AppWizard to create the basic application, called Newsread. You need an MDI application with a toolbar, just as with Mail. You won't be coding printing for this application; you'll save that for future enhancements.

So you turn off support for Print and Print Preview. Turn on Sockets support, either in AppWizard or by hand afterwards. When AppWizard summarizes the classes to be created, click Advanced and set the file extension to be .NWS, as shown in figure 12.2.

Fig. 12.2
This AppWizard dialog, Advanced Options, is where you specify the file extension that goes with your newsreader file.

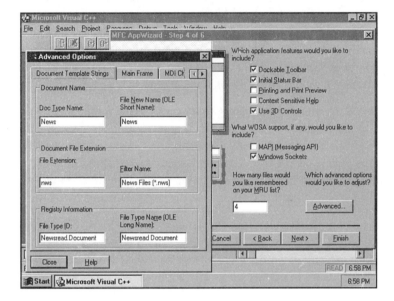

As usual, AppWizard creates a basic menu structure for you: File, Edit, View, Window, and Help. You'll need to add two menus: Article and Group. Group will have an item Display to show the articles in a selected group, and Article will have an item Display to show the selected article. Those are awfully short menus, but as you work through development you'll add a few more items. You use AppStudio to create them, as shown in figure 12.3.

While you're in AppStudio, you need a Setup dialog, like the one in figure 12.4. It needs to save three pieces of information: the NNTP host address, the user's e-mail address, and the user's real name. Give the controls the resource IDs IDC_NNTPHOST, IDC_USER, and IDC_USERNAME. Why NNTPHOST and not just HOST? Because if your product is going to be able to send mail, it will need the address of an SMTP host someday.

Then bring up ClassWizard from within AppStudio to create a CSetupDialog class (in the files SETUP.CPP and SETUP.H) with the controls hooked as CString values to the variables m_nntphost, m_user, and m_username.

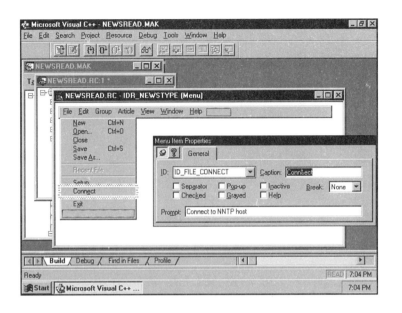

Fig. 12.3
You add menu
items in
AppStudio. The
Properties sheet
shows the resource
name, caption,
and prompt for
each menu item.

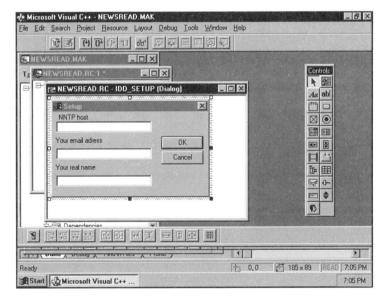

Fig. 12.4
The Setup dialog is
used to enter the
host and user
information.

Leave AppStudio and edit NEWSRDOC.H, adding three CString variables to
the class: NNTPHost, User, and Username. Inspired by CMailDoc::Serialize, from
Chapter 11, "Building an Internet Electronic Mail Application," write
CNewsreadDoc::Serialize like this:

```
void CNewsreadDoc::Serialize(CArchive& ar)
{
    if (ar.IsStoring())
    {
        ar << NNTPHost;
        ar << User;
        ar << Username;
    }
    else
    {
        ar >> NNTPHost;
        ar >> User;
        ar >> Username;
    }
}
```

Now wherever you put up the setup dialog, you fill it from the document variables and use it to set the document variables, just as you did with Mail.

Getting Connected and Set Up

You need to deal with that dialog right away. It will be brought up by a menu item: File, Setup. Add the item in AppStudio, then use ClassWizard to ensure that the message is caught by a CNewsreadDoc function called OnFileSetup. That function looks like this:

```
void CNewsreadDoc::OnFileSetup()
{
    CSetupDialog dialog;
      dialog.m_nntphost = NNTPHost;
      dialog.m_user = User;
      dialog.m_username = Username;

    if (dialog.DoModal() == IDOK)
    {
        NNTPHost = dialog.m_nntphost;
        User = dialog.m_user;
        Username = dialog.m_username;
        SetModifiedFlag();
    }

}
```

Now you know what site to connect to. To make the connection, you need a socket. Where will that socket be kept?

In most of the applications you've seen so far, all the socket handling was in a single view, like CFingerView or CFtpView. In Mail, many different views did socket work, but they each had their own pointer and made the connection fresh each time. Here in news, you're going to connect to the server at the beginning and stay connected. You have four different views and a document, all of which will need to access the connected socket.

The C programmers are all thinking at this point, "Use a global!" but there's a nicer way. If you add the socket pointer to the document, the views can all reach it with the function GetDocument().

What happens if one of the views sets the Receive Target for the socket, and sends a command, but before the response comes back another view changes the ReceiveTarget? A big mess is what happens. So you should add a flag (SocketAvailable) to the class too, and two functions, GetSocket and ReleaseSocket. So the lines you add to NEWSRDOC.H are:

```
private:
    CSocket* pSocket;
    BOOL SocketAvailable;
public:
    QSocket* GetSocket();
    BOOL IsSocketAvailable() {return SocketAvailable;}
    void ReleaseSocket();
```

SocketAvailable is set to FALSE in the constructor, and is set to TRUE after a successful connection. GetSocket uses it like this:

```
CSocket* CNewsreadDoc::GetSocket()
{
    if (SocketAvailable)
    {
        SocketAvailable = FALSE;
        return pSocket;
    }
    else
    {
        return NULL;
    }
}
```

SocketAvailable is set back to TRUE by ReleaseSocket, which doesn't do anything else:

```
void CNewsreadDoc::ReleaseSocket()
{
    SocketAvailable = TRUE;
}
```

You're all set for handling the socket once it's connected, but where will you connect it? The user should make the connection, once the setup is complete or the right file has been loaded, so you need to add a menu item. You add it to the File menu because it fits better there than elsewhere. Use AppStudio to add a menu item called Connect right after Setup, and use ClassWizard to connect that message to a function in CNewsreadDoc called OnFileConnect.

In the past, you've set a Receive Target before trying to connect, and the status change triggered a message, so the work of handling the connection was in OnSocket. But a document cannot be a message target, only a command target (a subtle Windows distinction) so you have to wait until the connection goes through.

 NOTE If you had designed QSocket to send commands rather than messages, this wouldn't be an issue. Sending commands is a little trickier than sending messages, but you're welcome to try it.

While you're waiting, you pump Windows messages. Here's OnFileConnect:

```
void CNewsreadDoc::OnFileConnect()
{
    delete pSocket;
    SocketAvailable = FALSE;  // Until we're connected.
    pSocket = new QSocket();

    if (pSocket->Connect(NNTPHost, 119))
    {
        while (pSocket->GetStatus() == CONNECTING)
        {
          for(;;)
          {
              MSG msg;
              if (PeekMessage(&msg, NULL, 0, 0, PM_REMOVE))
              {
                  TranslateMessage(&msg);
                  DispatchMessage(&msg);
              }
              else
              {
                  break;
              }
          }
        }
        if (pSocket->GetStatus() == CONNECTED)
        {
          CString response = AppSocket->GetLine();
            SocketAvailable = TRUE;
        }
    }

    if (!SocketAvailable)
    {
        CString message = "Can't connect to server.
          ➥Check File Setup settings";
        message += '\n';
        message += "and then do File Connect again.";

        AfxMessageBox(message,MB_OK¦MB_ICONSTOP);
    }
}
```

```
    else
    {
        AfxMessageBox("Connected", MB_OK¦MB_ICONINFORMATION);
    }
}
```

The loop that starts with `for(;;)` is called a *message pump*. It looks to see if
there are any messages waiting to be delivered to other windows, and if so it
dispatches them. Whenever there are no messages, it breaks from the `for`
loop, checks the socket status at the top of the loop, and if you're still CON-
NECTING, pumps some more messages. Eventually you are no longer CON-
NECTING and are instead CONNECTED or in an error state (the `enum` in
SOCKET.H lists all the Status values). If you are CONNECTED, you do a
`GetLine` to bring back the "hi there" message the server has surely given you.
You set the `SocketAvailable` flag so that other functions can use this con-
nected socket.

If the original `Connect` call failed, or the status was not CONNECTED, you end
up outside your first `if` with `SocketAvailable` still false. The user needs to
redo File, Setup and then try connecting again. If it's true, you're connected.
You put up a message box, because the connection can take quite a while and
so it's nice to tell the user when it's finally complete.

A List of Newsgroups to Choose From

You've already decided that you'll use the LIST command to get a list of
newsgroups from the NNTP server. But there are well over 10,000 newsgroups
on the net—should you really build such a list and show it to the user every
time? Getting this list every time makes startup very slow, and users will get
aggravated paging through 10 or 15 thousand groups to find the ones they're
interested in. It is much more convenient for the user to designate certain
groups as *subscribed*, and show only the subscribed ones to the user every
time. This concept is explored in more detail in Que's Using UseNet
Newsgroups.

You'll keep a list of subscribed groups in the application's document using
the MFC class `CStringArray`, then add two menu items, Group, Subscribe and
Group, Unsubscribe, to add and delete groups from the subscribed list. You'll
leave those aside for a moment and work on the main Group Selection View,
`CNewsreadView`.

You want the view to contain a list box, so you add a line to NEWSRVW.H
saying that the view has a list box called `GroupList`:

```
    CListBox GroupList;
```

Now, you need to make this box come up on-screen with group names in it. You add an override of the OnInitialUpdate method for your view, and have it call the list box Create method, which causes the list box to appear in the window:

```
void CNewsreadView::OnInitialUpdate()
{
    CRect rectangle;
    GetClientRect(rectangle);
    GroupList.Create(LBS_NOTIFY|WS_CHILD|WS_VISIBLE
                |WS_VSCROLL|WS_HSCROLL,
                rectangle, this,IDC_GROUPLISTBOX);
}
```

Most of the style flags in the Create call should be familiar, except perhaps the LBS_NOTIFY style. It asks the list box to pass along any notification messages it receives because of a user action such as clicking or double-clicking.

This creates the list box within the view, but it will be empty until you make some calls to GroupList.AddString. What strings will you be adding? The strings in your CStringArray, your subscribed groups, of course. You'll add this list of subscribed groups to your document. In NEWSRDOC.H add:

```
CStringArray SubscribedGroups;
```

You need to change the Serialize function for the document so that this list is read in when you open a document, and written out when you save one. The CStringArray class handles the IsStoring question for us, so you just add a call to its Serialize method before the if:

```
void CNewsreadDoc::Serialize(CArchive& ar)
{
    SubscribedGroups.Serialize(ar);
    if (ar.IsStoring())
    {
        ar << NNTPHost;
        ar << User;
        ar << Username;
    }
    else
    {
        ar >> NNTPHost;
        ar >> User;
        ar >> Username;
    }
}
```

How do you know whether your Serialize function should call an object's Serialize function or check ar.IsStoring and use << and >>? If the object has a Serialize function, use it! It makes your Serialize much easier to read. Once you get down to numbers, CStrings, and other low-level types, use << and >>.

Now, back in `CNewsreadView::OnInitialUpdate`, you put in some `AddString` calls to add one string for each entry in `SubscribedGroups`:

```
void CNewsreadView::OnInitialUpdate()
{
    CRect rectangle;
    GetClientRect(rectangle);
    GroupList.Create(LBS_NOTIFY¦WS_CHILD¦WS_VISIBLE
                ¦WS_VSCROLL¦WS_HSCROLL,
                rectangle, this,IDC_GROUPLISTBOX);
    for (int i = 0; i< ((CNewsreadDoc*)GetDocument())
        ➡->SubscribedGroups.GetSize(); i++)
    {
        GroupList.AddString(((CNewsreadDoc*)GetDocument())
            ➡->SubscribedGroups[i]);
    }
}
```

All views in MFC can find their documents with the method `GetDocument()`. You cast the returned pointer to a `CNewsreadDoc*` because you want to access a member of `CNewsreadDoc`. If you're thinking that you should really dereference that function call, saving the document pointer so you don't call the function at the top of each loop and again in the body of the loop, relax. `GetDocument` is an inline function, which means the compiler expands it like a macro. There's no function call overhead involved.

The `GetSize()` method of `CStringArray` returns the number of strings in the array, and the `[]` operator returns strings in the array. `SubscribedGroups[i]` is the i'th string (zero-based). You then pass that string to `AddString` and it goes into the list box for the user to see.

So it's time to fill that `CStringArray` by handling the <u>G</u>roup, <u>S</u>ubscribe menu item. Add <u>S</u>ubscribe and <u>U</u>nsubscribe to the <u>G</u>roup menu with AppStudio. Then use the Message Maps tab in ClassWizard to connect these menu items to functions in `CNewsreadView` called `OnGroupSubscribe` and `OnGroupUnsubscribe`. Since <u>G</u>roup, <u>D</u>isplay will be handled by the `CNewsreadView` as well, you might as well connect that message while you have ClassWizard up.

Next, you need a Group Subscribe dialog box to find out what group to add. Some users might want to choose from a list of valid groups, while others want to just type the name instead of waiting for that 10,000-item list to come across the phone wire. You'll arrange for both ways to work.

Follow these steps to create and flesh out the dialog box:

1. Create the dialog box in AppStudio. Give it the resource ID `ID_GROUP_SUBSCRIBE` and the caption Group Subscribe.

2. Add static text "Group Name:" an edit box (ID_GROUP_NAME), a button with the caption "Fill List Box" (ID_GROUP_FILL), and a list box (ID_GROUP_LIST) to the dialog, as shown in figure 12.5.

Fig. 12.5
The Group Subscribe dialog enables the user to type in a group name or choose it from the full list. Clicking the Fill buttons fills the list.

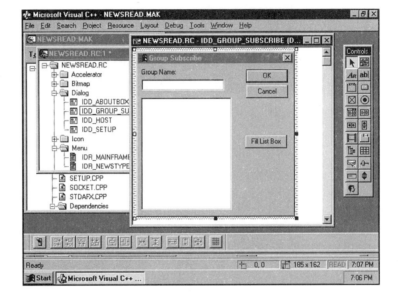

3. Bring up ClassWizard from within AppStudio and connect the dialog to a class called CGroupSubscribeDialog, in the files GROUPSUB.H and GROUPSUB.CPP.

4. Connect the edit box to a string called m_groupname in the usual way. For the list box, choose Control rather than Value, and connect the list box to a CListBox called m_grouplist.

You're not finished with this class yet. When the user clicks the Fill button, you want to catch that message right in this dialog and fill the list box by asking the server for a list of groups. Also, when the user clicks an entry in the list box, you want to catch that message and copy the selected item into the edit box. This confirms the selection for the user and makes it easier for you to find the selected group after the user clicks OK.

Don't leave OnGroupSubscribe dangling any longer. It needs to put up the dialog, and it can count on the edit box, which is connected to the member variable m_groupname, containing a group name that you need to add to your list of subscribed groups if the user clicked OK. This makes it a fairly simple function:

```
void CNewsreadView::OnGroupSubscribe()
{
    CGroupSubscribeDialog dialog(this);
    if (dialog.DoModal() == IDOK)
    {
        ((CNewsreadDoc*)GetDocument())->SubscribedGroups.Add(
            ➥dialog.m_groupname);
        GetDocument()->SetModifiedFlag();
        GroupList.AddString(dialog.m_groupname);
    }
}
```

You declare an instance of the dialog, and put it up with DoModal. If the
user clicks OK, you add the name of the selected group to the document's
SubscribedGroups and the list box GroupList. You also set the modified flag
for the document to trigger a save later.

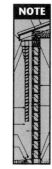

> **NOTE**
>
> A real newsreader would make sure this is a valid group; the user could have typed
> the group name directly into the edit box and made an error. The GROUP command
> enables you to check with the NNTP server, which tells you if the group exists on
> that server or not. You're going to skip this validation step for now, but by the end of
> this chapter you should feel confident enough to add it.
>
> If you were really feeling adventurous, you might consider saving this long list of
> newsgroups in a different file (there's no need to keep it in the document) and add a
> field to File, Setup so the user can indicate where this local copy is kept. Many people
> refer to this list of newsgroups as "the active file." It can take over ten minutes to
> bring the list down from the server.

Group, Unsubscribe is just the opposite:

```
void CNewsreadView::OnGroupUnsubscribe()
{
    int index = GroupList.GetCurSel();
    if (index < 0)
    {
        // User hasn't selected a group.
        return;
    }
    ((CNewsreadDoc*)GetDocument())->SubscribedGroups.RemoveAt(
        ➥index);
    GetDocument()->SetModifiedFlag();
    GroupList.DeleteString(index);
}
```

If the user has clicked a group in the list, you delete the group name from
SubscribedGroups and from the list box, and set the document's modified
flag.

Now, back to CGroupSubscribeDialog. You'll tackle the Fill button first. Use ClassWizard to arrange for the message to trigger a call to OnGroupFill. The function itself needs to get the socket, send it the LIST command, and add each group name to the list box as it comes in. But unfortunately, CGroupSubscribeDialog is not a view, and so it can't call its GetDocument() method to find the socket. You have to pass the socket pointer to the dialog when you construct it in OnGroupSubscribe. Change the CGroupSubscribeDialog constructor to take a QSocket* as well as a CWnd*, and add a QSocket* called Socket to the class. The constructor sets Socket to the passed pointer. You'll have to change OnGroupSubscribe so that it passes the socket pointer:

```
void CNewsreadView::OnGroupSubscribe()
{
    QSocket *socket = GetDocument()->GetSocket();

    if (socket)
    {
        CGroupSubscribeDialog dialog(socket, this);
        if (dialog.DoModal() == IDOK)
        {
            ((CNewsreadDoc*)GetDocument())->SubscribedGroups
                ➡.Add(dialog.m_groupname);
            GetDocument()->SetModifiedFlag();
            GroupList.AddString(dialog.m_groupname);
        }

        GetDocument()->ReleaseSocket();
    }
    else
    {
        AfxMessageBox("The connection is busy now.
            ➡Try again in a moment.",MB_OK¦MB_ICONSTOP);
    }
}
```

You try to get the socket pointer from the document, and if you can't ask the user to try later. If you got it, you declare the dialog (passing the extra parameter to the constructor), and proceed as before. After the dialog has been completed (either by OK or Cancel), you release the socket because the dialog no longer needs it.

You're ready to write OnGroupFill. The basic structure should look like this:

```
void CGroupSubscribeDialog::OnGroupFill()
{
    // Fill the list box with groupnames.
    CString response;
    if (Socket)
    {
        Socket->Send("LIST\r\n");
```

```
    response = Socket->GetLine();
    if ( atoi(response) == 215)
    {
        // Group names.
        while ( (response = Socket->GetLine()) != ".\r\n"
                && Socket->GetStatus() == CONNECTED)
        {
            // Add group name to list box.
            // Pump messages that may have accumulated.
        }
    }
}
```

The `while` block keeps going until the entire list has been received or the socket has somehow disconnected. Remember text responses are terminated with "." alone on a line.

Why are you using `GetLine` instead of just setting a Receive target and doing something else until the socket has some group names? Because you're expecting lots of little short lines, and it would be a lot of work to parse them into lines.

The group names are the first token in the response, so you need to extract the portion up to the first space. Adding the names to the list box doesn't always succeed—a lot of very long entries can use up the available memory. (In fact, for 16-bit applications only about 3,000 of the 13,000 or so newsgroups in existence will fit into the box.) You set up a flag called `keep_adding` and start it as `true`. If an `AddString` fails, you set that flag to `false` and avoid future adds. Adding the names to the list box looks like this:

```
length = response.Find(" ");
if (length >= 0 && keep_adding)
{
    if (m_grouplist.AddString(response.Left(
        ➥length)) < 0)
    {
        keep_adding = FALSE;
    }
}
```

Without a message pump in here, the user cannot even page up and down until the whole list has been retrieved—this can take several minutes, and a wait that long is not acceptable. The message pump code should look familiar from the "waiting to connect" code in `OnFileConnect`:

```
for(;;)
{
    MSG msg;

    if (PeekMessage(&msg, NULL, 0, 0,
```

```
                    PM_REMOVE))
            {
                TranslateMessage(&msg);
                DispatchMessage(&msg);
            }
            else
            {
                break;
            }
    }
```

Speaking of taking a long time, what if an impatient user clicks the Fill button while the list is still filling, or clicks OK or Cancel too soon? If you gray those buttons as you start this long process, and ungray them when you're finished, the user will get an obvious indication of how things are going.

Use ClassWizard to connect the Fill button to a CButton called m_ fillbutton, the OK button to m_okbutton, and the Cancel button to m_cancelbutton. Now, at the top of OnFill, gray all three of these:

```
    m_fillbutton.EnableWindow(FALSE);     // Gray the button.
    m_okbutton.EnableWindow(FALSE);       // Gray the button.
    m_cancelbutton.EnableWindow(FALSE);   // Gray the button.
```

At the very end of the function, enable them again:

```
    m_fillbutton.EnableWindow(TRUE);      // Ungray the button.
    m_okbutton.EnableWindow(TRUE);        // Ungray the button.
    m_cancelbutton.EnableWindow(TRUE);    // Ungray the button.
```

There, that's OnFill taken care of. You also said that when the user clicks a group in the list box, you want to copy it into the edit box. Clicking in a list box that was created with the LBS_NOTIFY flag, like this one, generates a LBN_SELCHANGE message. ClassWizard doesn't handle this message but that doesn't matter—you just add the message map entry as you did for socket messages in earlier chapters. In GROUPSUB.H:

```
    // Generated message map functions.
    //{{AFX_MSG(CGroupSubscribeDialog)
    afx_msg void OnGroupFill();
    //}}AFX_MSG
    afx_msg void OnSelect();
    DECLARE_MESSAGE_MAP()
```

In GROUPSUB.CPP:

```
    BEGIN_MESSAGE_MAP(CGroupSubscribeDialog, CDialog)
        //{{AFX_MSG_MAP(CGroupSubscribeDialog)
        ON_BN_CLICKED(IDC_GROUP_FILL, OnGroupFill)
        //}}AFX_MSG_MAP
```

```
        ON_LBN_SELCHANGE(IDC_GROUP_LIST, OnSelect)
END_MESSAGE_MAP()
```

This arranges for `OnSelect` to be called whenever the user clicks in the list box. `OnSelect` asks `m_grouplist`, the list box, to put the text of the currently selected item into the member variable `m_groupname`, then calls `UpdateData` to copy `m_groupname` into the edit box:

```
void CGroupSubscribeDialog::OnSelect()
{
     m_grouplist.GetText(m_grouplist.GetCurSel(),m_groupname);
     UpdateData(FALSE);  // Fills the edit box.
}
```

So your user can manage the list of subscribed groups using Group, Subscribe and Group, Unsubscribe. Once the user has this list of groups, the next step is to choose a group and get a list of articles, an Article Selection View.

A List of Articles to Choose From

A user clicks a group and chooses the menu item Group, Display. What should happen? A new window should appear with a list of articles in it. You've already arranged with ClassWizard that this menu item triggers a call to `CNewsreadView::OnGroupDisplay`, and you also want this to happen if the user double-clicks a group. You want the Windows event "double-clicking the list box contained in the `CNewsreadView` class" to trigger a call to the function `OnGroupDisplay` of `CNewsreadView`. ClassWizard won't do this, but you can. When you created the list box, you gave it a resource ID of `IDC_GROUP_LISTBOX`; now you're using that definition. The message for a double-click event is `LBN_DBLCLK`; you add an entry for this to the message map in NEWSRVW.CPP. (You don't need to change the message map in NEWSRVW.H because it is only declaring the functions that are called, and `OnGroupDisplay` has already been declared.)

```
BEGIN_MESSAGE_MAP(CNewsreadView, CView)
     //{{AFX_MSG_MAP(CNewsreadView)
     ON_COMMAND(ID_GROUP_SUBSCRIBE, OnGroupSubscribe)
     ON_COMMAND(ID_GROUP_DISPLAY, OnGroupDisplay)
     ON_COMMAND(ID_GROUP_UNSUBSCRIBE, OnGroupUnsubscribe)
     //}}AFX_MSG_MAP
     ON_LBN_DBLCLK(IDC_GROUPLISTBOX, OnGroupDisplay)
END_MESSAGE_MAP()
```

Your new entry translates as "when the left button is double-clicked in the list box `IDC_GROUPLISTBOX`, call `OnGroupDisplay`."

Now you need to write `OnGroupDisplay`. It needs to create a new view, an article selection view, and pass it the group name so that it can issue a

II

Developing Applications

NEWNEWS command to fill itself with the article headers. To create the new view, you use view templates as you did with the mail application.

The first step is to add a string to the AppStudio string table describing your new view. Select the IDR_NEWSTYPE string and use Edit, Copy to put it into the Clipboard. Change the IDR_NEWSTYPE string to IDR_ARTICLESELECT and then paste IDR_NEWSTYPE back in from the Clipboard. Remove the first instance of News Document from the long string of symbols under Caption (the Properties sheet is the best way to edit the caption). This trick keeps views other than the main view from appearing when the user chooses File, New. While you're here, add strings IDR_ARTICLE and IDR_COMPOSITION, also with that first "News Document" removed. You'll be setting up those views in parallel with the article selection view.

In NEWSREAD.CPP, find the existing code that sets up the view template, and copy it three times (once for each of our three extra views). Change the resource string for IDR_NEWSTYPE to the string we added earlier, and change the names of the frame window and view classes:

```
// Register the application's document templates.
// Document templates serve as the connection between
// documents, frame windows, and views.
//
// In a trick stolen from the CHKBOOK MFC sample, you omit
// the third string in the Resource strings of all templates
// except CNewsreadView, so that even though you add the
// templates here, the user won't get a menu on File, New.

CMultiDocTemplate* GSWTemplate;
GSWTemplate = new CMultiDocTemplate(
    IDR_NEWSTYPE,
    RUNTIME_CLASS(CNewsreadDoc),
    RUNTIME_CLASS(CMDIChildWnd),
    // Standard MDI child frame.
    RUNTIME_CLASS(CNewsreadView));
AddDocTemplate(GSWTemplate);

ASWTemplate = new CMultiDocTemplate(
    IDR_ARTICLESELECT,
    RUNTIME_CLASS(CNewsreadDoc),
    RUNTIME_CLASS(ArtSelMDIChildWnd),
    RUNTIME_CLASS(ArticleSelectionView));

ASWTemplate->m_hMenuShared = GSWTemplate->m_hMenuShared;
ASWTemplate->m_hAccelTable = GSWTemplate->m_hAccelTable;
AddDocTemplate(ASWTemplate);

AWTemplate = new CMultiDocTemplate(
    IDR_ARTICLE,
    RUNTIME_CLASS(CNewsreadDoc),
    RUNTIME_CLASS(ArtMDIChildWnd),
```

```
        RUNTIME_CLASS(ArticleView));
AWTemplate->m_hMenuShared = GSWTemplate->m_hMenuShared;
AWTemplate->m_hAccelTable = GSWTemplate->m_hAccelTable;
AddDocTemplate(AWTemplate);

CWTemplate = new CMultiDocTemplate(
        IDR_COMPOSITION,
        RUNTIME_CLASS(CNewsreadDoc),
        RUNTIME_CLASS(CompMDIChildWnd),
        RUNTIME_CLASS(CompositionView));
CWTemplate->m_hMenuShared = GSWTemplate->m_hMenuShared;
CWTemplate->m_hAccelTable = GSWTemplate->m_hAccelTable;
AddDocTemplate(CWTemplate);
```

Unlike the mail situation, here you are using a different frame window class
for each view. The mail views all used CMDIChildWnd, but because you want to
improve your interface, you create ArtSelMDIChildWnd, ArtMDIChildWnd, and
CompMDIChildWnd, all of which will inherit from CMDIChildWnd and override the
frame title code.

After you put this code into NEWSREAD.CPP, are you ready to bring the article selection view up in OnGroupDisplay? No. You first need to define the
classes ArtSelMDIChildWnd and ArticleSelectionView.

Use ClassWizard to create ArticleSelectionView and add it to the project.
Bring up ClassWizard, click Add Class and fill in the class name and file
names. (Use ARTSEL.CPP.cpp and ARTSEL.H.) The class should inherit from
CScrollView, since it is mainly a holder for another big list box. While you're
at it, create ArticleView and CompositionView, which both inherit from
CEditView as the mail MessageView and ComposeView did.

Next, you need the frame window class. This is so tightly tied to the view
that you should keep the code in ARTSEL.H and ARTSEL.CPP, after
ArticleSelectionView. To ARTSEL.H add the lines:

```
class ArtSelMDIChildWnd : public CMDIChildWnd
{
        DECLARE_DYNCREATE(ArtSelMDIChildWnd)
public:
        CString Group;
        virtual void OnUpdateFrameTitle(BOOL bAddToTitle);
};
```

This says that ArtSelMDIChildWnd is a CMDIChildWnd with an extra member
variable (Group) and an override of the function OnUpdateFrameTitle.

While you're editing ARTSEL.H, you need to add some things to the
boilerplate you got from ClassWizard. The view also has a groupname, and
it has a list box. You add a #define for the list box ID before the start of the
class:

```
#define IDC_ARTLISTBOX 201
```

and add two member variables:

```
public:
    CListBox ListBox;
    CString Group;
```

In ARTSEL.CPP the first thing you need to do is write OnUpdateFrameTitle. This is the function in CMDIChildWnd that puts the document name or other information in the title bar of each view's frame window. Remember that with Visual C++ you get the MFC source, so you should be able to find CMDIChildWnd::OnUpdateFrameTitle (it may be in WINMDI.CPP). Here's how it looks:

```
void CMDIChildWnd::OnUpdateFrameTitle(BOOL bAddToTitle)
{
    // Update your parent window first.
    GetMDIFrame()->OnUpdateFrameTitle(bAddToTitle);

    if ((GetStyle() & FWS_ADDTOTITLE) == 0)
        return;      // Leave child window alone!

    CDocument* pDocument = GetActiveDocument();
    if (bAddToTitle && pDocument != NULL)
    {
        TCHAR szText[256];
        lstrcpy(szText, pDocument->GetTitle());
        if (m_nWindow > 0)
            wsprintf(szText + lstrlen(szText), _T(":%d"),
                m_nWindow);

        // Set title if changed, but don't remove completely.
        SetWindowText(text);
    }
}
```

This code first updates the parent window, since this window may want to ask the parent for its title later. Then, if the FWS_ADDTOTITLE flag is not set, you return. If you were passed TRUE, you ask the document for the title, and if there is more than one window on the document, add a ":1" or ":2" or whatever, then call SetWindowText to put it into the caption.

Surely a nicer title for your article selection view would be the name of the newsgroup. Because people might have more than one document open at a time, you leave the first part of the title the same, just replacing the number with the newsgroup name. There's no need to test m_nWindow; since the CNewsreadView is always open, any function in ArticleSelectionView knows for a fact there are at least two views on this document.

```
void ArtSelMDIChildWnd::OnUpdateFrameTitle(BOOL bAddToTitle)
{
     // Update your parent window first.
     GetMDIFrame()->OnUpdateFrameTitle(bAddToTitle);

     if ((GetStyle() & FWS_ADDTOTITLE) == 0)
          return;       // Leave child window alone!

     CDocument* pDocument = GetActiveDocument();
     if (bAddToTitle && pDocument != NULL)
     {
          char szText[256];

          lstrcpy(szText, pDocument->GetTitle());
          wsprintf(szText + lstrlen(szText),": %s",
                     (LPSTR)((char*)Group));

          SetWindowText(text);
     }
}
```

Ugh! That's so hard to read. It looks like C code, not C++. Haven't you moved
beyond lstrcpy and wsprintf? Sure you have. Here's that last block translated
into C++:

```
CString text = pDocument->GetTitle();
text += ": ";
text += Group;
SetWindowText(text);
```

Much better. You can actually read what that does.

Now, ArticleSelectionView needs an OnInitialUpdate that creates the list
box. It looks like this:

```
void ArticleSelectionView::OnInitialUpdate()
{
     SetScrollSizes(MM_TEXT, GetTotalSize());
     Group = ((ArtSelMDIChildWnd*)GetParentFrame())->Group;
     ((ArtSelMDIChildWnd*) GetParentFrame())
        ➥->OnUpdateFrameTitle(TRUE);
     CRect rectangle;
     GetClientRect(rectangle);
     ListBox.Create(LBS_NOTIFY¦WS_CHILD¦WS_VISIBLE
                     ¦WS_VSCROLL¦WS_HSCROLL,
                     rectangle, this,IDC_ARTLISTBOX);
     // Fill the list box with article information.

     CScrollView::OnInitialUpdate();     // Will call Update() too.
}
```

What does this code do? It gets the group name from the frame (you'll see in
a moment how the frame got the name to begin with), creates the list box,

and fills the list box. Or at least, it will fill the list box after you write the
necessary code. The box is filled with "subject" and "from" information from
each of the articles that the NNTP server has for the group whose name is in
Group. You have already decided to use the NEWNEWS command, but you'll
have to figure out the parameters for it before you send it. Then you handle
the responses, a line at a time, and fill a CStringArray with the message IDs
the server is returning. (Add this array to the class, because you can use it
when the user selects an article to display.) Then when the list is complete,
you go through it sending HEAD commands to the server, parsing out the Subject: and From: headers and building a string to add to the list box. Here's the
structure of the fill code:

```
// Fill the list box with article information.
QSocket* Socket = GetDocument()->GetSocket();
CString response;
if (Socket)
{
    // Send NEWNEWS command.

    response = Socket->GetLine();
    if ( atoi(response) == 230)
    {
        // Message IDs follow.
        while ( (response = Socket->GetLine()) != ".\r\n"
            && Socket->GetStatus() == CONNECTED)
        {
        // Add this message ID to MessageIDs.
        }
    }
    for (int i = 0; i<MessageIDs.GetSize() ; i++)
    {
        // Send the HEAD command.

        response = Socket->GetLine();
        if ( atoi(response) == 221)
        {
        // Headers follow.
            while ( (response = Socket->GetLine())
                ➡!= ".\r\n"
                    && Socket->GetStatus() == CONNECTED)
            {
        // Record subject and from as they arrive.
            }

        // Build line and add to list box.
        }
        else      // If response = 221.
        {
                    // Handle error state.
        }             // If response = 221.
    } // For loop going through MessageIDs.
    GetDocument()->ReleaseSocket();
} // If Socket.
```

You'll start with "send NEWNEWS command." You need the group name and a date and time. What date and time will you use in the command? It should be the last time that the user read this group, so that the user doesn't get the same articles presented over and over again. But to be honest, using NEWNEWS and keeping track of date and time for each group is not really the way to do this. After all, what if someone wants to skip an article and read it the next day? Real newsreaders keep track of individual articles and whether or not they've been read, using the article number. So you won't get into saving dates and times; instead you'll just take today's date from GetCurrentTime() and subtract two days from it using CTimeSpan. You use the CTime method Format to get the date and time into NNTP format with almost no effort:

```
CTime date_time = CTime::GetCurrentTime()-CTimeSpan(2,0,0,0);
CString response;
int length;
if (Socket)
{
    CString command = "NEWNEWS ";
    command += Group;
    command += " ";
    command += date_time.Format("%y%m%d %H%M%S");
    command += "\r\n";
    Socket->Send(command);
```

Next, "add message ID to messageIDs," which goes in the while loop that processes the NEWNEWS response:

```
length = response.GetLength();
if (length >= 2
        && response[length-2] == '\r'
        && response[length-1] == '\n')
{
    MessageIDs.Add(response.Left(length-2));
}
```

(Declare the integer length outside the while loop.) This strips off the trailing \r\n from the response and calls the Add method of the CStringArray MessageIDs. Simple.

Now you need to "send the HEAD command" in the for loop that goes through all the message IDs.

```
CString command = "HEAD ";
command += MessageIDs[i];
command += "\r\n";
Socket->Send(command);
```

Next, "record subject and from as they arrive" looks like this (declare the CString variables subject and from outside the for loop):

```
subject = "";
from = "";
length = response.GetLength();
if (response.Left(9) == "Subject: ")
{
        subject = response.Right(length - 9);
        length = subject.GetLength();
        if (length >= 2
                && subject[length-2] == '\r'
                && subject[length-1] == '\n')
        {
                subject = subject.Left(length-2);
        }
}
if (response.Left(6) == "From: ")
{
        from = response.Right(length - 6);
        length = from.GetLength();
        if (length >= 2
                && from[length-2] == '\r'
                && from[length-1] == '\n')
        {
                from = from.Left(length-2);
        }
}
```

Here you simply look at each line to see if it starts with "Subject: " (that trailing space is important) and if so, put the part of the line after "Subject: " (but not including the trailing \r\n) into subject. Filling from goes much the same way.

Almost there! You just need to add a string to the list box for each header that has been returned:

```
line = from.Left(30); // So as not to overshoot tabstop.
line += '\t';          // Tab -- see Create.
line += subject;
ListBox.AddString(line);
```

The \t is a tab, just as in the list box in CMailView in the mail application. Way back up at the top of OnInitialUpdate (you're still working on OnInitialUpdate, remember?) was a call to ListBox.Create. You need to add LBS_USETABSTOPS to the flags, and then call the list box SetTabStops and SetHorizontalExtent methods:

```
ListBox.Create(LBS_NOTIFY¦LBS_USETABSTOPS¦WS_CHILD¦WS_VISIBLE
               ¦WS_VSCROLL¦WS_HSCROLL,
               rectangle, this,IDC_ARTLISTBOX);
#define tabwidth 30
    ListBox.SetTabStops(tabwidth*4); //dialog units
    ListBox.SetHorizontalExtent(LOWORD(GetDialogBaseUnits())
            *tabwidth*2); //pixels
```

If the response code was not 221, the article can't be retrieved even though the server reported its message ID as a recent one. Instead of a "from \t subject" line, you add a line explaining this:

```
else // If response = 221.
{
    line = MessageIDs[i];
    line += " cannot be retrieved.";
    ListBox->AddString(line);
} //if response = 221
```

Having finally finished ArticleSelectionView::OnInitialUpdate, you are ready to write CNewsreadView::OnGroupDisplay to bring up this frame window and view. It's much like the equivalent code in mail:

```
void CNewsreadView::OnGroupDisplay()
{
    CNewsreadApp* App = (CNewsreadApp*)AfxGetApp();
    if (!(GetDocument()->IsSocketAvailable()))
    {
        // We're not connected yet.
        AfxMessageBox("The connection is busy now.
            ➥Try again in a moment.",
            MB_OK¦MB_ICONSTOP);
        return;
    }

    int index = GroupList.GetCurSel();
    if (index < 0)
    {
        // User hasn't selected a group -- use the first one.
        index = 0;
    }

    CString selectedgroup;
    selectedgroup = ((CNewsreadDoc *)m_pDocument)
            ➥->SubscribedGroups[index];

    ArtSelMDIChildWnd* pNewFrame = (ArtSelMDIChildWnd*)App
        ➥->ASWTemplate->CreateNewFrame(m_pDocument,NULL);
    if (pNewFrame == NULL)
    {
        return;
    }
    pNewFrame->Group = selectedgroup;
    App->ASWTemplate->InitialUpdateFrame(pNewFrame, m_pDocument);
}
```

First you make sure the socket is free, so that ArticleSelectionView:: OnInitialUpdate can get it. Then you get the groupname, call CreateNewFrame, and set the frame's Group Variable. InitialUpdateFrame calls the view's OnInitialUpdate, which transfers the group name from the frame to the view.

II

Developing Applications

Now the user can make a list of subscribed groups, and select one group and see a summary of the articles in it. The next step is to display a selected article.

Threading, NOV, and XOVER

Your bare-bones newsreader presents this list of articles in the same order as they arrive from the server. Many users would rather see articles arranged in a more logical order. Some newsreaders can arrange the articles by the Subject or From headers, for example. But one of the most useful and popular ways of arranging messages is threading.

As mentioned earlier, a news article has a References header that lists the message IDs of articles that are logically connected to this one. Just to illustrate, imagine that message IDs are single letters. Someone posts an article, A. Two followups to A are posted: B and C. A followup to C is posted, with the message ID D. This article has a References header listing both C and A. These four articles belong together, even though hundreds of other articles may have been posted to the same group after article A. Threading pulls these related articles together.

A *thread* is a collection of articles arranged into a hierarchy with a single article at the root. Each "child" article has in its references the parent article's message ID. A threading newsreader would display our imaginary thread in this order: A, B, C, D, and would provide a way to skip or select entire threads at a time.

Threading is a lot of work, and so is building an article selection list like this one. Both jobs are made easier by using the News OverView (NOV) extensions to NNTP, accessible with the XOVER command. You can learn more about NOV from the NOV FAQ, posted to the newsgroups **news.software.nntp** and **news.software.readers** by Rob Robertson. If your NNTP server supports the XOVER command, rather than sending HEAD commands over and over again, you can get all the essential header information in a compact list, already parsed for you into a database form. The time savings are enormous, so if you want to make this a real newsreader, implementing XOVER support is a vital first step.

Displaying an Article

As was mentioned earlier, the article view is an edit view, like the message view in mail. It is brought up when the user chooses Article, Display or double-clicks an entry in the list box in the article selection view. Both these events should be caught by ArticleSelectionView, but ClassWizard only helps you catch the menu. Use ClassWizard to connect the menu item Article, Display to ArticleSelectionView::OnArticleDisplay, then add the extra line in the message map in ARTSEL.CPP catching the LBN_DBLCLK and triggering OnArticleDisplay as well.

`ArticleView` has already been created in ClassWizard, but you need to write `ArtMDIChildWnd` yourself. Just like `ArtSelMDIChildWnd`, it has one extra variable and overrides the frame title function:

```
class ArtMDIChildWnd : public CMDIChildWnd
{
    DECLARE_DYNCREATE(ArtMDIChildWnd)
public:
    CString MessageID;
    virtual void OnUpdateFrameTitle(BOOL bAddToTitle);
};
```

The `OnUpdateFrameTitle` method is just like the `ArticleSelectionView` version, except this puts the article's Message ID, rather than the group name, in the title:

```
void ArtMDIChildWnd::OnUpdateFrameTitle(BOOL bAddToTitle)
{
    // Update your parent window first.
    GetMDIFrame()->OnUpdateFrameTitle(bAddToTitle);

    if ((GetStyle() & FWS_ADDTOTITLE) == 0)
        return;      // Leave child window alone!

    CDocument* pDocument = GetActiveDocument();
    if (bAddToTitle && pDocument != NULL)
    {
        CString text = pDocument->GetTitle();
        text += ": ";
        text += MessageID;

        SetWindowText(text);      }
```

Once again, `OnInitialUpdate` is going to do your filling, and ask the server for the information you want. But you're not going to get it back a line at a time as you did for the list of message IDs: instead you're going to return to message-driven socket work. That means `OnInitialUpdate` will set up a receive target before sending the command:

```
void ArticleView::OnInitialUpdate()
{
    MessageID = ((ArtMDIChildWnd*)GetParentFrame())->MessageID;
    ((ArtMDIChildWnd*) GetParentFrame())
        ➥->OnUpdateFrameTitle(TRUE);
    GetEditCtrl().SetReadOnly(TRUE);
    CEditView::OnInitialUpdate();

    // Fill the edit box.
    QSocket* Socket = GetDocument()->GetSocket();
    if (Socket)
    {
        Socket->SetReceiveTarget(this, WM_SOCKET_RESPONSE);
```

```
                     CString command = "ARTICLE ";
                     command += MessageID;
                     command += " ";
                     command += "\r\n";
                     Socket->Send(command);
                     // Rest of the filling will be done in OnSocket.
              }
       }
```

The first half of OnInitialUpdate is just like the article selection view. In the
second half, you get a socket and tell it that when it has responses, it should
send the Windows message WM_SOCKET_RESPONSE to this window. Then you
build an ARTICLE command and send it to the NNTP server. To make sure that
OnSocket is called when this message arrives, add a #define for the message,
and message map entries. In ARTVIEW.H, before the class definition, add:

```
#define WM_SOCKET_RESPONSE WM_USER+201
```

After the AFX part of the message map in ARTVIEW.H add a declaration of
your OnSocket function:

```
       // Generated message map functions.
       //{{AFX_MSG(ArticleView)
       //}}AFX_MSG
       afx_msg LRESULT OnSocket(WPARAM wParam, LPARAM lParam);
       DECLARE_MESSAGE_MAP()
```

And in ARTVIEW.CPP:

```
BEGIN_MESSAGE_MAP(ArticleView, CEditView)
       //{{AFX_MSG_MAP(ArticleView)
       //}}AFX_MSG_MAP
       ON_MESSAGE(WM_SOCKET_RESPONSE, OnSocket)
END_MESSAGE_MAP()
```

At this point you make a tiny change to CNewsreadApp::ReleaseSocket, adding
a line to undo any SetReceiveWindow settings when the window releases the
socket:

```
void CNewsreadApp::ReleaseSocket()
{
       SocketAvailable = TRUE;
       AppSocket->SetReceiveTarget(NULL,0);
}
```

You only need to write OnSocket, to handle the response and put it into the
edit box. As you did for Mail's MessageView::OnSocket, you tack buffer on to
the end of windowtext (a CString you add to the class) and if it doesn't end
with \n.\r\n there is more to come, so you just return. Once windowtext contains the full message, there is work to do:

```
LRESULT ArticleView::OnSocket(WPARAM amount, LPARAM buffer)
{
    windowtext += (char *)buffer;
    if (windowtext.Right(4) == "\n.\r\n") // End of transmission.
    {
        // Remove trailing .\r\n.
        windowtext = windowtext.Left(windowtext.GetLength()-3);
        // Find .. at start of lines, and drop one .
        // First handle special case if first line starts ..
        if (windowtext.Left(2) == "..")
        {
            windowtext = windowtext.Right(windowtext
                ➥.GetLength()-1);
        }
        char* position;
        char* windowbuffer = windowtext.GetBuffer(0);
        position = windowbuffer;
        while (position = strstr(position,"\n.."))
        {
            int length = windowtext.GetLength();
            strcpy(position+1,position+2); // Skip second dot.
            position += 2; // Get past the \n. left behind.
        }
        GetEditCtrl().SetWindowText(windowtext);
        GetDocument()->ReleaseSocket();
    }
    return 0;
}
```

II

Developing Applications

First, that .\r\n at the very end is a signal to you, not part of the message, so you delete it. Next, if any lines start with .., the extra dot is from the server, and you need to take it away. Then you use SetWindowText to put the text on-screen, and release the socket. Done!

This code works, and puts an article on-screen. But there's an unexpected extra first line: a 220 status response. Like the .\r\n at the end, it's not really part of the article, but a signal to you. Stripping it away is harder than you might think, because the socket responses are not coming a line at a time; you might get half the first line the first time OnSocket is called, or ten lines, or a hundred. You need a flag called FirstCall—add it to the class and set it TRUE in the constructor. Once you've removed that first line you set it to FALSE. Then right after windowtext += buffer, you add this block of code:

```
if (FirstCall)
{
    // First line of response is status.
    int pos;
    if ( (pos = windowtext.Find("\r\n")) >= 0)
    {
        CString line = windowtext.Left(pos);
        if ( atoi(line) == 220)
        {
```

```
                       // Article follows -- strip out this line.
                       windowtext = windowtext.Right(
                               windowtext.GetLength()-pos-2);
                       FirstCall = FALSE;
                 }
                 else
                 {
                       // Error status of some sort.
                       AfxMessageBox("Article could not be retrieved");
                       // Close this article view.
                       ((CNewsreadApp*)AfxGetApp())->ReleaseSocket();
                       CWnd *wnd = GetParent();
                       wnd->DestroyWindow();

                 }
           }
           else
           {
                 return 0;
                 // No processing till we have the first line.
           }
     }
```

The first thing you need to find out is if you have the entire first line. If pos is
–1, you haven't received a \r\n yet, and should just return. Once you have
that whole first line in windowtext, you check the return code. If it's 220, there
will be an article following it and all you need to do is remove from 0 to
pos+1 from windowtext, then set FirstCall to FALSE so you won't go into this
block again. If it's not 220, there's no message following it, because there's
some sort of problem. Though it has nothing to do with removing the status
line, this is a problem you have to deal with. You put up an error box, release
the socket, and destroy the current view.

And now your newsreader actually works! As you can see in figure 12.6, you
have a list of groups; if you double-click a group in the list you get a new
view with a list of articles, and if you double-click an article in the list you get
a third view with the contents of the article.

 There is one problem with this approach for 16-bit programmers: you put the whole
response into a CString, and they can only be 32K long. The program will blow up
rather messily if you try to read a long article. Getting around this problem is beyond
the scope of this book; don't use the newsreader to read binary postings (GIFs, ZIP
files, and so on) or large FAQ (Frequently Asked Questions) postings unless you're
working with 32 bits.

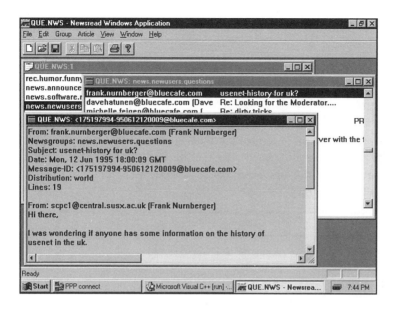

Figure 12.6
Your rudimentary
newsreader is in
action. This
question is at
home in
**news.newusers.
questions**, which
all new UseNet
users should read
at first.

Creating a New Article

Most news articles are in response to earlier articles: they answer a question,
or rebut an argument, or offer advice. Such articles are called followups. Our
newsreader should enable users to create both original articles and followups.
There are a few rules, laid out in RFC 1036, for the format of articles. In addition there are some generally accepted rules:

■ Original articles must not have Subject lines starting with "Re:. "

■ Original articles must have empty Reference headers.

■ Followup articles should have Subject lines that are the same as the
article that inspired them, unless that article's Subject does not begin
with "Re:.," in which case those four characters should be inserted at
the beginning of the Subject.

■ Followup articles should have a References header that is the same as
the article that inspired them, with the message ID of that article added
at the end.

■ Followup articles should have a Newsgroups header that includes all the
groups from the Followup-To header in the article that inspired them. If
that article had no Followup-To header, the followup article should
have the same Newsgroups header as the original article.

■ Followup articles should have the same Distribution and Keywords headers as the article that inspired them.

■ Followup articles often include quoted material from the articles that inspired them, according to a standard format described later in this chapter.

To create an original or followup article, your application needs to build an empty article, give it to the user for editing, and send the article to the NNTP server to be posted. You'll need to add three items to the Article menu, as shown in the following table:

Item	Usage
Post	Creates an original article
Followup	Creates a followup article
Send Post	Sends either kind of article to the NNTP server

Building an Original Article

Building an empty original article is quite simple. You create a new edit view (this one is not read-only!) and add lines to it. You need From, Subject, Date, and Newsgroups headers as an absolute minimum. The user can add extra headers such as Keywords or Organization if required. (The Message-ID header is a required header but the NNTP server will add it for you.)

Which view (or the document) should handle this menu item? It shouldn't matter whether the user is reading an article, choosing an article, or just looking at the list of groups. If any view caught this message, when that view did not have focus, the menu item would not be available. You could write three identical versions of the function, one for each view, or you could just have the document catch the message.

In ClassWizard, you get CNewsreadDoc to handle the Article, Post menu item. OnArticlePost creates a CompositionView in the same way as you've been creating article selection and article views:

```
void CNewsreadDoc::OnArticlePost()
{
    CNewsreadApp* App = (CNewsreadApp*)AfxGetApp();
    CompMDIChildWnd* pNewFrame = (CompMDIChildWnd*)App->
        CWTemplate->CreateNewFrame(m_pDocument,NULL);
    if (pNewFrame == NULL)
```

```
    {
        return;
    }
    App->CWTemplate->InitialUpdateFrame(pNewFrame, m_pDocument);
}
```

`OnInitialUpdate` now needs to create the blank and prefilled headers. The From header requires the user's e-mail address, which you get from the document. The Date header is based on today's data and time. You'll also provide blank Subject and Newsgroups headers.

Caution

Make sure you fill in your e-mail address properly (by choosing File, Setup) if you use this newsreader to post messages. Replies won't reach you if you enter only a partial address. And don't enter an address, say "**president@whitehouse.gov**," other than your own. You won't fool anyone, and the forgery will be easily traced back to you using other headers. Your joke might cost you your Internet access.

Here's `OnInitialUpdate` without the Date header:

```
void CompositionView::OnInitialUpdate()
{
    ((CompMDIChildWnd*) GetParentFrame())
        ➡->OnUpdateFrameTitle(TRUE);
    // Updates frame title.
    GetEditCtrl().SetReadOnly(FALSE);
    CEditView::OnInitialUpdate();

    CString text = "";
    text += "From: ";
    text += GetDocument()->User;
    text += " (";
    text += GetDocument()->Username;
    text += ")\r\n";

    text += "Newsgroups: \r\n";
    text += "Subject: \r\n";

    // Build Date header.

    text += "\r\n";   // Empty line between headers and body.

    GetEditCtrl().SetWindowText(text);
    int selchar = GetEditCtrl().LineIndex(GetEditCtrl()
        ➡.GetLineCount()-1);
    GetEditCtrl().SetSel(selchar,selchar);
}
```

Notice how you ask the document for the e-mail address and real name to build a From header like:

```
From: kate@gregcons.com (Kate Gregory)
```

A nice touch here is setting the selection in the edit control to the first position on the last line, to make it easier for the user to type in the article body. The integer selchar is the number of characters to the beginning of the last line—GetLineCount() returns the number of lines in the control (one-based) and LineIndex returns the number of characters to the start of the (zero-based) line number it is passed. They are both edit control functions, accessed with the edit control pointer the edit view gives you from the GetEditCtrl function.

Now, the Date header. It looks like this:

```
Date: Fri, 23 Jun 1993 23:59:30 -0500 (EST)
```

In other words, today's date and time converted to Universal time and followed by an indication of the local time zone. The format has to be just right; the comma after the weekday, for example, is not optional. You're going to use a great shortcut here: the CTime class has a FormatGmt function that converts to GMT (Universal Time) and prints the date using a sprintf-like format string:

```
//   Date: Mon, 17 Jan 1994 11:14:55 -0500 (EST)
     text += "Date: ";
     CTime time = CTime::GetCurrentTime();
     text += CString(time.FormatGmt("%a, %d %b %Y %H:%M:%S "));
     if (_timezone > 0)
     {
         text += "-";   //switch signs
     }
     else
     {
         text += "+";
     }
     text += CString(CTimeSpan((time_t)_timezone).Format("%H%M ("));
     text += CString(time.FormatGmt("%z"));
     text += ")";
//   Date: Mon, 17 Jan 1994 11:14:55 -0500 (EST)
```

The number following the time in a news Data header has the opposite sign convention to the _timezone variable. This sort of thing happens when programmers have to make arbitrary decisions about directions. Eastern Standard Time has a _timezone value of +5 hours, no minutes, but the news header for EST should read –0500. So, you switch the signs yourself. Notice the use of CTimeSpan; it has the same Format function as CTime. Having added the –0500 (or whatever), you use `FormatGmt` one more time, to get the common name for the time zone.

> If the user hasn't set the time zone, MFC assumes Pacific Time (PST or PDT, depending on today's date). To set the time zone, use the Date/Time portion of Control Panel. For Windows 95, select the Time Zone sheet. For NT, use the drop down box under the settings boxes for the date and the time.

> The Date/Time control panel doesn't handle time zones in Windows 3.1. Edit your AUTOEXEC.BAT to set the TZ environment variable. To set it to Eastern time, use this line:
>
> ```
> set TZ=EST+5EDT
> ```
>
> For other time zones, use your three-letter abbreviations and the time difference from Universal Time (don't make any allowance for Daylight Savings, that will be done automatically.)

Date is more work than any of the other headers, but just try doing it without `CTime` and `CTimeSpan`—only don't hold your breath while you're doing it.

Figure 12.7 shows a test post being composed with your newsreader. You'll see this post again very shortly.

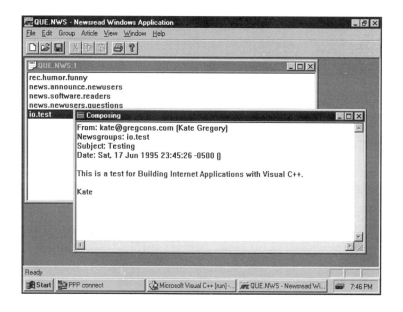

Fig. 12.7
Your newsreader can now be used to compose articles.

II

Developing Applications

Sending an Article to the NNTP Server

When the user chooses the Article Send Post menu option, you need to send the contents of the view to the NNTP server. An obvious enhancement here would be to do some validation on the article before sending it. Some things to check include:

- The Newsgroups line must not be blank, and must have no spaces in it.

- The From line must not be blank, and must contain a syntactically valid e-mail address. That means exactly one @, at least one . after the @, no commas, and so on. Any other text on the line must be enclosed in parentheses.

- The Subject line must not be blank.

- If the user has provided a Sender, Message-ID, Path, or Xref header, they should be removed and the user should be warned not to provide them.

Bring up ClassWizard and map the menu item Article, Send Post to CompositionView::OnArticleSendpost. This function sends a POST command to the NNTP server, and if the server responds 340, sends the rest of the article a line at a time, terminated by a "." alone as usual. If any line starts with a ".", you send an extra "." before the line. Here's how it looks:

```
void CompositionView::OnArticleSendpost()
{
    CNewsreadDoc *doc = GetDocument();
    QSocket* Socket = doc->GetSocket();
    if (Socket)
    {
        Socket->Send("POST\r\n");

        CString response = Socket->GetLine();
        char buffer[5004];
        // For \r, \n, zero term, and perhaps an extra .
        unsigned int line_length;
        unsigned int lines = GetEditCtrl().GetLineCount();
        if ( atoi(response) == 340)
        {
            CString command;
            for (unsigned int i = 0; i< lines; i++)
            {
                line_length = GetEditCtrl().GetLine(i,buffer,
                                        5000);
                buffer[line_length] = 0;
                if (buffer[0] == '.')
                {
                    command = '.' + buffer;
                }
                else
```

```
                                {
                                    command = buffer;
                                }
                                command += "\r\n";
                                Socket->Send(command );
                            }
                            Socket->Send(".\r\n");
                            response = Socket->GetLine();
                            if ( atoi(response) == 240)
                            {
                                AfxMessageBox("Posting succeeded.");
                                CWnd *wnd = GetParent();
                                wnd->DestroyWindow();
                            }
                            else
                            {
                                AfxMessageBox("The article was not accepted
                                    ➡by the NNTP server.");
                            }
                        }
                        else
                        {
                            AfxMessageBox("This NNTP server will not
                                ➡allow you to post.");
                            CWnd *wnd = GetParent();
                            wnd->DestroyWindow();
                        }

                        doc->ReleaseSocket();
                    }
                }
```

When transmission is complete the server responds 240 if the article was posted successfully. A response of 440 to the original POST command means that posting is not allowed, and a response of 441 after transmitting the article means that the posting attempt failed. After a successful post, or learning that you cannot post at all, you close the composition view with a call to DestroyWindow. You leave the view up after a failed post, because the failure may have been due to a simple error like a missing Subject header. The user can fix the error and resubmit.

One thing to note: you have to save the document pointer in a local variable, doc. That's because you want to release the socket after you may have destroyed the window. The alternative to this is to repeat the ReleaseSocket call after each AfxMessageBox, much as you did with the QUIT command in Mail's Message, Send function.

Figure 12.8 shows an article view in which you're reading the test article you composed in figure 12.7. This shows that your posting function really sends the article to the server, and from there out to the rest of the world.

II

Developing Applications

Fig. 12.8
Your test posting
reached the NNTP
server and is
publicly available
in the newsgroup
you posted it to.
Always use a test
group for test
postings.

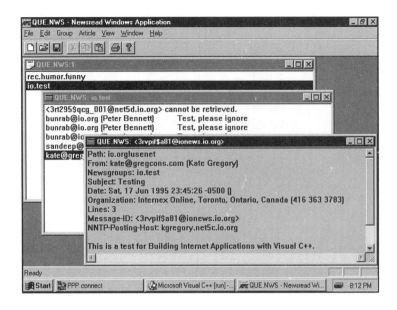

Building a Followup Article

When you build a followup, you can't just provide blank headers for the user
to fill in. You need to handle the Newsgroups header, build a References
header, and quote the inspiring article. Other than that the process is just
like building an original article.

The Newsgroups line must include all the groups from the Followup-To
header in the inspiring article. If that article had no Followup-To header, the
followup article should have the same Newsgroups header as the inspiring
article.

The References header is the same as that of the inspiring article, with the
message ID of the inspiring article added on at the end. If the inspiring article
had no References header you will need to start a new one.

Many newsreaders let the user choose whether or not to quote the inspiring
article. If you are going to quote, you will build an attribution line using the
Message-ID and From headers of the original article, then copy lines from the
inspiring article's edit box to this one, inserting a ">" character at the beginning of each line.

After the empty article is built and given to the user, the posting process is
the same for followups as for originals.

If you want to implement followups, here's what you need to do:

1. Connect the menu item Article Followup to a CNewsreadDoc function OnArticleFollowup.

2. Write OnArticleFollowup; it brings up a CompositionView.

3. Change CompositionView::OnInitialDialog to test whether this is a followup or original. Use a variable kept in both the frame and the view, like MessageID in the article view or Group in the article selection view.

4. Change the CompositionView class, adding member variables to view and frame for the parts of the inspiring article you'll need (or just its message ID, in which case you'll have to issue HEAD, BODY, or AR-TICLE commands to the NNTP server when you want the details).

5. Write the code to handle the Newsgroups, Subject, and References headers properly.

6. Write code to produce an attribution line and quote the body of the inspiring article.

Not a simple task! But if you've been following along this far, you can do this. It's painstaking, but manageable work.

Disconnecting

When you're completely finished you should send a QUIT command to the server and clean up the socket. What piece of code is involved when you're completely finished with a socket?

There is one socket per document, and as long as the document is open, the socket exists. When the document closes, the destructor for CNewsreadDoc is called. This is the perfect place for tidying up the socket:

```
CNewsreadDoc::~CNewsreadDoc()
{
    if (pSocket)
    {
        if (SocketAvailable && pSocket->GetStatus() == CONNECTED)
        {
            pSocket->Send("QUIT");
        }
        pSocket->Disconnect();
        delete pSocket;
    }
}
```

Assuming pSocket is not NULL, you send the QUIT if the socket is available and connected (it may have gone into an error condition while you've been running). You disconnect the socket no matter what, and delete pSocket.

There! You've got a working newsreader. You can't send mail messages or post followups automatically (though you can construct a followup by hand using a lot of cut and paste), but it does indeed read news. It needs a few nice touches though, and this is the place for them.

Menu Graying

In mail you needed to gray the Message Delete item when no message was selected. In news, if Message, Display or Article, Display is chosen with no selection you just use the first entry in the list box. Does that mean there's no extra graying needed? No; what happens if a user selects Group, Display before File, Connect? A strange message about the connection being busy, that's what.

Probably the easiest way to summarize which view catches which command, and the code for each, is just to present all the OnUpdate functions. So for example, because there is a function ArticleSelectionView::OnUpdate-ArticleDisplay, you should arrange in ClassWizard for ArticleSelectionView to catch the UPDATE_COMMAND_UI message for ID_ARTICLE_DISPLAY in addition to the COMMAND message it already catches. Here are the functions that gray or ungray according to whether or not a socket is available:

```
void ArticleSelectionView::OnUpdateArticleDisplay(CCmdUI* pCmdUI)
{
    pCmdUI->Enable(GetDocument()->IsSocketAvailable() );
}

void CNewsreadView::OnUpdateGroupDisplay(CCmdUI* pCmdUI)
{
    pCmdUI->Enable(GetDocument()->IsSocketAvailable());
}

void CNewsreadView::OnUpdateGroupSubscribe(CCmdUI* pCmdUI)
{
    pCmdUI->Enable(GetDocument()->IsSocketAvailable());
}

void CNewsreadDoc::OnUpdateArticlePost(CCmdUI* pCmdUI)
{
    pCmdUI->Enable(SocketAvailable);
}

void CompositionView::OnUpdateArticleSendpost(CCmdUI* pCmdUI)
{
    pCmdUI->Enable(GetDocument()->IsSocketAvailable());
}
```

This one insists that a group be selected:

```
void CNewsreadView::OnUpdateGroupUnsubscribe(CCmdUI* pCmdUI)
{
    pCmdUI->Enable(GroupList.GetCurSel() >= 0);
}
```

And finally, this one, for File, Connect, insists that there be no socket (the pointer is NULL) or the existing socket is not CONNECTED.

```
void CNewsreadDoc::OnUpdateFileConnect(CCmdUI* pCmdUI)
{
    pCmdUI->Enable(pSocket == NULL
                    || pSocket->GetStatus() != CONNECTED);
}
```

Sizing

The two edit views, ArticleView and CompositionView, handle sizing issues automatically, because they don't contain any other controls. The list box in CNewsreaderView does not need to be sized by the user—newsgroup names are all pretty well the same length. But the list box in ArticleSelectionView should be adjustable. Just as you did in mail, you catch the WM_SIZE message and arrange for OnSize to be called. In mail you carried a flag to indicate whether the list box had been created. Here you learn another way to do this. Change the CListBox to a CListBox*, still called ListBox. Change the declaration in ARTSEL.H, set the pointer to NULL in the constructor, delete it in the destructor, and change all the instances of ListBox. to ListBox-> throughout ArticleSelectionView. In OnInitialUpdate, add a call to new for the list box:

```
ListBox = new CListBox;
```

right before the Create. Now your OnSize function looks like this:

```
void ArticleSelectionView::OnSize(UINT nType, int cx, int cy)
{
    CScrollView::OnSize(nType, cx, cy);
    if (ListBox)
    {
        ListBox->MoveWindow(0,0,cx,cy);
    }
}
```

Which do you prefer? The ListCreated flag, or making the list box a pointer? As you can see, they both work fine.

II

Developing Applications

From Here...

You've seen a number of shortcomings, things you've glossed over, and places where you really should check what the user typed to make the program bulletproof. Here's a summary of those improvements:

- The group name entered on the Group Subscribe dialog should be validated before the dialog is closed, by sending a GROUP command to the server.

- The use of NEWNEWS should be abandoned and the ARTICLE commands should select articles by message number within a group, rather than by message ID. The document should save not only the names of subscribed groups, but what article numbers have been read in each group, so only unread articles are presented to the user to be selected for reading. Crossposted articles should be marked as read in all of their groups after they have been read in one group.

- The program should prepare followups according to the guidelines mentioned earlier, with automatic generation of Newsgroups, References, and Subject headers.

- A new menu item—Message, Reply—should prepare mail messages to be sent by SMTP. Since mail messages and news articles are so similar, it's probably best to add a flag to CompositionView that indicates whether the user is composing mail or news. Don't forget to add an SMTP entry to the File Setup dialog.

- Wherever the program has a slow wait, it should indicate to the user what is going on. A bare minimum would be to put up an hourglass cursor. A slightly nicer approach would be to report progress to the message area on the status bar.

There's much, much more you would have to do to create a newsreader that has the functionality of those on the market today.

- While reading an article, it should be easy for the user to move to the next one. Closing this article and double-clicking the next entry in the article list is not simple or easy.

- If a newsgroup is moderated, a user's posting to that group should be converted automatically to mail and sent to the moderator of the group. This requires keeping track of the moderated/unmoderated status of all the subscribed groups.

- Threading is almost a required feature today (see the Sidebar). Threading means true references-based threading, not just sorting by subject line. Some users do prefer as-arrived, sorted-by-subject, or sorted-by-from order, so the program should offer a choice.

- *Filtering* (sometimes called *kill files*) enables articles to be thrown away (or marked as interesting) based on simple criteria, such as having a certain text string in the Subject: header.

- Automatically adding a short signature file to all mail and news is something all users appreciate. Making it simple to use different signature files for different groups would be a very nice feature. And making it impossible to have a signature longer than four lines would endear you to everyone else on UseNet who has to read those 20-line monstrosities.

- Some postings are not text meant for human eyes, but rather encoded binary files: graphics or executables or sound files. They have to be translated with a technique called *uuencoding*, and split into several parts before they are posted. Good newsreaders prepare a binary file posting for you, and translate someone else's that you want to use, automatically.

- And don't forget the Good Netkeeping Seal of Approval and all the features it demands or suggests you include.

That "laundry list" of work will make your newsreader an acceptable, but not outstanding, piece of Internet software. There are still more features found in existing newsreaders that aren't listed here. But if you start using any existing newsreader and reading news regularly, you'll soon start thinking of neat features you'd add to your own reader. And you'll read other people's wish lists, too, in the newsgroup **news.software.readers**. Who knows? If you have the time to put into it, you might just create everyone's dream newsreader. Good luck!

II

Developing Applications

Chapter 13

Secure Communications on the Internet

As the Internet has become more and more popular, concern about Internet security has increased. Companies, schools, and individual users are all worried about protecting the privacy of their data as well as protecting it against attack—and with good reason, as you'll see. You may even know of attacks mounted against corporate, university, or service-provider computers that you use.

The Internet's like a large city in many respects: there are brightly lit shopping areas, great halls of learning and knowledge, entertainment of every shape and size, and dark alleys that are best avoided. There are easy steps you can take to reduce the risk of, or the damage from, an attack. This chapter will teach you enough about security culture, security tools, and security programming to give you a good start on building more secure applications.

The chapter won't teach you to build military-level security into each and every application (although that would be a great boon to the Net community, as you'll see in a minute). Instead, you'll learn enough to understand the basics and be able to improve the security and privacy-protecting features in the tools you build. Most programmers favor technical solutions to problems; after all, that's what programmers *do*. Rather than relying on political, social, or legal protection to safeguard your data, you'll do better to take a proactive stance and secure the data yourself. Here's what you'll learn in this chapter:

- What the real risks are

- How to talk like a cryptographer

- Basics of data security and privacy

- How to build in security

- How to build an encrypting socket class

- Security in action: building and using an encrypting talk client

- The politics of encryption

First, an important distinction: this chapter *will not* tell you how to protect your individual computer from crackers. That's well outside the scope of this book; besides, how to do so depends on which operating system you're running and a host of other things. However, the chapter will explain how you can protect data stored and transmitted by your application from thieves, eavesdroppers, and tamperers.

Although this chapter includes source code for some cryptographic software, that source is *not* included on the CD. To find out why, see the section "The Politics of Encryption" later in this chapter.

What Are the Real Risks?

As you no doubt know, today's Internet grew out of the needs of research sponsored by the U.S. Department of Defense. The researchers' goal was to build a network of networks that could route traffic from host to host and coast to coast regardless of any damage to some parts of the network. In the same way, when you make a long-distance call today, the phone system can complete your call even if part of the phone network between you and your destination is damaged.

By and large, the Internet wasn't designed to be especially secure. Its original users were professors and researchers, not the general public—the businessmen, engineers, and millions of other people who now use it daily. The TCP/IP protocol has some limited security features built in, as does UNIX (which is still the dominant operating system on the Net). The rapid growth in the number of computers on the Net, and the passage of years since TCP/IP and UNIX were first fielded, have made those once-robust security systems more vulnerable to attack.

Some types of attacks are *passive:* attackers intercept data, but they don't actively interfere with your network communications. *Active* attackers get in the middle of protocols and transactions and disrupt, degrade, or falsify communications. This chapter will examine both kinds of attacks and tell how to blunt them.

Most Internet communications are safe from these attacks—for now. The increasing amount of valuable data passed over the Net makes future attacks more likely. For example, sites that sell valuable data or that accept unencrypted credit-card transactions are tempting targets precisely because stealing Internet data is much easier than stealing most kinds of physical goods.

Besides the specter of attackers trying to steal data, there's another, more insidious, risk of communicating on the Internet. It can be difficult or impossible to be sure that your communications and traffic stay private. If you've ever hunted for a new job from your current workplace or exchanged e-mail containing other confidential information about yourself, imagine how you'd react if you knew that some third party knew what you'd said, where you'd visited, and what you'd done while there.

Laws exist that are supposed to protect the privacy of your electronic communications, but they're spottily enforced, and require that a spy be caught in the act. Electronic spies don't leave fingerprints, so there's no way to catch the spy. It's up to you to take affirmative action to keep your private communications private. It's also up to you as a programmer to give your users reliable, secure privacy tools.

Talking Like a Cryptographer

Vocabulary tip: *Codes* replace words or phrases with code words (or code numbers). *Ciphers* use mathematical formulae to transform letters, bytes, or bits; they ignore words, phrases, and sentences.

It seems that there are some things the U.S. government would prefer that you forget: cryptography has been in the hands of private citizens for over 4,000 years. If you're like most people, you might think of cryptography as an enormously complex field, interesting only to spies and the military. You'd be half right: cryptography, the study of designing and implementing cipher systems, *is* a very complex subject. It's interesting to note that, besides his better-known accomplishments, Thomas Jefferson designed a cipher that was independently rediscovered in the 1930s and used by the U.S. Navy during World War II.

Although cryptography is a complex field, even novice programmers can use very powerful ciphers in their programs with a minimum of design work. You don't have to have an electrical engineering degree to program computers, and you don't need a degree in advanced math to apply crypto to your own software.

Designing ciphers is hard work. There are many subtle traps that can make a seemingly impenetrable scheme completely useless, and there are a lot of very smart researchers who make their living by dissecting new systems to see if they're really secure. Therefore, there are two things you should *never* do:

- Don't make up your own ciphers. Because the art of cryptography has been in existence for more than 4,000 years, it's unlikely that you'll come up with anything new, and the odds that your cipher can be easily broken are overwhelming.

- Don't use a cipher whose basic design (or *algorithm*) you can't examine or don't trust. If the vendor, or a government agency, says "Our cipher is based on a secret method, but trust us, it's secure," that should be a danger signal to you. The practice of believing something is secure because it's hidden is commonly called "security through obscurity"— and it's not secure at all.

One of the first steps in exploring a new field is to learn the lingo. Before you can walk the crypto walk, you'll need to at least understand these bits of crypto talk:

- A *cipher* is a method for scrambling information. Ciphers use *keys* to secure data. Unencrypted data is called *plaintext*, and the encrypted version is called *ciphertext*. A key is just a string of bytes used as input to the cipher. Exactly how the data is scrambled depends on the design of the algorithm.

- *Secret-key* (also called *symmetric-key*) ciphers use a single key to encrypt and decrypt messages. (In some symmetric-key ciphers there are two keys, and each can be calculated from the other.) The security of messages depends entirely on the key; anyone who has the key can read the message. These ciphers require that you have a secure way to send the key to the recipient, which is inconvenient. They can be very fast when implemented on modern 32- or 64-bit processors.

- *Public-key* ciphers use two keys: a *private* key, which you keep secret, and a *public* key, which you give to others. The two keys are mathematically related, but you can't calculate one from the other. The security of messages depends on the security of the private key. To encrypt a message, you use the recipient's public key; only the corresponding private key can decrypt it. Public-key algorithms tend to be somewhat slower than symmetric-key ciphers, but they remove the need for a separate secure channel for passing the keys.

- *Key-exchange* protocols allow two or more parties to generate a symmetric key over an insecure channel. The best-known key exchange protocol, Diffie-Hellman, allows two or more parties to agree on a key without providing an eavesdropper enough information to reconstruct the key.

- *Digital signature* protocols supply a way to verify that a document or block of data hasn't been changed. They can be used like paper signatures: to seal contracts, make promises, or notarize stored copies of data.

The Crypto++ Class Library

Throughout this book, you've been using C++ classes, in the form of the MFC, to keep from having to do the same work over and over. In this chapter, you'll use Crypto++, a library encapsulating ciphers into C++ classes. Written by Wei Dai, Crypto++ offers reusable components for many secure ciphers, plus the Diffie-Hellman key exchange protocol and some other useful components. You'll use a couple of the ciphers, plus a simple key exchange similar to Diffie-Hellman, in the programming part of the chapter later on.

Because of the warning a few pages ago not to use unproved ciphers, you might wonder why the application uses someone else's library instead of one of mine. Dai has implemented well-known and well-analyzed ciphers in Crypto++, not home-brewed methods of uncertain pedigree. Because the source code for each algorithm is available, anyone can verify that the code matches the process described by the ciphers' inventors.

If you want to consult a tutorial on how these ciphers work or to independently verify this code, Schneier's book (see the end of the chapter for a full citation) is an excellent resource.

NOTE Because of a dispute between the author of Crypto++ and the corporation which holds patents on the Rivest-Shamir-Adelman (RSA) cryptosystem, Crypto++ is not presently distributable in the US. However, a subset of Crypto++ without the disputed RSA bits should be available on the Internet by the time this goes to print.

In this chapter you'll integrate some of those ciphers into an offshoot of QSocket and build a secure chat program from them. Before you begin coding, however, you need to understand what these ciphers are good for.

Data Security and Privacy: The Basics

When designing security, a helpful concept to know about is the idea of *threat models*. That is, you should figure out who might try to eavesdrop on users of your application or disrupt its data, so that you'll know what level of protection your application needs. For example, an application that protects internal information for a large bank is more likely to face certain kinds of attacks than one that implements a Web-based chat forum. The threat model used in this chapter covers three threats: eavesdropping, traffic analysis, and impostors. After reading this chapter, you'll be able to determine on your own which of these three to include in your own threat model.

Many security experts also believe that it's not a good idea to distribute information about security weaknesses. Taking this approach is figuratively like hiding money in a mattress and being able to trust that its obscurity will protect it. In contrast, making security information available to people is like enabling them to lock their money in a bank vault and thus to use real security that can withstand a concerted attack. Currently, widespread reliance on "security through obscurity" means that many successful breaches of security aren't ever publicized, for fear that other miscreants will harness the same methods to attack other systems.

The nature of the Internet makes it vulnerable to the three types of attacks discussed below. The Internet Engineering Task Force (IETF) and other standards groups are in the process of developing more secure Internet protocols, but it's wise to be aware of these tricks in the meantime.

Eavesdropping

First, estimate the likelihood that someone will intercept your data traffic without your consent or knowledge. Because the Internet was designed to route traffic over any available path, it's difficult to predict where packets sent from your computer will travel en route to their destination. As they travel, they can encounter *packet sniffers*—programs or hardware devices that, like TCP/IP wiretaps, can record all packets sent from or to an individual network address. An individual anywhere on the network between your host and your destination can sniff your packets if they pass through his or her section of the network.

The idea that your packets are vulnerable may seem farfetched, but consider this: whether you're using a corporate or university network or a commercial Internet provider, many other people on *your local network* can see your data. Most (but not all!) packet sniffing attacks are not run by some shadowy evildoer on another continent, but by someone within a small section of the network neighborhood. Of course, the potential for large-scale sniffing exists. Several commercial Internet providers have been attacked by organized sniffers since 1991, and there have probably been other, less publicized incidents.

To protect against eavesdroppers, programmers do what they do with ordinary paper mail: seal it in an opaque wrapper. For regular mail, that wrapper is an envelope; for data, it's encryption. If an eavesdropper does sniff encrypted packets, he or she won't be able to decipher them. If you encrypt all the data your application sends and receives, you'll also make it easier to resist the next method of attack.

Traffic Analysis

Urban legend has it that reporters in Washington, D.C., knew that something unusual was happening in August, 1990, when Iraq was preparing to invade Kuwait. How did they achieve this magic? By watching the number of pizza trucks making deliveries at the Pentagon. Just as journalists correctly inferred lots of after-hours activity at the Pentagon, monitoring where data goes can tell you a lot about what the data is or might be. This process is called *traffic analysis*. For example, packets flowing from `somehost.bigcorp.com` to `www.jobs-r-us.com` is a good indication that someone at BigCorp might be looking for a new job. Television rating companies also offer services that tell how many hosts accessed a given Web page—they also tell which domains those hosts are from. That's great for advertisers, but most people don't want their visits to the Playboy or Christian Coalition Web pages to be public record.

Gathering data for traffic analysis is easy; some packet sniffers can do the job automatically. Foiling traffic analysis is somewhat harder. Not only do the source and destination of messages give away information, so do their length and frequency. It's hard to conceal the source and destination of packets, but you can disguise the length (by padding all messages to a uniform length) and frequency (by sending dummy messages in idle periods). Overall, the key is to make your real messages blend in with other traffic. Having data security code in your Internet application is advantageous to others besides your users; it helps users of all other programs that incorporate encryption by providing them with additional camouflage against traffic analysis. It's hard to blend in with a crowd of other similar packets unless those other packets exist—otherwise, it's like standing in the middle of a football stadium by yourself.

Impostors

TCP/IP offers a wonderful set of utilities for converting machine names to IP addresses, and vice versa. Most network hosts also have some way to identify a particular user who's communicating over the network. The one thing these different services have in common is that they can all be deceived. A dedicated attacker can create fake Domain Name Service records for a particular host so that his packets appear to be coming from a trusted host, and a really determined cracker can use other types of complex attacks that involve putting bogus data inside the TCP/IP packets themselves.

A number of protocols can fix this problem by allowing one party to authenticate commands or data sent by another. For example, you could use the popular Rivest-Shamir-Adelman (RSA) public-key algorithm, which uses two keys. In this method, if you encrypt a request with your private key and send it to a host computer, the host can decrypt it with your public key to verify that you, and only you, had sent it.

Other protocols provide undeniable signatures, so that there's no way to deny a signature once it's made. Some specialized challenge-response protocols allow you to make sure that a "man in the middle" isn't interfering with a session or impersonating either end of a session; others allow you to prove that someone holds a piece of information (like a password) without making the person disclose the information over the network.

 The cipher is only part of the overall cryptosystem. A strong cipher is useless if you give it a weak key or otherwise compromise its security.

Building in Security

As in the other programming chapters of this book, in this chapter designing comes before coding. Now that you know what threats may face your applications, you can start planning how to add security to them. It's important to think carefully about your plan so that you "build in security" instead of "building insecurity." Here are some rules that should be helpful:

1. *Lean toward pessimism.* Assume that your users need maximum security, and that there are plenty of potential attackers out there. A good general rule: if the data goes over the network or onto disk, you should allow users to encrypt it if they choose.

2. *Extra security doesn't always impose extra speed burdens.* The difference in speed between a marginally secure algorithm, like the Data Encryption Standard (DES), and a more secure one, like the Improved Data Encryption Algorithm (IDEA) or triple-DES (a variation of DES that repeats each round of encryption three times), is often small—especially compared to the gain in security. As computer power grows, so does the chance that a brute-force attack will be able to crack particular algorithms. Build in more security than you need now so that future users will have it when they need it.

3. *Don't cut corners.* It doesn't do much good to use a secure cipher if you store the password as part of the file. If you're serious about security, take the time to think about how you use the cipher in the program. If you feed a very secure algorithm like IDEA a precomputed key, or if you store the key in the file, the security of the algorithm is nullified. (Several major Windows applications do just that; don't rely on them to secure your critical data.)

4. *Make encryption easy for the user.* If you can, make it completely transparent. This application's new version of the Qsocket class uses randomly generated keys for each session and distributes them. The user doesn't have to do anything special to make this work. If encryption is difficult, people won't use it. This goes for programmers, too; if you're writing a DLL, OCX, VxD, or another tool that programmers will use, make it easy for them, or they won't use it either.

In the next section, you'll apply these principles to building a socket class that knows how to send and receive encrypted data automatically. As you create the application, the chapter will point out the use of these principles.

Building an Encrypting Socket Class

So far throughout the book, you've used the Qsocket class to simplify your socket communications. Although Qsocket neatly wraps up all the methods and behaviors that you need from a socket into one easy-to-use class, one thing it *doesn't* do is provide data security. You can remedy that by creating a new class, based on QSocket, which I'll call EQSocket (the E is for Encrypting). You'll add the security you need to EQSocket so that making an application secure is almost as simple as replacing one source file with another.

EQSocket will do all the things that QSocket does now, but it will have some new methods to let the application work with encrypted connections. Rule #1 says to add all the security you can, so to help prevent traffic analysis, pad all messages to make them a uniform size.

Rather than add separate member functions for encrypted connections, you'll control encryption on a socket-by-socket basis by adding a flag to the constructor. That way, your application can become crypto-enabled by changing one line of code! Rule #4 strikes again. You'll also modify the Send(), SendRaw(), and GetLine() methods to automatically encrypt or decrypt messages.

What about choosing the key? You could argue that for maximum usefulness we should use the Diffie-Hellman algorithm to automatically generate and exchange keys—and you'd be right. Unfortunately, the DH algorithm is patented in the US, so I can't use it here. (The patent expires in 1997, though.) You may be able to use DH in your own programs; for more details, check out RSA Labs' Web page (it's in the references).

Because we can't use DH, we'll add a SetKey() method to use a user-specified key. All is not lost, though; we can let the user type in an arbitrarily long *passphrase* (like a password, only longer), and crunch the passphrase down to a 128-bit key.

The EQSocket class will depend on Crypto++, which I built as a statically linked library for this chapter. You need to pick a default cipher from the wide array that Crypto++ offers. This application uses the IDEA cipher (but you can choose another cipher if you prefer, as you'll see).

Why IDEA? First, it has withstood intense scrutiny, and the crypto community believes it to be secure. Second, it's relatively fast; and third, it's free for noncommercial use (it *is* patented, so don't use it for a commercial product without a license). It's well-documented, simple, and reliable—perfect for the task at hand.

Creating a New Encrypted Socket

Before you can do anything else, you'll need to be able to create a new instance of EQSocket. Because you'll want existing programs to function pretty much unchanged, create a new class derived from our own QSocket. The following listing shows the header file which defines the new EQSocket class.

```
#include "socket.h"
#include "cryptlib.h"
#include "misc.h"
#define kCipherBits        128
#define kCipherBytes       16

class EQSocket : public QSocket
{
public:
    EQSocket(BOOL fCreateSocket);
    void EQSocket::InitEncryption(const byte *key);
private:
    BlockTransformation *pCipherIn;
    BlockTransformation *pCipherOut;

public:
    BOOL fIsEncrypted;
public:
    virtual ~EQSocket();
    BOOL EQSocket::Disconnect(void);
    EQSocket *EQSocket::Accept(void);
    void EQSocket::Send(const CString& data);
    void EQSocket::SendRaw(const void *data,
                  const int dataLen);
protected:
    void EQSocket::OnReceive(int error);
    void EQSocket::OnAccept(int error);
};
```

The two #defines tell us how many bits, and bytes, of key the chosen cipher uses. In IDEA's case, it's 128 bits, or 16 bytes. You'll need to change these definitions if you change to another cipher.

The constructor is just like the QSocket constructor, which only makes sense! We'll talk more about each of the other member functions (both the new ones and those we inherit from QSocket) below.

The purpose of fIsEncrypted is to tell the application whether the socket is handling encrypted data. The key, obviously, is the encryption and decryption key. The other two lines of code need a bit of explanation. Because Crypto++ provides so many different algorithms, you'll want to be able to choose one easily. BlockTransformation is an abstract class from which all the block ciphers in Crypto++ descend. Instead of keeping a pointer typed to, say, Blowfish * for the Blowfish cipher, or IDEA * for the IDEA cipher, keep a pointer to the abstract base class and typecast it where needed. Crypto++ sensibly splits up encryption and decryption, so you need two cipher objects, each with a different direction specified. (See Crypto++'s misc.h file for more details.)

NOTE All the ciphers discussed in this chapter are block ciphers, and they're implemented as subclasses of Crypto++'s `BlockTransformation` class. `BlockTransformation` encapsulates the notion of a cipher that operates on fixed-size blocks; for every chunk of plaintext that goes in, an equivalently sized block of ciphertext comes out, and vice versa.

First, lay the groundwork for modifying the socket class. Add these `#includes` to `socket.h`.

```
#include "cryptlib.h"
#include "misc.h"
```

You'll also need to tell Visual C++ where the library's `include` files are. Here's how to do that. Figure 13.1 shows the result.

Fig. 13.1

Visual C++'s "Project Settings" dialog box has many options; here, you've told the compiler where to find additional `include` files.

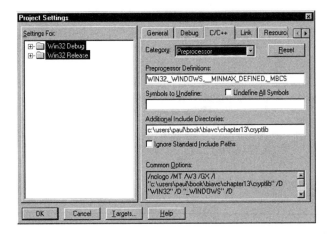

1. Choose Project, Settings. The Project Settings dialog box will appear.

2. Click the "C/C++" tab, then select "Preprocessor" from the Category pulldown. (You'll have to scroll down a few lines to see it.)

3. In the field labeled "Additional Include Directories," type the full path to the Crypto++ include files. In this case, that was
   `c:\biavc\chapter13\cryptlib`.

Since the constructor is very simple, we'll start there. In fact, it's hard to get much simpler than this:

```
EQSocket::EQSocket(BOOL fCreateSocket)
    :fIsEncrypted(FALSE),
     pCipherIn(NULL), pCipherOut(NULL)
{
}
```

We don't want to create the crypto objects yet, because we need to pass the
key to the `BlockTransformation` constructor, and we don't have a key yet.
We'll leave it up to the programmer to get a key from somewhere and pass
it to `InitEncryption()`.

Preparing for Encrypted Communications

To provide automatic key exchange, you might consider using the Diffie-
Hellman (or DH) algorithm, named for its inventors, Martin Hellman and
Whitford Diffie. It allows two users (say, Alice and Bob) to negotiate a key
over an insecure channel. An eavesdropper (say, Eve) won't be able to rebuild
the key on her own. Explaining the math of the DH algorithm is beyond the
scope of this chapter, but the basics are that Alice and Bob agree on two large
integers and share them. Each then computes another large integer and keeps
it secret. Finally, they each do some computations to combine their secret
and public numbers and generate a *public value*. Alice and Bob can use each
others' public values to independently compute a secret key.

In this case, the DH algorithm is patented in the US, so it can't be used here.
Instead, you'll add code to let each user specify a passphrase, which will be
converted to a 128-bit IDEA key. DH is a much better solution, though.

> If you read any of the references listed at the end of the chapter, you'll meet Alice,
> Bob, and Eve again, plus a whole host of others, including Peggy the prover, Mallet
> the malicious attacker, and Victor the verifier.

Ideally we'd have one function that would set up all the crypto objects and
do any needed key management, like a DH exchange. Since the key management scheme we're using here is very simple, you might wonder whether a
whole Init routine is necessary, but you can always customize it to add more
meat later. Here's what `InitEncryption()` looks like:

```
void EQSocket::InitEncryption(const byte *key)
{
    pCipherIn = new IDEADecryption(key);
    pCipherOut = new  IDEAEncryption(key);
    gCipherBlockLen = pCipherIn->BlockSize();
    gCipherBlockBytes = gCipherBlockLen / 8;
    fIsEncrypted = TRUE;
}
```

You need to create new cipher objects for the incoming and outgoing ends of the socket. Notice how the IDEA class from Crypto++ gives you separate objects for encryption and decryption; these two objects can share the same key or have different keys. Set the global variables for cipher size and set the socket's isEncrypted flag, and that's it!

Accepting Incoming Encrypted Connections

Before we can call InitEncryption(), we must figure out how to accept, or start, encrypted connections— but before we can accept a connection, someone has to initiate it. Let's defer that problem for right now, since we'll actually solve it in the dialog's socket handler. Luckily, QSocket offers us an easy hook: you can override the OnAccept() function so that it'll do what the right thing whenever the socket gets an accept message.

You also need to override the QSocket::Accept() method, since it creates a new QSocket. We want a new EQSocket, so we have to do that ourselves. The following listing shows the new Accept() and OnAccept() functions.

```
EQSocket *EQSocket::Accept()
{
    EQSocket *return_socket = new EQSocket(FALSE);
    return_socket->m_hSocket = INVALID_SOCKET;

    // do not get the address of remote end.
    if (!CSocket::Accept(*return_socket, NULL, NULL))
    {
        delete return_socket;
        return_socket = 0;
        SetErrorVars(__FILE__, __LINE__);
    }

    return_socket->CurrentStatus = CONNECTED;
    return return_socket;
}
```

The big part of this routine is actually the two first lines. Instead of creating a new QSocket, as does QSocket::Accept(), this function creates a new EQSocket and sets its socket pointer to a special value, INVALID_SOCKET. The MFC socket libraries expect us to set the pointer to INVALID_SOCKET before trying to use that socket in an accept() call. The rest of the function is just like what's in QSocket::Accept().

Speaking of similarities, now is a good time to talk about OnConnect(). The only difference between the EQSocket and QSocket versions is that the EQSocket version should call EQSocket::Accept. Just copy QSocket::OnAccept(), then edit the line that says:

```
QSocket *new_socket = Accept();
```

so that it calls `EQSocket::Accept()` instead, like this:

```
EQSocket *new_socket = Accept();
```

Now the application can accept incoming requests for secure connections.
Next you'll look at how to send and receive encrypted data over the socket.

Sending Encrypted Data

Chapter 8, "Building an Internet HTTP Server," showed you how to send
non-`CString` data by adding a `SendRaw()` method to the `QSocket` class. You'll
use that method again now, because all of the `BlockTransformation` derivatives want data in discrete blocks, not `CStrings`. Therefore, you'll need to
break the send data down into blocks, encrypt each block, and send it. If the
data size isn't an even multiple of the block size, pad the last block before
transmitting it. The following listing shows the new version of `SendRaw()`:

```
void EQSocket::SendRaw(const void *data, const int dataLen)
{
    int amt = dataLen;

    if (dataLen == 0)
        return;

    if (fIsEncrypted)
    {
        int idx=0, numBlocks = 0;
        int nLeftOver = 0;
        unsigned char *p = (unsigned char *)data;
        unsigned char *pBlock = NULL;

        numBlocks = dataLen / gCipherBlockLen;
        nLeftOver = dataLen % gCipherBlockLen;
        pBlock = (unsigned char *)malloc(gCipherBlockLen);
        memset(pBlock, 0, gCipherBlockLen);

        for ( ; idx < numBlocks; idx++, p += gCipherBlockLen)
        {
            memcpy(pBlock, p, gCipherBlockLen);
            pCipherOut->ProcessBlock(pBlock);
            QSocket::SendRaw((const void *)pBlock,
            ➥gCipherBlockLen);
        }

        memset(pBlock, 0, gCipherBlockLen);
        memcpy(pBlock, p, nLeftOver);
        pCipherOut->ProcessBlock(pBlock);
        QSocket::SendRaw((const void *)pBlock, gCipherBlockLen);
        free(pBlock);
    }
    else
```

```
                        QSocket::SendRaw((const void *)data, dataLen);

        if (amt == SOCKET_ERROR)
        {
            int error = WSAGetLastError();
            if (error != WSAEWOULDBLOCK && error != WSAEINPROGRESS)
                QSocket::SetErrorVars(__FILE__, __LINE__);
        }
    }
```

This routine looks like the original SendRaw at the beginning and the end, but the middle is quite different. If the socket's encrypted, then we need to know how many blocks of data we're sending. The block size varies, because different ciphers use different block sizes. Use the BlockSize() member function to tell us how big ciphertext blocks are. Then use the block size to calculate the number of full blocks, plus the number of leftover bytes at the end. Having done that, allocate and clear a buffer to hold the block data, and then enter a loop for processing the blocks.

Each loop iteration encrypts one block of data by calling the ProcessOut() method of the BlockTransformation object (which, in this case, is IDEA). Once the application has encrypted the block, send *that block only* over the socket and go back to the start of the loop.

Once we've finished the loop, we reset the buffer and send any leftover bytes, padded on the right with 0. IDEA's default block size is 8 bytes, so for a 92-byte message, we'd send a total of 12 8-byte blocks. The receiving end is responsible for stripping off the padding, if necessary. That's why you use 0; since we're sending strings, the receiving end can decrypt the block without worrying about where the padding lies.

NOTE If you want to be really careful, make sure that none of your plaintext gets swapped to disk by the Windows virtual memory subsystem. Windows NT provides calls that let a user keep certain data in physical RAM at all times, but there isn't space to discuss them here. Rules #1, #2, and #4 collide here; it's bad practice to ever allow plaintext to get written out by the OS, but we don't want to complicate things unnecessarily. Be careful!

Of course, we also need to be able to send plain old CStrings, so we should provide a new Send() as well. In this case, we want to call the inherited Send() if the socket's not encrypted; if it is encrypted, we'll just pass the CString data to SendRaw() for transmission. The following listing shows the new EQSocket::Send() method.

```
void EQSocket::Send(const CString& data)
{
    if (data.GetLength() == 0)
        return;
    if (fIsEncrypted)
        SendRaw(data, data.GetLength());
    else
        QSocket::Send(data);
}
```

Receiving Encrypted Data

Receiving encrypted data is pretty much the inverse of sending it. You need to split the received data into discrete chunks of ciphertext, decode them, and pass them on. Once again, a QSocket member function does almost what we want. QSocket::OnReceive() gets called when new data arrives on a socket, so it's a logical place for us to decrypt that data. The easiest way to implement this is to make a copy of the QSocket::OnReceive() function, then add the necessary decrypting code just below the line that reads "temp[amt] = 0;"

```
 if (fIsEncrypted)
 {
     int idx=0, numBlocks = 0;
     int nBlkSize = pCipherIn->BlockSize();
     unsigned char *p = (unsigned char *)temp;
     numBlocks = amt / nBlkSize;
     for (; idx < numBlocks; idx++, p += nBlkSize)
         pCipherIn->ProcessBlock(p);
 }
```

This looks suspiciously like the code given previously, and with good reason. The program should decode all the full blocks it receives; because the sender pads all messages before sending them, the blocks will always be full. The existing code in OnSocketMessage() will either pass the decrypted plaintext on to a user-specified handler (set with SetReceiveTarget), or it will put the plaintext into the line buffer for retrieval with GetLine().

Switching to a Different Cipher

What if you have a requirement to interoperate with a system that uses DES instead of IDEA? Rather than rewriting all the code you've already completed, you can simply change the cipher that EQSocket uses. These #defines tell the application how large the cipher's keyspace and block size are:

```
int gCipherBlockLen;
int gCipherBlockBytes;
#define kCipherBits       128
#define kCipherBytes    16
```

First, change the `#include` in `eqsocket.cpp` to include the class definitions for the cipher you want to use. Immediately below that, adjust the definitions for `kCipherLen` and `kCipherBytes`. `kCipherBits` is the number of bits in the cipher's key, and `kCipherBytes` is `kCipherLen` divided by 8. The final step is to edit `EQSocket::InitEncryption()` so that it creates objects of the new cipher type, instead of using IDEA as before.

Security in Action: Building a Talk Client

Now you're ready to learn how to apply `EQSocket` to a real-world problem: talking with a user on another host. You could always use IRC, and Chapter 9, "Building an Internet IRC Application," explained how to write an IRC client. Alternatively, most UNIX systems provide a simpler solution for those times when you want to talk with one other person: the `talk` command. `Talk` allows you and another user to chat back and forth via your keyboards. In this section, you'll combine `EQSocket` with the things you've learned in previous chapters to write a Windows-based talk utility.

Designing the Talk Program

As always, make sure you think through your application's design before you plunge into coding. What you want is a mini-IRC client that can either make or receive calls—sort of like a keyboard telephone. Its key feature is encryption support, but it still needs some minimal functionality to make it useful:

- a way for the user either to listen for incoming calls, or to start a call to another user

- a way for the user to set an encryption key, unless you're using a key-exchange protocol

- a place to type in messages that the other user can see

- a place to display what the other user has typed

Creating the User Interface

Using AppWizard, create a dialog box-based application; this one is called "Secret Sharer," since that's what it's for. Make sure to tell AppWizard that you want Windows Socket support. As usual, the next step is to create your dialog boxes, including member variables and linked message-map functions. Here's what to do:

1. Modify the main dialog box that AppWizard created for you. Figure 13.2 shows the completed main dialog box.

2. Rename the OK button to "Call..." and the Cancel button to "Quit." Make a member variable, m_Call, for the Call button. Add accelerators for them (or any of the buttons below) if you'd like.

3. Add two new buttons: Hang Up (resource ID IDC_HANGUP) and Listen (resource ID IDC_LISTEN). Create member variables named m_Hangup and m_Listen to point to the button objects. Use the Properties palette to disable IDC_HANGUP.

4. Add a large edit control (resource ID IDC_INCOMING) to display text from the other end of the connection; make sure to set its style to "multiline" and "read-only." Give the control two member variables: m_Incoming should point to the CEdit control, and m_IncomingText will hold the control's text.

5. Add a smaller edit control (resource ID IDC_OUTGOING) to give the user a place to type. Set its state to disabled; you'll enable it only when the user is connected. This edit control also gets two member variables: m_ Outgoing should point to the CEdit control, and m_ OutgoingText will hold the control's CString value.

6. Use ClassWizard to create message map functions for the Listen, Hang Up, and Call buttons. Name them OnListen, OnHangUp, and OnCall.

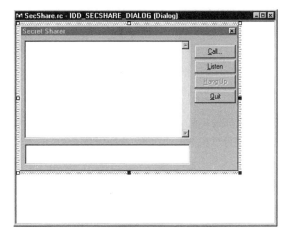

Fig. 13.2
The completed main dialog box provides several controls for conducting a talk session.

Next, you need a dialog box to let the user specify whom to call when the Call button is triggered. This one is simple enough—just create a dialog box (name it `IDC_CALL_DLG` or something similar) and add one text field named `IDC_CALLEE`. When you use ClassWizard to build a new class for the dialog box, name it `CCallDialog` and give the `IDC_CALLEE` field a member variable to hold its contents. Now add code for the message map functions you added above.

Finally, create a dialog box so the user can specify a key. It needs an edit control (single-line, please) and a member variable to hold that control's text. In this example, the dialog's named CLoadKeyDlg.

Handling User Commands

If Alice wants to use the chat program, there are six basic things that she can do. The code needs to handle each of them:

1. Alice and Bob can independently set keys. Of course, they need to use the same key! We'll use `OnKey()` to do this, and we'll automatically call `OnKey()` if no key has been set when the user starts or accepts a call.

2. Alice can call Bob. The `OnCall()` function should handle this.

3. She can also start listening for a call from Bob. `OnListen()` is responsible for this case.

4. Once connected, she can type messages to Bob, as well as seeing what Bob types. You need a new message map entry for the typing, as well as support for sending and receiving socket data.

5. At any time, Alice can hang up (provided she's connected!) `OnHangup()` takes charge of this case.

6. She can quit the application. You need to provide for a clean disconnection regardless of whether Alice is listening or talking, but MFC already handles the dialog box-related work.

The first step is setting the key. Because we created a dialog box just to get the key, the `OnKey()` routine is pretty simple, but there's one neat twist. Here's the code:

```
void CSecShareDlg::OnKey()
{
    CLoadKeyDlg theDlg;

    if (theDlg.DoModal()==IDOK)
    {
        MD5 keyHash;

        keyHash.Update((unsigned char*)(LPCTSTR)theDlg.m_Passphrase,
                        theDlg.m_Passphrase.GetLength());
```

```
        memset(appKey, 0, kCipherBytes);
        keyHash.Final(&appKey[0]);
    }
}
```

As we've done many times before, we toss up a dialog box and take some action if the user presses OK. In this case, we're going to take the user's key and transmogrify it. IDEA uses 128 bits of key, but because English text carries lots of information (remember the "f u cn rd this u cn b n rtst" subway signs?) even a long phrase may actually not carry much unique information.

The MD5 message-digest algorithm, produced by RSA Data Security, takes an arbitrary block of plaintext in and produces a 128-bit *hash* as output. Changing one bit of plaintext usually results in changing many bits of the hash, and that's what we want here.

Using the Crypto++ MD5 is simple: create the object, call MD5::Update() with each block of plaintext you want hashed, then call MD5::Final() to get the actual hash value. We store the hash value in a global which stores the key. We'll use the key later, when we call InitEncryption().

> For improved security, the code above should use a salt value to keep Mallet from precomputing the MD5 hashes of common passphrases and mounting a dictionary attack. If you know what this means, then fix the code; if not, see Schneier for a lucid explanation.

Next comes starting a new call to Bob. Here's what the OnCall() function looks like:

```
void CSecShareDlg::OnCall()
{
    CCallDialog callee;
    if (callee.DoModal()==IDOK)
    {
        pCallingSocket = new EQSocket(TRUE);
        pCallingSocket->Connect(callee.m_CalleeText, kTalkPort);
        pCallingSocket->SetReceiveTarget(this,
                        WM_CALLING_SOCKET_RESPONSE);
    }
}
```

> kTalkPort is a #define that sets the port number. Because you're implementing a new service, you can't use any existing service number. I chose 2159 for the program on the CD.

Present the `CCallDialog` dialog box, which lets Alice choose a host to call; if she confirms her choice, the application creates a new, encrypted socket and uses `Connect()` to connect it to her specified host. You should also link the `OnCallingSocket()` function to the socket with a call to `SetReceiveTarget()`.

Being able to make a call implies that there's someone listening on the other end—that would be the `OnListen()` function. It's a bit longer, so it's shown in the following listing. You may find it very reminiscent of the `OnStart()` function from the HTTP server dialog box shown in Chapter 8, "Building an Internet HTTP Server."

```
void CSecShareDlg::OnListen()
{
    pListeningSocket = new EQSocket(TRUE);
    if (pListeningSocket)
    {
        pListeningSocket->SetReceiveTarget(this,
                        WM_LISTENING_SOCKET_RESPONSE);
        SOCKADDR theAddr;
        theAddr.sa_family = AF_INET;
        memset(theAddr.sa_data, 0, sizeof(theAddr.sa_data));
        *(u_short *)(&theAddr.sa_data[0]) = htons(kTalkPort);

        if (pListeningSocket->Bind(&theAddr, sizeof(theAddr)))
        {
            if (pListeningSocket->Listen(0))
            {
                fIsListening = TRUE;
                fIsConnected = FALSE;
                UpdateControls();
            }
        }
    }
}
```

Begin by creating a new encrypted socket, then calling `SetReceiveTarget()` to make the listening socket send its events to the dialog box. The new socket then gets bound as a listening socket (with a call to `Bind()`). Finish up by calling `Listen()`, which waits for incoming connections. Because this application allows only one conversation at a time, the parameter to `Listen()` specifies that no backlogged connections are allowed. Once done, set the flags and dialog box buttons to reflect what you just did.

See the section "Starting, Stopping, and Quitting" in Chapter 8, "Building an Internet HTTP Server," for a more thorough explanation of what this code does.

Now, on to hanging up. All the `OnHangup()` routine needs to do is dispose of the sockets and set the state flags to reflect that you're not connected *or* listening. Here's how:

```
void CSecShareDlg::OnHangup()
{
    if (fIsListening)
    {
        if (pListeningSocket)
            delete pListeningSocket;
        fIsListening = FALSE;
    }
    else
    {
        if (pCallingSocket)
            delete pCallingSocket;
    }
    fIsConnected = FALSE;
    UpdateControls();
}
```

Quitting is easy. Use the ClassWizard to add a function (call it `OnQuit`) to be invoked when `IDCANCEL` gets a `BN_CLICKED` event. All that function needs to do is call the `OnHangup()` method if we're connected, followed by a call to `CDialog`'s default `OnCancel()` method. Here's what the code looks like.

```
void CSecShareDlg::OnQuit()
{
    if (fIsListening ¦¦ fIsConnected)
        OnHangup();
    CDialog::OnCancel();
}
```

You might wonder what to do about letting Alice and Bob type back and forth. Before you can do that you need to finish providing socket I/O support. You also need to learn how to update the dialog box controls to keep the dialog box items properly enabled and disabled:

```
void CSecShareDlg::UpdateControls(void)
{
    m_Listen.EnableWindow((!fIsConnected) && (!fIsListening));
    m_Hangup.EnableWindow(fIsConnected ¦¦ fIsListening);
    m_Call.EnableWindow((!fIsConnected) && (!fIsListening));
    m_Outgoing.EnableWindow(fIsConnected);
}
```

Using the Socket to Send and Receive Data

You still need to make the main dialog box class able to handle both incoming and outgoing connections; then you need to add code so that the text that one person types appears on the other person's screen. Chapters 7

("Building an Internet FTP Application") and 8 ("Building An Internet HTTP Server") explained how to do this.

Setting Up

First, you'll need to fix up the dialog box class's header file. `#define` the socket messages by adding these statements to the dialog box class's header file:

```
#define WM_LISTENING_SOCKET_RESPONSE WM_USER+201
#define WM_CALLING_SOCKET_RESPONSE WM_USER+202
```

You need message map entries in the class message map. Still in `secshdlg.h` (the name may vary depending on what you chose to name your application), add these prototypes just before `DECLARE_MESSAGE_MAP`:

```
afx_msg LONG OnListeningSocket(WPARAM amount, LPARAM buffer);
afx_msg LONG OnCallingSocket(WPARAM amount, LPARAM buffer);
```

Your last task in the header file is to declare the private member variables your dialog box needs. You've already seen all of them, but here they are again:

```
private:
    EQSocket *pCallingSocket;
    EQSocket *pListeningSocket;
    BOOL fIsConnected;
    BOOL fIsListening;
```

You know enough now to be able to make sure that the class destructor and constructor do the right thing with these members.

Now you need to work on the dialog box class `.cpp` file. First off, tie the socket functions into the class message map. Insert these two lines into the `CSecShareDlg` message map, just before the `//}}AFX_MSG_MAP` line:

```
ON_MESSAGE(WM_LISTENING_SOCKET_RESPONSE, OnListeningSocket)
    ON_MESSAGE(WM_CALLING_SOCKET_RESPONSE, OnCallingSocket)
```

OnListeningSocket() and OnCallingSocket()

To actually send and receive data, you'll need to provide code for the `OnListeningSocket()` and `OnCallingSocket()` functions. For variety, you might start by describing `OnListeningSocket()` first this time. It's shown in the following listing.

```
afx_msg LONG CSecShareDlg::OnListeningSocket(WPARAM amount,
                            LPARAM buffer)
{
    if ((int)amount > 0)
```

```
        {
        }
        else
        {
            switch((SocketReceiveCmd)amount)
            {
                case NewSocketAccepted:
                {
                     pCallingSocket = (EQSocket *)buffer;
                    pCallingSocket->SetReceiveTarget(this,
                            WM_CALLING_SOCKET_RESPONSE);
                    if (!appKey[0])
                            OnKey();
                    pCallingSocket->InitEncryption(&appKey[0]);
                    fIsConnected = TRUE;
                    UpdateControls();
                    m_Outgoing.SetFocus();
                    break;
                }
                case SocketStatusChanged:
                default:
                        break;
            }
        }
        return 0;
    }
```

You saw this code first in Chapter 7's ("Building an Internet FTP Application") FTP client and then in Chapter 8's ("Building an Internet HTTP
Server") HTTP server. In this case, the EQSocket::Accept() method has already
taken care of creating the actual encrypted socket, but you still need to turn
on its encryption code. After you tie the new socket into the existing window, check to see if the user's set a key. If not, make them set one before
continuing on and calling InitEncryption(). Once the encryption objects
have been created, update the controls and state flags, and continue.

Now for OnCallingSocket(). This routine isn't too different from its ancestors
in other chapters, even though it handles an encrypted socket. Here's why.
One of this application's design goals, in accordance with Rule #4, was for
EQSocket to be a drop-in replacement for QSocket. That means that the
EQSocket::OnSocketMessage() function is actually decrypting the data; by
the time it gets to OnCallingSocket, it's plaintext.

The new features of this OnCallingSocket are that it knows how to hang up if
the other end of the connection disconnects; it can automatically put incoming text into the CEdit control, à la the IRC client's view class, and it turns on
encryption automatically when the connection first completes. The code for
the new and improved OnCallingSocket is in the following listing.

```
afx_msg LONG CSecShareDlg::OnCallingSocket(WPARAM amount,
                    LPARAM buffer)
{
    if ((int)amount > 0)
    {
        int tLen = m_Incoming.GetWindowTextLength();
        char *bufText = (char *)malloc(amount+4);

        m_Incoming.SetSel(tLen, tLen);
        int s = strlen((char *)buffer);
        memcpy(bufText, (char *)buffer, s);
        if (bufText[s-1] == '\n')
        {
            bufText[s-1] = '\r';
            bufText[s] = '\n';
            bufText[s+1] = 0;
        }
         m_Incoming.ReplaceSel((char *)bufText);
        free(bufText);
    }
    else
        switch((SocketReceiveCmd)amount)
        {
            case SocketStatusChanged:
                switch (pCallingSocket->GetStatus())
                {
                    case DISCONNECTED:
                    {
                        fIsConnected = FALSE;
                        OnHangup();
                        break;
                    }

                    case CONNECTED:
                    {
                        fIsConnected = TRUE;
                        UpdateControls();
                        m_Outgoing.SetFocus();
                        if (!appKey[0])
                            OnKey();
                        pCallingSocket->
                            InitEncryption(appKey);
                        break;
                    }

                    default:
                        break;
                }
                break;

            default:
                break;
        }
    return 0;
}
```

If the application gets incoming data, it will copy it into a private buffer and fiddle with the newline and carriage return characters at the end, so that when the screen displays the text it will look OK. Afterwards, set the CEdit's selection to the end of its text and append the new text. If we get a status change instead of data, we use it to either call OnHangup() (if it was a disconnect) or start the connection (if it was a connection). If we're starting a new connection, we create a key if needed before calling InitEncryption().

Alice and Bob: Together at Last

Now you're almost done. All you have left to do is add some code that will actually send what Alice and Bob type; OnCallingSocket() will take care of displaying the text when it comes in over the socket. Because Windows' edit controls don't have a way to let you know when the users hit the Enter key, you have to find another way.

The following listing shows the (somewhat unusual) solution. Make the edit control a multiline field using AppStudio; then have the program check to see whether the control has more than one line. If so, the user will have hit return, so have the application extract the text and send it to the other end.

```
void CSecShareDlg::OnChangeOutgoing()
{
    if (fIsConnected)
        if (m_Outgoing.GetLineCount()>1)
        {
            char *pLine = NULL;
            int nLen = 0;
            int tLen = m_Incoming.GetWindowTextLength();
            CString sOutText = "( ";

            nLen = m_Outgoing.LineLength(0);
            pLine = (char *)malloc(nLen+2);
            memset(pLine, 0, nLen+2);

            m_Outgoing.GetLine(0, pLine, nLen+1);
            pLine[nLen] = '\n';

            pCallingSocket->Send(pLine);
            m_Outgoing.SetSel(0, -1);
            m_Outgoing.Clear();

            pLine[nLen] = 0;

            m_Incoming.SetSel(tLen, tLen);
            sOutText += pLine;
            sOutText += " )\r\n";
            m_Incoming.ReplaceSel(sOutText);
            free(pLine);
        }

}
```

The application is now complete. You are now able to talk securely with anyone you please.

Using Secret Sharer

As you've seen, this chat program is pretty simple. If you want to call someone else, click Call and provide a hostname. If you want to wait for someone to call you, click Listen instead. In either case, you can use Hang Up to stop the call or Quit to stop the call and exit.

Once you're connected to someone, you can type messages into the lower CEdit; your message will appear on in the upper CEdit control (surrounded by parentheses), as will the text that your correspondent types.

Please remember that this is a demo application. Because of political and legal reasons, I can't add as much security as I would like, or I couldn't get the chapter included in the book. Why is that? Read on to find out.

The Politics of Encryption

As you might expect, the U.S. government has strict regulations to prevent the export of military information and material, including "technical data"— a catch-all term for books, papers, drawings, articles, or anything that describes how to build any item which is restricted itself, like fighter planes and tanks. These regulations, called the International Traffic in Arms Regulations, or ITARs, are enforced by the full power of the U.S. Government, which takes them very seriously.

The ITARs put cryptographic software in the same category as an M-1 tank, an aircraft carrier, or a fighter jet. Exporting crypto software itself, whether on a floppy or via the Internet, is punishable by time in a Federal prison. However, the government claims that the technical data clauses cover the source code for, *and articles about,* such materials.

The First Amendment to the U.S. Constitution prohibits the government from restricting the content of citizens' speech— including printed speech. The wide-ranging ban resulting from the application of the ITARs to printed matter is felt to be blatantly unconstitutional by many scholars and legal experts. The missing link is that no legal precedent has equated text on a floppy or FTP site with text on paper, even though most reasonable people would see no significant difference between the two media.

When Bruce Schneier wrote his landmark *Applied Cryptography* in 1994, no one even thought of asking for government permission to publish such a book; after all, the government isn't allowed to exercise prior restraint of the free press. However, requests sent to the U.S. Departments of State and Commerce asking for permission to legally export floppies of *the same source code contained in Schneier's book* have been consistently denied since the book was published.

As I write this, the current state of case law says that if I put crypto source code in a paper book, it enjoys the same protection as any other expressive material—it's covered by the First Amendment. If, however, I take the *same code* and place it on a CD or floppy, it becomes subject to export control, and I (and the publisher) can go to jail if that floppy or CD finds its way outside the U.S. or into the hands of a non-U.S. citizen within the U.S. This is the reason there's no crypto source code on the CD included with this book.

Patents

There's another reason why even the innocuous, non-crypto code from Crypto++ isn't on the CD, either: patents. Patent law restricts how and when you can use a patented invention without licensing it, and RSA Data Security, Inc. (RSADSI) claims patent protection for the RSA and Diffie-Hellman algorithms. I couldn't include a patented device (like, say, a machine tool) in this book, and I equally can't include source code for a patented algorithm.

RSADSI has freely released the MD5 message-digest algorithm (provided I acknowledge their creation, which I just did), and the inventors of IDEA allow you to make non-commercial use of their patented algorithm without paying a license fee.

If you plan to incorporate crypto into shareware or commercial tools, be careful. RSADSI has very aggressive lawyers, but their licensing terms are said to be reasonable, and both DH and RSA are too useful to not use. Check out their web site at `http://www.rsa.com`. Good news: the Diffie-Hellman patent expires 4/29/97, and the RSA patents expire in the year 2000.

What You Can Do

When the ITARs were written, just after World War II, cryptographic tools were among the nation's most closely held secrets. Since then, an explosion in research activity in the civilian cryptographic community, combined with the dizzying increase in affordable computer power, has put military-grade security into the hands of ordinary citizens.

II

Developing Applications

Of course, some people find that a disquieting thought. They argue that "national security" or "protection against criminals" requires the government to have access to any encryption key used within the U.S. The FBI and National Security Agency have begun quietly laying the groundwork for a ban on any private encryption system not approved by the U.S. Government. To put this in more easily visible terms, imagine having to protect your home with locks to which the government had a key, and imagine that it was illegal to use any other kind of lock.

If you want to continue to have the freedom to protect your data and your privacy, do us all a favor: distribute your crypto software widely *within the limits of the law*. Give it to your friends and colleagues. Explain why they should protect their privacy if they don't already know. Write magazine articles. Give lunchtime talks at your office. Spread the word.

From Here...

Although it's hard to cover such a complex and broad subject in a single chapter, hopefully it has equipped you to add security to your Internet applications. If you're motivated to learn more about the technology, policies, and public policy implications of privacy protection, see the references below.

Suggested Improvements

The chat program is a simple (not to say simple-minded!) example of a secure communications tool. The security is pretty good, but the user interface and feature set could use some work—but hey! I wouldn't want to finish everything for you, because you'd quickly get bored.

Here are some areas where the application could be improved or expanded. Try as many as you find interesting.

- Polish the user interface. You could even reuse the code from the IRC client and build an SDI talk application. Add a status bar to show the connection and conversation status.

- Let your users choose whether to encrypt their chat or not. While you're at it, add compatibility with the UNIX talk protocol so that they can talk to a UNIX user.

- Provide support for key verification. Right now, two users of your application can be spoofed by Mallet with a man-in-the-middle attack. (You'll need to read up in Schneier for this one.)

Recommended Reading

Because this topic is so complex, this book has a "Recommended Reading" section. The following references provide more detail on the history, politics, implementation, and implications of privacy-protection software. I recommend skimming through them to see which ones fit your interests and then absorbing all the learning you can.

- Bruce Schneier's *Applied Cryptography* (John Wiley & Sons, 1994; ISBN 0-471-59756-2). Subtitled "Protocols, Algorithms, and Source Code in C," this book is the single most important book you can own if you want to secure your applications.

- If you need some crypto source code, there's an excellent archive created by Klaus Pommerening and served by Win Treese at `http://www.openmarket.com/info/cryptography/applied_cryptography.html`. Notice that these pages only contain pointers to sites outside the U.S., so it's OK for you to import the code you find.

- David Kahn, *The Codebreakers: The Story of Secret Writing* (Macmillan & Co., 1967). Kahn has written the definitive history of codes and ciphers, starting some 4,000 years ago and continuing through the early 1960s. Highly recommended, especially if you're a history buff.

- Francis Litterio keeps a thorough and engaging collection of pages on "Cryptography, PGP, and Your Privacy" at `http://draco.centerline.com:8080/~franl/crypto.html`. PGP, of course, is Phil Zimmerman's Pretty Good Privacy, an outstanding data security program for Windows, DOS, Macintosh, and UNIX computers.

- John Gilmore's "Cryptography and Export Control" archives, located on the Web at `http://www.cygnus.com/~gnu/export.html`, are an excellent source of information on the bizarre world of the ITARs.

- The Electronic Frontier Foundation (EFF) has joined two private citizens in filing lawsuits challenging the constitutionality of ITAR restrictions. See EFF's "Legal Alerts" page at `http://www.eff.org/pub/Alerts`.

- If you want to use the RSA or Diffie-Hellman algorithms in a real product, you'll want to visit RSA Labs at `http://www.rsa.com`. They offer reference toolkits and a wealth of other useful technical data there.

- The Cypherpunks is an informal group of people interested in the technical implementation of crypto and privacy software. Their unofficial rallying cry is "Cypherpunks write code." Visit their mailing list (send mail to `cypherpunks—request@toad.com`), and don't miss their Frequently Asked Questions list (at `http://www.apocalypse.org/pub/u/nelson/bin.cgi/cyphernomicon`).

Chapter 14

Building an Unique Internet Application— QSend

So far all of the applications you have developed have been "standard" applications. Clients are widely available for a variety of operating systems, and servers run on many, if not all, sites on the Internet. In this chapter, you will write both a server and a client for an application that is not in standard use: QSend, which transfers an object between two sites. In this chapter you'll cover:

- What QSend is for
- How to design QSend
- How to build QSend
- How to use QSend

What *QSend* Does

QSend is an *OLE container* application. OLE, Object Linking and Embedding, enables Windows programs to cut, copy, and paste entire *objects*, such as images, sounds, charts, or wordprocessing documents directly between applications. A container application can contain an OLE object and access the menus and commands of the application that created the object.

QSend allows OLE objects to be transferred from one site to another. For example, say you are designing a large image in an image-manipulation tool. Without QSend, you could save the image to a file, start up a mail program, such as Eudora, that can send attachments and send it to the other person. That person would start Eudora, receive the message, and then load the saved attachment into their image-management program. Or you could start QSend, bring the image in with OLE, and send it to the other person who could look at it and use it right away.

Designing *QSend*

Because you're writing both ends of this application, you can use a very nice technique that Microsoft recommends for sockets. You attach the socket to an archive and use Serialize to send and receive data over the connection. This means that the code in this chapter will only work for those of you using Visual C++ 2.1 or later. You use Microsoft's CSocket and CSocketFile classes, not included in earlier versions.

You'll turn on OLE container support, but not server or automation, and you'll need one other menu option: Network, Send to send an object. That process opens a dialog box prompting for the host name. This is actually a very simple application.

Building *QSend*

As usual, you'll use AppWizard to build the skeleton application, AppStudio to change the menu and build the dialog, ClassWizard to connect the menu and dialog to code, and then do some real coding to make the program do the transfer.

AppWizard
First, you use AppWizard to create the basic application, called QSend. You need an MDI OLE container application with a toolbar, but without printing. Turn on Sockets support, either in AppWizard or by hand afterwards.

AppStudio
Open the IDR_QSENDTYPE menu in AppStudio and add a new menu, Network. Add one item, Send, to it. Then add the same menu and item to IDR_QSENDTYPE_CNTR_IP. (Use the same resource ID.) This menu is used when there is an embedded object (your application is functioning as a container, hence CNTR) being edited in place (IP).

Place <u>S</u>end in a menu of its own to make it stand out better.

Create a simple dialog IDD_SELECT_HOST, with one edit field, for the host name, like the one shown in figure 14.1.

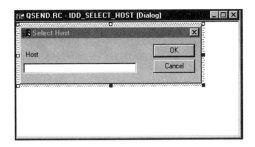

Fig. 14.1
The dialog specifies the host where the embedded object will be sent.

ClassWizard

Connect the IDD_SELECT_HOST dialog to a class called SelectHost, and the IDC_SELECTED_HOST control (the edit box with the host name) to a CString member variable called m_selected_host. Arrange for CQSendDoc to catch the menu item <u>N</u>etwork, <u>S</u>end.

Coding the Client Portion

It's not a simple matter to define client and server in this context: If you believe that clients receive and servers send, you give a different definition than if you believe that clients initiate action and servers wait for actions to be requested. The latter definition is preferable, and so it is the client part of this program that handles <u>N</u>etwork, <u>S</u>end.

Getting a Socket

You need a socket, as usual. But since you're going to create it, connect it, and then get rid of it, you don't need a socket pointer stored in the class as you usually do. Instead you can just create one on the stack. You call Create and Connect, in the old familiar way, and then comes some really neat stuff, courtesy of MFC. First, the general structure of OnNetworkSend:

```
void CQsendDoc::OnNetworkSend()
{
    SelectHost select_host;
```

```
if (select_host.DoModal() == IDOK)
{

    CSocket sockClient;

    sockClient.Create();

    if (!sockClient.Connect(select_host.m_selected_host,
            QSEND_PORT))
    {
        AfxMessageBox("Host is unreachable.");
        return;
    }
    // Send the embedded object.

}
}
```

This code puts up the SelectHost dialog, and if the user clicks OK, declares a
CSocket. You can't use QSocket easily here because you'll be passing this
socket to some functions that are expecting a CSocket. Rather than casting,
since you don't need the extra functionality of QSocket, just use a CSocket.
Having declared it, you call the Create method, and then connect it to
m_selected_host.

Connecting the Socket

You call connect as usual, with the port QSEND_PORT. You've used a variation
on the usual #define for the port—add the line

```
const int QSEND_PORT = 5500;
```

to QSEND.H. Really, const int is better than #define. When you need to
interact with Windows (for example, message-handling), stick with #define,
but when you just need to attach a name to a number, use const int. It's
typesafe (triggers a compiler error or warning if used somewhere an int
shouldn't be used) and reliable (it can't be overridden later as a #define can).

How did you choose the port number to use for this application? RFC 1700 is
the key. This RFC lists the ports that are used by standard applications like
NNTP, Finger, or SMTP, and also those that are not used for standard applications but are registered for use with certain specific Internet applications. This
RFC, like all the others, is on the CD-ROM that comes with this book.

The *Internet Assigned Numbers Authority* (*IANA*) keeps track of port assignments and makes sure that each application has a unique port number. If this
chapter's application, QSend, were to become an ongoing part of your Internet
life, you would want to be sure that the port number you were using did not

conflict with the port being used by another user on your machine for a different application. For example, if you chose port 25, whenever SMTP traffic arrived you would think it was yours.

Ports in the range 1,024 to 65,635 are not controlled by the IANA, they are "up for grabs" but as a convenience they keep track of which ones are being used and include them in RFC 1700. Almost every number is used up to 2070, then things get a little sparse. There's nothing between 5303 and 6000, so 5500 is a good choice. By the way, this RFC is updated regularly (with a new RFC number) and someday 5500 may be taken.

Sending the Data

You may have noticed that you didn't call SetReceiveTarget for the socket before the call to Connect. You are going to use archives to handle the send. This is the MFC-recommended way when you are writing both ends of the application as Windows programs. Usually, archives are connected to files, and the connection is done by the framework. Your Serialize function is called with a CArchive object whenever the document needs to be opened or saved. Here, you do it a little differently. This is the code to send the embedded object:

```
CSocketFile sockFile(&sockClient);
CArchive arSend(&sockFile, CArchive::store);
Serialize(arSend);
```

You declare a CSocketFile first, passing it a pointer to the socket you've already declared. A CSocketFile inherits from CFile and provides a neat way to talk to a socket (write to the socket file) and listen to one (read from the socket file).

Next, you declare a CArchive, passing it the socket file and the "store" flag to indicate you plan to send data to the archive (and so to the socket file and so to the socket and so to the other machine).

Finally, in a truly neat trick, you call the Serialize function of this document, passing it the archive that's connected to the socket file that's connected to the socket that's connected to the other machine. After all, you need a way to get the object embedded in the document passed to an archive, and later you'll need a way to fill a document from an archive. That function is already written: it's called Serialize. Why reinvent the wheel?

AppWizard gave you a Serialize that does just what you want with no extra code and it can still be used for saving and opening the document from a disk file—obviously it would be passed a different CArchive in that case.

II

Developing Applications

There! You've written everything you need to do to send the embedded object across the Internet. Less than 20 lines of code! One thing though: the receiving user will know when the receive is complete because the screen will change. How will the sender know? You add a line to the very end of OnNetworkSend:

```
AfxMessageBox("Send Complete");
```

Because Windows is message-driven, adding this box causes a minor problem—the last socket message doesn't finish going out while the box is on-screen. You can prevent this by causing the destructor for the archive to go off before calling the message box. Simply wrap everything in the "guts" of this routine, except the message box call, in another layer of brace brackets:

```
void CQsendDoc::OnNetworkSend()
{
    SelectHost select_host;

    if (select_host.DoModal() == IDOK)
    {

        {
            CSocket sockClient;

            sockClient.Create();

            if (!sockClient.Connect(
              select_host.m_selected_host, QSEND_PORT))
            {
                int err = sockClient.GetLastError();
                AfxMessageBox("Host is unreachable.");
                return;
            }

            CSocketFile sockFile(&sockClient);

            CArchive arSend(&sockFile, CArchive::store);

            Serialize(arSend);
        }

        AfxMessageBox("Send Complete");
    }
}
```

Now sockFile and arSend will go out of scope at that "extra" closing brace bracket, and their destructors will run before the message box. The CSocketFile destructor is irrelevant here, but look at the CArchive destructor:

```
CArchive::~CArchive()
{
    // Close makes m_pFile NULL. If it is not NULL,
    // you must Close the CArchive.
```

```
        if (m_pFile != NULL && !(m_nMode & bNoFlushOnDelete))
            Close();

        Abort();    // Abort completely shuts down the archive.
    }
```

So what does `Close` do?

```
    void CArchive::Close()
    {
        ASSERT_VALID(m_pFile);

        Flush();
        m_pFile = NULL;
    }
```

And what does `Flush` do?

```
    void CArchive::Flush()
    {
        ASSERT_VALID(m_pFile);
        ASSERT(m_bDirectBuffer || m_lpBufStart != NULL);
        ASSERT(m_bDirectBuffer || m_lpBufCur != NULL);
        ASSERT(m_lpBufStart == NULL ||
            AfxIsValidAddress(m_lpBufStart,
                    m_lpBufMax - m_lpBufStart, IsStoring()));
        ASSERT(m_lpBufCur == NULL ||
            AfxIsValidAddress(m_lpBufCur,
                    m_lpBufMax - m_lpBufCur, IsStoring()));

        if (IsLoading())
        {
            // Unget the characters in the buffer,
            // Seek back unused amount.
            m_pFile->Seek(-(m_lpBufMax - m_lpBufCur),
                        CFile::current);
            m_lpBufCur = m_lpBufMax;    // Empty
        }
        else
        {
            if (m_lpBufStart == NULL
                || m_lpBufCur != m_lpBufStart)
            {
                if (!m_bDirectBuffer)
                {
                    // Write out the current buffer to file.
                    m_pFile->Write(m_lpBufStart,
                      m_lpBufCur - m_lpBufStart);
                }
                else
                {
                    // Commit current buffer.
                    m_pFile->GetBufferPtr(CFile::bufferCommit,
                            m_lpBufCur - m_lpBufStart);
```

```
                              // Get next buffer.
                              VERIFY(m_pFile->GetBufferPtr(
                                 CFile::bufferWrite, m_nBufSize,
                                 (void**)&m_lpBufStart,
                                 (void**)&m_lpBufMax) == (UINT)m_nBufSize);
                              ASSERT((UINT)m_nBufSize == (UINT)(m_lpBufMax
                                 - m_lpBufStart));
                           }
                           m_lpBufCur = m_lpBufStart;
                        }
                     }
                  }
```

After asserting various things to make sure you got to this function in the usual way, if you are storing (which you are), this code writes out the final buffer of data to the file, which is really a socket file, which is really a socket. Only once this process is complete is it really OK to put up that message box saying the send is complete. And that's why you put an extra set of brace brackets into the body of OnNetworkSend.

Coding the Server Portion

Coding the server is a little more work. (It could hardly be less.) It needs to wait for a connection to come through, then handle the data when it arrives.

Waiting for a Connection

Where should the code that watches for an incoming connection go? Not in the view, for no matter what view has focus you want to catch the message. Not in the document; what if there's no document open? (The user can use File, Close to close the Qsend1 document they always start with.) Perhaps the application itself? Applications inherit from CWinApp and can be command targets but not message targets. You need a window that is always open—the mainframe window.

You use a listening socket, as you have done before when the connection is started from the other end. In MAINFRM.H add to the class:

```
private:
     QSocket *pListeningSocket;
```

Set this pointer to NULL in the constructor and delete it in the destructor.

When the application first starts, the mainframe window is created with a call to CMainFrame::OnCreate. You need to add a call at the end of this function to set up the listening socket. Add:

```
Listen();
```

This function looks like this:

```
void CMainFrame::Listen()
{
    delete pListeningSocket;
    pListeningSocket = new QSocket;
    SOCKADDR_IN sock_address;
    int addr_size = sizeof(sock_address);
    sock_address.sin_family = AF_INET;
    sock_address.sin_addr.s_addr = htonl(INADDR_ANY);
    sock_address.sin_port = htons(QSEND_PORT);
    pListeningSocket->Bind((SOCKADDR*)&sock_address, addr_size);
    pListeningSocket->SetReceiveTarget(this, WM_SOCKET_LISTEN);
    pListeningSocket->Listen();

}
```

This is the same method of setting up a listening socket as you have used
before. You allocate the socket, build an address and port (using INADDR_ANY
and QSEND_PORT—this is why the definition of QSEND_PORT had to be in
QSEND.H, where all the objects would see it), allocate, build, and bind the
socket to the address you built. Then you call SetReceiveTarget to send a
WM_SOCKET_LISTEN message to this class when there is activity on the socket.
Don't forget to define WM_SOCKET_LISTEN in QSEND.H:

```
#define WM_SOCKET_LISTEN WM_USER+201
```

and add the entry to both message maps. The MAINFRM.H message map
becomes:

```
// Generated message map functions.
protected:
    //{{AFX_MSG(CMainFrame)
    afx_msg int OnCreate(LPCREATESTRUCT lpCreateStruct);
    //}}AFX_MSG
    afx_msg LRESULT OnListeningSocket(WPARAM wParam,
            LPARAM lParam);
    DECLARE_MESSAGE_MAP()
```

and the mainframe.cpp message map becomes:

```
BEGIN_MESSAGE_MAP(CMainFrame, CMDIFrameWnd)
    //{{AFX_MSG_MAP(CMainFrame)
    ON_WM_CREATE()
    //}}AFX_MSG_MAP
    ON_MESSAGE(WM_SOCKET_LISTEN, OnListeningSocket)
END_MESSAGE_MAP()
```

Handling Received Data

The next step is to write CMainFrame::OnListeningSocket to handle the message when the listening socket receives something. It's much like previous

II

Developing Applications

`OnListeningSocket` functions except for what it does with the new data
socket:

```
LRESULT CMainFrame::OnListeningSocket(WPARAM amount, LPARAM buffer)
{
    if ((int)amount > 0)
    {
    }
    else
    {
        // If amount < 0 it is a receive command.
        switch ( (SocketReceiveCmd)amount )
        {
            case SocketStatusChanged:
                break;
            case NewSocketAccepted:
                // The only function of this listening socket
                // is to tell you where to find the data
                // socket that the server connected to. After
                // that you work with the data socket.

                QSocket *pSockRecv = (QSocket *)buffer;

                // Handle incoming data.
                delete pSockRecv;

                break;              }
    }
    return 0;
}
```

The way it handles the data on the data socket is the same chain of objects as
you used on the send:

```
{
    CSocketFile sockFile(pSockRecv);
    CArchive arRecv(&sockFile, CArchive::load);
    ASSERT(!AfxGetApp()->m_templateList.IsEmpty());
    // Should have one template.
    CDocTemplate *pTemplate = (CDocTemplate *)AfxGetApp()
        ➥m_templateList.GetHead();

    CDocument *pDocument = pTemplate->OpenDocumentFile(NULL);
    // Get a new document.
    arRecv.m_pDocument = pDocument;

    pDocument->Serialize(arRecv);

    pDocument->UpdateAllViews(NULL);
    pDocument->SetModifiedFlag(TRUE);
}
```

You declare a `CSocketFile` connected to the data socket, and an archive connected to the socket file. You make sure that there is at least one document
template defined for this application (in other words, that no one has deleted

the AppWizard template code from QSEND.CPP) and then get a pointer to the first template. At the moment, it's the only template. Then you get a pointer to a CDocument by calling OpenDocumentFile(NULL)—normally this function takes a string that holds the file name, but if it is passed NULL it makes one of those "empty" documents that are usually created with File, New.

The archive holds a pointer to its document, so you set that to point to the new empty document, and then a call to Serialize deals with the data as it comes over the socket. When that is complete, a call to UpdateAllViews makes sure the screen is changed to reflect this new object, and you set the modified flag—after all, dumping an entire object into the document surely does modify it.

This whole block is wrapped in brace brackets to make the CArchive object go out of scope and trigger the destructor, as you did before. But there's another reason for it this time: the CSocketFile destructor contains an ASSERT statement that the socket is still around, so you have to be sure that this destructor goes off before you delete pSockRecv. The brace brackets ensure this.

Using *QSend*

This program now works. It was quick and simple to write because the MFC OLE code does all the work. To test it, you would ideally use two machines, each connected to the Internet and each with a different address. If you don't have that, you can use the "loopback" address 127.0.0.1 that you first learned about all the way back in Chapter 5, "Building an Internet Finger Application."

Run the program from within Visual C++. To embed an object, choose Edit, Insert New Object, then select the object. Do not set the Link check box—you want to make a copy of this to send across the network. Figure 14.2 shows the program with the embedded object. Up to this point none of your new code has been involved—all this functionality came from AppWizard and MFC.

Now, choose Network, Send. Fill in **127.0.0.1** as the host address, and click OK. A new window appears, with the document name QSend2, with a copy of the chart object, as shown in figure 14.3.

That's all there is to using the program. The receiving user can save the document by choosing File, Save as usual. You've simply extended OLE to transfer objects over the Internet.

II

Developing Applications

Fig. 14.2
QSend acts as an OLE container with a Microsoft Chart object being edited in place. Notice that the menus are Microsoft Chart menus, not the smaller menus you defined for this program, but that your Network menu is still there. The toolbar is also a Chart toolbar.

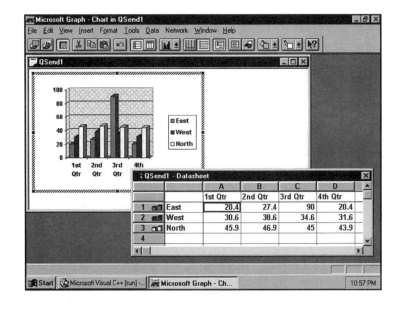

Fig. 14.3
A copy of the chart object has been sent to this site through the loopback address. The message box confirms the send is complete. Note the menu is back to the simple QSend one.

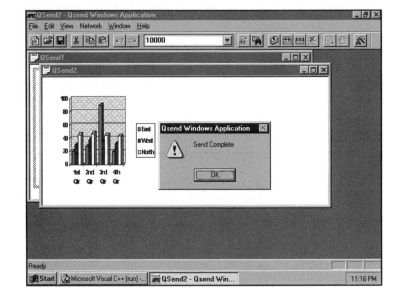

From Here...

You haven't put much work into this application, and yet it works and is useful. It's not e-mail, yet in some ways it's quicker and neater than e-mail because you can edit the object in place and don't need to save it before sending. If you want to embellish it a little, here are a few tips:

- Change the edit box on the Select Host dialog to a drop-down list box. Save (in the .INI file) a list of sites this user has sent objects to in the past, and use this list to fill the box.

- Check Chapter 18 of *Introducing Visual C++* (one of the many many manuals that come with Visual C++) and read through the list of enhancements to the default OLE container implementation that are discussed there. Most if not all of those suggestions are appropriate for this container class too: handling sizing more neatly, allowing multiple embedded objects in a single document, and deleting embedded objects from a document.

- Chapter 19 of that manual also covers implementing copy and paste for embedded objects, faster redraw code, and an even nicer resizing approach.

- Add an item to the toolbar for <u>N</u>etwork, <u>S</u>end.

- Set up an icon for the application that looks different from the usual icon, and have the application change to this icon when a receive is complete. This means that the user can keep the application open on the desktop, and get a visual prompt when an object arrives.

This is a neat little application that runs over the Internet and yet is unique. You won't find a description of it, or a version of it, anywhere else. If you can think of a neat Internet application of your own, there's nothing stopping you from writing a client and a server for it (or a combination client and server, also known as a *peer* application, as you've done here) and spreading the word. You don't need to send the entire document object, as you have done here. You can send any object that has a `Serialize` function (and you can always write a `Serialize` function if you need to) or that has the `<<` and `>>` operators defined. Remember that those operators are provided for `CString` objects, so you could have an interactive session with `CStrings` being sent back and forth through `CArchive` and `CSocketFile` objects.

II

Developing Applications

Because you're handling both ends, the Internet traditions of ending each line with \r\n and ending multiline transmissions with a "." alone on a line aren't necessary in this case. But then again, your application will only work if both machines are running Windows, both running the same version of the software (the `Serialize` functions must be identical at both ends, at least). Traditional Internet applications function perfectly when the machines at either end have different operating systems, different file systems, different character representations, and so on. You won't replace the traditional services, but who knows, you may create a brand-new "standard" Internet service of your very own! (Make sure I get a copy.)

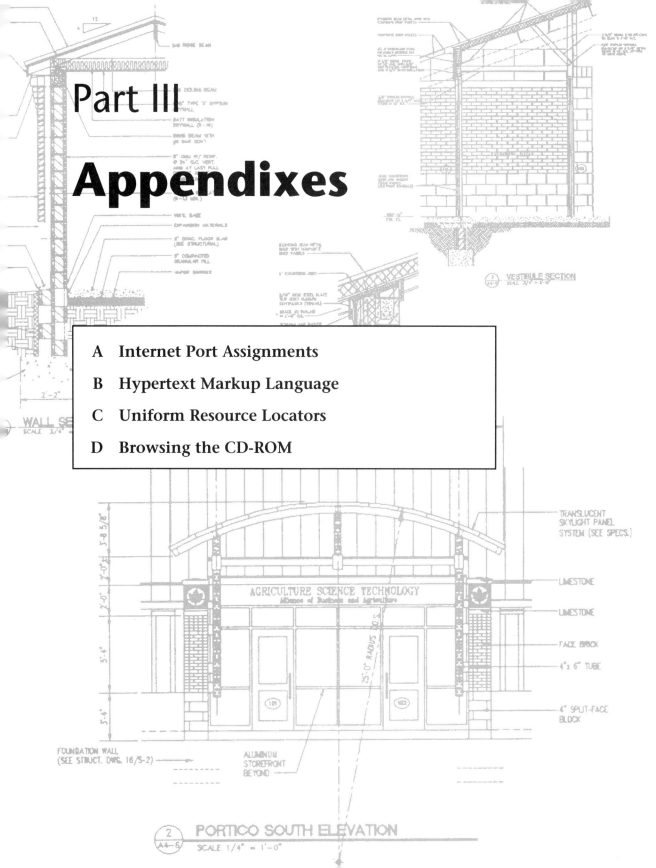

Part III

Appendixes

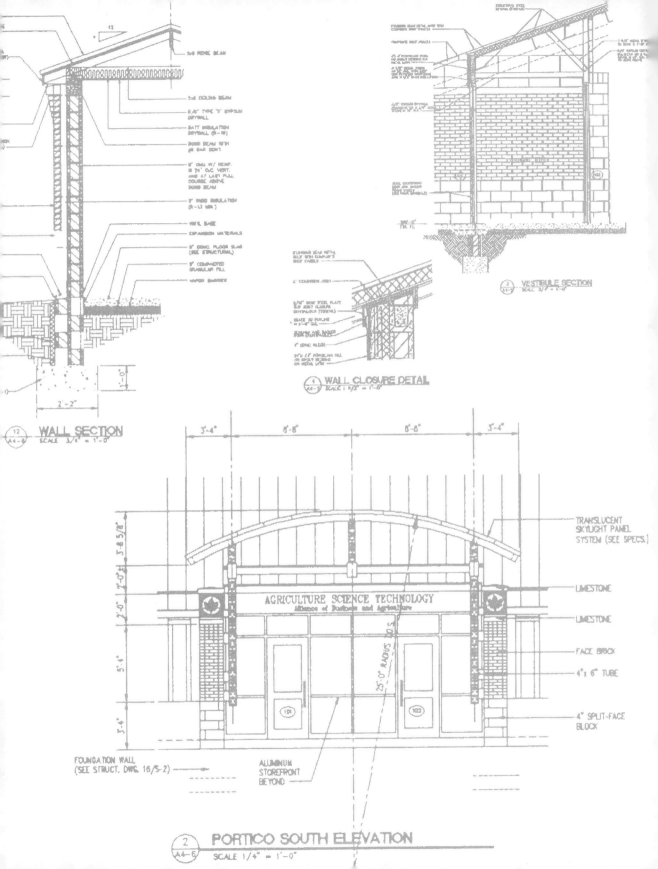

Appendix A

Internet Port Assignments

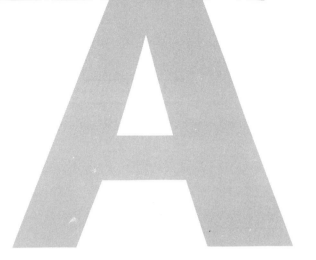

Throughout this book specific port numbers that are used for specific Internet services have been mentioned; for example, port 25 is used for SMTP. These port numbers are provided in the RFC for the particular service. This appendix summarizes the port numbers and also provides standard service names for use in a WSAAsyncGetServByName function call. (The names must also appear in the SERVICES file provided with your TCP/IP stack.)

Service	Port	Protocol	Description
ECHO	7	TCP/UDP	Sends you everything you send to it—used for diagnostics
DISCARD	9	TCP/UDP	Eats everything you send to it—used for diagnostics
DAYTIME	13	TCP/UDP	Returns the time and date
QOTD	17	TCP/UDP	Returns the quote of the day
FTP-DATA	20	TCP	Data channel for the *File Transfer Protocol*
FTP	21	TCP	Command channel for the *File Transfer Protocol*
TELNET	23	TCP	Remote terminal login (like connecting by modem)
SMTP	25	TCP	*Simple Mail Transfer Protocol*—transfers Internet mail from system to system
TIME	37	TCP/UDP	Gets the system time

(continues)

Service	Port	Protocol	Description
RLP	39	UDP	*Resource Location Protocol*—locates resources such as domain name servers and gateways
FINGER	42	TCP/UDP	Gives you information about users, using the FINGER (or NAME) protocol
WHOIS	43	TCP	Gets user information from the SRI-NIC server
DOMAIN	53	TCP/UDP	Retrieves information from a domain name server
NAMESERVER	53	TCP/UDP	Same as DOMAIN
MTP	57	TCP	*Mail Transfer Protocol*—transfers mail from one system to another
BOOTP	67	UDP	*Bootstrap Protocol*—provides a way for diskless workstations to boot from a server
TFTP	69	UDP	*Trivial File Transfer Protocol*—transfers files to and from servers
FINGER	79	TCP	Gets information about users of a host system
SUPDUP	95	TCP	Similar to Telnet, it provides a terminal emulation to remote users
HOSTNAMES	101	TCP	Returns a host name on the SRI-NIC server
POP2	109	TCP	*Post Office Protocol 2*—gets Internet mail from a mail server (obsolete protocol)
POP3	110	TCP	*Post Office Protocol 3*—gets Internet mail from a mail server
SUNRPC	111	TCP/UDP	*Sun Microsystems' Remote Procedure Call* protocol—passes messages between processes
PORTMAP	111	TCP/UDP	Maps RPC program and version numbers to their corresponding port number
AUTH	113	TCP	Returns the identity of a user that owns a specific Internet address

Service	Port	Protocol	Description
SFTP	115	TCP	*Simple File Transfer Protocol*—like TFTP and FTP, transfers files
UUCP-PATH	117	TCP	Enables a user to get the e-mail address of someone on a system that's not connected to the Internet, but who has access to Internet mail through UUCP or some other protocol
NNTP	119	TCP	*Network News Transfer Protocol*— retrieves news from a UseNet server
NTP	123	UDP	*Network Time Protocol*—gets system time
SGMP	153	UDP	*Simple Gateway Monitoring Protocol*—manages gateways remotely
TCPREPO	158	TCP	PC-based mail distribution often referred to as PCMAIL
SNMP	161	UDP	*Simple Network Management Protocol*—allows remote users to modify attributes of a network
SNMP-TRAP	167	UDP	Used by the *Simple Network Management Protocol*
BIFF	512	UDP	Used by mail systems to tell users that they've received new mail
EXEC	512	TCP	Provides a way to execute programs or processes remotely
LOGIN	513	TCP	Telnet-type connection with automatic user and password verification
WHO	513	UDP	Provides a list of who is currently signed onto a system. Also provides some statistical information
SHELL	514	TCP	Provides a way to execute programs or processes remotely and verifies the user automatically
PRINTER	515	TCP/UDP	Used by print spoolers
TALK	517	TCP/UDP	Part of *Internet Relay Chat*

(continues)

III

Appendixes

Service	Port	Protocol	Description
NTALK	518	TCP/UDP	Part of *Internet Relay Chat*
EFS	520	TCP	*Extended Filename Servers*—resolves names
ROUTE	520	UDP	Local routing process. Uses a form of the *Routing Information Protocol*
TIMED	525	TCP/UDP	Provides system time and date information
TEMPO	526	TCP/UDP	Enables someone to change the time and date on a system
COURIER	530	TCP/UDP	Used by RPC (the *Remote Procedure Call* protocol)
CONFERENCE	531	TCP/UDP	*Internet Relay Chat*
NETNEWS	532	TCP/UDP	Network news
NETWALL	533	TCP/UDP	Used for emergency broadcasts
UUCP	540	TCP/UDP	Used by the *UNIX to UNIX Copy* protocol—the mail interchange protocol
KLOGIN	543	TCP/UDP	Kerberos automated sign-on
KSHELL	544	TCP/UDP	Kerberos remote command and process execution with automatic verification
NEW-RWHO	550	UDP	Provides a list of who is currently signed onto a system
REMOTEFS	556	TCP/UDP	Used in the management of a file system from a remote location
RMONITOR	560	TCP/UDP	Provides a way to monitor processes remotely
MONITOR	561	TCP/UDP	Provides a way to monitor processes from a terminal that's local to the process (on the same host)
ELCSD	704	TCP/UDP	Error log copy/server daemon

If you're interested in more information regarding the assigned TCP/IP ports, you can contact:

> Internet Assigned Numbers Authority
> USC Information Sciences Institute
> 4676 Admiralty Way
> Marina del Rey, CA 90292-6695

Port numbers above 1024 are not used by standard Internet applications, but many of them are in use and it's better to choose a unique port number if possible. Use a number above 7,000 in the absence of any other information. This issue is discussed in more detail in Chapter 14, " Building a Unique Internet Application—QSend."

Appendix B

Hypertext Markup Language

The Hypertext Markup Language (HTML) is a standard way of distributing hypermedia documents. Think of HTML as a primitive RTF format, but with extensions to handle features such as hyperlinks, images, tables, and interactive forms. The HTML language continues to grow, and will soon support extensions such as movies and sound, file upload, text wrap around images, and style sheets.

HTML Markup

An HTML document is really just a plain text document with HTML *tags* embedded within it. HTML tags inform the client that a particular section of the document should be displayed in a certain way. How the client displays the characters is really up to the client. Most clients enable the user to select the font, size, and color of any displayed text.

HTML markup is simple enough to code by hand and can be authored using many word processing tools. HTML tags are codes encapsulated within angle brackets "<" and ">". HTML tags are case-insensitive; in other words, both lowercase and uppercase tags are treated the same. Some tags require an end tag, where a tag's effect is terminated. For instance, the <b> tag is used to mark when text should be bold and the </b> tag is used to mark the end of the bold text. Nesting tags are not guaranteed to produce the desired effect, such as the following example: <i><b>Hopefully italicized bold text</b></i>. Some World Wide Web Browsers display this correctly, while others display it using italics only. When nesting tags, be sure to terminate them in the right order—from the inside out.

In HTML, text is free-format, as consecutive spaces, tabs, and newlines are compressed to single spaces. Adding additional spaces, tabs or newlines may improve readability of the HTML source at the expense of increasing the size of the file and network bandwidth required to transfer the file.

With HTML, it is important to code for content and not appearance. The appearance of an HTML document depends on several things, including which World Wide Web browser is used, and the specific browser configuration. Many browsers enable the user to define the way that documents are displayed, such as the typeface, font size, and whether round or dashed bullets are used.

Document Structure

There is a small number of tags that define the overall structure of an HTML document. The `<html>` and `</html>` tags enclose the entire HTML document. Within the `<html>` and `</html>` tags are the actual document heading and body. The `<head>` and `</head>` tags are used to enclose the document heading, and the `<body>` and `</body>` tags are used to enclose the document body. As a rule, the title of the document is specified in the document heading enclosed by the `<title>` and `</title>` tags.

If you want to include comments within your HTML document, enclose the comment text with the `<!—` and `—>` tags. Any text between these will be ignored when the document is displayed.

For example, the following HTML code serves as an overall template for the HTML document structure:

```
<html>
<head>
<title>Document Title</title>
</head>
<body>
This is where the content of the document goes.
<!— Use comments to explain awkward formatting or structure —>
</body>
</html>
```

The actual content of the document belongs within the `<body>` and `</body>` tags.

Headings

HTML defines six levels of heading tags. First level headings should be enclosed by the `<h1>` and `</h1>` tags. Second level headings use `<h2>` and `</h2>`. The series continues up to sixth level headings, using the `<h6>` and `</h6>` tags. World Wide Web browsers typically render headings on a line by themselves, starting with a large font size for first level headings, decreasing to a smaller font size for sixth level headings. The user can often change the specific typeface and font for each heading level.

Line Breaks, Paragraphs, and Horizontal Rules

Since HTML is free format and ignores multiple whitespace and newlines, special markup codes are used to define line breaks and paragraph breaks. A line break is indicated by the <br> tag. Line breaks force text to the next line with no additional vertical spacing. Note that there is no end tag.

A paragraph break is marked by the <p> tag, again without an end tag. The paragraph break results in vertical spacing that signifies the end of a paragraph and the beginning of another.

A horizontal rule is simply a line drawn across the screen. The <hr> tag is used to mark where a horizontal rule is displayed. The <hr> tag does not require an end tag either.

Lists

HTML provides several ways to define lists. The most used list types are ordered and unordered. Variations on the unordered list include a menu list and a directory list. Lists can be nested.

An ordered, or numbered list is introduced by the <ol> tag and terminated by the </ol> tag. Within <ol> and </ol> are the actual list items, each introduced by the <li> tag. The <li> tag has no end tag. Paragraph <p> marks are not required to separate the list items. When a World Wide Web browser displays an ordered list, each list item will be numbered, starting at number one and incremented automatically for each item.

For example, the following HTML code defines an ordered list:

```
<h1>Top three reasons to get connected to the Internet</h1>
<ol>
<li>Gain access to a lot of information
<li>Get to surf the web and check out the competition's home page
<li>Get to send e-mail to friends and family
</ol>
```

Unordered lists are formatted the same as ordered lists, except that the <ul> and </ul> tags replace the <ol> and </ol> tags. Alternatively, use the <menu> and </menu> or <dir> and </dir> tags for a slightly different appearance. When displaying unordered lists, World Wide Web browsers introduce each list item with a bullet or a dash. Some browsers track the nesting level and display a different symbol for each level.

For example, the following HTML code defines an unordered list:

```
<h1>Things to pack for a day at the beach:</h1>
<ul>
<li>Bathing suit
<li>Sunglasses
<li>Towel
<li>Suntan lotion
<li>Cooler
<li>Radio
<li>Frisbee
<li>Volleyball
</ul>
```

A third type of list that HTML defines is known as a definition list, where each list item is composed of a title and description. The description is displayed indented under the item title. Definition lists are enclosed by the <dl> and </dl> tags. Title items are introduced by the <dt> tag, and the descriptions are introduced by the <dd> tag. Some browsers allow multiple <dd> tags for each <dt>.

For example, the following HTML code defines a definition list:

```
Internet buzzwords:
<dl>
<dt>URL
<dd>Uniform Resource Locator
<dt>WWW
<dd>World Wide Web
<dt>MIME
<dd>Multipurpose Internet Mail Extensions
</dl>
```

Character Formatting

HTML provides a small set of character markup tags. The tags are used to change the appearance of the enclosed text. Character markup is an area where the HTML specification continues to change as demand for new character formatting codes arises, such as blinking text, and finer control of font size. See Table B.1 for the list of HTML character markup tags.

It is important to note that some browsers do not always produce the desired results when used with nested character markup, such as Bold Italic . Also, when nesting tags, be sure to terminate them in the right order, as in from the inside out.

Table B.1   HTML character markup tags

Formatting Tag	Description
<TT>...</TT>	Typewriter text, typically displayed in a fixed-width (or monospaced) font
<PRE>...</PRE>	Pre-formatted ASCII text, typically displayed in a fixed-width font, and also recognizes horizontal tabs
<B>...</B>	Bold
<I>...</I>	Italic
<U>...</U>	Underline
<EM>...</EM>	With Emphasis, typically displayed in an italic font
<STRONG>...</STRONG>	With strong emphasis, typically displayed in a bold font
<CODE>...</CODE>	Code example, typically displayed in a fixed-width font
<SAMP>...</SAMP>	A sequence of literal characters
<KBD>...</KBD>	Identify text typed by the user, as in an instruction manual
<VAR>...</VAR>	Identify a variable name
<DFN>...</DFN>	Identify the defining instance of a term. Typically displayed in a bold or bold italic font
<CITE>...</CITE>	Identify a citation. Typically displayed in an italic font

Hyperlinks

HTML enables you to define text that form hyperlinks to other documents or resources. World Wide Web browsers display the hyperlinks in a bright color or underlined, to set them apart from the rest of the document text. When a user selects the link, the browser fetches the new document and displays it.

To create a hyperlink, or anchor, enclose the hyperlink text with the `<a href="URL">` and `</a>` tags, placing the actual URL within the quotes of the opening tag. If you know the target document is on the same server as the document that is currently displayed, you can use a relative URL. If the document is on a different server, use a full, or absolute, URL.

III

Appendixes

For example, the following HTML anchors identify the same document, given that the first anchor is referenced from a document on **http:// www.intergraph.com**:

```
See <a href="news.shtml">what's new</a> at Intergraph.
See <a href="http://www.intergraph.com/news.shtml">
    ➥what's new</a> at Intergraph.
```

HTML also allows *inter-document links*, also known as *named anchors*. These anchors are useful for a table of contents at the beginning of a long document, for instance. You can also define URLs that link to named anchors in other documents. Named anchors are defined by enclosing the target text with the <a name="any name"> and </a> tags. To create a hyperlink to the named anchor, use "#any name" in the URL.

For example, the following HTML code identifies a link to an inter-document anchor, and a link to a named anchor in another document.

```
<h1>Table Of Contents</h1>
Section 1: <a href="#intro">Introduction</a><br>
Section 2: <a href="#conn">Connecting to the Internet</a><br>
<!— ... more table of contents listings ... —>
Section 99: <a href="http://www.intergraph.com/webmaster.
    ➥html#brady">About the Author</a><p>
<hr>
<h2><a name="intro">Introduction</a></h2>
<!— ... the content of the introduction ... —>
<h2><a name="conn">Connecting to the Internet</a></h2>
<!— ... more content ... —>
```

Inline Images

Inline images are pictures that are referenced from within HTML documents. Inline images can be UNIX XBM format, as well as GIF and JPEG. In the near future, HTML may include support for inline movies and sound files that are played when the HTML document is displayed.

To include an inline image in your HTML document, define the location of the image file inside an <img src="URL" alt="caption"> tag. The alt="caption" option defines a textual caption that is displayed when the user does not wish to view the images. Each inline image is fetched using a separate connection to the server.

For example, the following HTML code references a picture that is fetched and displayed when the document is displayed.

```
<img src="golden/thumb.gif"" alt="Award winning picture">
    ➥ This month's featured Golden Mouse Award goes to ...
```

Inline images can also perform hyperlinks to other documents depending on the coordinates of the user's mouse when the image is clicked. This capability is called an *image map*. Image maps are defined by using the "ismap" option in a hyperlink anchor.

For example, the following HTML code defines an image map:

```
<a href="/cgi-bin/imagemap/usa" ismap><img src="usa.gif"></a>
```

When the image is clicked, the coordinates are passed to the server, which uses an external program to translate the coordinates into an URL. The URL is returned to the browser which performs a transparent fetch for the actual document.

Interactive Forms

One of the most powerful features of HTML is the capability to define interactive user interfaces, or forms. Forms are used to collect user input through the use of text fields, lists, checkboxes, and buttons, then send the input to the server for processing. The following are some general notes about forms:

■ More than one form can appear in an HTML document

■ HTML forms cannot be nested

■ World Wide Web browsers display form elements differently

■ HTML markup can be used within the form definition

All HTML forms are enclosed by the <form> and </form> tags. Inside the <form> tag is an action attribute, which defines the URL of the server program to process the data. Another attribute defines the method of passing the input to the server program.

There are two types of form methods, GET and POST. Using POST is preferable, since the GET method can cause problems for servers that have limited environment memory. The difference between the GET and POST methods is how the form input is passed back to the server, and how the server passes the input to the server program. For the GET method, form input is passed as part of the URL and appears in the environment of the server program. Using the POST method, the form input appears to the server program as a separate file. Most World Wide Web browsers can handle either GET or POST forms, but the server program must be written correctly to use the method chosen.

The following HTML code shows the usage of the opening and closing form tags:

```
<form action="process.pl" method="POST">
<!— ... Interactive elements and HTML markup ... —>
</form>
```

HTML supports a rich set of interactive form elements. Each element must have a unique name. The element name is used to identify the input associated with that element.

Submit and Reset Buttons

Every HTML form must have a submit button. When the user selects the submit button, the World Wide Web browser sends the input from the interactive elements to the action URL specified in the opening form tag.

A reset button is optional. When selected, the reset button causes the form to reset to its original values.

The value="caption" attribute defines the text that displays within the button.

The submit and reset buttons are coded in HTML forms as follows:

```
<input type="submit" name="SUB" value="Select to Show Form Input">
<input type="reset" value="Reset Form">
```

Text Input Fields

For single-line text fields, use the <input type="text"> tag. You can also specify the text which appears pre-loaded in the field with the value="" attribute. The size of the text field is defined by the size=nn, where nn represents the number of characters. Control the maximum number of characters with the maxlength=nn attribute. Instead of type="text", use the type="password" attribute when a field contains sensitive input which should not be displayed when entered.

For multi-line text fields, use the <textarea>...</textarea> tags. Any text within the tags will be pre-loaded into the field. Control the size of the textarea by specifying the rows=nn and cols=nn attributes, where nn represents the number of lines and characters, respectively.

Text, password and textarea fields are coded in HTML forms as follows:

```
<input type="text" name="ORG" value="Intergraph Corporation"
    ➥ size=40 maxlength=50>
<input type="password" name="PW" value="mypassword" size=10
maxlength=10>
<textarea name="textarea" rows=10 cols=50>Default Text</textarea>
```

Checkboxes

For simple checkboxes, use the `<input type="checkbox">` tag. The `value="somevalue"` attribute defines the text returned when the checkbox is selected. The optional checked attribute selects the checkbox when the form is loaded.

Checkboxes are coded in HTML forms as follows:

```
<input type="checkbox" name="BCC" value="YES" checked>
    ➥ Copy me on the order
```

Radio Buttons

Radio buttons enable the user to select one choice from a set of choices. World Wide Web browsers use the name attribute to identify all the radio buttons in a set. The `value="somevalue"` attribute defines the text returned when the radio button is selected. The optional checked attribute identifies the radio button that is selected when the form is loaded.

Radio buttons are coded in HTML forms as follows:

```
How would you like to pay for that?<br>
<input type="radio" name="PAYMENT" value="CC">Credit Card or
<input type="radio" name="PAYMENT" value="CB" checked>
    ➥Cyber Bank Account?<br>
```

Selection Lists

Selection lists enable the user to select one or many choices from a set of choices. Use the `<select>` and `</select>` tags to enclose the items. Each item is introduced by the `<option>` tag. Specify the multiple attribute to enable multiple selections. The `size=nn` attribute defines the number of rows displayed for the selection list.

A single selection list is coded in HTML forms as follows:

```
How would you like that shipped?<br>
<select name="SHIPBY" size=1>
<option selected>UPS
<option>Federal Express
<option>U.S. Postal Service
<option>E-mail
</select>
```

A multiple selection list is coded in HTML forms as follows:

```
What else would you like on that (select all that apply)?<br>
<select name="ADD" multiple size=3>
<option selected>Lettuce
<option selected>Tomato
<option>Onions
<option selected>Pickles
```

```
<option>Relish
<option selected>Ketchup
<option>Mustard
<option>Mayonnaise
</select><br>
```

Hidden Information

To define form input that is not displayed as an interactive element, use the type="hidden" attribute in an <input> tag. Hidden elements can contain name and value attributes, which are sent to the server program when the form is submitted. Although hidden elements are not displayed, they are not secret, as they can be displayed using a World Wide Browser's "View Document Source" function.

A hidden element is coded in HTML forms as follows:

```
<input type="hidden" name="SHOPPER" value="54366">
```

Listing 2.1 shows a sample HTML form.

Listing 2.1 sugg.html

```
<html>
<head>
<title>Suggestion Box</title>
</head>
<body>
<img src="sugg.gif">
<h1>Suggestion Box</h1>
<strong>We encourage your input!</strong>
If you want to file a problem report instead, please use the
<a href="ws.pl">Problem Report</a> form.<p>
<hr>
<form action="send-sugg.pl" method="POST">
<input type="text" name="NAME" size=40 maxlength=50> Your Name<br>
<input type="text" name="EMAIL" size=40 maxlength=50>
        ➥ Your E-mail address<p>
Your suggestion:<br>
<textarea name="DESC" rows=10 cols=40></textarea><p>
<input type="checkbox" name="CC" value="YES" checked>
        ➥ Copy me on the e-mail<br>
Is this a <input type="radio" name="TYPE" value="S"
checked>Suggestion,
<input type="radio" name="TYPE" value="C">Comment or
<input type="radio" name="TYPE" value="G">Gripe?<br>
How would you rate your knowledge of the World Wide Web?
<select name="WWW" size=1>
<option selected>End User
<option>Know HTML
<option>Webmaster
<option>Wavemaker
```

```
    </select>
    <input type="hidden" name="RECIPIENT" value="webmaster@myorg.com">
    </form>
    <hr>
    MyOrg / <a href="mailto:webmaster@myorg.com">
        ➥websmater@myorg.com</a>
    </body>
    </html>
```

HTML Entities

HTML defines several character sequences, or entities, for common characters that are not represented in the ASCII character set. Entity names are prefixed by an ampersand (&) and followed by a semicolon. Alternatively, entity can be specified by their numerical equivalent, prefixed with the # pound character. Many of these entities are defined in the ISO Latin 1 character set. Table B.2 lists the HTML character entities and their numerical equivalents.

Table B.2   HTML Entities

Entity Description	Char	Entity Code	Numeric Entity Code
less than sign	<	&lt;	&#62;
greater than sign	>	&gt;	
ampersand	&	&amp;	
double quote	"	&quot;	
capital AE diphthong (ligature)	Æ	&Aelig;	&#198;
capital A, acute accent	Á	&Aacute;	&#193;
capital A, circumflex accent	Â	&Acirc;	&#194;
capital A, grave accent	À	&Agrave;	&#192;
capital A, ring	Å	&Aring;	&#197;
capital A, tilde	Ã	&Atilde;	&#195;
capital A, dieresis or umlaut mark	Ä	&Auml;	&#196;
capital C, cedilla	Ç	&Ccedil;	&#199;
capital Eth, Icelandic	_	&ETH;	&#208;

III

Appendixes

(continues)

Table B.2 Continued

Entity Description	Char	Entity Code	Numeric Entity Code
capital E, acute accent	É	&Eacute;	&#201;
capital E, circumflex accent	Ê	&Ecirc;	&#202;
capital E, grave accent	È	&Egrave;	&#200;
capital E, dieresis or umlaut mark	Ë	&Euml;	&#203;
capital I, acute accent	Í	&Iacute;	&#205;
capital I, circumflex accent	Î	&Icirc;	&#206;
capital I, grave accent	Ì	&Igrave;	&#204;
capital I, dieresis or umlaut mark	Ï	&Iuml;	&#207;
capital N, tilde	Ñ	&Ntilde;	&#209;
capital O, acute accent	Ó	&Oacute;	&#211;
capital O, circumflex accent	Ô	&Ocirc;	&#212;
capital O, grave accent	Ò	&Ograve;	&#210;
capital O, slash	Ø	&Oslash;	&#216;
capital O, tilde	Õ	&Otilde;	&#213;
capital O, dieresis or umlaut mark	Ö	&Ouml;	&#214;
capital THORN, Icelandic	Ð	&THORN;	&#222;
capital U, acute accent	Ú	&Uacute;	&#218;
capital U, circumflex accent	Û	&Ucirc;	&#219;
capital U, grave accent	Ù	&Ugrave;	&#217;
capital U, dieresis or umlaut mark	Ü	&Uuml;	&#220;
capital Y, acute accent	Y	&Yacute;	&#221;
small a, acute accent	á	&aacute;	&#225;
small a, circumflex accent	â	&acirc;	&#226;
small ae diphthong (ligature)	æ	&aelig;	&#230;
small a, grave accent	à	&agrave;	&#224;
small a, ring	å	&aring;	&#229;

Entity Description	Char	Entity Code	Numeric Entity Code
small a, tilde	ã	&atilde;	&#227;
small a, dieresis or umlaut mark	ä	&auml;	&#228;
small c, cedilla	ç	&ccedil;	&#231;
small e, acute accent	é	&eacute;	&#233;
small e, circumflex accent	ê	&ecirc;	&#234;
small e, grave accent	è	&egrave;	&#232;
small eth, Icelandic	∂	&eth;	&#240;
small e, dieresis or umlaut mark	ë	&euml;	&#235;
small i, acute accent	í	&iacute;	&#237;
small i, circumflex accent	î	&icirc;	&#238;
small i, grave accent	ì	&igrave;	&#236;
small i, dieresis or umlaut mark	ï	&iuml;	&#239;
small n, tilde	ñ	&ntilde;	&#241;
small o, acute accent	ó	&oacute;	&#243;
small o, circumflex accent	ô	&ocirc;	&#244;
small o, grave accent	ò	&ograve;	&#242;
small o, slash	ø	&oslash;	&#248;
small o, tilde	õ	&otilde;	&#245;
small o, dieresis or umlaut mark	ö	&ouml;	&#246;
small sharp s, German (sz ligature)	ß	&szlig;	&#223;
small thorn, Icelandic	þ	&thorn;	&#254;
small u, acute accent	ú	&uacute;	&#250;
small u, circumflex accent	û	&ucirc;	&#251;
small u, grave accent	ù	&ugrave;	&#249;
small u, dieresis or umlaut mark	ü	&uuml;	&#252;
small y, acute accent	y	&yacute;	&#253;
small y, dieresis or umlaut mark	ÿ	&yuml;	&#255;

Appendix C

Uniform Resource Locators

Uniform Resource Locators (URLs) specify the exact location of any resource on the Internet that is part of the World Wide Web. The format of an URL is fairly straightforward.

The first part of an URL defines the application protocol. Most Internet application protocols are supported, such as HTTP, FTP, and Gopher. You also find URLs that reference other protocols, like WAIS (Wide-Area Information Search) or NNTP. The number of supported application protocols is growing, and you may find URLs that are not listed in the following examples. A colon delimits the application protocol from the remainder of the URL.

What follows the application protocol depends on which protocol is used. Most URLs introduce a server name by double-slashes. Server names are fully qualified domain names. If an application protocol is running on a non-standard TCP/IP port, then the port number can follow the server name, delimited by a colon. If no port number is defined, the standard port number for that protocol is used instead.

Paths to specific files, directories, or programs on the server follow the server name. Finally, arguments or parameters to server programs may be passed at the end of the URL.

Consider the following examples of URLs:

http://www.intergraph.com/index.html

This URL identifies a file named "index.html" on the www.intergraph.com server, using the HTTP application protocol.

http://www.intergraph.com/bbs/

When a directory is specified with no document, the HTTP server usually returns a default file or a listing of the files in the directory, depending on how the HTTP server is configured.

ftp://ftp.intergraph.com/help/FAQ

This URL identifies a file named "FAQ" in the "help" directory on the ftp.intergraph.com anonymous-ftp server. Note that no username and password is supplied. In this case, the FTP connection is established using the username "anonymous," and some identifier as the password, such as the user's e-mail address.

If required, the username and password can be specified before the host name, as in **ftp://myuserid@mypassword:ftp.intergraph.com/help/FAQ**.

gopher://gopher.intergraph.com:70/pub/win32

This URL requests a Gopher listing of the /pub/win32 directory on the Gopher.intergraph.com server. The additional ":70" after the server name identifies the IP port number to connect to. This port number is optional in the URL.

news:news.answers

The "news:" URL identifies a UseNet newsgroup. In this case, World Wide Web browsers connect to an NNTP server that is configured in some other area of the browser. The "news:" URL does not allow the specification of the NNTP server, only the requested newsgroup.

nntp://news.uu.net/news.answers

The "nntp:" URL is similar to the "news:" URL, but it allows the user to define the NNTP server along with the UseNet newsgroup.

mailto:info@intergraph.com

The "mailto:" URL identifies an e-mail address. Usually, World Wide Web browsers display a form which enables the user to fill in a subject, return e-mail address, and message. When submitted, the form input is used to create an e-mail message and send it via the SMTP application protocol. Most World Wide Web browsers forward the message through an SMTP server whose address is configured in some other area of the browser.

file:/usr/htdocs/index.html,
file:c\\htdocs\\default.htm, and
file://ftp.intergraph.com/help/FAQ

To reference local files, as opposed to those on the network, use a "file:" URL. When you drag a file from Windows Explorer and drop it onto a World Wide Web browser, the browser references the document with a "file:" URL. The first example is a UNIX reference, while the second is a Microsoft Windows reference. Notice that back-slashes are used, and the pipe symbol is used after the drive identifier instead of a colon. In general, URLs always use forward slashes, but some browsers allow backslashes as well.

Some World Wide Web browsers allow the "file:" URL to behave as an "ftp:" URL when a server is introduced with double-slashes, as in the third example.

telnet://ausername:apassword@archie.sura.net

The "telnet:" URL identifies a host to invoke a Telnet session connection, including the username and password. Typically, World Wide Web browsers do not have inherent Telnet terminal emulation, and spawn an external Telnet application to handle the request.

wais://waishost/database?search-text

WAIS is an acronym for *Wide-Area Information Search*. Basically, WAIS servers act as index hosts for Internet documents. The "wais:" URL enables a user to perform a search on a WAIS server and return the results as document links, or enables the user to further refine the search criteria.

RFC 1738 contains many examples of URLs and the syntax for using them.

Appendix D

Browsing the CD-ROM

This appendix explains the contents of the CD-ROM that's included with your copy of *Building Internet Applications with Visual C++*. As you learned throughout the book, all of the code and all of the relevant RFCs are on this CD. But there's much, much more.

There are five main folders on the CD: Apps, Code, Docs, RFC, and Webpages:

■ These contain more than 80 Internet applications for you to try. Besides being fun and useful, these applications will give you ideas for more clients or servers that you could develop yourself. If there's already a terrific application that does just what you planned, you'd better make a new plan.

This appendix gives a short description of each application stored on the CD. Additional information can be accessed by pointing your Web browser at the APPCD.HTM Web page in the root of the CD. This page lets you select links to pages that describe each application on the CD.

Feel free to give your opinions on any of these applications to their authors—we've provided contact information.

■ All of the code, plus executable programs, for the sample applications discussed in this book are in subfolders of their own under the CODE folder. The Socket subfolder contains the socket class that does not inherit from CSocket; you may copy into those subfolders if you are not using a recent version of Visual C++, as discussed in Chapter 3, "Windows Sockets (WINSOCK.DLL)."

If you are working with 16 bits, you need a 16-bit executable to run the program and a 16-bit makefile to change the program or load it into Visual C++. These are kept in a subfolder for each application called 16BIT; for example, the 16-bit executable for mail is in \CODE\MAIL\16BIT\MAIL.EXE while the 32-bit version is in \CODE\MAIL\MAIL.EXE.

■ Documents, explanations, and lists that are not RFCs are in the DOCS folder.

■ The RFC folder provides indexes linked to the RFC documents. Simply click the link, and you'll be presented with the RFC document that you want.

If you want to see the RFC documents themselves in HTML format with links to related documents and information, please let us know. Send a note to **webmaster@mcp.com**. If enough readers are interested, Que can add HTML versions of the RFC documents to the Que Web site (**http://www.mcp.com**).

■ The WEBPAGES folder contains, well, Web pages. These are designed to be read with your browser (Netscape, or one of the simple browsers included on this CD) as local files. The links are to other places on the CD, and they make the CD easy to explore. The detailed lists that follow refer to the location of both the Web page and the actual application. The most important Web page, however, isn't in this folder: APPCD.HTM is in the root folder, and it is the road map to the whole CD.

Useful Applications

We've collected software from all over the Net and put it on this CD to save you the time of exploring and downloading. Included here are full client or server applications, neat Internet-related utilities, and accessories, such as file converters, compressors, and image viewers.

What Is Shareware?

Much of the software on the CD is *shareware*. Shareware was developed as an alternative to traditional methods of software distribution. The basic idea is that you can try a software package—usually for 30 days—before paying for it. Initially, the number of programs available in the shareware market was quite small, and they were distributed mainly through local bulletin board systems.

With the vast popularity of the Internet and the ease of connecting to FTP sites, the quantity and quality of shareware has gotten dramatically better.

The retail distribution channels are just starting to offer large numbers of Internet applications. Most of the commercial activity is focusing on suites of applications that include Telnet, FTP, e-mail, Gopher, and a Web browser. However, there still are plenty of opportunities to create new programs that expand the market and create profits.

Most of the software on the CD includes some type of file (or instructions in the software itself) that tells you how to register the software. *Please remember that you're obligated to register any shareware software that you plan to use regularly.* You gain many benefits by registering the shareware:

- You have a clean conscience, knowing that you've paid the author for the many hours spent to create such a useful program.

- Registering the software can give you additional benefits, such as technical support from the author, a printed manual, or additional features that are available only to registered users. Consult the individual programs for details about what bonuses you may receive for registering.

- Registering puts you on the author's mailing list so that you will be up-to-date about new versions of the software, bug fixes, compatibility issues, and so on. Again, the benefits of registration vary from product to product. Some authors even include, in the cost of registration, a free update to the next version.

- If the license agreement states that you must pay to continue using the software, you're violating the license if you don't pay. In some cases, unregistered use may be a criminal offense. Wise individuals, corporations, and businesses register shareware to avoid any chance of legal problems.

Several of the authors and companies that provided software for this CD-ROM asked that a notice of their copyright, shareware agreement, or license information be included in this book. The lack of such a statement printed in this book doesn't mean that the software isn't copyrighted or doesn't have a license agreement. Please see the text or help files for specific copyright or licensing information.

III

Appendixes

Getting Updates for Software

The documentation that accompanies the programs on the CD-ROM usually tells you where to find updated versions. However, it isn't exactly easy to continually look at 10 or 20 FTP sites to monitor new versions.

Que has come up with a solution: A special FTP site has been created so that readers of this book can get new versions of the software on the CD. As soon as an update is received, it's posted on the FTP site, and you can download it by anonymous FTP. The FTP address for this site is **ftp.mcp.com**. (MCP stands for Macmillan Computer Publishing, the company that owns Que.)

Also, Macmillan maintains several mailing lists to automatically notify subscribers when programs are updated. By pointing your Web browser at **http://www.mcp.com**, choosing Reference Desk, and then selecting Information SuperLibrary Reports, you'll learn how to subscribe to the various mailing lists. Pick the one that fits your needs.

Many of the authors and companies asked that an e-mail or postal address where they can be contacted be included in this book. If you don't find a specific e-mail address listed here, you can find an e-mail address for nearly every program on the CD in the program's documentation, in the program itself (often by choosing <u>H</u>elp, <u>A</u>bout), or on the Web pages describing the applications on the CD.

Installing Software from the CD-ROM

Before using any software on the CD, you need to install it. Many of the programs come with their own installation program. If a program includes an installation program, its description on the Web page will give you the directions you need to install it.

For programs that don't have an installation program, the installation process is straightforward. To install a program that doesn't have an installer, follow these steps:

1. Create a folder on your hard drive for the software.

It's a good idea to create one main folder (such as \INTERNET) in the root of your hard drive for all your Internet software, and then create subfolders for individual programs in that folder. This keeps the root folder of your hard drive less cluttered.

2. Copy all the files and subfolders from the program's folder on CD to the folder you created on your hard drive. Remember to reset the Read Only attribute after copying the files. After switching to the folder (using the DOS CD command) that contains the newly copied files, type the following command, which uses the DOS ATTRIB function to reset the Read Only attribute from all the files in a folder:

   ATTRIB –r *.*

Each application on the CD has a Web page associated with it. You might want to look at the Web page for the application that you want to install to see whether any late-breaking news has been added. Also, special installation instructions are located there. You can read the Web pages by starting at the home page of \APPCD.HTM on the CD.

3. After all the files are copied, create an icon for each program you plan to run in Windows. An easy way to do this is to drag the program file from the folder on your hard drive under My Computer to your desktop or the folder where you want the icon.

Some people find that it's a good idea to create a program group to hold all their Internet program icons.

That's all there is to it. Repeat these steps for any software you want to install.

Internet Applications

This section describes the many applications that have been included on the CD. These applications are grouped by subject so that you can quickly find the programs you need.

Connection Software. This category of software enables you to make the physical connection to the Internet through a phone line or a local area network.

Core Internet-Connect v2.0 Trial Version (\WEBPAGES\APPS\INETCON2.HTM, \APPS\CONNECT\INETCON2). This program, which provides Winsock and TCP/IP for networks, is designed to help end users connect. It's also designed for developers who want to build other TCP/IP applications.

This package contains the Internet-Connect® Trial Copy program. Internet-Connect is developed and marketed by Core Systems, 245 Firestone Drive, Walnut Creek, CA 94598, (510) 943-5765.

Crynwr Packet Drivers (\WEBPAGES\APPS\CRYNWR.HTM, \APPS\CONNECT\CRYNWER). This collection of drivers is required by most DOS-based (and some Windows-based) Internet applications. The collection serves as an interface between established network software and packet-based Internet connections. A wide range of drivers is included in these archive files for most popular network packages, such as Novell NetWare and Artisoft LANtastic. The source code for each driver is also included.

NetDial (\WEBPAGES\APPS\NETDIAL.HTM, \APPS\CONNECT\NETDIAL). NetDial is an Internet dial-up program with many features. NetDial can call, connect to your Internet host, log you in, and run your TCP/IP program at the click of a mouse. Other features include baud-rate support of up to 256K baud, as many as 99 redial attempts, automatic dialing on startup, sound support, support for up to five separate configurations, cumulative timer window (tracks all time online), built-in call log viewer/editor, supports up to five startup programs on startup, and additional modem support.

Slipper/CSlipper v1.5 (\WEBPAGES\APPS\SLIPPR.HTM, \APPS\CONNECT\SLIPPTR). Slipper/CSlipper version 1.5 is a DOS-based replacement application for SLIP8250. Slipper and CSlipper were written to provide Internet connections through a packet-driver interface. Both applications are very small and command-line driven.

Trumpet Winsock v2.0b (\WEBPAGES\APPS\TWSK20B.HTM, \APPS\CONNECT\TWSK20B). Trumpet Winsock is the most widely used shareware Winsock package. The software supports modem and network connections. This version features firewall support and improved scripting and routing capabilities.

The Trumpet Winsock is now distributed as shareware. You may use the Trumpet Winsock program for 30 days to evaluate its usefulness. If at the end of that time you're satisfied with the product, you need to register it.

Trumpet Winsock v2.0b has a Send Registration option that automatically posts encrypted credit-card details to Trumpet Software International. Choose File, Register to take advantage of this feature.

E-Mail and Accessories. E-mail is one of the most popular features on the Internet. You'll be sending a lot of mail, so pick a program that you feel comfortable with.

Eudora v1.4.4 (\WEBPAGES\APPS\EUDORA.HTM, \APPS\EMAIL\EUDORA). Eudora is an e-mail package that offers many features. It supports private mailboxes, reply functions, periodic mail checking, and many more features that make this software one of the best mail packages on the market. For a detailed exploration of this product and Internet e-mail, see *Using Eudora* by Dee-Ann and Robert LeBlanc (Indianapolis: Que Corporation, 1995).

> You can get information about Eudora 2, the commercial version, on the Web page for Qualcomm's QUEST group. The URL is **http://www.qualcomm.com/quest/QuestMain.html**. Alternatively, you can get information about the commercial version by sending e-mail to **eudora-sales@qualcomm.com** or by calling (800) 2-EUDORA—that is, (800) 238-3672.

Pegasus Mail (\WEBPAGES\APPS\PEGASUS.HTM, \APPS\EMAIL\PEGASUS). Pegasus Mail is a powerful, easy-to-use e-mail program. Several add-ins for Pegasus make it easier to send attachments of popular document types, such as Word Pro and Word for Windows. One add-in, Mercury (a mail transport system), is included in the \APPS\EMAIL\PEGASUS\MERCURY folder. Pegasus is free software that can be used without restriction.

RFD Mail (\WEBPAGES\APPS\RFDMAIL.HTM, \APPS\EMAIL\RFDMAIL). RFD MAIL is a Windows off-line mail reader that supports many online services, including CompuServe, Delphi, GEnie, MCI Mail, World UNIX, the Direct Connection, MV Communications, Panix, the Well, the Portal System, NETCOM, CRL, INS, and the Internet Access Company. The program's other features include, support for scripts; an address book; folders with drag-and-drop and search capability; backup and restore capability; polling; and multiple signature blocks.

WinSMTP (\WEBPAGES\APPS\WINSMTP.HTM, \APPS\EMAIL\WINSMTP). WinSMTP is a mail server, or *daemon*. It sends and receives SMTP mail and also acts as a POP3 mailbox. If you have a SLIP account now, your provider holds your mail for you in a mailbox you can reach with SMTP or POP3. By using WinSMTP, you can have multiple users on your site without buying multiple accounts from your ISP. Also, you can administer mailing lists and debug mail clients that you are writing. The

III

Appendixes

registered version includes several enhancements including a finger server. The author, Jack De Winter, can be reached at **wildside@wildside.kwnet.on.ca**, and more information is also available at **http://wildside.kwnet.on.ca**.

Transfer Pro (\WEBPAGES\APPS\XFERPRO.HTM, \APPS\EMAIL\XFERPRO). Transfer Pro is a Windows-based shareware tool that enables you to send text, application data, messages, images, audio, video, executable files, and other data types by way of e-mail using the latest MIME 1.0 standards according to RFC 1341. The program supports UU and XX encoding and decoding.

WinMIME (\WEBPAGES\APPS\WINMIME.HTM, \APPS\EMAIL\WINMIME). WinMIME includes some utilities that are useful with .WAV and .GIF attachments. It records or plays MIME attachments. There's no documentation provided, but play around with it a little and you'll get the hang of it.

Finger/WHOIS. Finger and WHOIS applications are used to get information about a user.

CFinger v1.1 (\WEBPAGES\APPS\CFINGER.HTM, \APPS\FINGER\CFINGER). This Finger application is truly Windows-based, enabling you to select users for fingering with a mouse click. It can use any WHOIS database and allows searching of the search results.

Finger 1.0 (\WEBPAGES\APPS\FINGER10.HTM, \APPS\FINGER\FINGER10). Finger 1.0 is a simple Finger client. It is written for Borland C++ 3.1 using OWL, and the source code is included. The documentation is rather sketchy, but how much documentation does such a simple application need?

WinWHOIS (\WEBPAGES\APPS\WINWHOIS.HTM, \APPS\FINGER\WINWHOIS). WinWHOIS is a very easy-to-use, Windows-based WHOIS search front-end application. The program keeps a log of responses, so you can copy and paste an address if you find what you're looking for.

WinSock Finger Daemon (\WEBPAGES\APPS\WFNGRD.HTM, \APPS\FINGER\WFNGRD). This Windows Finger server can be set up to deliver information about multiple users on the same machine or for a single user. It's a server, which means it runs on your machine to deliver information about you.

The software is written by Jim O'Brien of Tidewater Systems. Please note that inclusion of this program on the CD doesn't grant a license for continued use.

FTP. File-transfer clients are used to download files from FTP sites.

WS_FTP (\WEBPAGES\APPS\WS_FTP.HTM, \APPS\FTP\WS_FTP16, \APPS\FTP\WS_FTP32). This FTP client is extremely easy to use. It comes preconfigured with many popular FTP sites, and you can add more. It also has support for advanced features, such as firewalls. The CD includes 16-bit and 32-bit versions.

WinFTP (\WEBPAGES\APPS\WINFTP.HTM, \APPS\FTP\WINFTP). This client is based on WS_FTP but with some additional features. With the history dialog box, you can select a folder that you've already visited without having to traverse the entire folder tree. There are filters to enable you to look for specific file types, such as *.TXT or *.ZIP, in the local and remote hosts, and many other features. The CD includes 16-bit and 32-bit versions.

WFTPD v2.0 (\WEBPAGES\APPS\WFTPD, \APPS\FTP\WFTPD). WFTPD is the first shareware FTP server (also called a daemon) that was written specifically for Winsock. An FTP server enables your machine to be an FTP site to which others can point their client programs and download files from you. WFTPD supports anonymous access, access from Mosaic/Netscape/other WWW browsers, folder-based per-user security, and configurable on-screen and to-file logging.

The registered version, which costs $15, includes the following features:

- No limits on the numbers of GETs or PUTs per login or per run of the program
- Customizable greeting and farewell messages (The unregistered version has fixed messages that identify your site as using unregistered shareware.)

Most information required to use this product is in the supplied help file, but additional queries may be addressed to the author, Alun Jones, at **alun@texis.com,** or faxed to (512) 346-2803.

Gopher. Gopher clients enable you to search for information stored on Gopher servers.

Gopher for Windows (\WEBPAGES\APPS\WGOPHER.HTM, \APPS\GOPHER\WGOPHER). The Chinese University of Hong Kong created this simple little Gopher client. If you're looking for something fancy,

III

Appendixes

this program may not be the ticket for you. If you want something fast and simple, though, this program is the perfect Gopher client.

Hampson's Gopher v2.3 (\WEBPAGES\APPS\HGOPHER.HTM, \APPS\GOPHER\HGOPHER). This is a small, yet powerful, Windows-based Gopher client that enables a user to search the many Gopher servers scattered around the Internet. Extensive help is available in the application.

 Version 2.4 of Hampson's Gopher has been licensed by FTP Software and is no longer available for free distribution.

Go4Ham (\WEBPAGES\APPS\GO4HAM.HTM, \APPS\GOPHER\GO4HAM). This application is a Gopher server, and it lets your site be a Gopher site. Other people throughout the Internet can access your Gopher documents using any Gopher client.

HTML Conversion. Some documents that you want to publish on the Web may already exist in another format. These applications enable you to convert documents to the HTML format for use on the Web.

RTF To HTML (\WEBPAGES\APPS\RTF2HTML.HTM, \APPS\HTML\RTF2HTML). This is a utility for converting documents from Rich Text Format (RTF) to HTML. RTF is a format that many word processors—including Word for Windows—can import and export. The package also includes a Word for Windows 2.0 template for writing HTML.

Tex2RTF (\WEBPAGES\APPS\TEX2RTF.HTM, \APPS\HTML\TEX2RTF). This utility is a handy way to convert LaTeX files to HTML in Windows. (It also converts LaTeX to Windows Help file format if you need that capability.) LaTeX is a format that's very popular for files created in print and online, and is also a common language used for technical documents. This program has a very good help system that you should read through to help you make the most of it.

HTML Editors. HTML documents are the heart of the Web. Whether you're creating a Web site for a major corporation or just putting up a few personal pages, you'll need an HTML editor or translator (unless you plan to hire someone else to do the work for you). The applications in this section are stand-alone editors for creating HTML documents.

HTML Assistant for Windows (\WEBPAGES\APPS\HTMLASST.HTM, \APPS\HTML\HTMLASST).

This program is a simple shareware HTML document editor. Most commands are implemented by way of a huge toolbar. The program is a good editor for small documents, but this version limits file size to 32K. (A professional version that loads larger documents is available; see the help file for ordering information.) One neat feature is the program's capability to convert files that contain URLs (for example, Cello bookmarks and Mosaic .INI files) to HTML documents that can be read with any Web browser.

HTMLed (\WEBPAGES\APPS\HTMLED.HTM,\APPS\ HTML\ HTMLED).

HTMLed is a powerful shareware HTML document editor. The interface features a toolbar for ease of use, and the abundant and clear menus make it easy to find the features that you need.

HTML Writer (\WEBPAGES\APPS\HTMLWRIT.HTM, \APPS\HTML\HTMLWRIT).

HTML Writer is a stand-alone HTML authoring program. Most HTML tags can be inserted through an extensive set of menu choices. It has a nice toolbar for implementing many HTML tags. Another good feature is the support of templates, which you can use to help design and create HTML documents with a consistent look and feel.

SoftQuad HoTMetaL (\WEBPAGES\APPS\HOTMETAL.HTM, \APPS\HTML\HOTMETAL, \WWW\HOTMETAL).

This freeware program is a full-featured, professional-quality HTML editor for Windows. With this program, you can edit multiple documents at the same time, use templates to ensure consistency between documents, and use the powerful word processor-like features to do such things as search and replace.

The commercial version, HoTMetaL PRO, includes the following new features:

- A cleanup filter called TIDY for any invalid legacy HTML files

- Bit-mapped graphics in-line in your documents

III

Appendixes

- Macros to automate repetitive tasks and reduce errors

- Rules checking and validation to ensure correct HTML markup

- A built-in graphical table editor

- The capability to fix invalid HTML documents and import them (with the Interpret Document command)

- A URL editor

- Full table and forms support

- Macro creation and editing support

- Document-validation commands

- Support for Microsoft Windows Help

- A printed manual and access to support personnel

- Home-page templates

- Editing tools

- Spell checking

- A thesaurus

- Full, context-sensitive search-and-replace capability

 You can order a copy of HoTMetaL PRO from SoftQuad for $195.

WebEdit v1.0c (\WEBPAGES\APPS\WEBEDIT.HTM, \APPS\HTML\WEBEDIT). This editor allows editing multiple documents at once and has a very clean simple interface that hides powerful features.

HTML Editors for Microsoft Word. These template files have been designed to work with Microsoft Word for Windows (version 2 or 6). If you like the Microsoft Word editing environment, give some of these templates a try. Essentially, they enable you to insert HTML codes into any new or existing Word document.

**ANT_HTML (\WEBPAGES\APPS\ANT.HTM,
\APPS\HTML\ANT_DEMO).** ANT_DEMO.DOT is a template designed to work in Word for Windows 6.x and Word 6.x for the Macintosh to facilitate the creation of hypertext documents. You can insert HTML codes into any new or existing Word document or into any ASCII document.

ANT_DEMO is a demonstration version of the ANT_PLUS conversion utility and the ANT_HTML package. ANT_HTML and ANT_PLUS work in all international versions of Word 6.x.

> ANT_HTML.DOT and ANT_DEMO.DOC are copyright © 1994 by Jill Swift. For more information, contact Jill Swift, P.O. Box 213, Montgomery, TX 77356, or **jswift@freenet.fsu.edu**.

**GT_HTML (\WEBPAGES\APPS\GT_HTML.HTM,
\APPS\HTML\GT_HTML).** This is another Word 6.x template for creating HTML documents. Only a small number of HTML tags are now supported, but they are the most common tags and should be useful for many basic HTML documents.

**HTML Author (\WEBPAGES\APPS\HTMLAUTH.HTM,
\APPS\HTML\HTMLAUTH).** This is another template for creating HTML documents in Word for Windows 6.x.

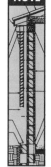

> The HTML Author software and its associated manual are copyright © 1995 by Grahame S. Cooper. You may copy and use them provided that you don't modify them (other than to change the paragraph styles).
>
> The HTML Author software is provided *as is* without warranty or guarantee. Neither Grahame S. Cooper nor the University of Salford accept any liability for errors or faults in the software or any damage arising from the use of the software.
>
> New versions and updates of the software may be obtained from the University of Salford at the following Web address:
>
> **http://www.salford.ac.uk/docs/depts/iti/staff/gsc/htmlauth/
> summary.html**

**WebWizard (\WEBPAGES\APPS\WEBWIZA.HTM,
\APPS\HTML\WEBWIZA).** This is another HTML authoring system that works as a template in Word for Windows 6.x. It adds a new toolbar with some HTML commands and a new WebWizard menu to the menu bar when loaded.

III

Appendixes

Miscellaneous. The applications listed in this section enable you to track IP addresses and talk to someone else over the Internet, keep your system time correct, and help you keep organized.

IP Manager (\WEBPAGES\APPS\IPMGR.HTM, \APPS\MISC\IPMGR). IP Manager helps you keep track of IP addresses, ensures that you don't have duplicate addresses, and even launches FTP and Telnet sessions.

This trial version is limited to only 25 devices. You may try IP Manager for 21 days. If at the end of the trial period you decide not to buy IP Manager, it should be deleted.

Internet Voice Chat (\WEBPAGES\APPS\IVC.HTM, \APPS\MISC\IVC). Internet VoiceChat enables two users connected to the Internet to talk to each other by way of their PCs. The program requires both PCs to have sound cards, microphones, and speakers.

The current version of IVC doesn't transmit the conversation in real time. It waits for a pause (such as the pause at the end of a sentence) and transmits the whole phrase at once. Audio quality isn't affected by a SLIP connection, but you can choose a lower sampling rate to speed transmission. Even so, the sound should be telephone quality or better. See the IVC.FAQ file for more information about using this interesting application.

If you use Trumpet Winsock, be sure to upgrade to Version 2.0b, because IVC isn't compatible with earlier versions.

NOTE Internet VoiceChat is copyright © 1994 by Richard L. Ahrens. The unregistered version of IVC may be used on an evaluation basis for no more than 30 days. Continued use after the 30-day trial period requires registration, which is $20 for individual users. Site licenses are negotiable. When you register, you get additional features, such as answering-machine and fax modes. Contact the author at 7 Omega Court, Middletown, NJ 07748.

Name Server Lookup Utility (\WEBPAGES\APPS\NSLOOKUP.HTM, \APPS\MISC\NSLOOKUP). This program is a simple but powerful little utility for looking up information about a specific machine or domain on the Internet. The program reports the numeric IP address and other information for the site or machine name.

Sticky (\WEBPAGES\APPS\STICKY.HTM, \APPS\MISC\STICKY). This interesting application lets you post little "sticky notes" on other users' computers via the Internet. You can create a small database of other users to send these notes to.

Time Sync (\WEBPAGES\APPS\TSYNC.HTM, \APPS\MISC\TSYNC).
Time Sync Version 1.4 is a Windows-based application that's designed to synchronize your PC's clock with the time on a UNIX host. This program, which relies on an established WinSock connection, is written in Visual Basic.

U2D (\WEBPAGES\APPS\U2D.HTM, \APPS\MISC\U2D). This handy program converts UNIX text-file line endings to DOS text-file format. All you have to do is drag a file (or files) from File Manager to the U2D icon to process them.

WebWatch (\WEBPAGES\APPS\WEBWATCH.HTM, \APPS\MISC\WEBWATCH). WebWatch is an Internet utility from Specter Inc., that you use to track changes in selected Web documents. WebWatch generates a local HTML document containing links only to those documents that were updated after the given date. You use this local file to navigate to the updated documents, using any Web browser.

In a typical scenario, you would set the anchor document (the local file, parsed for your URLs) to your Netscape BOOKMARK.HTM file and the result file (the file where the program generates its output) to your home page. This way, your home page will always contain links to the fresh, "must-see" documents, and you still can use your bookmarks in the usual way.

The CD-ROM contains a pre-release limited edition of WebWatch. The full, final release:

- Gives you the option to have WebWatch use your "last visit" date as it's stored by Netscape, rather than your having to specify a general "update" date.

- Doesn't contain a limitation on the number of URLs you can visit in one run.

To learn more about WebWatch, visit **http://www.specter.com/users/ janos/webwatch/index.html**. You can download your free evaluation copy of the final release from **ftp://ftp.specter.com/users/janos/ webwatch/wwatch10.zip**.

Windows Sockets Host (\WEBPAGES\APPS\WSHOST.HTM, \APPS\MISC\WSHOST). Windows Sockets Host is a simple utility that determines a host computer's name based on a dotted-decimal IP address, or vice versa.

III

Appendixes

Windows Sockets Net Watch (\WEBPAGES\APPS\WSWATCH.HTM, \APPS\MISC\WS_WATCH).

This program makes active checks on Internet hosts that are listed in its database file. This is useful for monitoring a host to see whether it's functioning. This program is designed to work on any Winsock DLL, but the documentation has some notes on which Winsocks it works well on and which ones it has problems with.

Windows Sockets Ping (\WEBPAGES\APPS\WSPING.HTM, \APPS\MISC\WS_PING).

Windows Sockets Ping is an uncomplicated Windows application used to test an Internet connection. The author wrote the program to test whether his two computers were connected on the Internet; you can use it to do the same thing. The source code is included in the archive, and the author grants you permission to alter it, if necessary. Windows 3.1 and Windows NT versions are included.

 Because Windows Sockets Ping uses non-standard Winsock calls, this application may not run on every Winsock stack.

WSArchie (\WEBPAGES\APPS\WSARCHIE.HTM, \APPS\ARCHIE\WSARCHIE).

Archie clients enable you to connect to an Archie server and search for a file. Most programs come preconfigured with the locations of several servers; try to pick a server near you. When a search is successful, you can simply click the file to start downloading.

WSArchie is a Winsock-compliant Archie program that enables you to connect to an Archie server and search for a file by using the familiar Windows interface. You can configure WSArchie to transfer files directly from the list of found files so that you don't have to open your FTP client manually and then re-enter the address and directory information.

WSIRC (\WEBPAGES\APPS\WSIRC.HTM, \APPS\IRC\WSIRC).

Internet Relay Chat is a real-time way to carry on a conversation with one or more people via computer over the Internet. Whatever you type, everyone else sees. Not very much software is available for the PC for IRC, but this program is very good.

This product is available in three versions: a freeware version, a shareware version that provides more functions when it's registered, and retail versions for personal and corporate use. The program's author also can custom-design an IRC client for special needs.

The freeware and shareware versions are both included on the CD. In this release, the shareware version has all the features enabled, but only for a limited time; after 30 days, you must register the shareware version to continue using it. The freeware version has no such limitations.

Newsreaders. There are many ways to read UseNet newsgroups. Using a dedicated reader usually makes for faster and easier reading.

NewsXpress (\WEBPAGES\APPS\NXPRESS.HTM, \APPS\NEWS\NXPRESS). This is one of the latest Windows newsreaders, but it's quickly becoming very popular. It has all the features found in the traditional leaders in this category and adds a more pleasant interface.

Paperboy v2.05 (\WEBPAGES\APPS\PBOY205.HTM, \APPS\NEWS\PAPERBOY). This is a Windows-based off-line news reader. It accepts "packets" created by a host program such as UQWK in the Simple Offline UseNet Packet format (SOUP) and downloaded from that host to your PC.

Trumpet News Reader (\WEBPAGES\APPS\WTWSK.HTM, \APPS\NEWS\WTWSK). This program is a full-featured shareware Winsock newsreader for Windows. You can use this program to perform all the expected functions, such as reading, posting, and replying (as a follow-up post or by e-mail). You also can save messages and decode attached files.

> Three other versions of this software are available for other types of Internet connections. All of these versions are similar in function to the Winsock version:
>
> ■ WT_LWP requires Novell LWP DOS/Windows and is located in the folder \APPS\NEWS\WT_LWP.
>
> ■ WT_ABI requires the Trumpet TSR TCP stack and is located in the folder \APPS\NEWS\WT_ABI.
>
> ■ WT_PKT works with a direct-to-packet driver (internal TCP stack) and is located in the folder \APPS\NEWS\WT_PKT.

WinNews Server (\WEBPAGES\APPS\WINNEWS.HTM, \APPS\NEWS\NNTP). This application is a news server. You can use it to collect news so that several different users at your site can read without downloading each article again and again, or to test your news client. This is an early beta copy and the product should be significantly improved by the time this book reaches the shelves. The author, Harold Bunskoek, can be reached at **cis@cis.iaf.nl**.

III

Appendixes

WinVN Newsreader (\WEBPAGES\APPS\WINVN16.HTM, \APPS\NEWS\WINVN16). This program is a full-featured, public-domain Winsock newsreader for Windows. The WinVN program and UseNet Newsgroups are discussed in detail in *Using UseNet Newsgroups*, published by Que Corporation.

Yarn (\WEBPAGES\APPS\YARN.HTM, \APPS\NEWS\YARN). YARN is a freeware, offline program for UseNet mail and news. It runs in DOS 3.0 or higher—it does not run in Windows. YARN accepts "packets" created by a host program such as UQWK in the Simple Offline UseNet Packet format (SOUP). It's better than the common QWK format readers for UseNet use because it preserves more of the unique UseNet header information when posting replies.

Telnet. Telnet enables you to log in to a remote server and use a text-based terminal session. It's one of the simplest interfaces to a remote computer over the Internet.

COMt (\WEBPAGES\APPS\COMT.HTM, \APPS\TELNET\COMT). COMt is a shareware program that enables a standard Windows-based communication program to act as a Telnet client in a TCP/IP environment. It enables you to use the more powerful features of your communication program in a Telnet session.

EWAN (\WEBPAGES\APPS\EWAN.HTM, \APPS\TELNET\EWAN). In a typical setting, this program is used primarily for Telnet; you can save configurations for several different Telnet sites. The program supports a capture log, and you can perform the usual copy-and-paste operations from the text to the capture log.

TekTel (\WEBPAGES\APPS\TEKTEL.HTM, \APPS\TELNET\TEKTEL). TekTel is a simple Telnet application with Textronix T4010 and VT100 emulation, a little rough around the edges, but functional. The source code (in Visual Basic) is included.

YAWTELNET (\WEBPAGES\APPS\YAWTEL.HTM, \APPS\TELNET\YAWTEL). YAWTELNET (Yet Another Windows Socket Telnet) is a freeware Telnet client designed specifically to work well with Mosaic. Many of the menu commands aren't functional, but you can select text in the active window and copy it to another application.

 NOTE   YAWTELNET is copyright © 1994 by Hans van Oostrom. Refer to LICENSE.TXT in the \YAWTEL folder for complete copyright information.

WEB Browsers. Most of the Web browsers have recently become commercialized. You can still find shareware versions of Windows-based browsers on the Web. However, all the newest features are being incorporated into commercial browsers.

Lynx (\WEBPAGES\APPS\LYNX.HTM, \APPS\WWW\LYNX). This program is a Web client for DOS machines. Lynx is an alpha release and doesn't support forms at present. On the positive side, each URL you access is opened in a separate window so that you can have several documents open at once. It also has support for displaying in-line images.

SlipKnot (\WEBPAGES\APPS\SLIPKNOT.HTM, \APPS\WWW\SLIPKNOT). SlipKnot is a graphical Web browser specifically designed for Microsoft Windows users who have UNIX shell accounts with their service providers. SlipKnot's primary feature is that it doesn't require SLIP, PPP, or TCP/IP services. It also provides background retrieval of multiple documents and storage of complete documents on users' local hard disks.

WEB Servers. These programs enable your Windows-based PC to act like a Web site that other Web browsers can access.

Web4Ham (\WEBPAGES\APPS\WEB4HAM.HTM, \APPS\WWW\WEB4HAM). Web4Ham is a Web server for Windows. The program enables your Windows PC to act like a Web site that other Web users can access with any Web client software.

Windows HTTPD v1.4 (\WEBPAGES\APPS\WHTTPD.HTM, \APPS\WWW\WHTTPD). This Web server for Windows has very extensive online documentation in HTML format. It's designed to be small and very fast with features such as form support, image mapping, and folder-level security.

WEB Accessories. These applications help you with your Web surfing by enabling you to launch other applications or store URLs for future reference.

Launcher (\WEBPAGES\APPS\LAUNCHER.HTM, \APPS\WWW\LAUNCHER). This freeware program is a neat utility that enables you to launch a Windows application from a link in a Web browser such as Mosaic. This feature enables you to open an application (such as WordPerfect or Excel) without having to create a link to a particular document. Source code is supplied on the CD-ROM.

URL Grabber Demo (\WEBPAGES\APPS\GRABDEMO.HTM, \APPS\WWW\GRABDEMO). Have you ever read an article in a UseNet newsgroup or an e-mail message and seen a URL that you wanted to save for further reference? Sure, you can copy and paste the URL into a browser and then save it in a hotlist or bookmark, but this handy little utility makes this process even easier. The URL Grabber toolbar lets you grab URLs from documents as you read them and then save a collection of addresses as HTML documents that you can open in any Web browser. You then have a Web document that contains all the links to the URL addresses that you saved, enabling you to jump to those URLs quickly and easily. In this demo version, you're limited to grabbing three addresses each time you run the program.

OLE Custom Controls (OCXs)

An OLE custom control is an OLE object with an extended interface that makes it behave like a Windows control. Like Visual Basic controls (VBXs), OCXs can be used in your program anywhere you'd use a standard control such as an edit box or a radio button. Many of them perform quite complex tasks.

With the evolution of component software, users have come to appreciate the ability to simply connect components together to create a seamless application that meets their specific needs. The Connectivity Custom Control Pack provides you with that plug-and-play capability for network communications across the Information Superhighway.

The advantage to the Connectivity Custom Control Pack is that it can be used by anyone with any level of programming knowledge. The management of communications and application protocols are encapsulated into small control libraries which enable you to connect to and manage information on the Information Superhighway.

All you need to use the Connectivity Custom Control Pack is Windows Sockets v1.1, a container/controlling application for 32bit operating systems, and an Internet connection.

The Connectivity Custom Control Pack comes with the following controls:

Control	Description
GETHOST	Address and name resolution using the Domain Name System
FINGER	Query hosts for user information

Control	Description
WHOIS	Locate hosts and users on the Internet
GOPHER	Access GOPHER services
FTP	File Transfer Protocol
MAIL	Send (SMTP) and receive (POP3) electronic mail
NEWS	UseNet newsgroups
TIME	Set your computer's time from a remote host
SOCKET	Develop low-level socket applications

Installation. To install the custom control, you should perform the following steps:

Copy the custom control and the help file into a directory of your liking. Normally this directory is the Windows system subdirectory. The control must be registered into the system registry before it can be used by any application. (If you move the control you must reregister the control in the new directory.) Using the included REGSVR32.EXE application, type the following command line:

REGSRVR32 <directory>\ FNAME.OCX

From within your container application, include the custom control and access the methods and members of the control for your custom Internet application.

Additional information on any of these custom controls is available by email: **etoupin@toupin.com**. You can also fill out a problem report at **http://www.toupin.com/~etoupin/welcome.html**. These controls are not freeware and do require registration if you use them.

The GetHost Custom Control (\OCX\GETHOST). The 32-bit TTC GetHost Custom Control v2.50a custom control encapsulates the function of name and address resolution on the Internet. The GetHost Custom Control is actually two controls in one. The first control, GetName, allows you to retrieve the name of a network host from a given Internet address. The second, GetAdrs, allows you to retrieve the Internet address of a network host from a given name.

To register on CompuServe, GO SWREG: # 6390.

You have access to the following members for the control:

```
GETNAME.AboutBox()
GETNAME.ErrorNum
GETNAME.HostAddress
GETNAME.GetHostName(HostAddress As String)
GETADRS.ErrorNum
GETADRS.AboutBox()
GETADRS.HostName
```

The Finger Custom Control (\OCX\FINGER). The 32-bit TTC Finger Custom Control v2.00a encapsulates the Finger protocol used to query Internet hosts for information about users. The Finger Custom Control enables you to retrieve information about a user from a selected host and works in conjunction with GetHost for address resolution.

As with the other controls of the Connectivity Custom Control Pack, you simply plug the Finger Custom Control into your 32-bit container and develop your Internet application. Once added, the custom control's functionality is available to your container environment. Combining the functionality of multiple controls provides you with a fully functional Internet connectivity application.

To register on CompuServe, GO SWREG: # 6392

You have access to the following members for the control:

```
FINGER.ErrorNum
FINGER.AboutBox()
FINGER. RequestData(FingerAdrs As String, FingerRequest As String)
```

The Whois Custom Control (\OCX\WHOIS). The 32-bit TTC Whois Custom Control v2.00a encapsulates the Whois protocol used to query Whois servers for users, hosts, and businesses on the Internet. The Whois Custom Control enables you to retrieve information about hosts or users from a selected host and works in conjunction with GetHost for address resolution.

To register on CompuServe, GO SWREG: # 6391

You have access to the following members for the control:

```
WHOIS.ErrorNum
WHOIS.AboutBox()
WHOIS. RequestData(WhoisAdrs As String, WhoisRequest As String)
```

The Gopher Custom Control (\OCX\GOPHER). The 32-bit TTC Gopher Custom Control v1.00a encapsulates the Gopher Protocol used to provide access to the morass of documents, files, and search databases available on the Internet. Originally developed at the University of Minnesota, Gopher enables you to access the wealth of information available on the Internet by way of a simple textual interface.

To register on CompuServe, GO SWREG: # 6394

You have access to the following members for the control:

```
GOPHER.ErrorNum
GOPHER.AboutBox()
GOPHER.QueryServer(SrvrAdrs As String, Query As String,
        OutApp As String, PortNum As String)
```

The FTP Custom Control (\OCX\FTP). The 32-bit TTC FTP Custom Control v2.05a encapsulates the File Transfer Protocol (FTP) used to transfer files between Internet hosts. The FTP Custom Control enables you to log onto remote hosts to transfer files to and from the remote host. The custom control works in conjunction with the GetHost custom control for address resolution.

To register on CompuServe, GO SWREG: # 6393

You have access to the following members for the control:

```
FTP.ErrorNum
FTP.AboutBox()
FTP.GetFile(localfile As String, remotefile As String,
    mode As Integer)
FTP.SendFile(localfile As String, remotefile As String,
    mode As Integer)
FTP.RenameFile(fromname As String, toname As String)
FTP.DeleteFile(filename As String)
FTP.ChangeDir(remotedir As String)
FTP.GetDir()
FTP.GetStatus()
FTP.ParentDir()
FTP.Logout()
FTP.GetSystem()
FTP.Help(topic As String)
FTP.Logon(hostadrs As String, uname As String,
    password As String, account As String)
```

The Mail Custom Control Module (\OCX\MAIL). The 32-bit TTC Mail Custom Control v2.00a encapsulates the Simple Mail Transfer Protocol (SMTP) and the Post Office Protocol (POP3) to enable you to exchange e-mail on the Internet. The Mail Custom Control Module enables you to send mail to Internet users with SMTP and receive mail from Internet users with POP3. This control can work in conjunction with the GetHost custom control for address resolution.

To register on CompuServe, GO SWREG: # 6395

III

Appendixes

The SMTP Custom Control (\OCX\SMTP). The SMTP Custom Control enables you to send e-mail to your SMTP server. The following members are available:

```
SMTP.AboutBox()
SMTP.ErrorNum
SMTP.OrigAdrs
SMTP.OrigName
SMTP.SmtpSrvrAdrs
SMTP.Subject
SMTP.DestUserList
SMTP.MailData
SMTP.DomainName
SMTP.CCUserList
SMTP.MailDate
SMTP.MailTime
SMTP.SendMail()
```

The POP Custom Control (\OCX\POP). The POP Custom Control enables you to retrieve e-mail from your POP server. The following members are available:

```
POP.AboutBox()
POP.ErrorNum
POP.UserName
POP.Password
POP.PopSrvrAdrs
POP.POPLogon()
POP.POPLogoff()
POP.ListMail()
POP.GetMail(MsgNum As Integer)
POP.DelMail(MsgNum As Integer)
POP.GetStatus()
```

The News Custom Control (\OCX\NEWS). The 32-bit TTC News Custom Control V1.00A encapsulates the Network News Transfer Protocol (NNTP) to enable you to retrieve and post UseNet articles from supporting hosts on the Internet.

To register on CompuServe, GO SWREG: # 6964.

You have access to the following members for the control:

```
NEWS.AboutBox()
NEWS.ErrorNum
NEWS. ConnectNewsService(hostadrs As String)
NEWS. DisconnectNewsService()
NEWS. ListArticles(groupname As String, daydiff As Integer)
NEWS.ArticleStatus(articlenumber As String)
NEWS.GetArticle(articlenumber As String)
NEWS.SelectGroup(groupname As String)
NEWS.GetPreviousHeader()
NEWS.GetNextHeader()
```

```
NEWS.ListNewsGroups(daydiff As Integer)
NEWS.PostArticle(fromuser As String, username As String,
     fromhostname As String, newsserver As String, newsgroups
     As String, subject As String, organization
     As String, body As String)
```

The Time Custom Control (\OCX\TIME). The 32-bit TTC Time Custom
Control v2.00a encapsulates the Network Time Protocol (NTP) to enable you
to retrieve the Greenwich Mean Time from supporting hosts on the Internet.
The Time Custom Control enables you to retrieve the Universal Coordinated
Time from a remote host on the Internet. The custom control works in con-
junction with the GetHost custom control for address resolution.

To register on CompuServe, GO SWREG: # 6524

You have access to the following members for the control:

```
TIME.ErrorNum
TIME.AboutBox()
TIME.RequestTime(TimeAdrs As String)
```

The Socket Custom Control (\OCX\SOCKET). The 32-bit TTC Socket Custom Control v1.51a encapsulates much of the functionality of the Windows
Sockets API to provide a simple, yet robust, means of accessing and communicating across the Internet from any 32-bit container / development environment. The Socket Custom Control encapsulates the low-level functions
required to perform communications on the Internet. The control enables
you to open a socket, connect to a remote host, send and receive information, and wait for connections from remote hosts.

To register on CompuServe, GO SWREG: # 6389

You have access to the following members for the control:

```
SOCKET.ErrorNum
SOCKET.AboutBox()
SOCKET.OpenSocket(AdrsFmt As Integer, SocketType
     As Integer, Protocol As Integer)
SOCKET.RecvRemote(TimeOut As Integer)
SOCKET. SendRemote(Buffer As String, TimeOut As Integer)
SOCKET.ConnectRemote(AdrsFmt As Integer, IPPort
     As Integer, IPAdrs As String)
SOCKET.CreateListenSocket(IPPort As Integer, AdrsFmt
     As Integer, SocketType As Integer, Protocol As Integer)
SOCKET.WaitForConnect()
SOCKET.CloseSocket()
```

Other Applications

The following sections list an eclectic mix of programs including graphics
and sound editors, compression software, and other useful utilities. While no

one is likely to use all these programs, you should find at least one you can use.

Compression Software. To save on download time over the Internet and disk space on servers, most applications are compressed into archives. These applications will help you decompress these archives so that you can run the applications you've downloaded.

ArcMaster (\WEBPAGES\APPS\ARCMASTR.HTM, \APPS\COMPRESS\ARCMASTR). This is a handy utility for compressing and decompressing files using many popular compression formats. Formats that are supported include ZIP, LHZ, and ARJ. You need to have the file compression/decompression utilities for each of these, as this is just a front end to make it easier to use the DOS utilities. It supports drag-and-drop, enables you to conveniently manipulate compressed files, and converts files from one compression format to another.

ArcShell (\WEBPAGES\APPS\ARCSHELL.HTM, \APPS\COMPRESS\ARCSHELL). ArcShell is a Windows shell for ZIP, LHZ, ARC, and ARJ compression files. You need to have the file compression/decompression utilities for each of these, as this is just a front end to make it easier to use the DOS utilities.

Drag And Zip (\WEBPAGES\APPS\DRAGZIP.HTM, \APPS\COMPRESS\DRAGZIP). Drag And Zip is a set of utilities that turns the Windows 3.1 File Manager into a file manager for creating and managing ZIP, LHZ, and GZ files. With its built-in routines to zip and unzip files, Drag And Zip makes it very easy to compress files into ZIP files and to extract files from ZIP files from any Windows File Manager that supports drag-and-drop. Drag And Zip also supports use of copies of PKZIP, LHA, and GUNZIP to manage compressed files. Drag And Zip has a built-in virus scanner that you can use to scan the files in the compressed file for possible viruses.

WinZip v5.6 (\WEBPAGES\APPS\WINZIP.HTM, \APPS\COMPRESS\WINZIP). WinZip is a Windows ZIP archive-managing program that no Internet user should be without. This application provides a pleasant graphical interface for managing many archive-file formats, such as ZIP, ARJ, ARC, and LZH. WinZip enables you to open text files from an archive directly to the screen so that you can read a file in an archive without actually extracting it.

Version 5.6 has the added support of archives using the GZIP, TAR, and Z formats that are very common on the Internet. You can now manage these files just as easily as ZIP files. It's common to find files on the Internet that have been stored as TAR files and then compressed with GZIP or Z. WinZip handles these multiple formats with no problems. This support is unique among the other ZIP file utilities discussed in this appendix.

Zip Manager (\WEBPAGES\APPS\ZIPMGR, \APPS\COMPRESS\ZIPMGR). Zip Manager is a standalone Windows ZIP utility. PKZIP and PKUNZIP aren't required to use this, which sets it apart from most other Windows-based ZIP utilities. It's 100 percent PKZIP 2.04-compatible, and the compression utilities are designed especially for Windows. ZMZIP and ZMUNZIP are built into Zip Manager.

Zip Master (\WEBPAGES\APPS\ZIPMASTR, \APPS\COMPRESS\ZIPMASTR). This is another Windows ZIP utility that doesn't require you to also have PKZIP or PKUNZIP. You can use it to add to, freshen, or update existing ZIP files; create new ZIP files; extract from or test existing ZIP files; view existing ZIP file contents, and many other functions.

File Readers: PostScript, Sound, Images, and Video. If you frequently download graphics, sound, or specially formatted files, you need software to view, listen, or otherwise manipulate these files.

Media Blastoff (\WEBPAGES\APPS\BLASTOFF.HTM, \APPS\READERS\BLASTOFF). This viewer provides support for several popular graphics formats, as well as sound and movies. The file formats that probably will be of most use to you with the Internet are .GIF, .AVI, and .WAV.

GhostView v1.0 (\WEBPAGES\APPS\GSVIEW.HTM, \APPS\READERS\GSVIEW). GhostView version 1.0, a Windows 3.1 application, can be used to view printer files that conform to GhostScript 2.6 or later standards. GhostScript is an interpreter for the PostScript page-description language used by many laser printers. GhostView also can be used to print GhostScript-embedded documents. Source code for this application is part of the archive. GhostView is the interpreter that NCSA recommends for use with Mosaic for viewing PostScript files with GhostScript.

Jasc Media Center (\WEBPAGES\APPS\JASC.HTM, \APPS\READERS\JASCMEDI). If you have many multimedia files you've collected from the Web, you'll find this utility useful for keeping them organized. It supports 37 file formats, including .GIF, JPEG, MIDI, .WAV, and .AVI. Formats that aren't supported can still be used if you have an external file filter for them.

PlayWave (\WEBPAGES\APPS\PLAYWAVE.HTM, \APPS\READERS\PLAYWAV). PlayWave is a simple Windows application for playing .WAV sound files. The program requires fewer mouse clicks for playing waves and can be set to loop a wave file continuously.

The program's author states that this application may not work on all systems. To use it, choose View, Options under My Computer and use the File Types sheet to "associate" .WAV files with PlayWave, not the Sound Recorder. Then, when you double-click .WAV file names, PlayWave comes up, not the Sound Recorder. To use it with your Web browser, designate it as the viewer for .WAV files, and when you download a .WAV format sound, it will start.

VuePrint (\WEBPAGES\APPS\VUEPRINT.HTM, \APPS\READERS\VUEPRINT). VuePrint is a graphics viewer that opens, saves, and prints graphics in JPEG and .GIF formats, as well as several other popular formats. It includes a screen saver that displays collections of these file formats. It also has a built-in UUEncoder and UUDecoder, which makes it pretty much an all-in-one graphics solution for most of your Internet graphics needs.

WinECJ (\WEBPAGES\APPS\WINECJ.HTM, \APPS\READERS\WINECJ). WinECJ is a fast JPEG viewer. The program can open multiple files and has a slide-show presentation mode.

WPlany (\WEBPAGES\APPS\WPLANY.HTM, \APPS\READERS\WPLANY). This sound utility plays sound files through a Windows .WAV output device (such as a SoundBlaster card). NCSA recommends WPlany for use with Mosaic. The program supports several sound-file formats (including most formats that are used on the Net) and is very easy to use. However, once a sound file begins to play, you can't stop it until it's done.

File Encryption. You may have sensitive information that you want to send to someone over the Internet. If you do, you'll need an encryption program to ensure that unauthorized individuals can't read your documents. Here are two encryption applications that provide this protection.

Crip for Windows (\WEBPAGES\APPS\CRIP.HTM, \APPS\ENCRPYT\CRIPWIN). This Windows-based text-encryption program was designed for use over the Internet. It has options for dealing with PC line feeds in files that are sent over the Internet. (See the README file for information on this.)

Enigma for Windows (\WEBPAGES\APPS\ENIGMA.HTM, \APPS\ENCRYPT\ENIGMA). This file-encryption program supports the DES encryption standard used by many U.S. government agencies. Although it isn't designed for sending encrypted messages by way of Internet e-mail, you can use it for transferring files through any protocol that supports binary transfer. You can encrypt files on an FTP site, send encrypted files as attachments to e-mail using UUEncode or MIME, or make encrypted files available by way of the Web as links from an HTML document.

This isn't a public key system, so the same password is used to encode and decode files. This limits its security for Internet usage, because anyone who would be receiving a file would need your password.

Picture Conversion/Manipulation. In addition to applications or text information files, the Internet offers a wealth of images in many different formats. These applications will help you convert images to a format that you can use.

Image'n'Bits (\WEBPAGES\APPS\IMA.HTM, \APPS\CONVERT\IMA). This is a graphics manipulation and conversion utility. Among the formats supported are .BMP and .GIF. Some of the special effects it includes are dithering, pixelizing, and solarizing, just to name a few. If you're working with artistic images or photographs as Web images, this program is very useful.

Murals (\WEBPAGES\APPS\MURALS.HTM, \APPS\CONVERT\MURALS). Murals enables you to use JPEG and .GIF images as wallpaper directly, without converting them to .BMP format. This capability saves you a great deal of disk space.

Paint Shop Pro (\WEBPAGES\APPS\PAINTSHP.HTM, \APPS\CONVERT\PAINTSHP). This is a powerful graphics viewing and editing utility. It supports about 20 different graphics file formats, including the common .GIF and JPEG formats found on the Web. It has a host of features for editing and manipulating graphics, and rivals commercial packages with the number and variety of filters and special effects. It also includes a screen-capture program.

WinJPEG (\WEBPAGES\APPS\WINJPEG.HTM, \APPS\CONVERT\WINJPG). WinJPEG is a Windows-based graphics-file viewer and converter. You can read and save TIFF, .GIF, .JPG, .TGA, .BMP, and .PCX file formats with this viewer/converter. WinJPEG has several color-enhancement and dithering features that allow the user to alter a graphics file slightly. The program also supports batch conversions and screen captures.

III

Appendixes

WinLab (\WEBPAGES\APPS\WINLAB.HTM, \APPS\CONVERT\WINLAB). This is a powerful graphics viewer and editor. In addition to the image-processing features, it has built-in TWAIN and network support and a Winsock-compliant application for sending and receiving images.

Grabbit Pro (\WEBPAGES\APPS\GRABPRO.HTM, \APPS\CAPTURE\GRABPRO). If you're putting Web pages together for software documentation, you'll find this Windows screen-capture utility to be an invaluable aid in creating pages with embedded screen shots. (It doesn't save files in .GIF format, so if you want to use saved images as in-line images, you need to convert them by using one of the other utilities discussed here.) There are Windows 3.1 and Windows NT versions, both of which are included here.

UUEncode/UUDecode. UUEncoding converts binary files (programs and archives) to text so that they can be transmitted over the Internet via messages. After receipt, the message files must be converted back (UUDecoding) to their original binary form.

Batch UUD for DOS (\WEBPAGES\APPS\BATCHUUD.HTM, \APPS\UUENCODE\BATCHUUD). As the name implies, this program is a batch UUDecoder that runs in DOS. With UUD, all you have to do is type **UUD *.*** in DOS or choose File, Run in Windows, and all saved files in UUEncoded format are decoded. The program is smart, as well: By alphabetizing all entries, UUD can make a logical guess at the order of split files.

Extract v3.04 (\WEBPAGES\APPS\EXTRACT.HTM, \APPS\UUENCODE\EXTRACT). Extract is a Windows application for encoding and decoding UU-embedded files.

 The documentation with this software is slightly out-of-date. The author requests that e-mail regarding the program be sent to **dpenner@msi.cuug.ab.ca**.

UUCode (\WEBPAGES\APPS\UUCODE.HTM, \APPS\UUENCODE\UUCODE). UUCode is a Windows-based application used to decode UUEncoded files sent over the Internet in messages. This application also UUEncodes a binary file so that it can be inserted into a message and sent over the Internet in this manner. The program's configuration options include file overwriting, default file names, and status messages.

WinCode (\WEBPAGES\APPS\WINCODE.HTM, \APPS\UUENCODE\WINCODE). WinCode is a great utility for UUEncoding and UUDecoding files. Two of its really nice features are the way that the program handles multiple files (effortlessly) and its capability to tie its menus to other programs. The program decodes many poorly encoded files that other decoders can't handle.

Internet Documents

The \DOCS folder and its subfolders contain quite a bit of information. Not all files are described here due to lack of space. Go ahead and explore the \DOCS folder to find some of the more esoteric files.

FAQs (\DOCS\FAQ)

Some Frequently Asked Questions documents (FAQs) are on the CD for ease of reading. You should be aware that there are FAQ documents on nearly every subject relating to the Internet, and plenty more that have nothing to do with the Internet itself, but are popular with Netters. The ones included on the CD are:

- Emily Postnews Answers Your Questions on Netiquette (EMILYPST.FAQ)

- How to find the right place to post (FINDPOST.FAQ)

- The "Good Net-Keeping Seal of Approval" for UseNet Software (GNKSA.TXT)

- How to Create a New UseNet Newsgroup (HOWCREAT.FAQ)

- IRC Frequently Asked Questions (IRC.FAQ)

- IRC Undernet Frequently Asked Questions (IRC.UND1 FAQ and IRC.UND2 FAQ)

- Answers to Frequently Asked Questions about UseNet (NETFAQ.FAQ)

- Hints on writing style for UseNet (NETSTYLE.FAQ)

- Introduction to news.announce (NEWSANCE.FAQ)

- Introduction to the *.answers newsgroups (NEWSANSW.FAQ)

■ A Primer on How to Work With the UseNet Community
(NEWSPRIM.TXT)

■ Rules for posting to Usenet (NEWSRULE.FAQ)

■ Usenet Software: History and Sources (NEWSSOFT.FAQ)

All FAQs are updated regularly. Check the Newsgroups: header in these
postings and look in those groups for more recent copies before acting on the
information you find in them. Thousands of FAQs are posted to the UseNet
group **news.answers** every month.

List of FTP Sites (\DOCS\FTPSITES)

This folder contains several files that list FTP sites. Each site listing includes
the country of origin, a comment about the site, and the types of files that
the site holds.

FYIs (\DOCS\FYI)

An FYI document is published strictly for its information content. It isn't
meant to be a standard. FYIs tend to be less technical than RFCs or STDs.

Provider List (\DOCS\PROVIDER)

This folder contains several text files listing companies and providers that
supply a constant Internet connection. Many sites listed in this text file also
have dial-up access to the Internet. Information such as contact name, phone
number, Internet address, and system information is listed for each site in the
provider lists, which are arranged by region. The lists are compiled and main-
tained by InterNIC.

Lists of Internet providers in the United States, Africa, Asia, Australia, Canada,
the former Soviet bloc, Latin America, the Middle East, and Western Europe
are included.

STDs (\DOCS\STD)

An STD document is an RFC document that has been accepted as a standard.
STDs tend to be technical.

RFCs (\RFC)

The RFC documents are the working notes of the committees that develop
the protocols and standards for the Internet. They're numbered in the order
in which they were released. Numbers that have been skipped represent RFCs
that are outdated, have been replaced by newer ones, or were never issued.

The CD Home Page (APPCD.HTM) allows various ways to look at the RFC list. In addition to having the RFC sorted by author and by number, you can view some humorous RFCs, which have been highlighted in their own section.

While many RFCs make for dry reading, and some are almost impenetrably dense, they define the specification for the part of your software that talks to the Internet, and that makes them "must" reading for you.

III

Appendixes

Index

G

GET CONNECTED
to the ultimate source of computer information!

The MCP Forum on CompuServe

Go online with the world's leading computer book publisher!
Macmillan Computer Publishing offers everything
you need for computer success!

Find the books that are right for you!
A complete online catalog, plus sample
chapters and tables of contents give
you an in-depth look at all our books.
The best way to shop or browse!

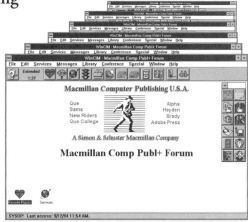

➤ Get fast answers and technical support for
MCP books and software

➤ Join discussion groups on major computer
subjects

➤ Interact with our expert authors via e-mail
and conferences

➤ Download software from our immense
library:

   ▷ Source code from books
   ▷ Demos of hot software
   ▷ The best shareware and freeware
   ▷ Graphics files

Join now and get a free CompuServe Starter Kit!

To receive your free CompuServe Intro-
ductory Membership, call **1-800-848-
8199** and ask for representative **#597**.

The Starter Kit includes:
➤ Personal ID number and password
➤ $15 credit on the system
➤ Subscription to *CompuServe Magazine*

Once on the CompuServe System, type:

GO MACMILLAN

for the most computer information anywhere!

MACMILLAN
COMPUTER
PUBLISHING

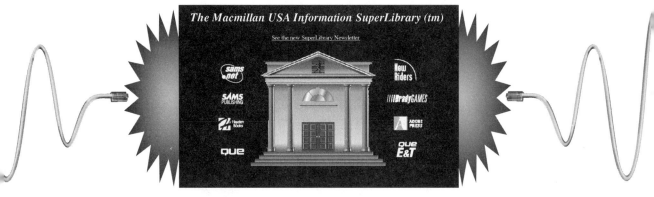

Licensing Agreement

By opening this package, you are agreeing to be bound by the following: